WELCOME no.6 | TOMO TAKEUCHI
to the BALLROOM

# Contents

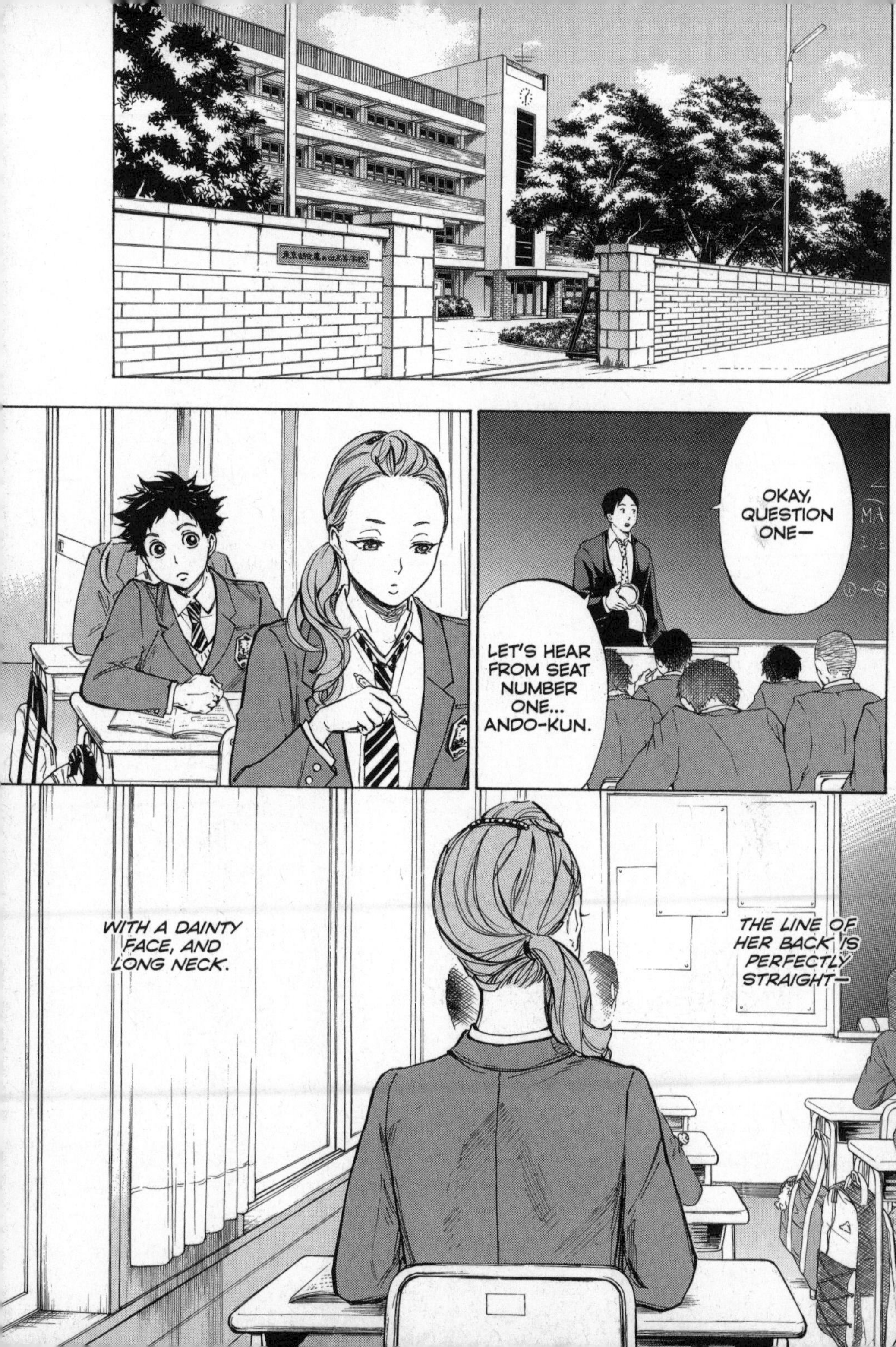
OKAY, QUESTION ONE—
LET'S HEAR FROM SEAT NUMBER ONE... ANDO-KUN.
THE LINE OF HER BACK IS PERFECTLY STRAIGHT—
WITH A DAINTY FACE, AND LONG NECK.

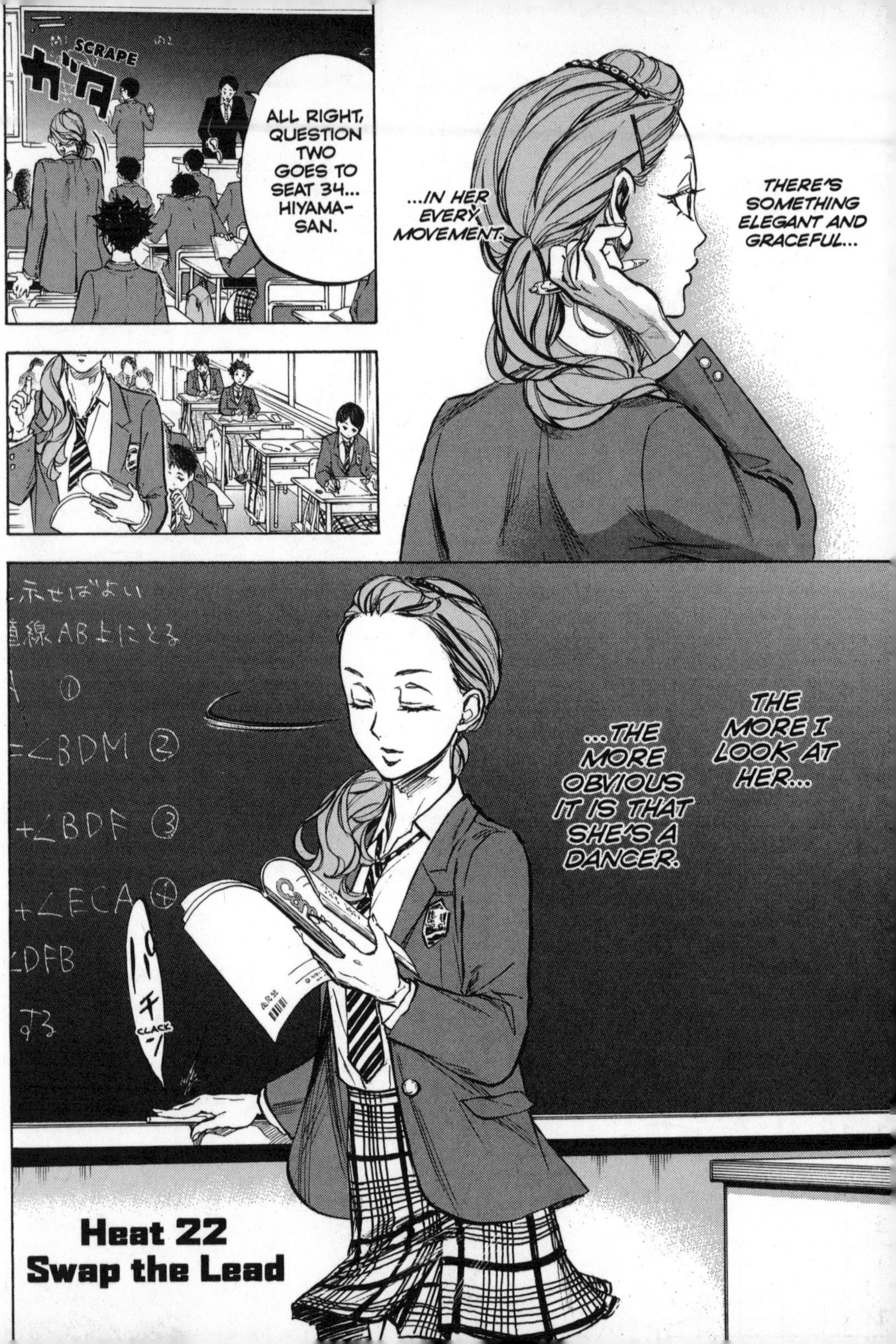
THERE'S SOMETHING ELEGANT AND GRACEFUL...
...IN HER EVERY MOVEMENT.
SCRAPE
ALL RIGHT, QUESTION TWO GOES TO SEAT 34... HIYAMA-SAN.
THE MORE I LOOK AT HER...
...THE MORE OBVIOUS IT IS THAT SHE'S A DANCER.
CLACK
Heat 22
Swap the Lead

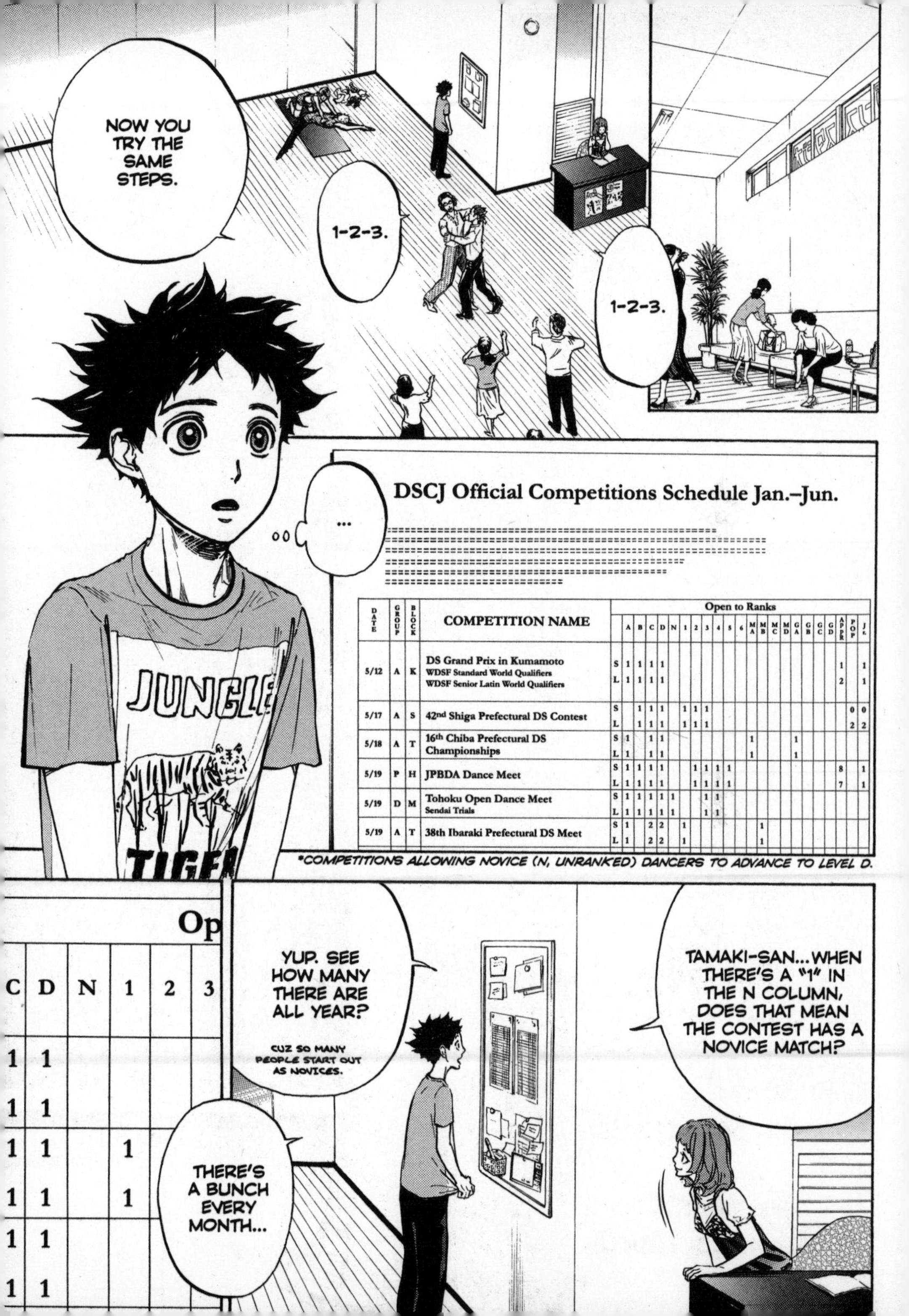
1-2-3.
1-2-3.
NOW YOU TRY THE SAME STEPS.
DSCJ Official Competitions Schedule Jan.–Jun.

| DATE | GROUP | BLOCK | COMPETITION NAME | Open to Ranks | | | | | | | | | | | | | | | | | | | | | | |
|---|---|---|---|---|---|---|---|---|---|---|---|---|---|---|---|---|---|---|---|---|---|---|---|---|---|---|
| | | | | | A | B | C | D | N | 1 | 2 | 3 | 4 | 5 | 6 | MA | MB | MC | MD | GA | GB | GC | GD | APPR | POP | Jr. |
| 5/12 | A | K | DS Grand Prix in Kumamoto<br>WDSF Standard World Qualifiers<br>WDSF Senior Latin World Qualifiers | S | 1 | 1 | 1 | 1 | | | | | | | | | | | | | | | | 1 | | 1 |
| | | | | L | 1 | 1 | 1 | 1 | | | | | | | | | | | | | | | | 2 | | 1 |
| 5/17 | A | S | 42nd Shiga Prefectural DS Contest | S | | 1 | 1 | 1 | | 1 | 1 | 1 | | | | | | | | | | | | | 0 | 0 |
| | | | | L | | 1 | 1 | 1 | | 1 | 1 | 1 | | | | | | | | | | | | | 2 | 2 |
| 5/18 | A | T | 16th Chiba Prefectural DS Championships | S | 1 | | 1 | 1 | | | | | | | | 1 | | | | 1 | | | | | | |
| | | | | L | 1 | | 1 | 1 | | | | | | | | 1 | | | | 1 | | | | | | |
| 5/19 | P | H | JPBDA Dance Meet | S | 1 | 1 | 1 | 1 | | | 1 | 1 | 1 | 1 | | | | | | | | | | 8 | | 1 |
| | | | | L | 1 | 1 | 1 | 1 | | | 1 | 1 | 1 | 1 | | | | | | | | | | 7 | | 1 |
| 5/19 | D | M | Tohoku Open Dance Meet<br>Sendai Trials | S | 1 | 1 | 1 | 1 | 1 | | | 1 | 1 | | | | | | | | | | | | | |
| | | | | L | 1 | 1 | 1 | 1 | 1 | | | 1 | 1 | | | | | | | | | | | | | |
| 5/19 | A | T | 38th Ibaraki Prefectural DS Meet | S | 1 | | 2 | 2 | | 1 | | | | | | | 1 | | | | | | | | | |
| | | | | L | 1 | | 2 | 2 | | 1 | | | | | | | 1 | | | | | | | | | |

...
*COMPETITIONS ALLOWING NOVICE (N, UNRANKED) DANCERS TO ADVANCE TO LEVEL D.
JUNGLE TIGER
TAMAKI-SAN...WHEN THERE'S A "1" IN THE N COLUMN, DOES THAT MEAN THE CONTEST HAS A NOVICE MATCH?
YUP. SEE HOW MANY THERE ARE ALL YEAR?
CUZ SO MANY PEOPLE START OUT AS NOVICES.
THERE'S A BUNCH EVERY MONTH...
Op
C D N 1 2 3
1 1
1 1
1 1 1
1 1 1
1 1
1 1

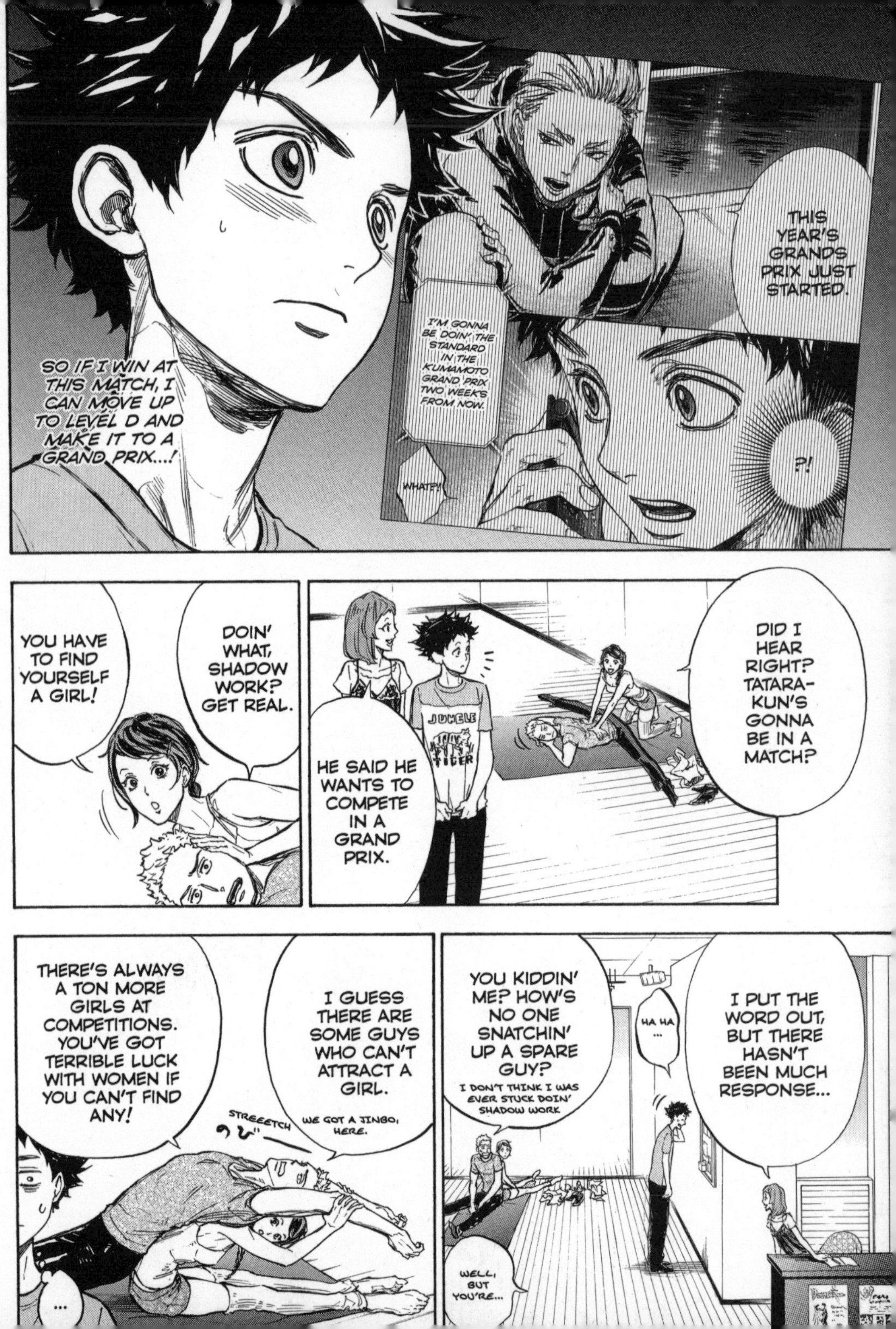
THIS YEAR'S GRANDS PRIX JUST STARTED.
I'M GONNA BE DOIN' THE STANDARD IN THE KUMAMOTO GRAND PRIX TWO WEEKS FROM NOW.
?!
WHAT?!
SO IF I WIN AT THIS MATCH, I CAN MOVE UP TO LEVEL D AND MAKE IT TO A GRAND PRIX...!
DID I HEAR RIGHT? TATARA-KUN'S GONNA BE IN A MATCH?
HE SAID HE WANTS TO COMPETE IN A GRAND PRIX.
DOIN' WHAT, SHADOW WORK? GET REAL.
YOU HAVE TO FIND YOURSELF A GIRL!
I PUT THE WORD OUT, BUT THERE HASN'T BEEN MUCH RESPONSE...
HA HA ...
YOU KIDDIN' ME? HOW'S NO ONE SNATCHIN' UP A SPARE GUY?
I DON'T THINK I WAS EVER STUCK DOIN' SHADOW WORK
WELL, BUT YOU'RE...
I GUESS THERE ARE SOME GUYS WHO CAN'T ATTRACT A GIRL.
WE GOT A JINBO, HERE.
THERE'S ALWAYS A TON MORE GIRLS AT COMPETITIONS. YOU'VE GOT TERRIBLE LUCK WITH WOMEN IF YOU CAN'T FIND ANY!
STREEETCH
...

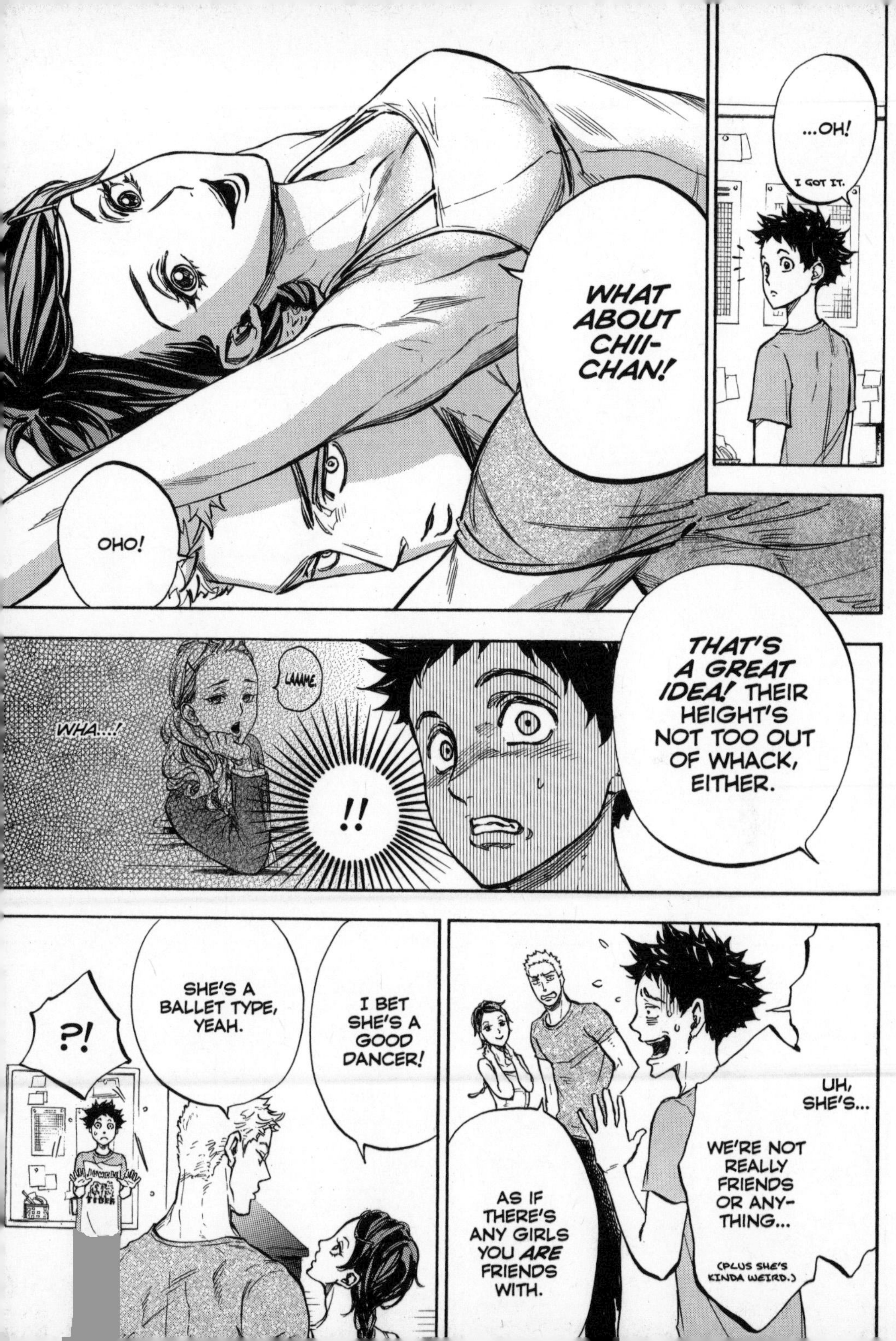
...OH!
I GOT IT.
WHAT ABOUT CHII-CHAN!
OHO!
THAT'S A GREAT IDEA! THEIR HEIGHT'S NOT TOO OUT OF WHACK, EITHER.
!!
LAAAME.
WHA...!
UH, SHE'S...
WE'RE NOT REALLY FRIENDS OR ANY-THING...
(PLUS SHE'S KINDA WEIRD.)
AS IF THERE'S ANY GIRLS YOU ARE FRIENDS WITH.
I BET SHE'S A GOOD DANCER!
SHE'S A BALLET TYPE, YEAH.
?!

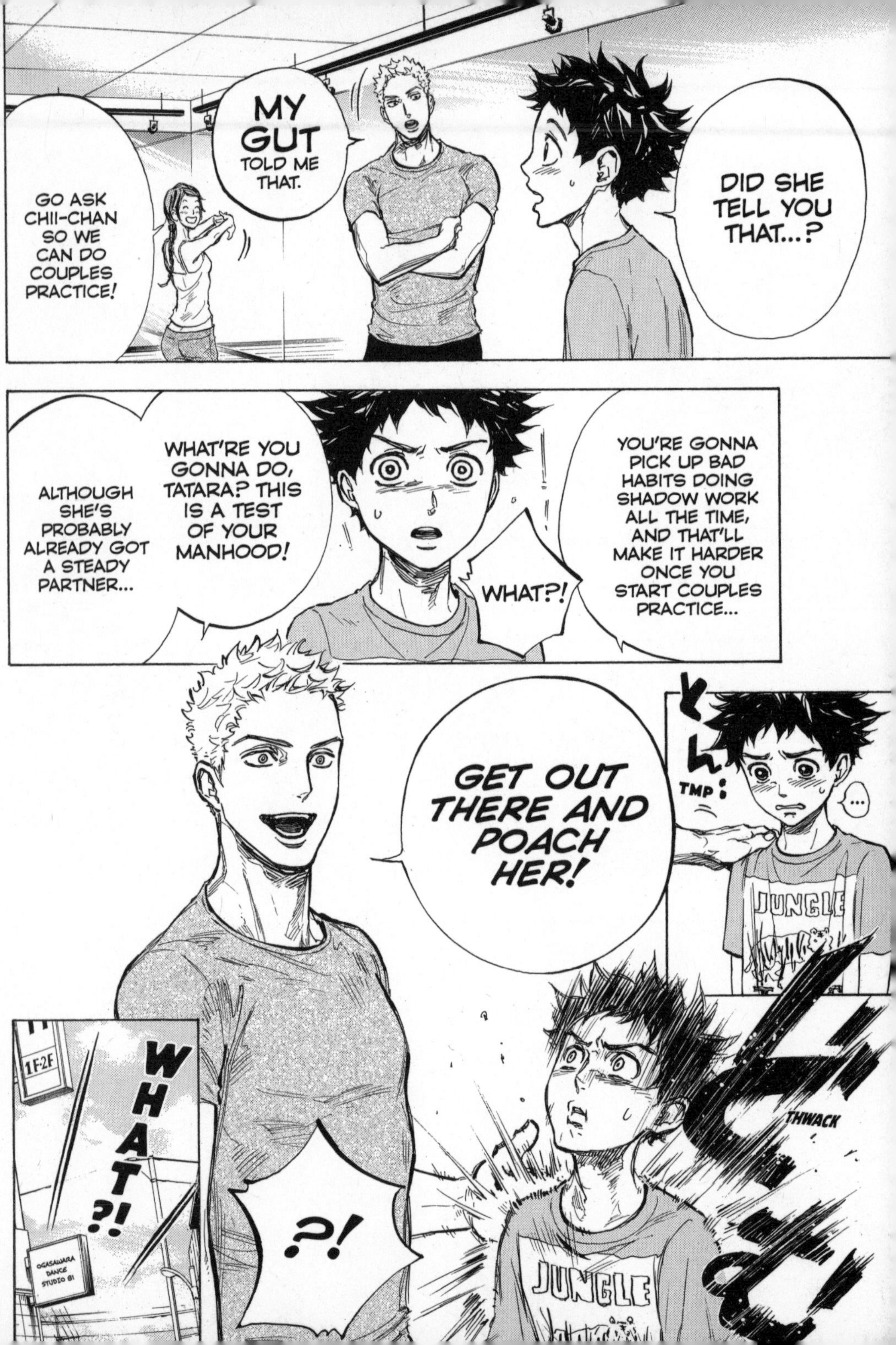

DID SHE TELL YOU THAT...?
MY GUT TOLD ME THAT.
GO ASK CHII-CHAN SO WE CAN DO COUPLES PRACTICE!
YOU'RE GONNA PICK UP BAD HABITS DOING SHADOW WORK ALL THE TIME, AND THAT'LL MAKE IT HARDER ONCE YOU START COUPLES PRACTICE...
WHAT?!
WHAT'RE YOU GONNA DO, TATARA? THIS IS A TEST OF YOUR MANHOOD!
ALTHOUGH SHE'S PROBABLY ALREADY GOT A STEADY PARTNER...
TMP
...
GET OUT THERE AND POACH HER!
THWACK
?!
WHAT?!
1F-2F
OGASAWARA DANCE STUDIO 81
JUNGLE

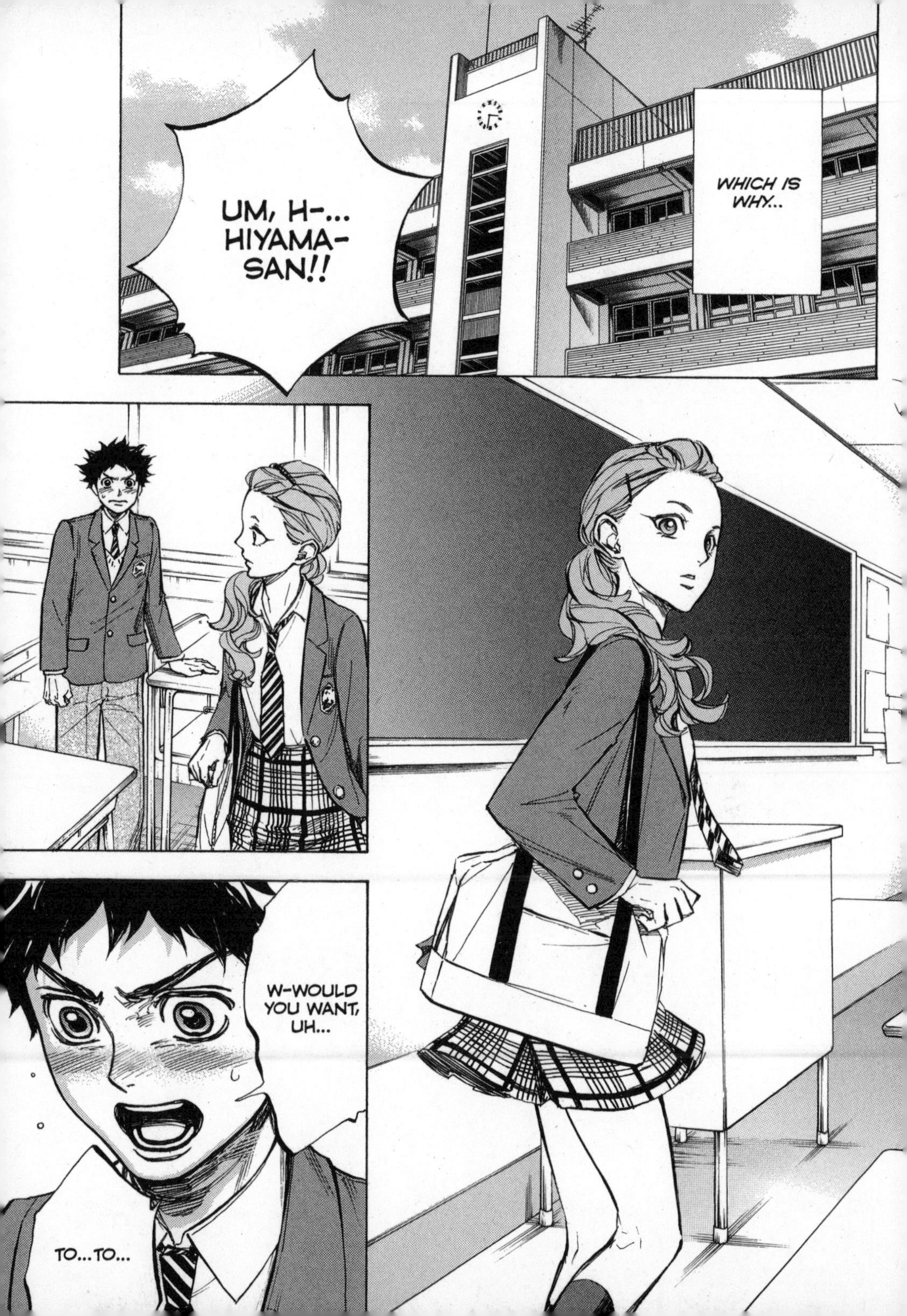
WHICH IS WHY...
UM, H-... HIYAMA-SAN!!
W-WOULD YOU WANT, UH...
TO... TO...

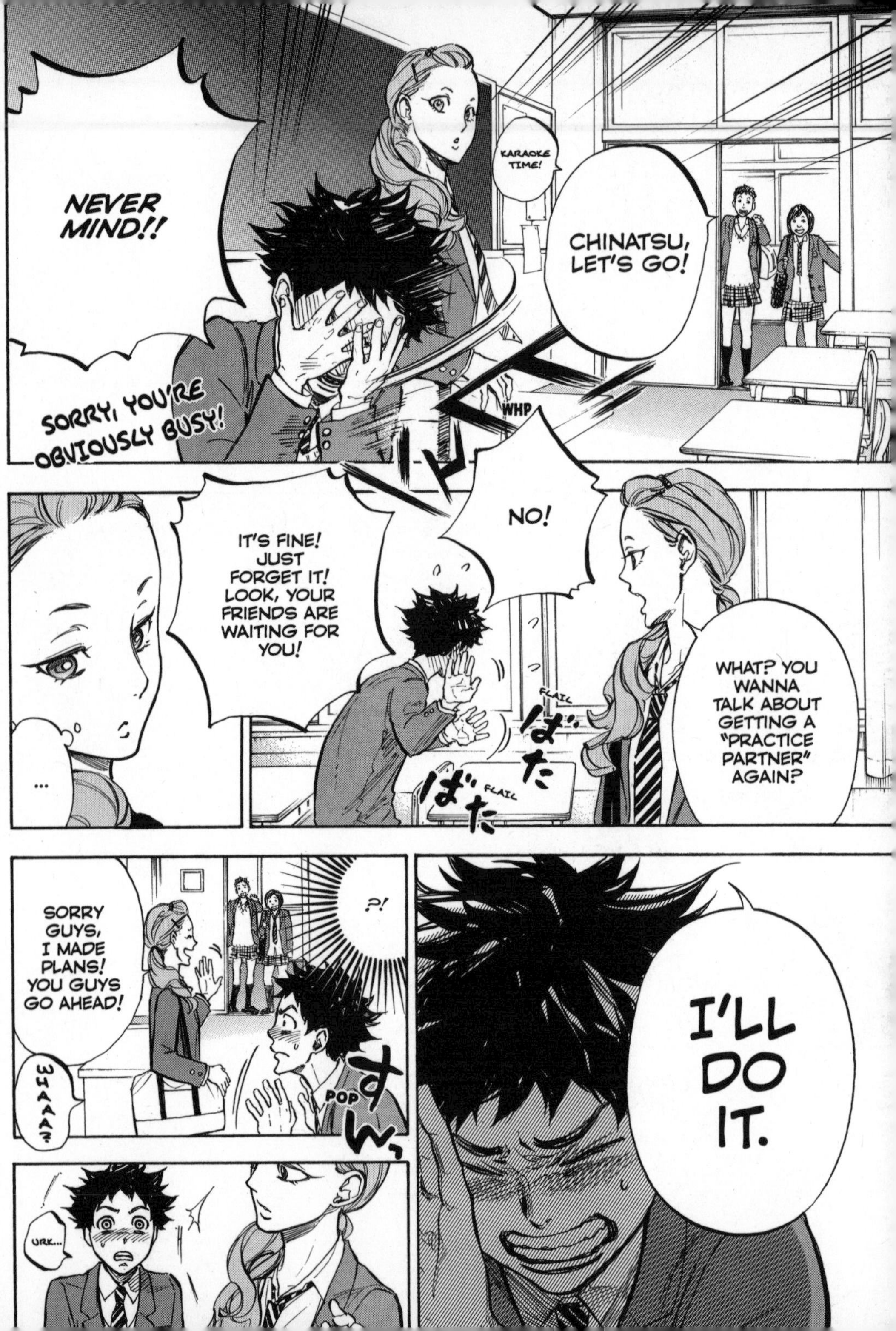
KARAOKE TIME!
CHINATSU, LET'S GO!
NEVER MIND!!
SORRY, YOU'RE OBVIOUSLY BUSY!
WHP
NO!
WHAT? YOU WANNA TALK ABOUT GETTING A "PRACTICE PARTNER" AGAIN?
IT'S FINE! JUST FORGET IT! LOOK, YOUR FRIENDS ARE WAITING FOR YOU!
ばた FLAIL
ばた FLAIL
...
I'LL DO IT.
?!
SORRY GUYS, I MADE PLANS! YOU GUYS GO AHEAD!
WHAAAA?
すん POP
URK...

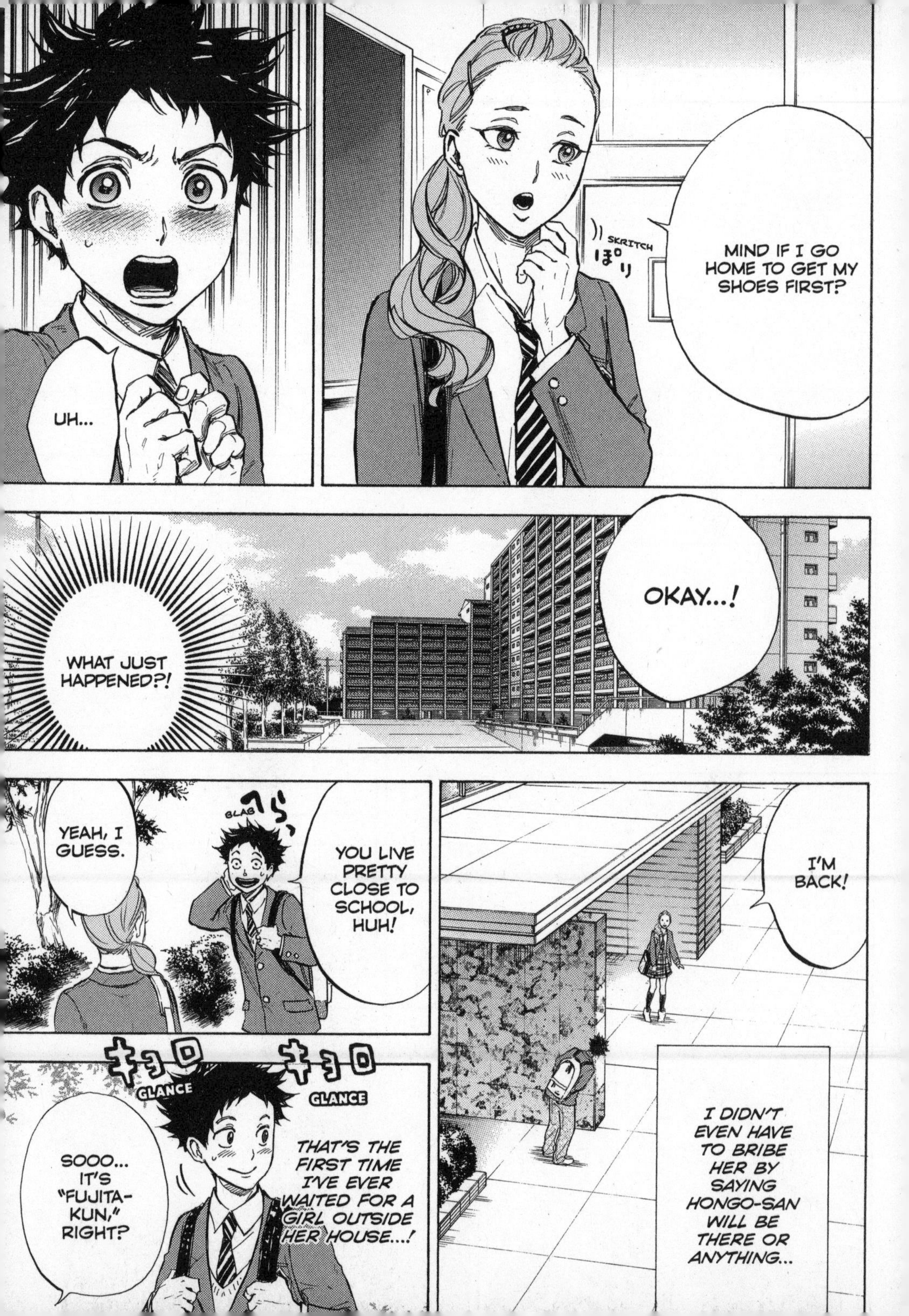
ぽり
SKRITCH
MIND IF I GO HOME TO GET MY SHOES FIRST?
UH...
OKAY...!
WHAT JUST HAPPENED?!
I'M BACK!
I DIDN'T EVEN HAVE TO BRIBE HER BY SAYING HONGO-SAN WILL BE THERE OR ANYTHING...
へら
GLAB
YOU LIVE PRETTY CLOSE TO SCHOOL, HUH!
YEAH, I GUESS.
キョロ
GLANCE
キョロ
GLANCE
THAT'S THE FIRST TIME I'VE EVER WAITED FOR A GIRL OUTSIDE HER HOUSE...!
SOOO... IT'S "FUJITA-KUN," RIGHT?

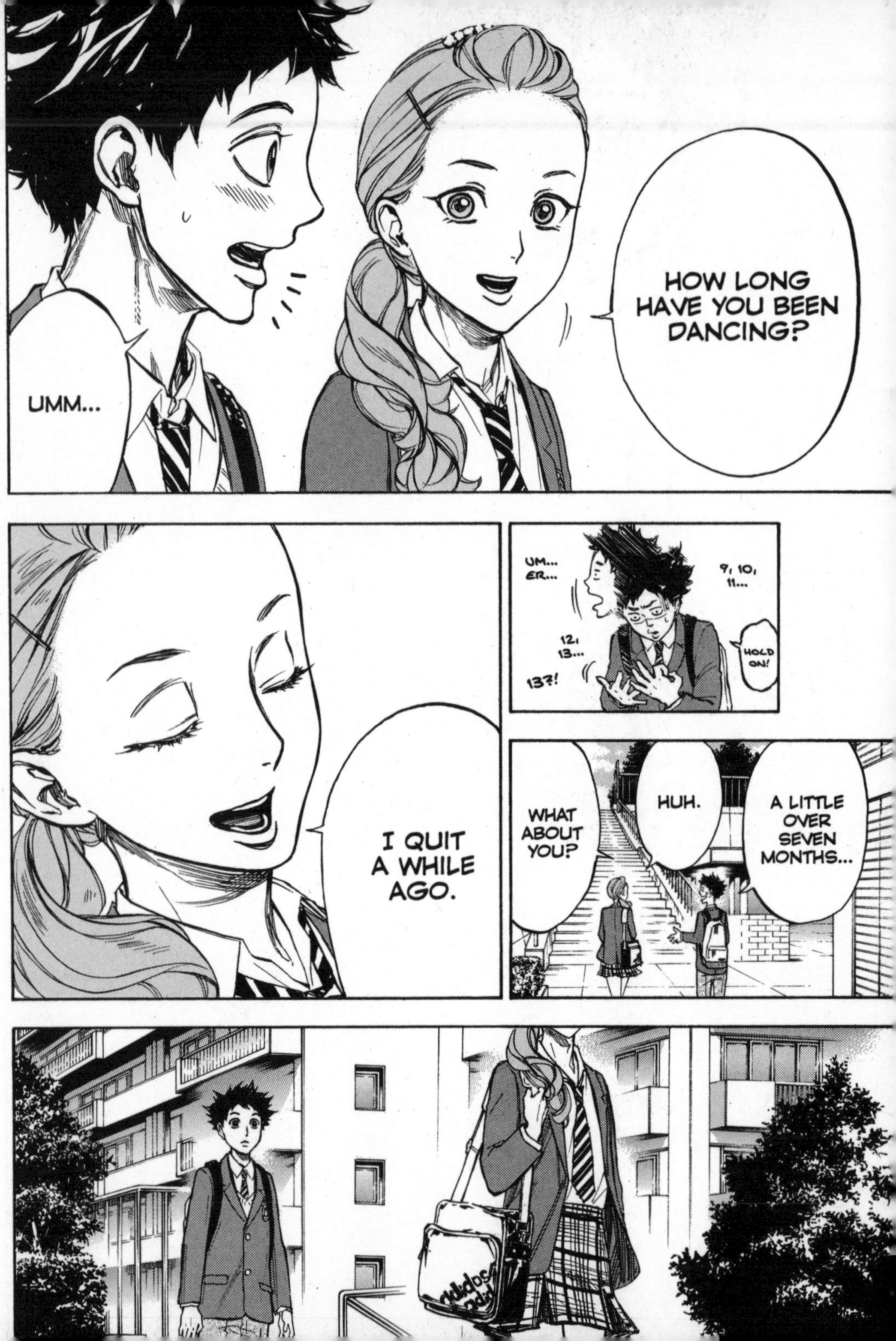
HOW LONG HAVE YOU BEEN DANCING?
UMM...
9, 10, 11...
UM... ER...
HOLD ON!
12, 13...
13?!
A LITTLE OVER SEVEN MONTHS...
HUH.
WHAT ABOUT YOU?
I QUIT A WHILE AGO.

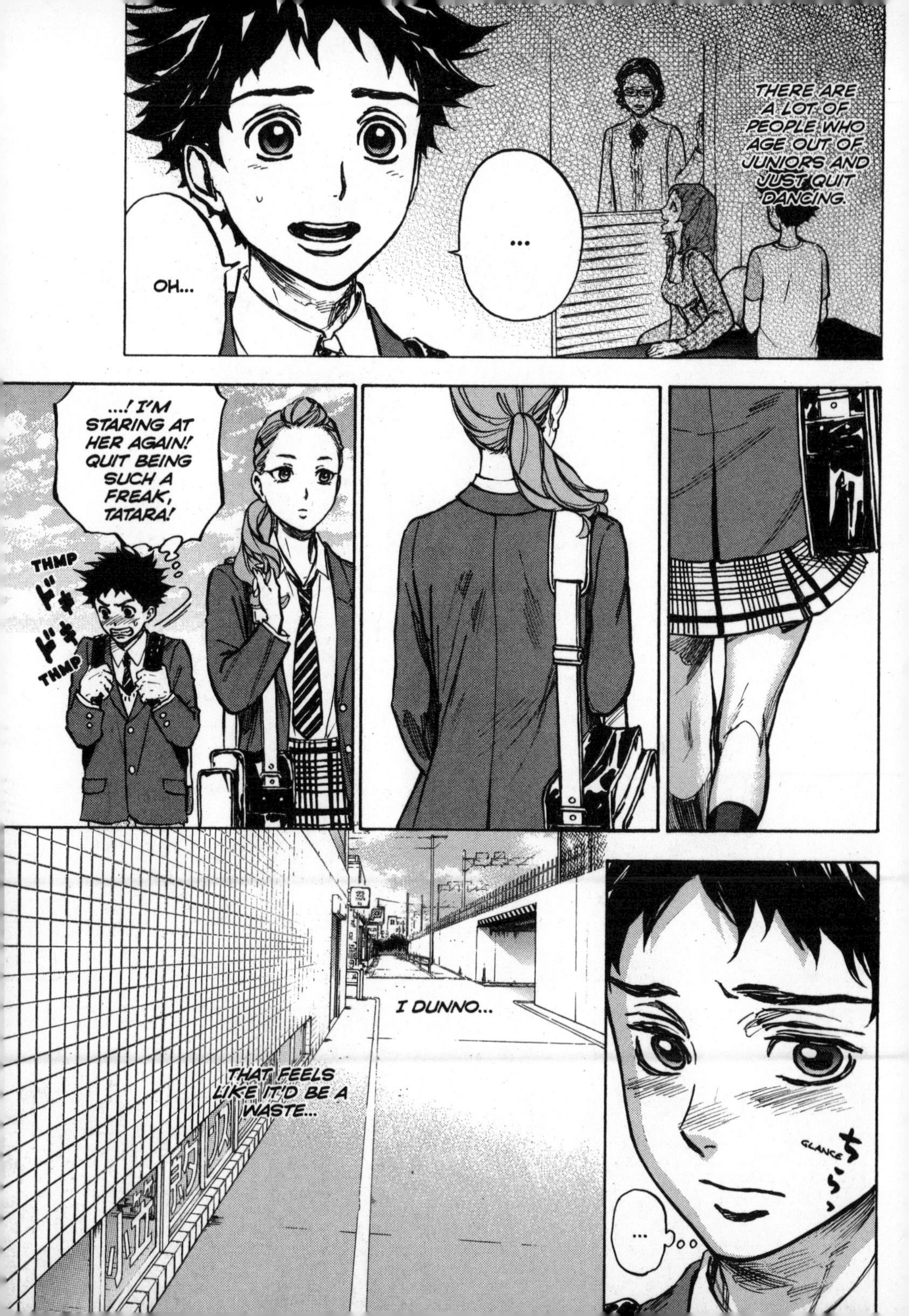
THERE ARE A LOT OF PEOPLE WHO AGE OUT OF JUNIORS AND JUST QUIT DANCING.
...
OH...
...! I'M STARING AT HER AGAIN! QUIT BEING SUCH A FREAK, TATARA!
THMP
ドキ
ドキ
THMP
GLANCE
ちらっ
...
I DUNNO...
THAT FEELS LIKE IT'D BE A WASTE...

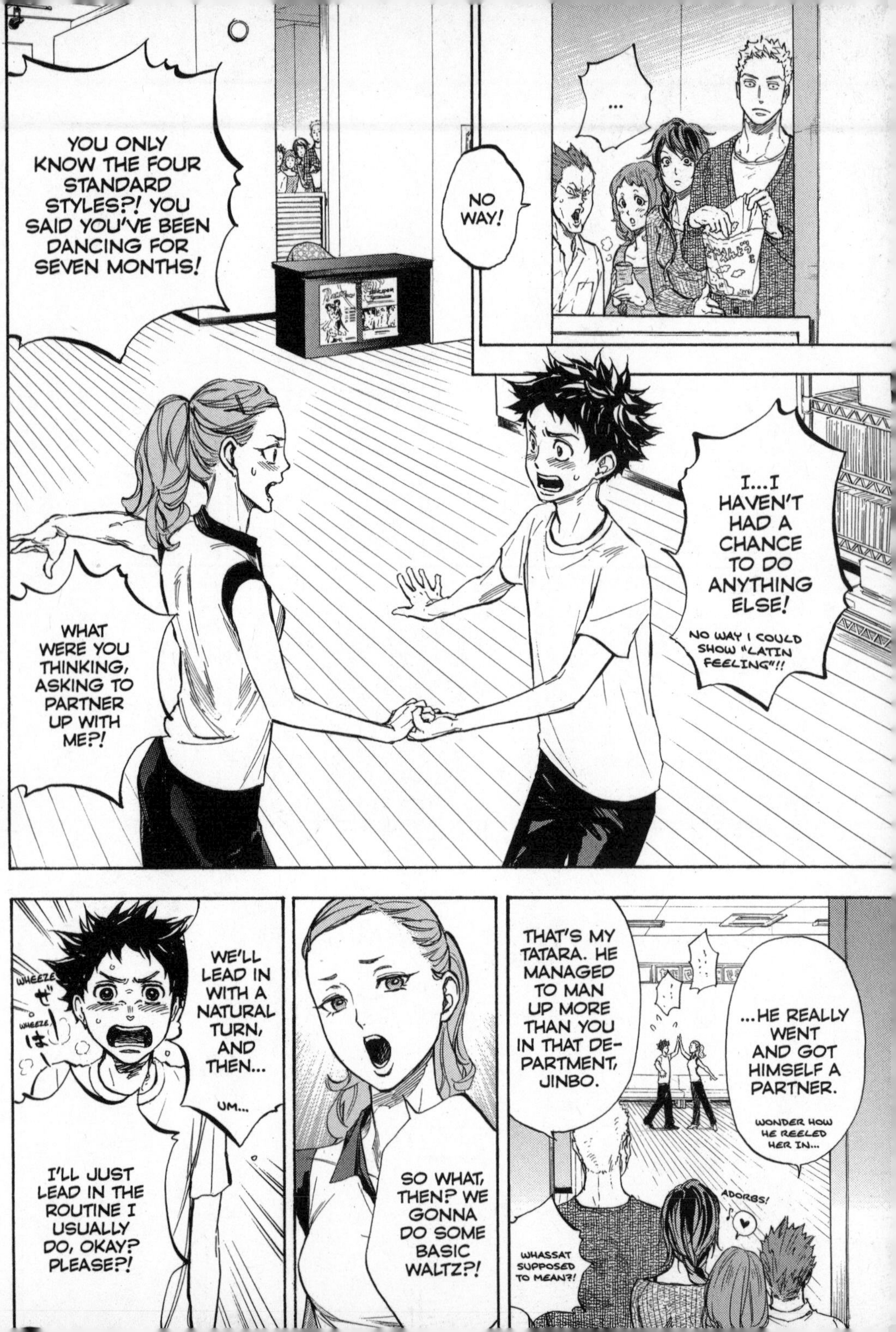
...
NO WAY!
YOU ONLY KNOW THE FOUR STANDARD STYLES?! YOU SAID YOU'VE BEEN DANCING FOR SEVEN MONTHS!
I...I HAVEN'T HAD A CHANCE TO DO ANYTHING ELSE!
NO WAY I COULD SHOW "LATIN FEELING"!!
WHAT WERE YOU THINKING, ASKING TO PARTNER UP WITH ME?!
...HE REALLY WENT AND GOT HIMSELF A PARTNER.
WONDER HOW HE REELED HER IN...
ADORBS!
THAT'S MY TATARA. HE MANAGED TO MAN UP MORE THAN YOU IN THAT DE-PARTMENT, JINBO.
WHASSAT SUPPOSED TO MEAN?!
SO WHAT, THEN? WE GONNA DO SOME BASIC WALTZ?!
WE'LL LEAD IN WITH A NATURAL TURN, AND THEN...
WHEEZE ぜ
WHEEZE は
UM...
I'LL JUST LEAD IN THE ROUTINE I USUALLY DO, OKAY? PLEASE?!

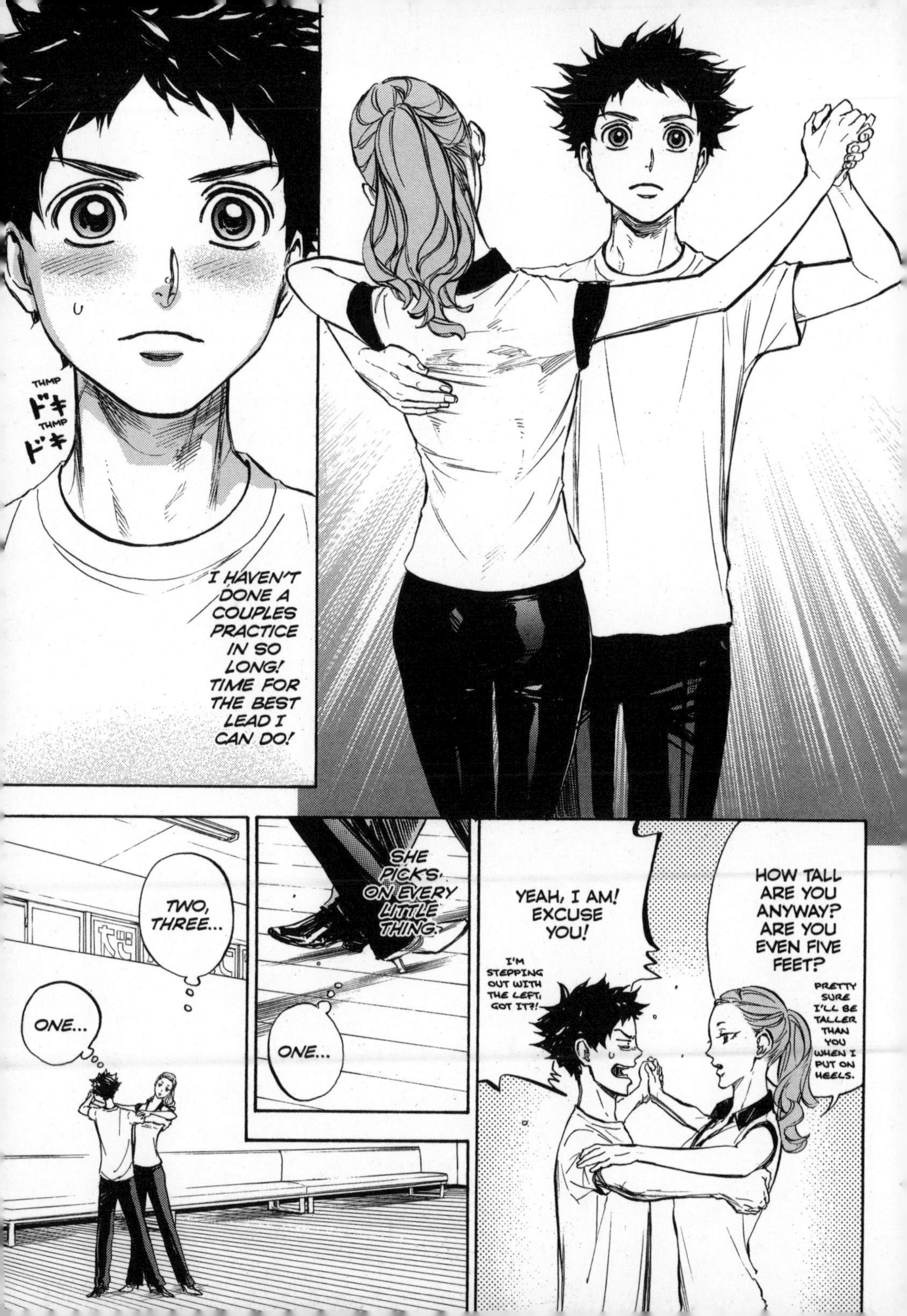
THMP
ドキ
THMP
ドキ
I HAVEN'T DONE A COUPLES PRACTICE IN SO LONG! TIME FOR THE BEST LEAD I CAN DO!
HOW TALL ARE YOU ANYWAY? ARE YOU EVEN FIVE FEET?
PRETTY SURE I'LL BE TALLER THAN YOU WHEN I PUT ON HEELS.
YEAH, I AM! EXCUSE YOU!
I'M STEPPING OUT WITH THE LEFT, GOT IT?!
SHE PICKS ON EVERY LITTLE THING.
ONE...
TWO, THREE...
ONE...

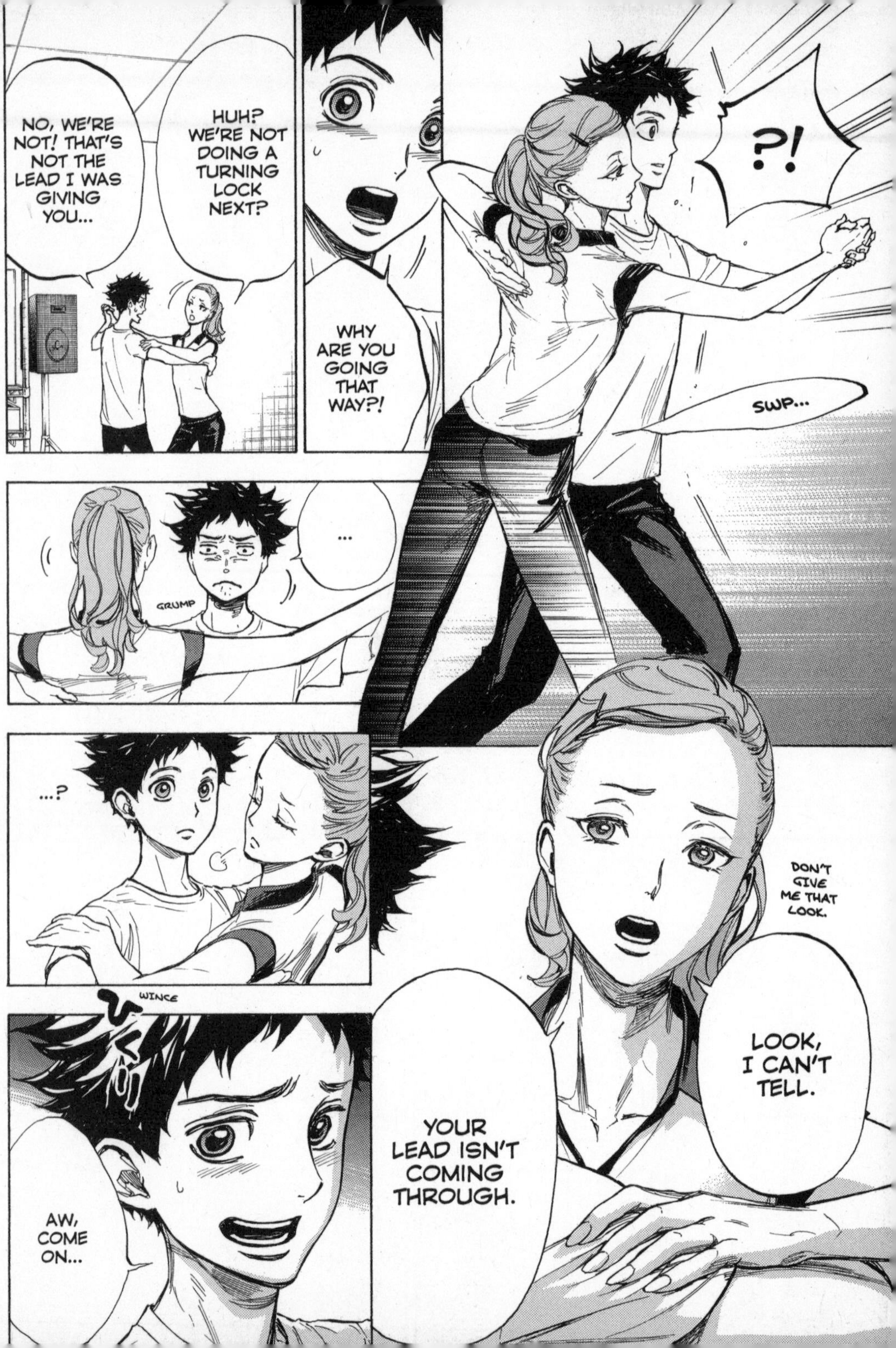
?!
SWP...
WHY ARE YOU GOING THAT WAY?!
HUH? WE'RE NOT DOING A TURNING LOCK NEXT?
NO, WE'RE NOT! THAT'S NOT THE LEAD I WAS GIVING YOU...
...
GRUMP
DON'T GIVE ME THAT LOOK.
LOOK, I CAN'T TELL.
YOUR LEAD ISN'T COMING THROUGH.
...?
WINCE
AW, COME ON...

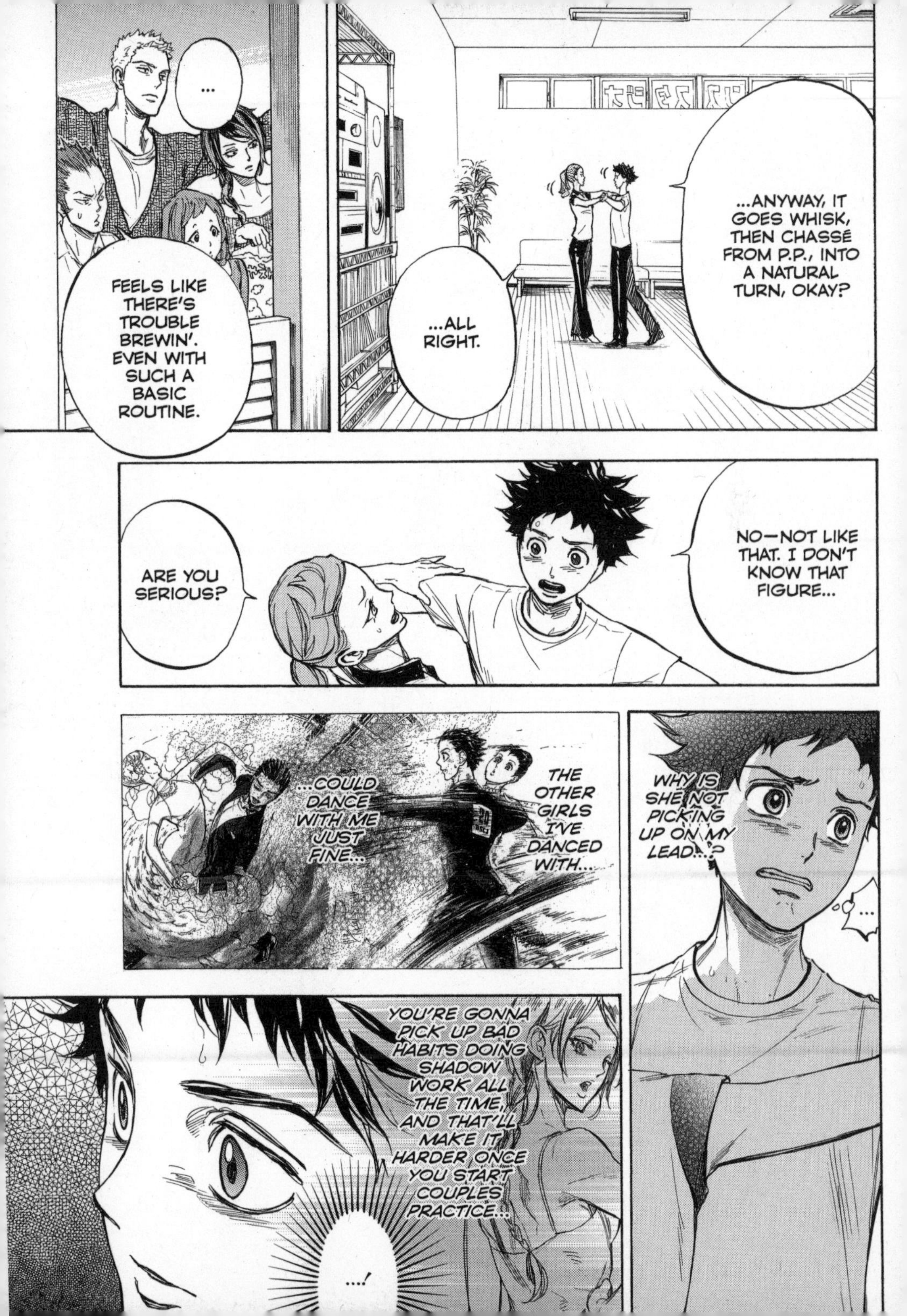
...ANYWAY, IT GOES WHISK, THEN CHASSÉ FROM P.P., INTO A NATURAL TURN, OKAY?
...ALL RIGHT.
...
FEELS LIKE THERE'S TROUBLE BREWIN'. EVEN WITH SUCH A BASIC ROUTINE.
NO—NOT LIKE THAT. I DON'T KNOW THAT FIGURE...
ARE YOU SERIOUS?
WHY IS SHE NOT PICKING UP ON MY LEAD...?
...
THE OTHER GIRLS I'VE DANCED WITH...
...COULD DANCE WITH ME JUST FINE...
YOU'RE GONNA PICK UP BAD HABITS DOING SHADOW WORK ALL THE TIME, AND THAT'LL MAKE IT HARDER ONCE YOU START COUPLES PRACTICE...
...!

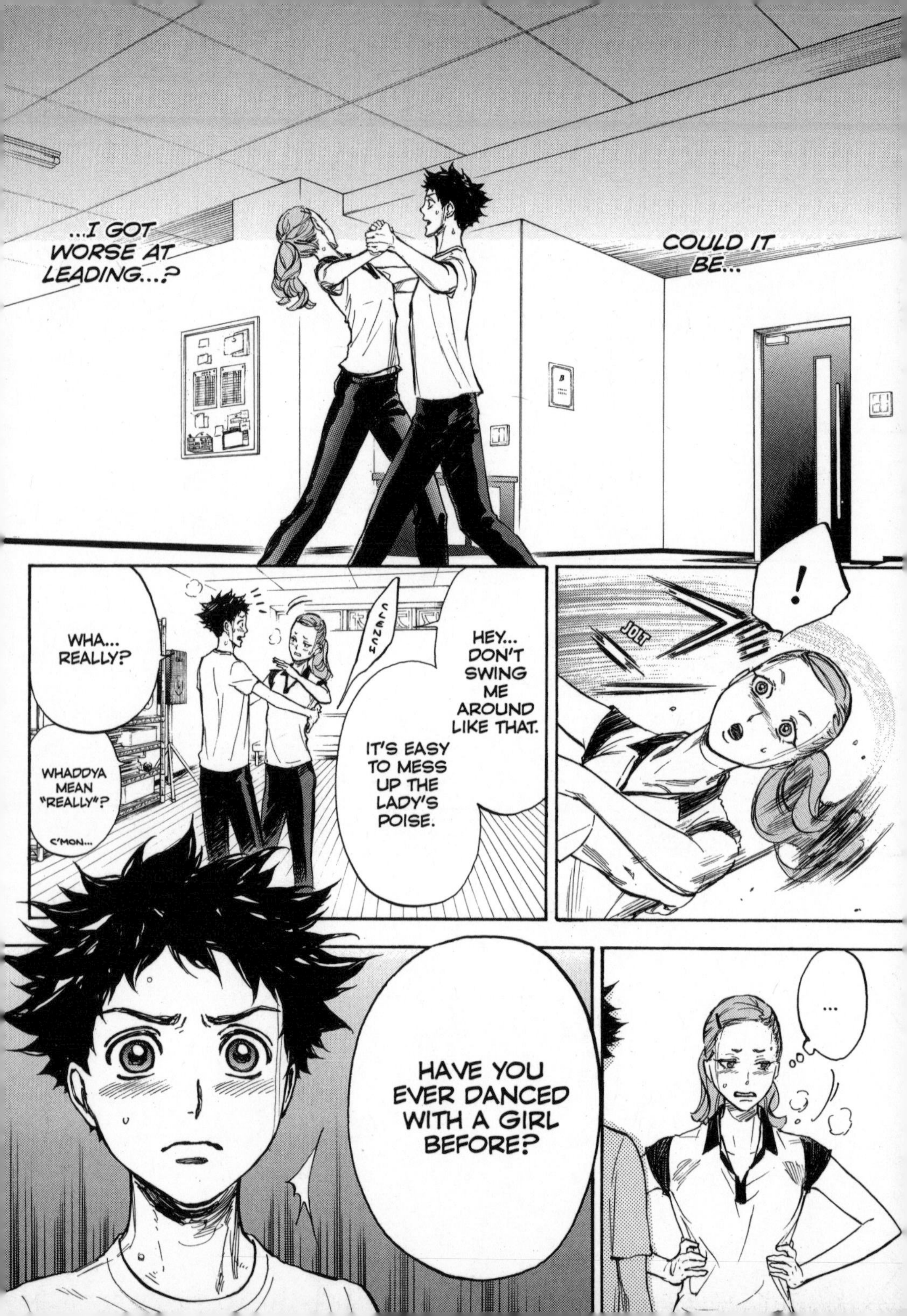
COULD IT BE...
...I GOT WORSE AT LEADING...?
!
JOLT
HEY... DON'T SWING ME AROUND LIKE THAT.
CLENCH
IT'S EASY TO MESS UP THE LADY'S POISE.
WHA... REALLY?
WHADDYA MEAN "REALLY"?
C'MON...
...
HAVE YOU EVER DANCED WITH A GIRL BEFORE?

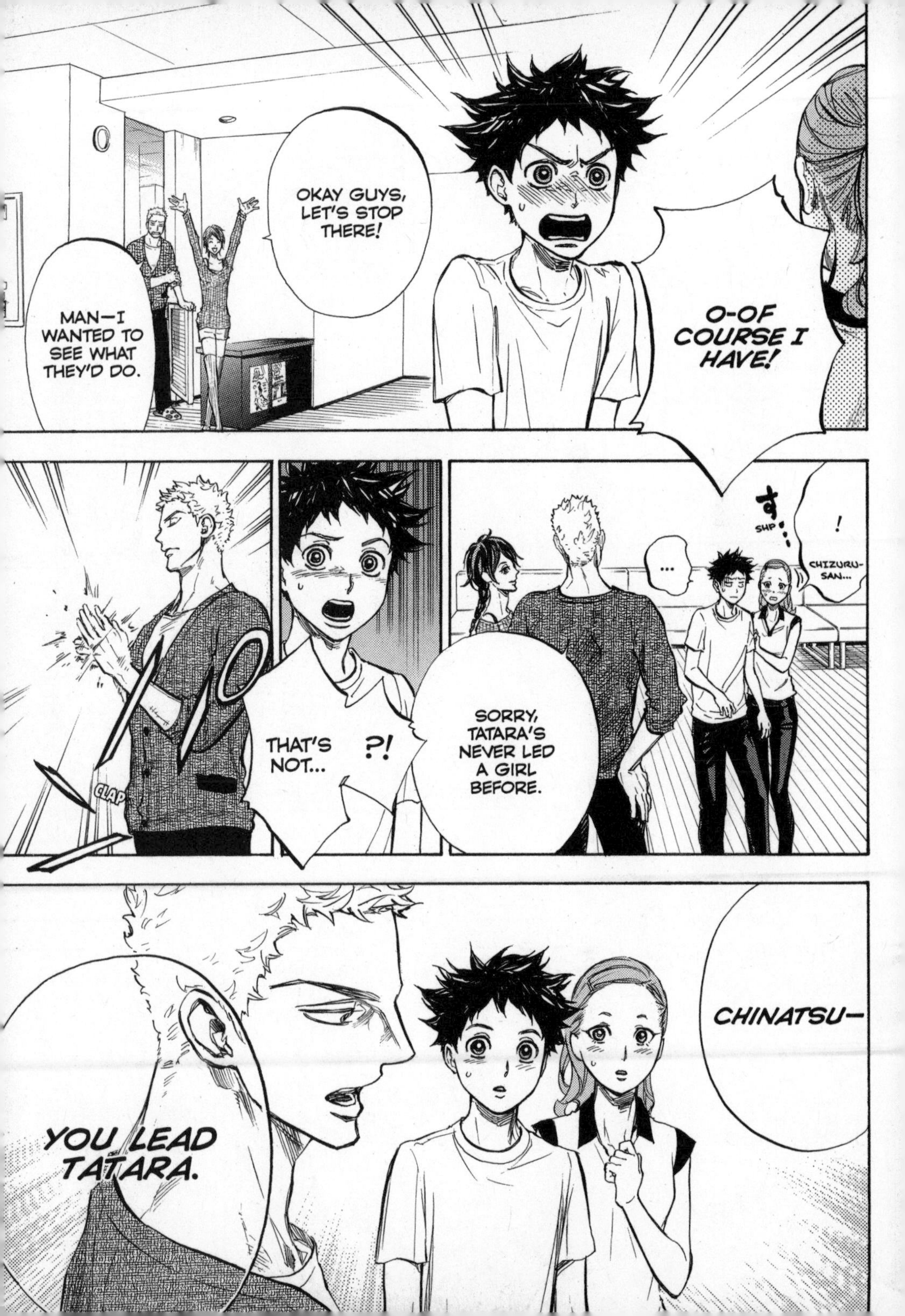
O-OF COURSE I HAVE!
OKAY GUYS, LET'S STOP THERE!
MAN—I WANTED TO SEE WHAT THEY'D DO.
す
SHP
!
CHIZURU-SAN...
...
SORRY, TATARA'S NEVER LED A GIRL BEFORE.
?!
THAT'S NOT...
CLAP
CHINATSU—
YOU LEAD TATARA.

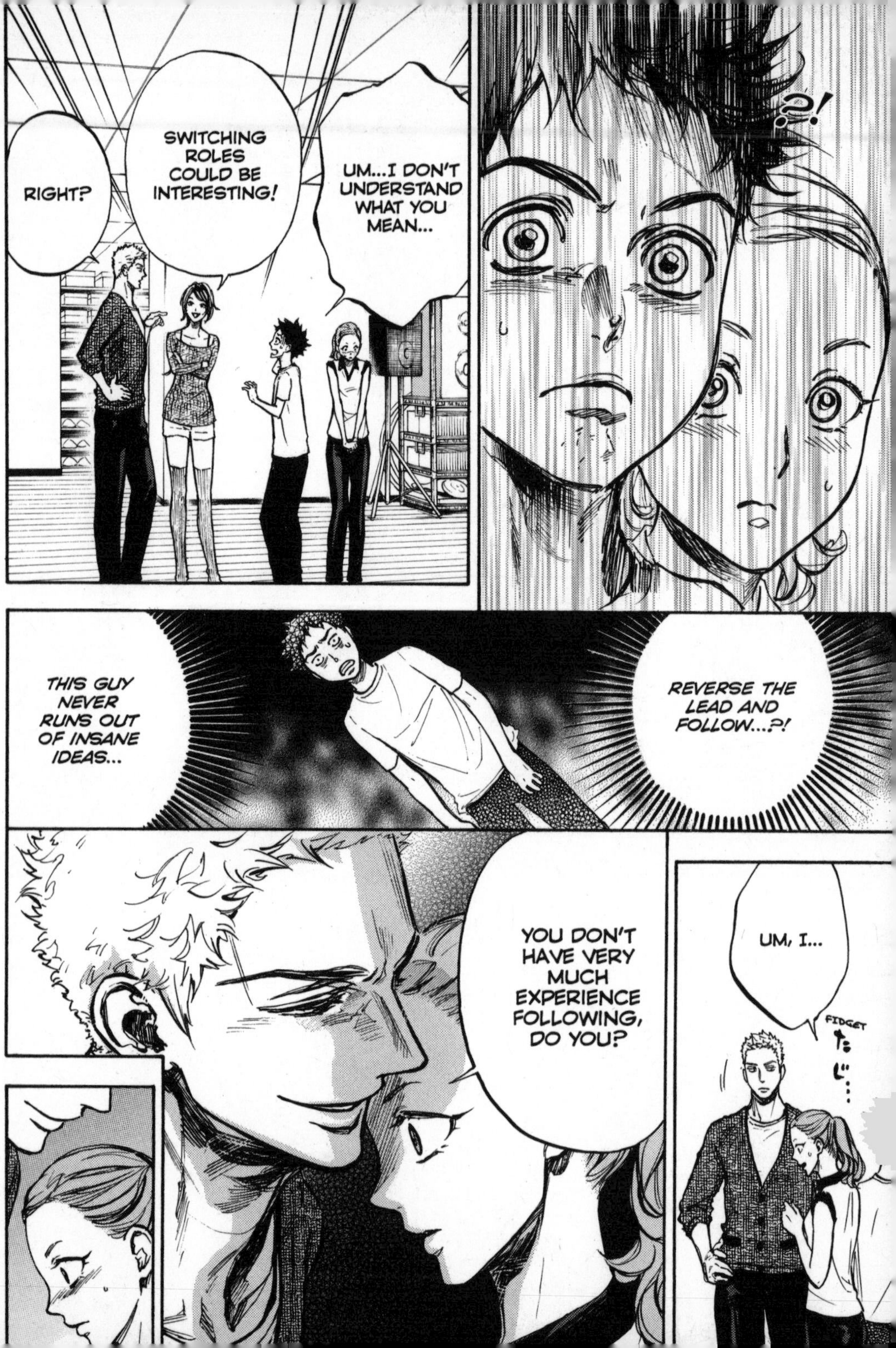
?!
UM...I DON'T UNDERSTAND WHAT YOU MEAN...
SWITCHING ROLES COULD BE INTERESTING!
RIGHT?
REVERSE THE LEAD AND FOLLOW...?!
THIS GUY NEVER RUNS OUT OF INSANE IDEAS...
UM, I...
FIDGET
YOU DON'T HAVE VERY MUCH EXPERIENCE FOLLOWING, DO YOU?

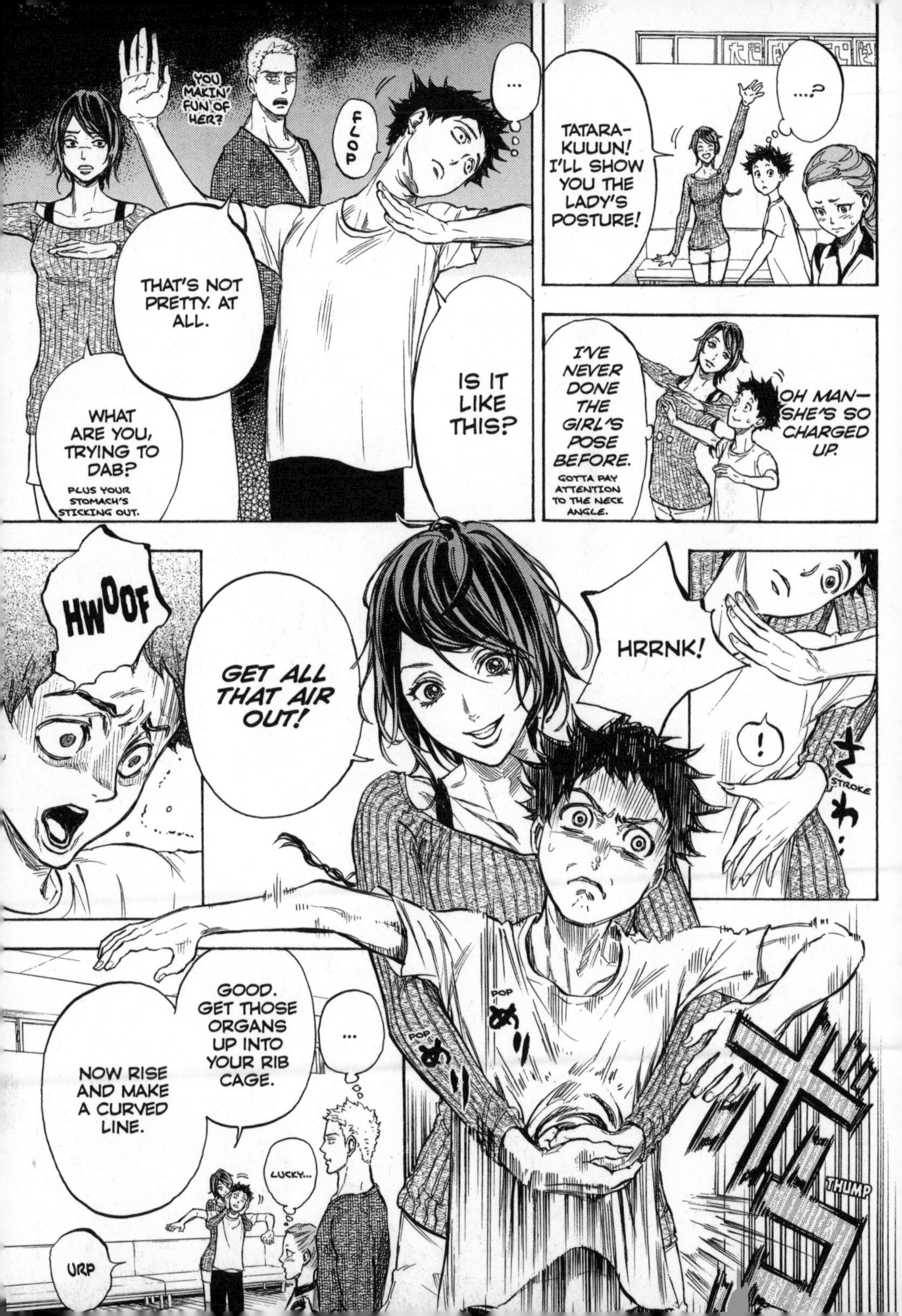
TATARA-KUUUN! I'LL SHOW YOU THE LADY'S POSTURE!
...?
I'VE NEVER DONE THE GIRL'S POSE BEFORE.
GOTTA PAY ATTENTION TO THE NECK ANGLE.
OH MAN—SHE'S SO CHARGED UP.
...
FLOP
IS IT LIKE THIS?
YOU MAKIN' FUN OF HER?
THAT'S NOT PRETTY. AT ALL.
WHAT ARE YOU, TRYING TO DAB?
PLUS YOUR STOMACH'S STICKING OUT.
HRRNK!
!
さわ
STROKE
GET ALL THAT AIR OUT!
HWOOF
THUMP
めり
POP
めり
POP
GOOD. GET THOSE ORGANS UP INTO YOUR RIB CAGE.
...
NOW RISE AND MAKE A CURVED LINE.
LUCKY...
URP

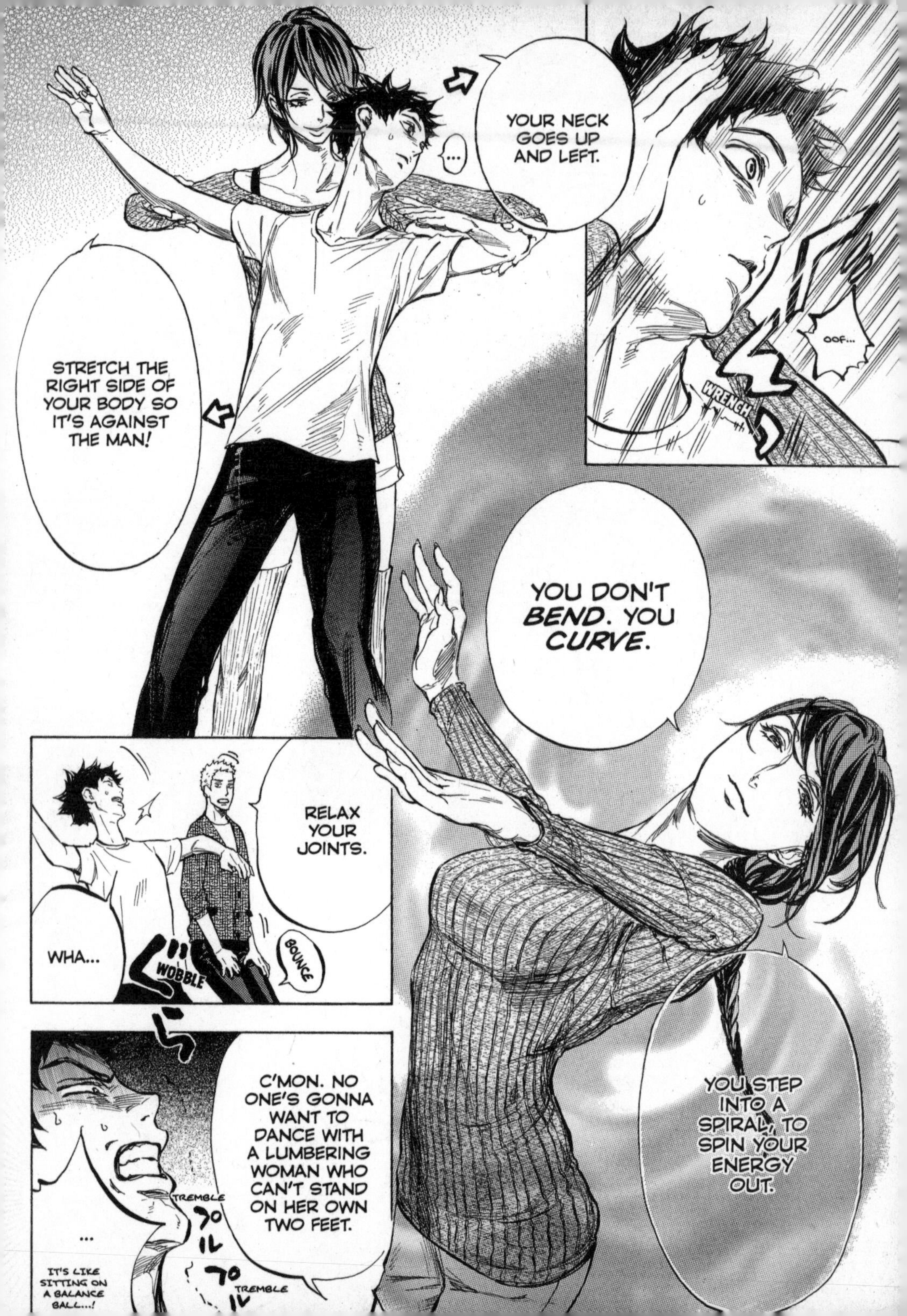
YOUR NECK GOES UP AND LEFT.
WRENCH
OOF...
...
STRETCH THE RIGHT SIDE OF YOUR BODY SO IT'S AGAINST THE MAN!
YOU DON'T *BEND*. YOU *CURVE*.
YOU STEP INTO A SPIRAL, TO SPIN YOUR ENERGY OUT.
RELAX YOUR JOINTS.
BOUNCE
WOBBLE
WHA...
C'MON. NO ONE'S GONNA WANT TO DANCE WITH A LUMBERING WOMAN WHO CAN'T STAND ON HER OWN TWO FEET.
TREMBLE
TREMBLE
...
IT'S LIKE SITTING ON A BALANCE BALL...!

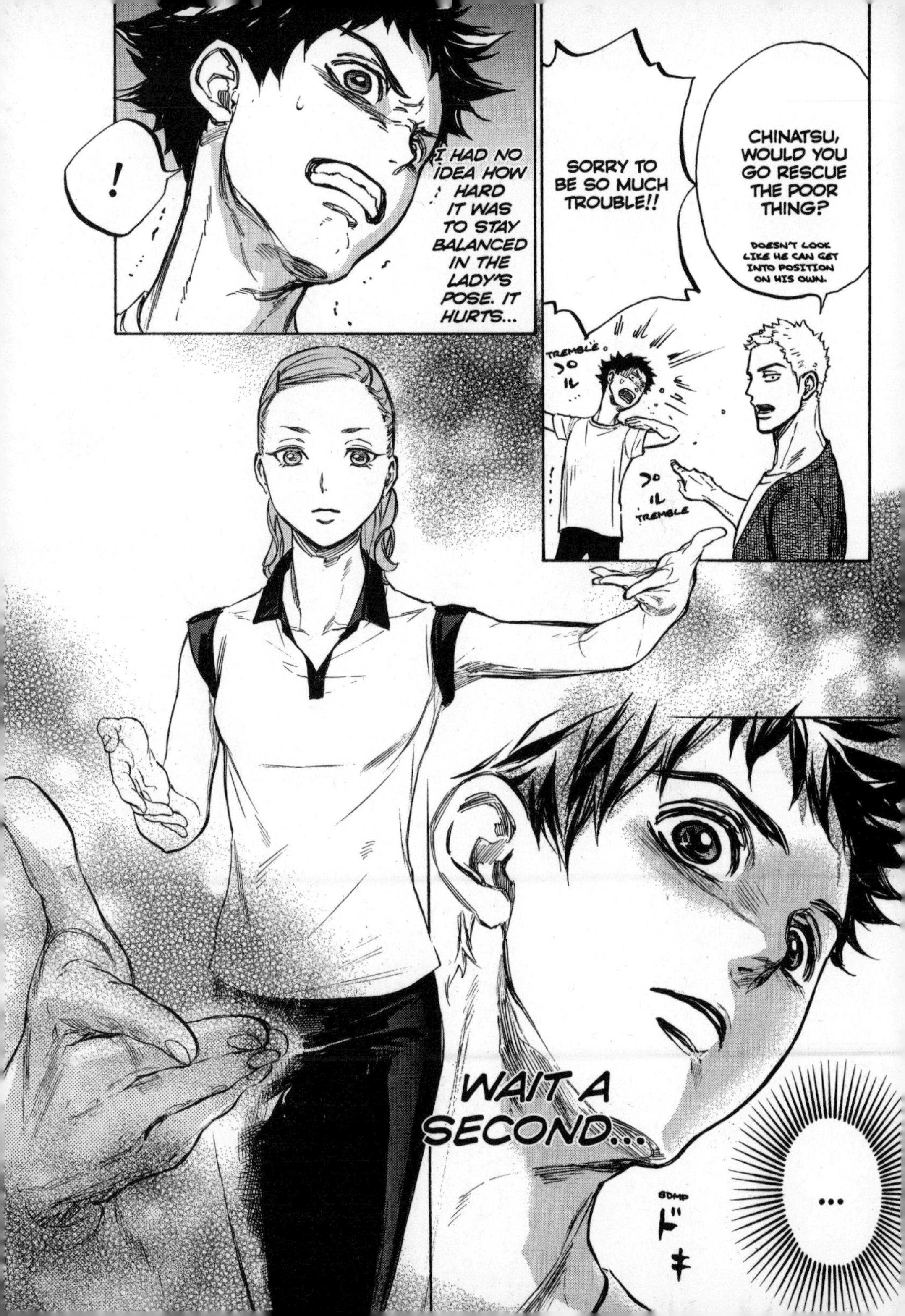

CHINATSU, WOULD YOU GO RESCUE THE POOR THING?
DOESN'T LOOK LIKE HE CAN GET INTO POSITION ON HIS OWN.
SORRY TO BE SO MUCH TROUBLE!!
TREMBLE
TREMBLE
I HAD NO IDEA HOW HARD IT WAS TO STAY BALANCED IN THE LADY'S POSE. IT HURTS...
!
...
SDMP
ドキ
WAIT A SECOND...

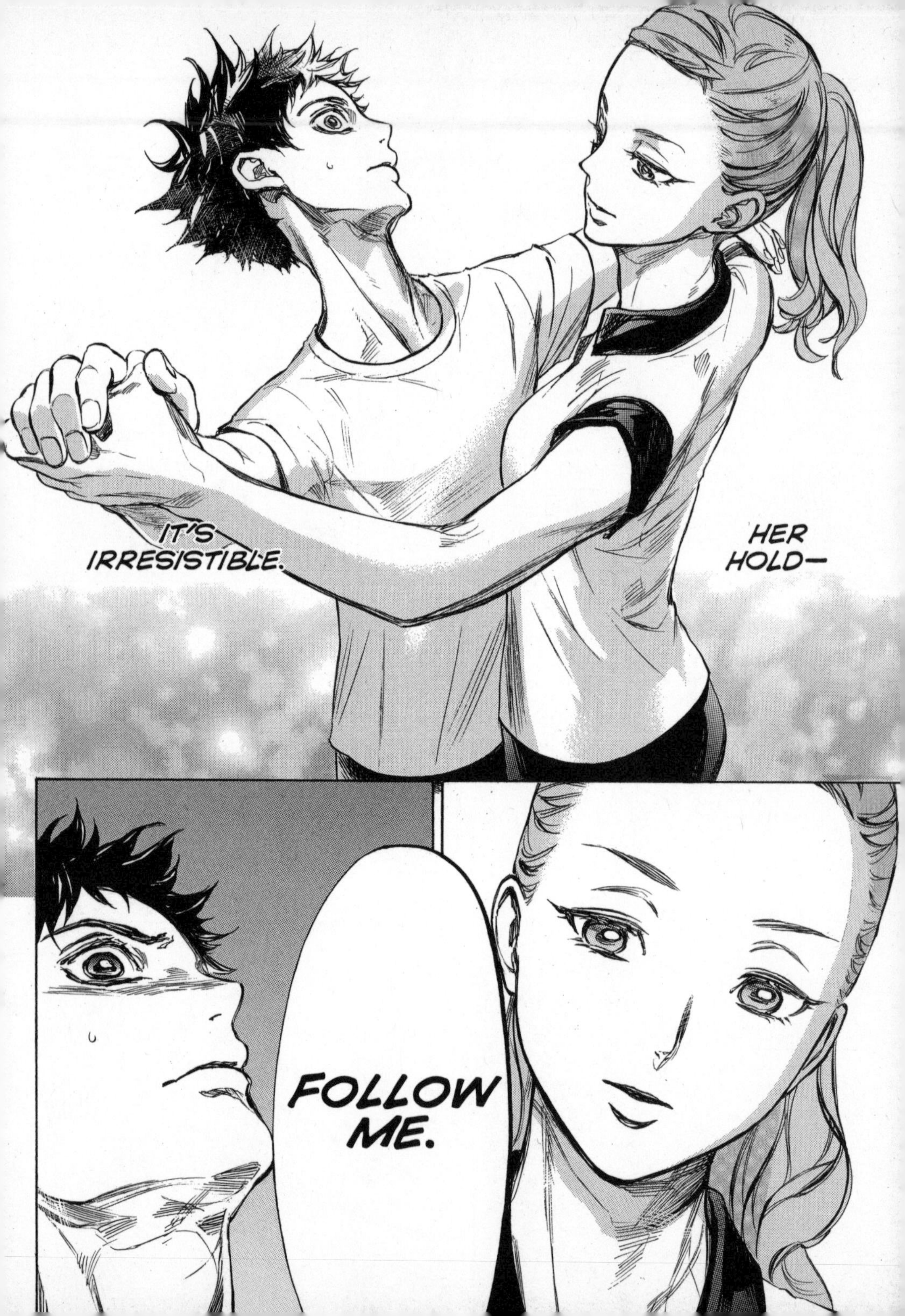
HER HOLD—
IT'S IRRESISTIBLE.
FOLLOW ME.

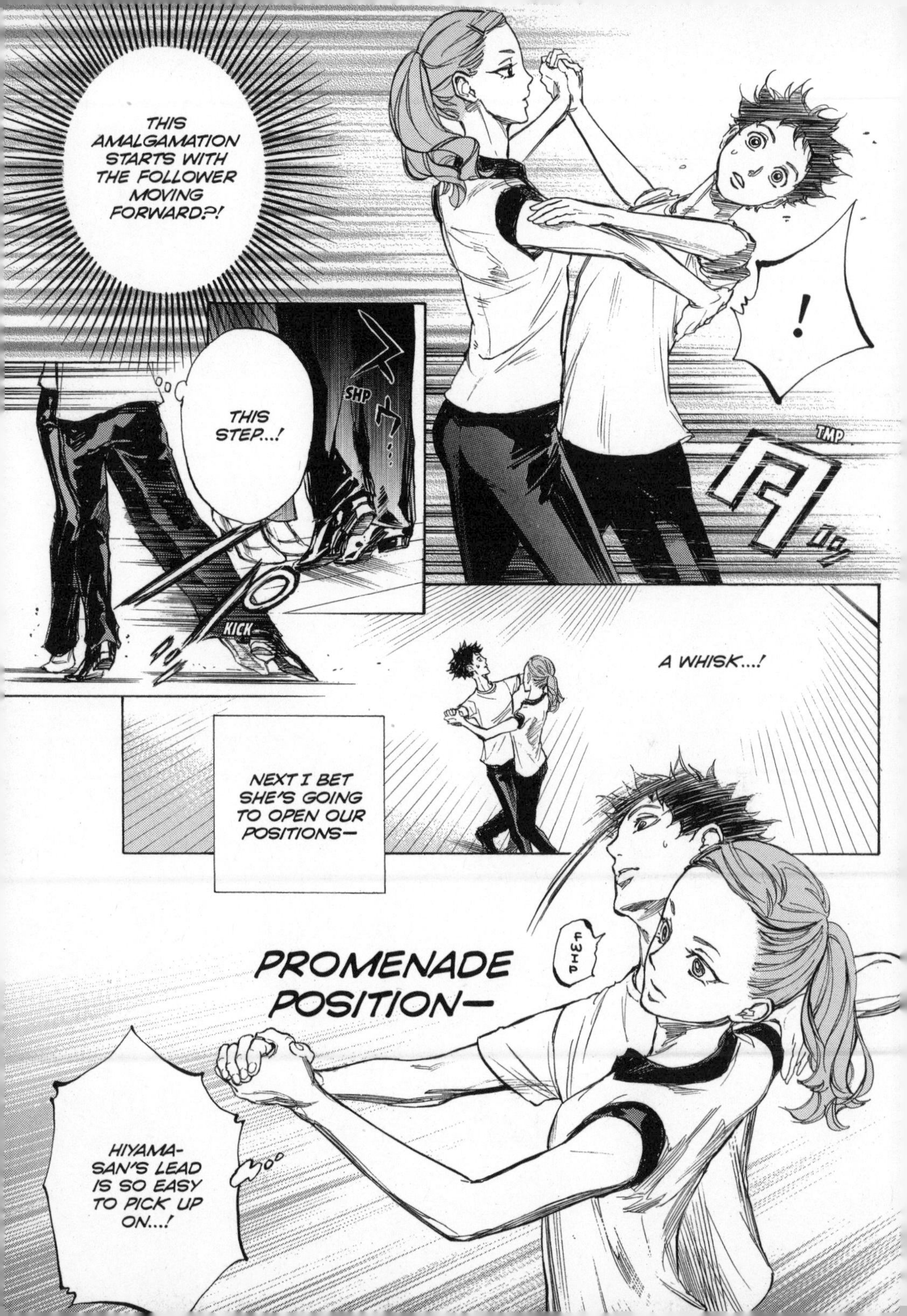
THIS AMALGAMATION STARTS WITH THE FOLLOWER MOVING FORWARD?!
!
TMP
SHP
THIS STEP...!
KICK
A WHISK...!
NEXT I BET SHE'S GOING TO OPEN OUR POSITIONS—
PROMENADE POSITION—
FSHP
HIYAMA-SAN'S LEAD IS SO EASY TO PICK UP ON...!

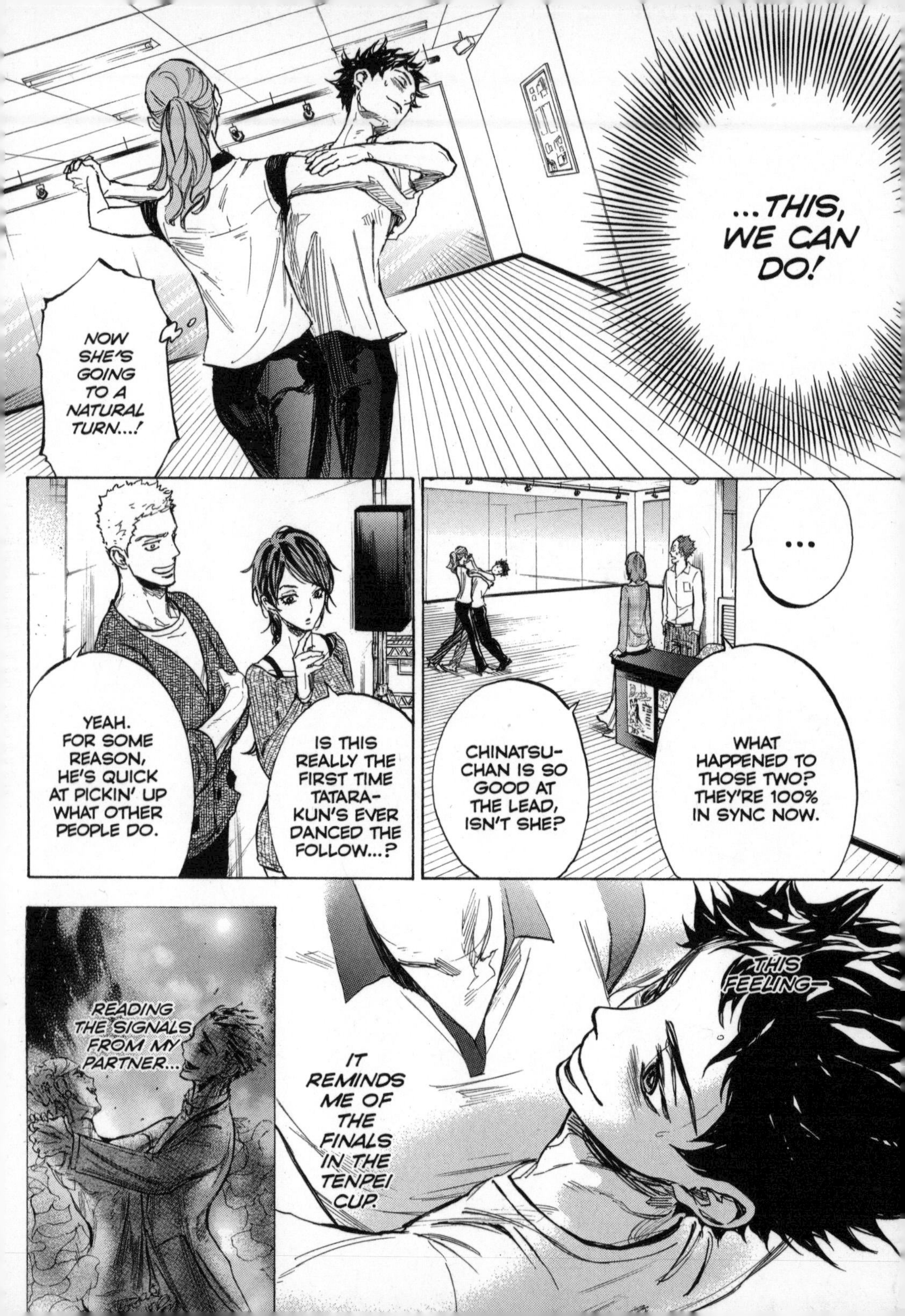
...THIS, WE CAN DO!
NOW SHE'S GOING TO A NATURAL TURN...!
...
WHAT HAPPENED TO THOSE TWO? THEY'RE 100% IN SYNC NOW.
CHINATSU-CHAN IS SO GOOD AT THE LEAD, ISN'T SHE?
IS THIS REALLY THE FIRST TIME TATARA-KUN'S EVER DANCED THE FOLLOW...?
YEAH. FOR SOME REASON, HE'S QUICK AT PICKIN' UP WHAT OTHER PEOPLE DO.
THIS FEELING—
IT REMINDS ME OF THE FINALS IN THE TENPEI CUP.
READING THE SIGNALS FROM MY PARTNER...

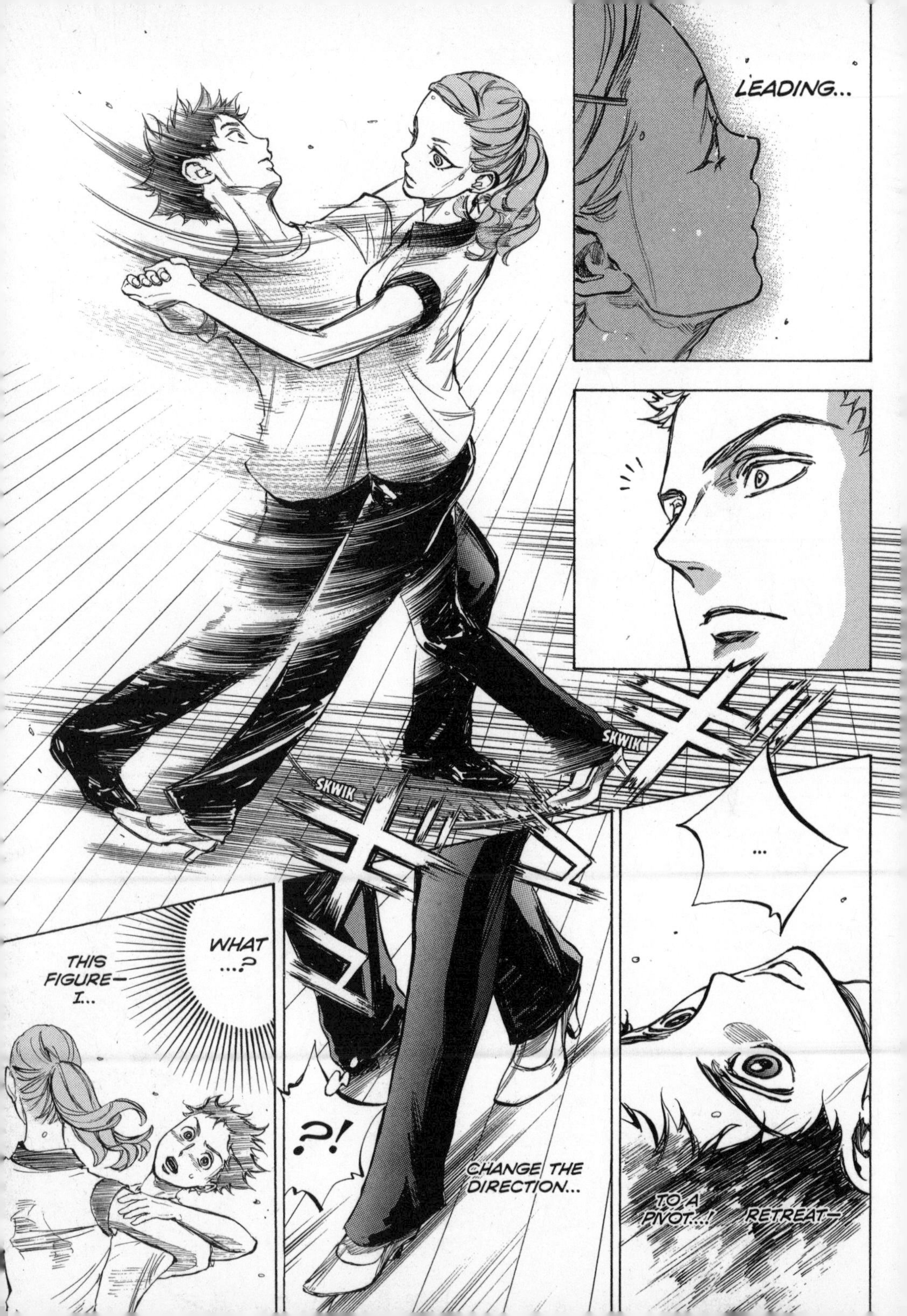
LEADING...
...
RETREAT—
TO A PIVOT...!
SKWIK
SKWIK
?!
CHANGE THE DIRECTION...
WHAT ...?
THIS FIGURE— I...

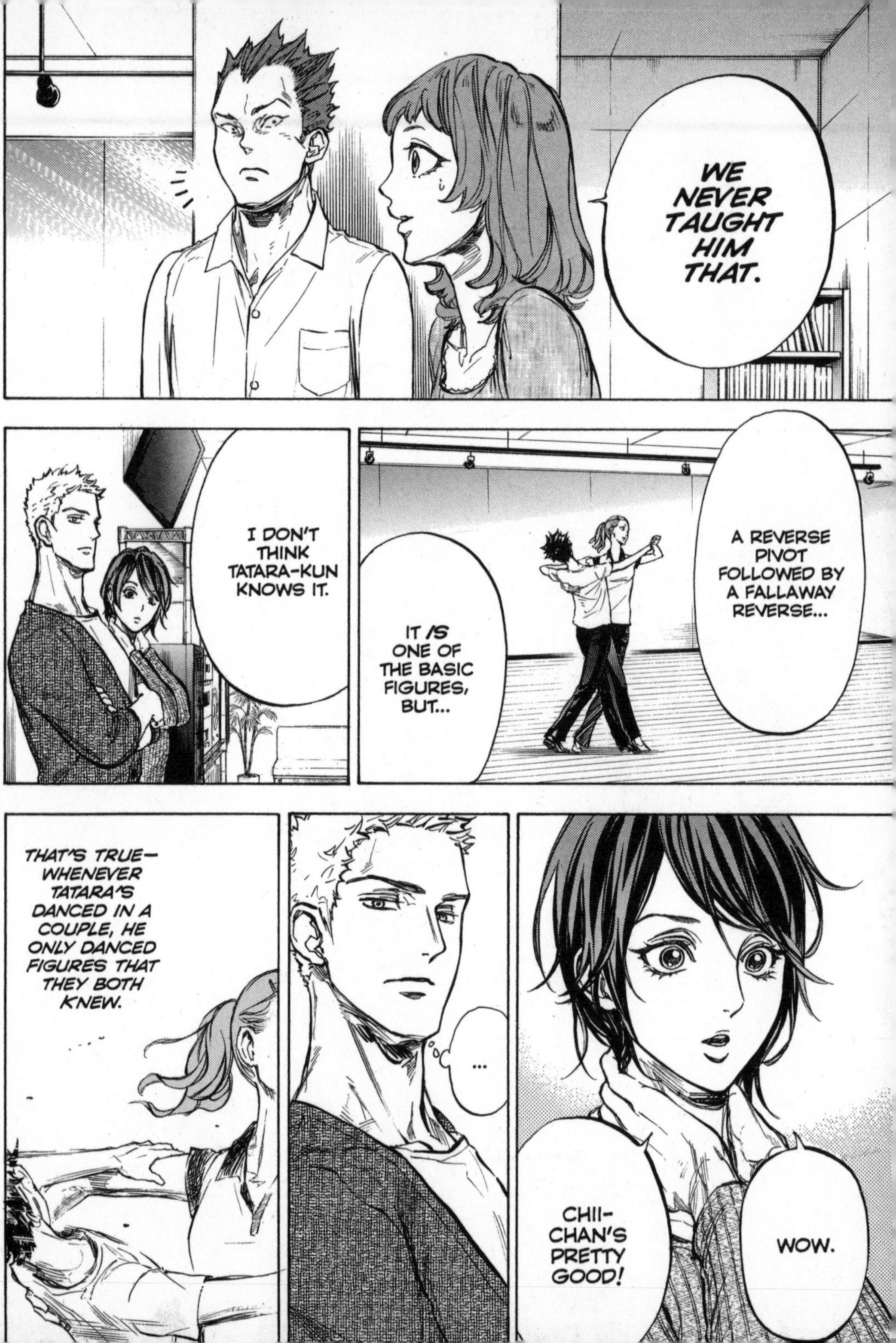
WE NEVER TAUGHT HIM THAT.
A REVERSE PIVOT FOLLOWED BY A FALLAWAY REVERSE...
IT IS ONE OF THE BASIC FIGURES, BUT...
I DON'T THINK TATARA-KUN KNOWS IT.
WOW.
CHII-CHAN'S PRETTY GOOD!
...
THAT'S TRUE—WHENEVER TATARA'S DANCED IN A COUPLE, HE ONLY DANCED FIGURES THAT THEY BOTH KNEW.

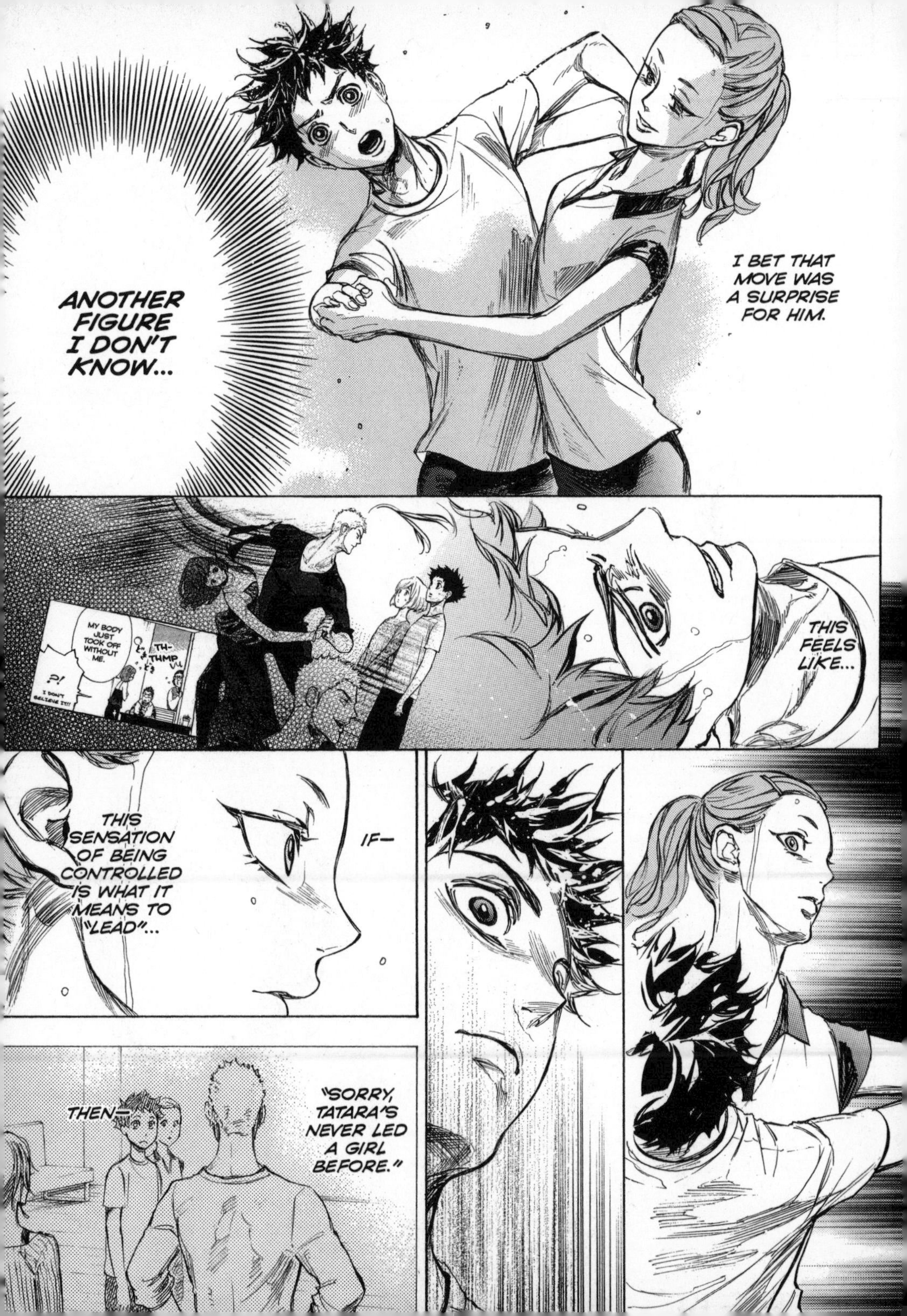
I BET THAT MOVE WAS A SURPRISE FOR HIM.
ANOTHER FIGURE I DON'T KNOW...
THIS FEELS LIKE...
TH-THUMP
MY BODY JUST TOOK OFF WITHOUT ME.
?!
I DON'T BELIEVE IT!!
IF—
THIS SENSATION OF BEING CONTROLLED IS WHAT IT MEANS TO "LEAD"...
"SORRY, TATARA'S NEVER LED A GIRL BEFORE."
THEN—

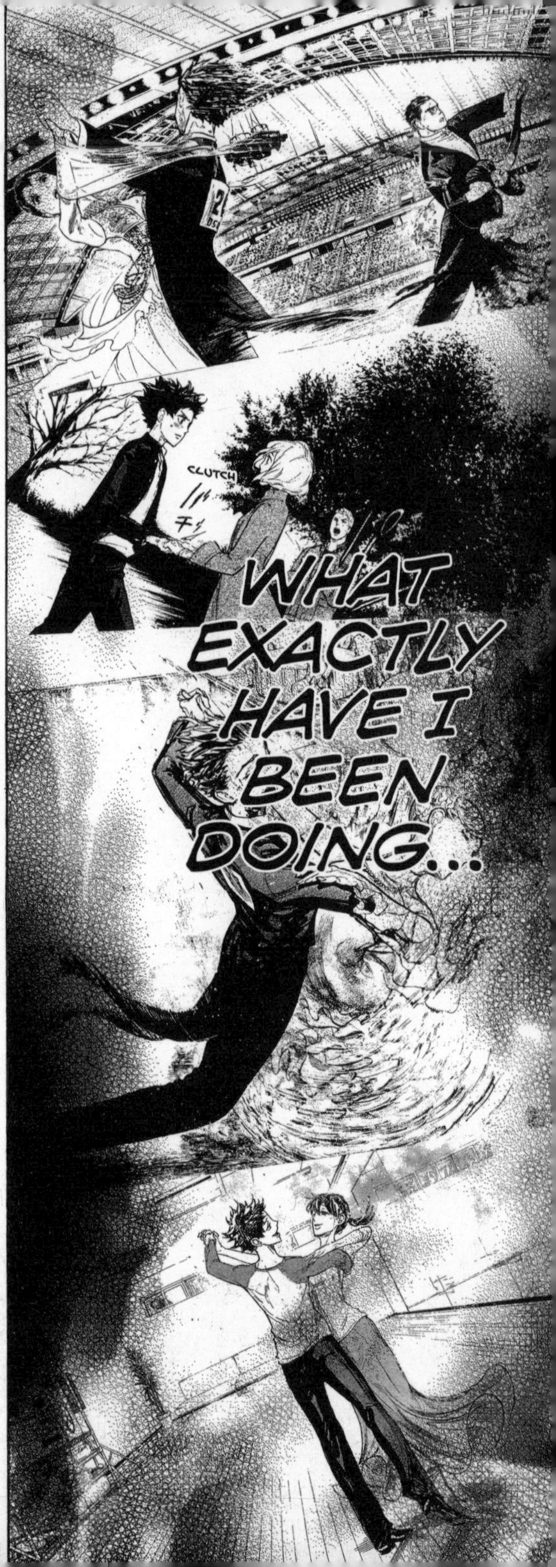
CLUTCH
WHAT EXACTLY HAVE I BEEN DOING...

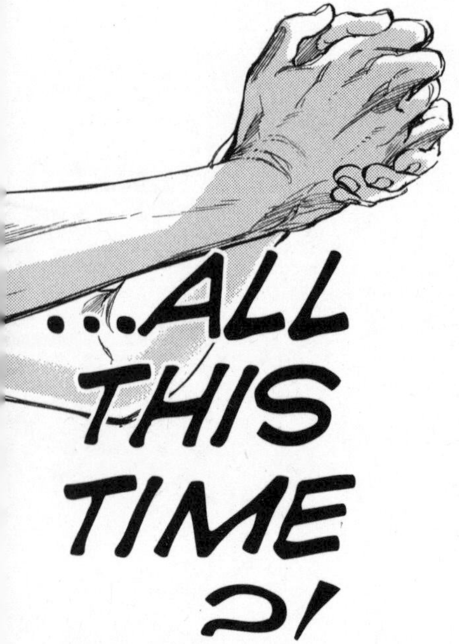
...ALL THIS TIME ...?!

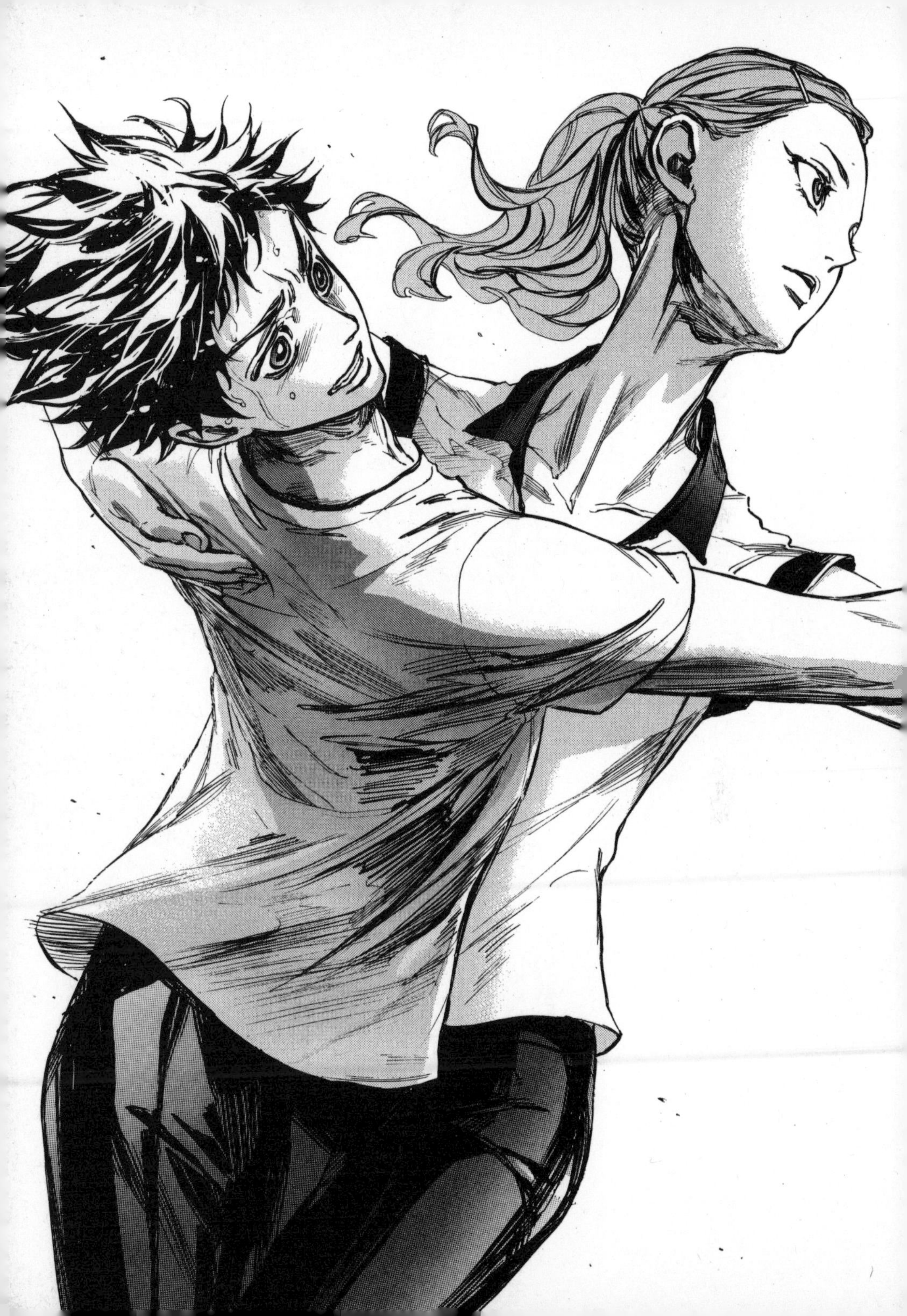

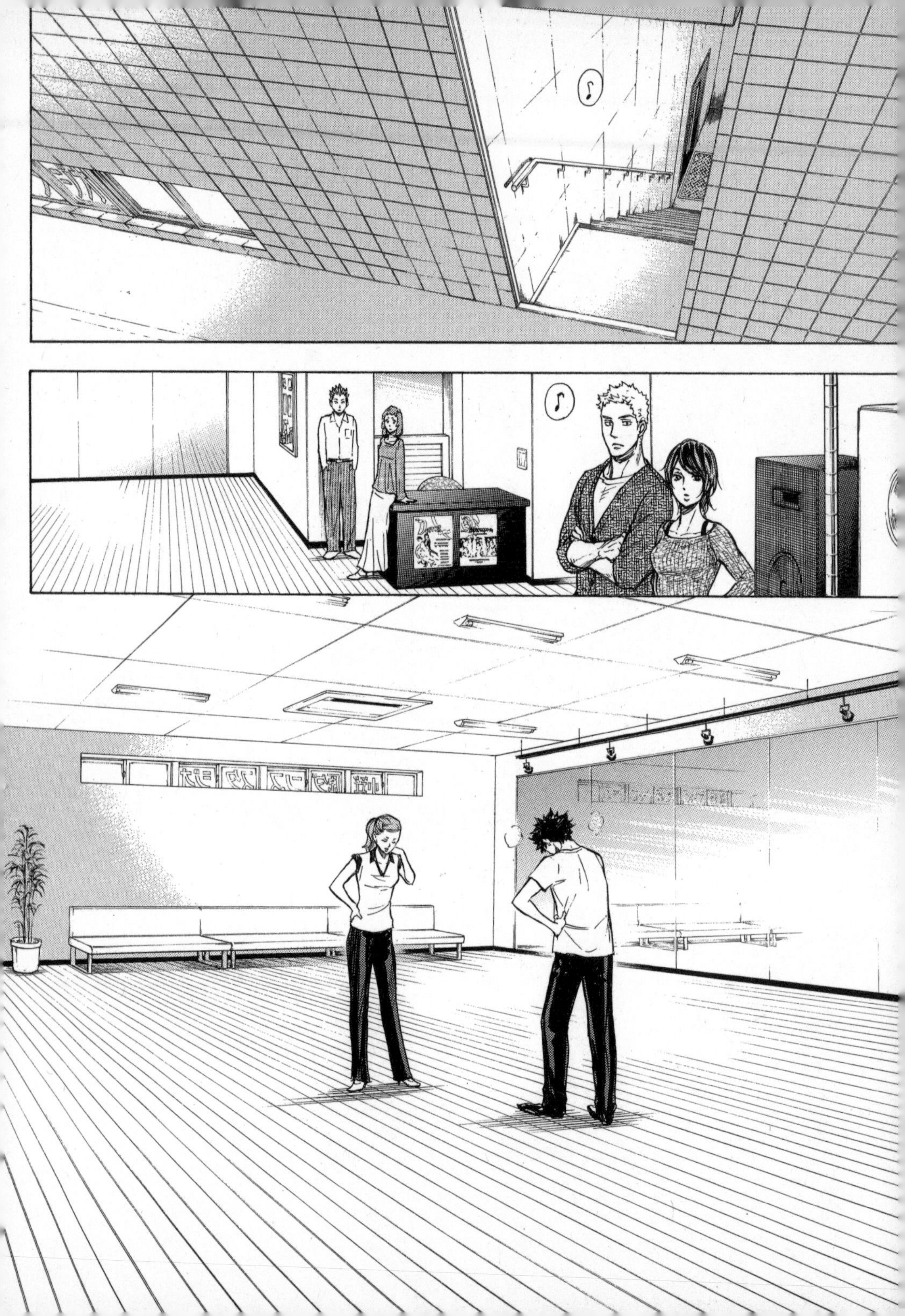

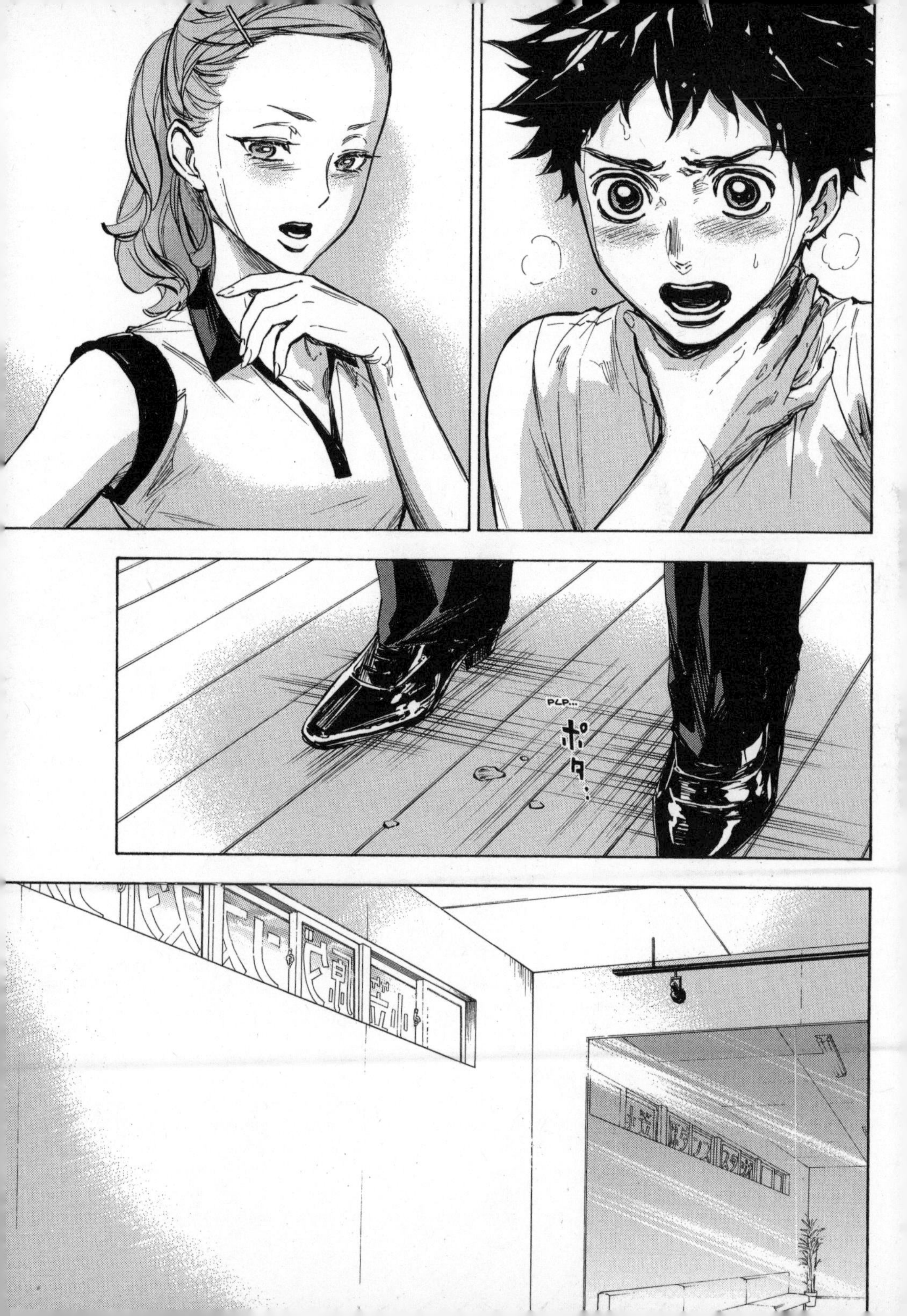
PLP...
ポタ‥

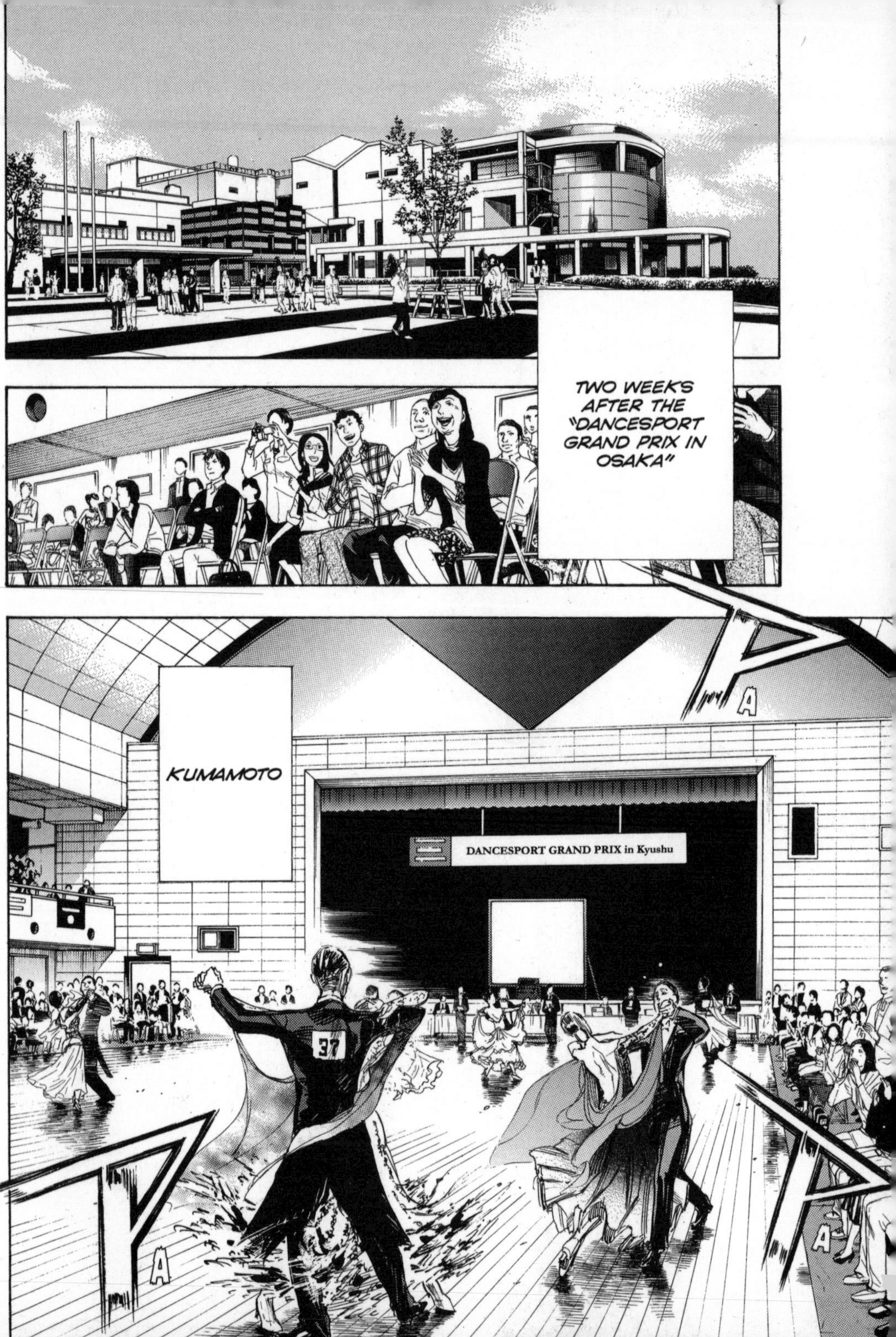

TWO WEEKS AFTER THE "DANCESPORT GRAND PRIX IN OSAKA"
PA
KUMAMOTO
DANCESPORT GRAND PRIX in Kyushu
PA
37
PA

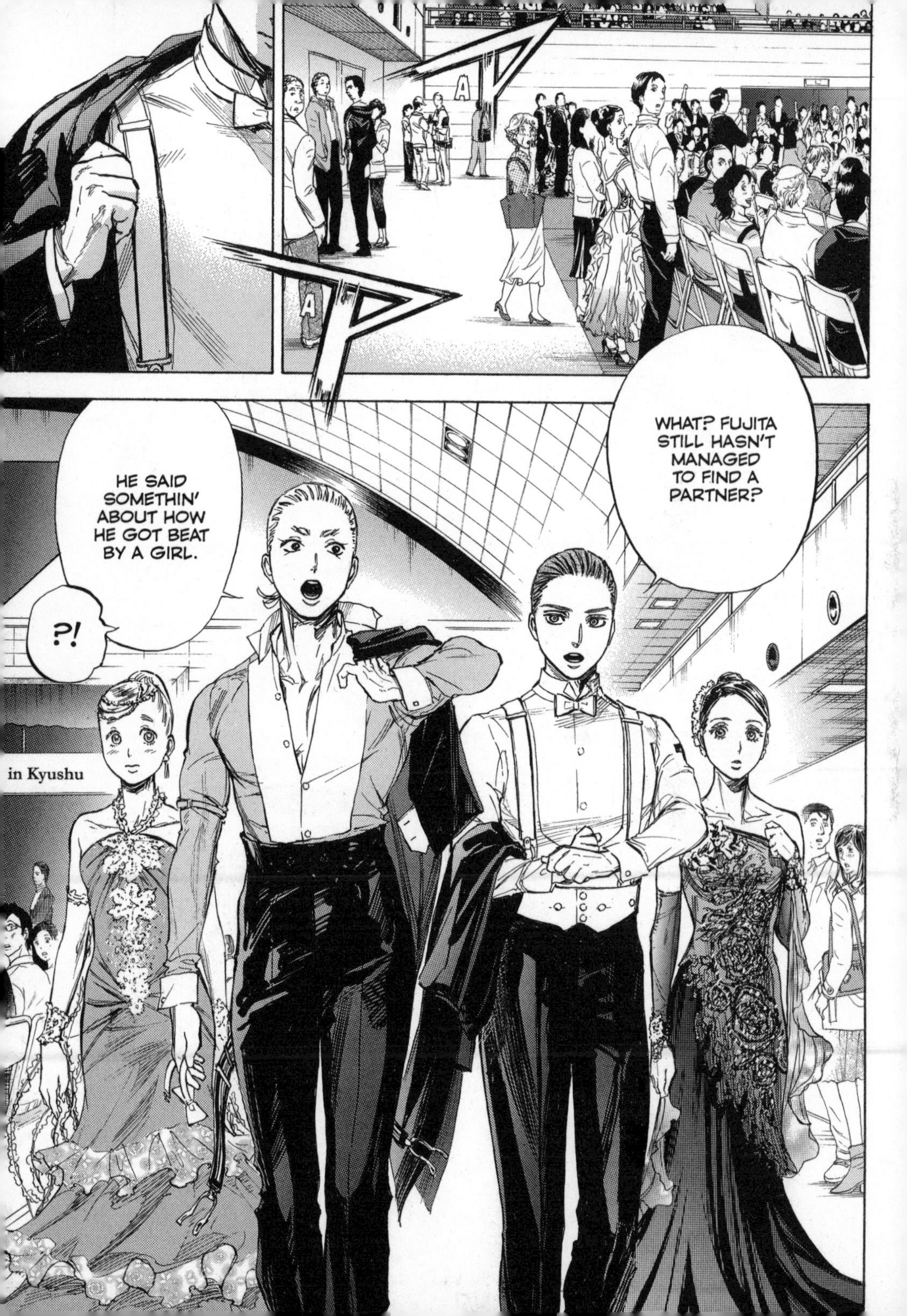
WHAT? FUJITA STILL HASN'T MANAGED TO FIND A PARTNER?
HE SAID SOMETHIN' ABOUT HOW HE GOT BEAT BY A GIRL.
?!
in Kyushu

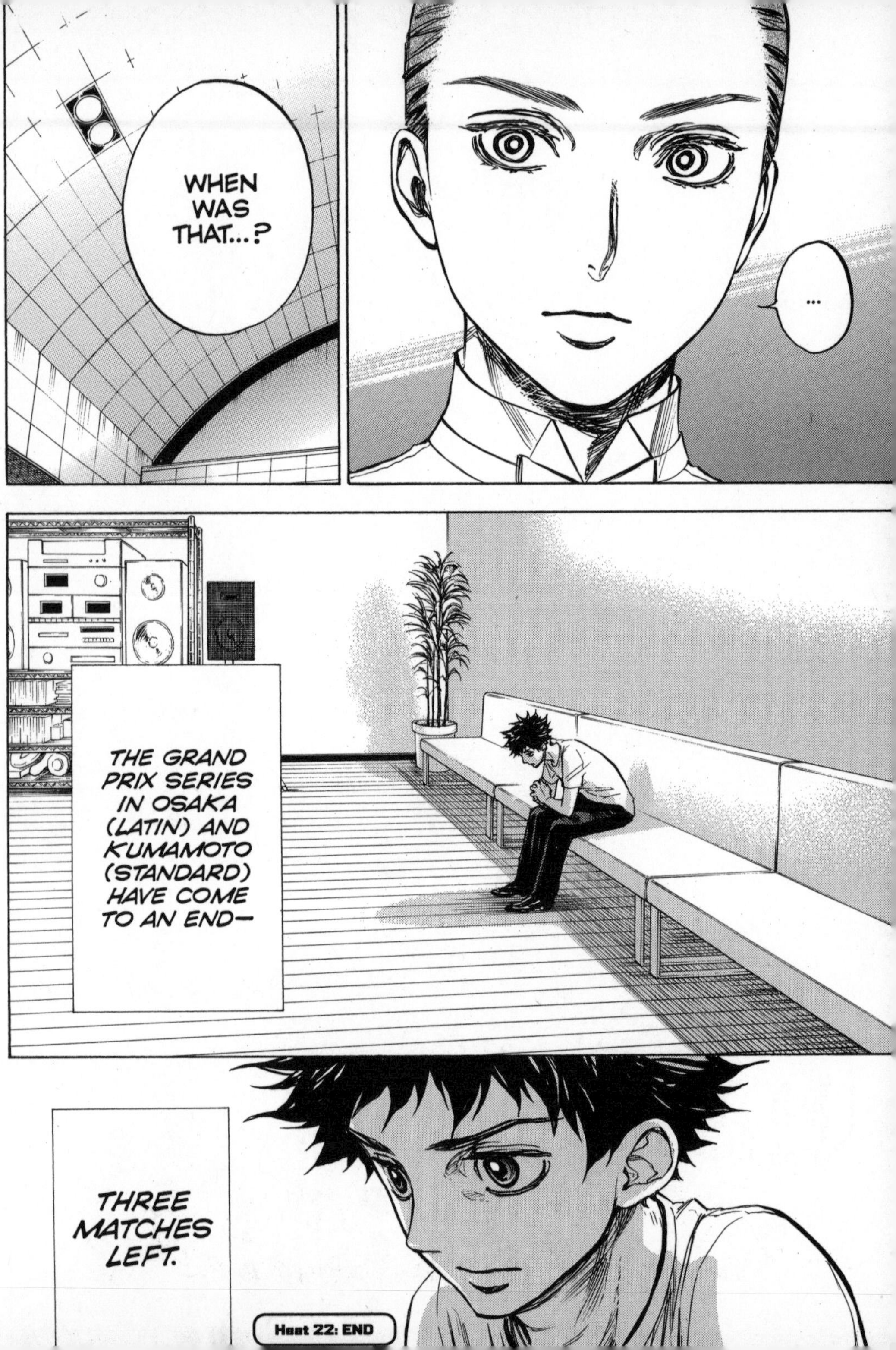
...
WHEN WAS THAT...?
THE GRAND PRIX SERIES IN OSAKA (LATIN) AND KUMAMOTO (STANDARD) HAVE COME TO AN END—
THREE MATCHES LEFT.
Heat 22: END

# WELCOME TO THE BALLROOM

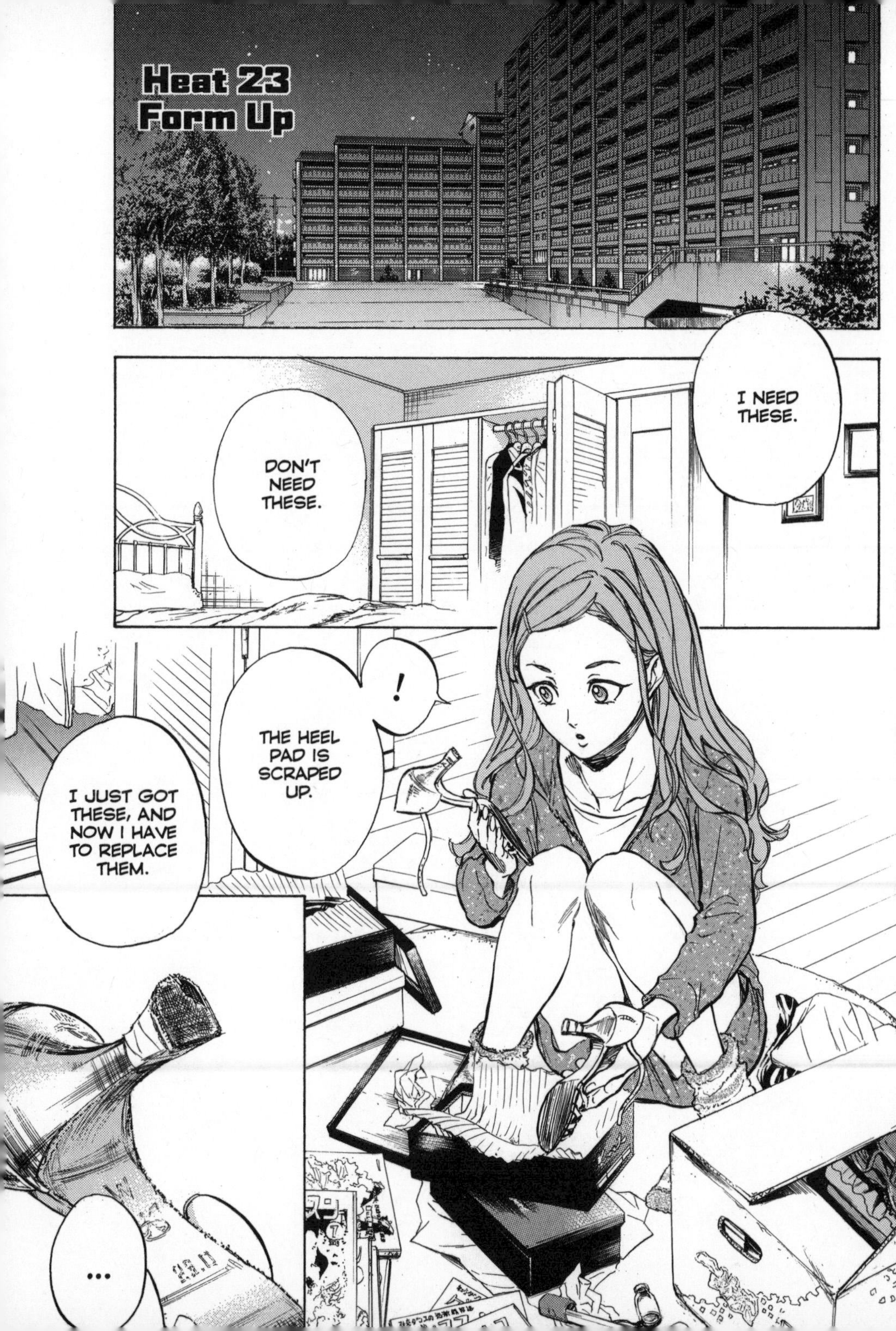
Heat 23
Form Up
I NEED THESE.
DON'T NEED THESE.
!
THE HEEL PAD IS SCRAPED UP.
I JUST GOT THESE, AND NOW I HAVE TO REPLACE THEM.
...

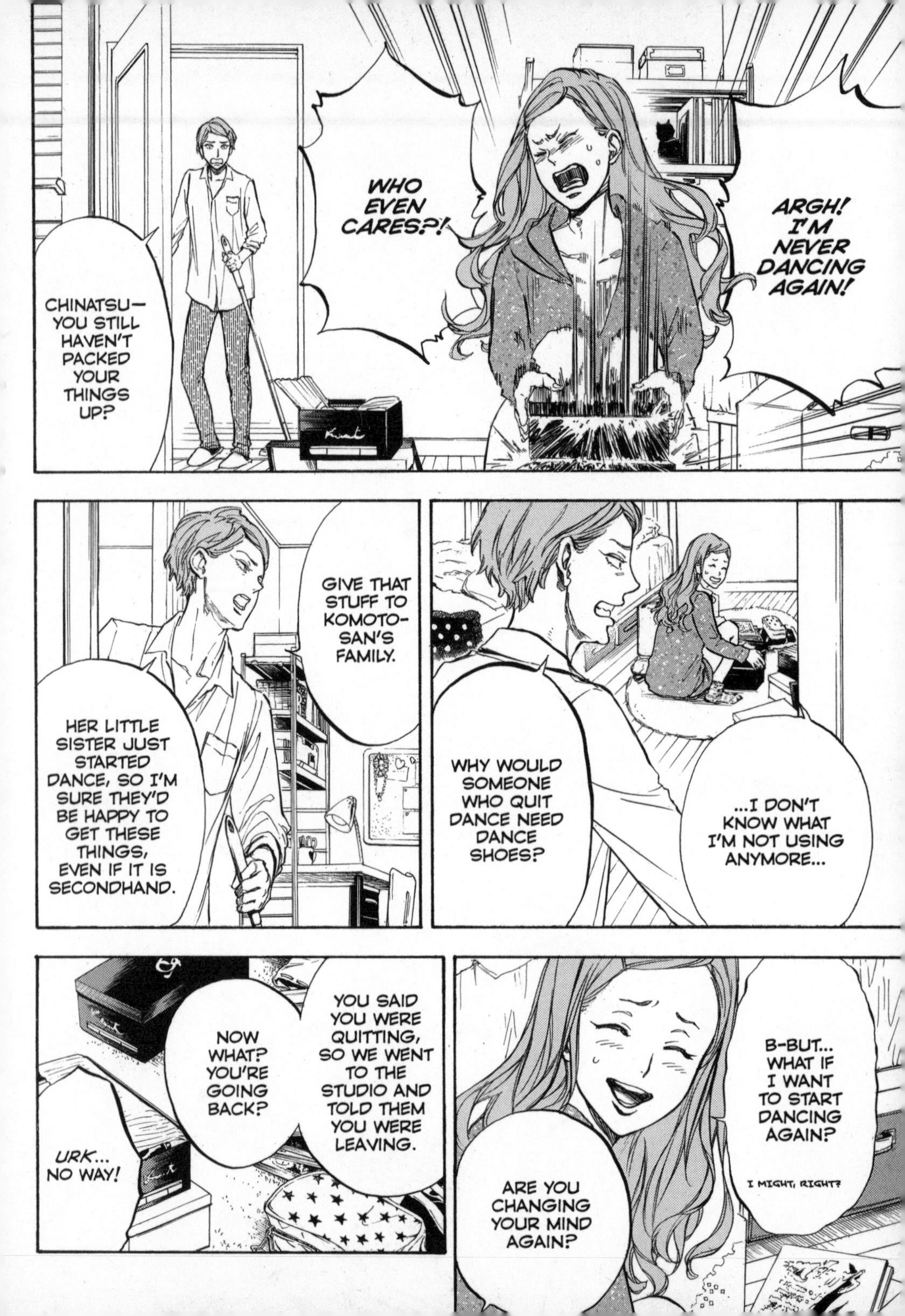
ARGH! I'M NEVER DANCING AGAIN!
WHO EVEN CARES?!
CHINATSU— YOU STILL HAVEN'T PACKED YOUR THINGS UP?
...I DON'T KNOW WHAT I'M NOT USING ANYMORE...
WHY WOULD SOMEONE WHO QUIT DANCE NEED DANCE SHOES?
GIVE THAT STUFF TO KOMOTO-SAN'S FAMILY.
HER LITTLE SISTER JUST STARTED DANCE, SO I'M SURE THEY'D BE HAPPY TO GET THESE THINGS, EVEN IF IT IS SECONDHAND.
B-BUT... WHAT IF I WANT TO START DANCING AGAIN?
I MIGHT, RIGHT?
ARE YOU CHANGING YOUR MIND AGAIN?
YOU SAID YOU WERE QUITTING, SO WE WENT TO THE STUDIO AND TOLD THEM YOU WERE LEAVING.
NOW WHAT? YOU'RE GOING BACK?
URK... NO WAY!

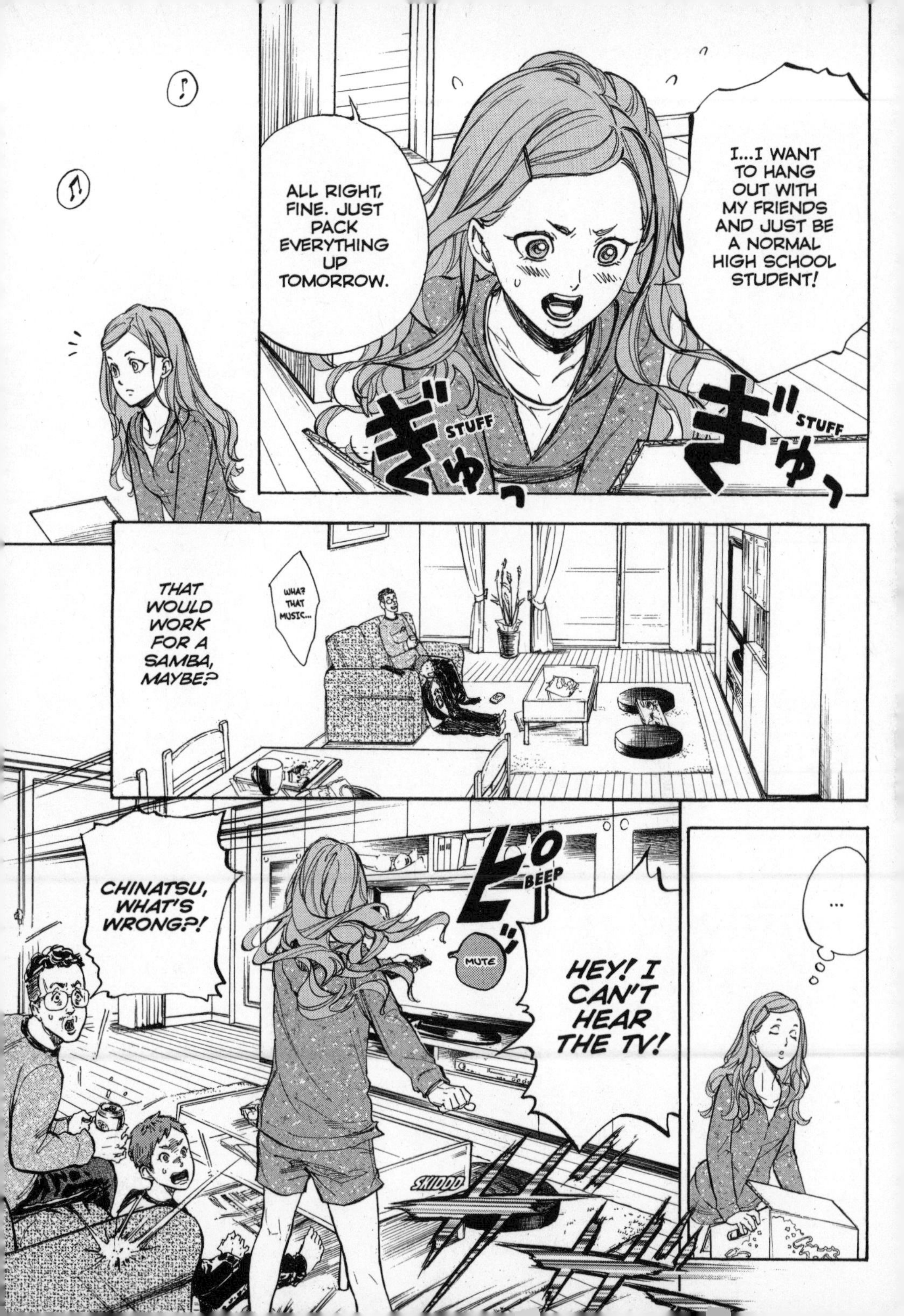
I...I WANT TO HANG OUT WITH MY FRIENDS AND JUST BE A NORMAL HIGH SCHOOL STUDENT!
ALL RIGHT, FINE. JUST PACK EVERYTHING UP TOMORROW.
ぎゅっ
STUFF
ぎゅっ
STUFF
♪
♪
WHA? THAT MUSIC...
THAT WOULD WORK FOR A SAMBA, MAYBE?
...
ピッ
BEEP
HEY! I CAN'T HEAR THE TV!
MUTE
CHINATSU, WHAT'S WRONG?!
SKIDDD

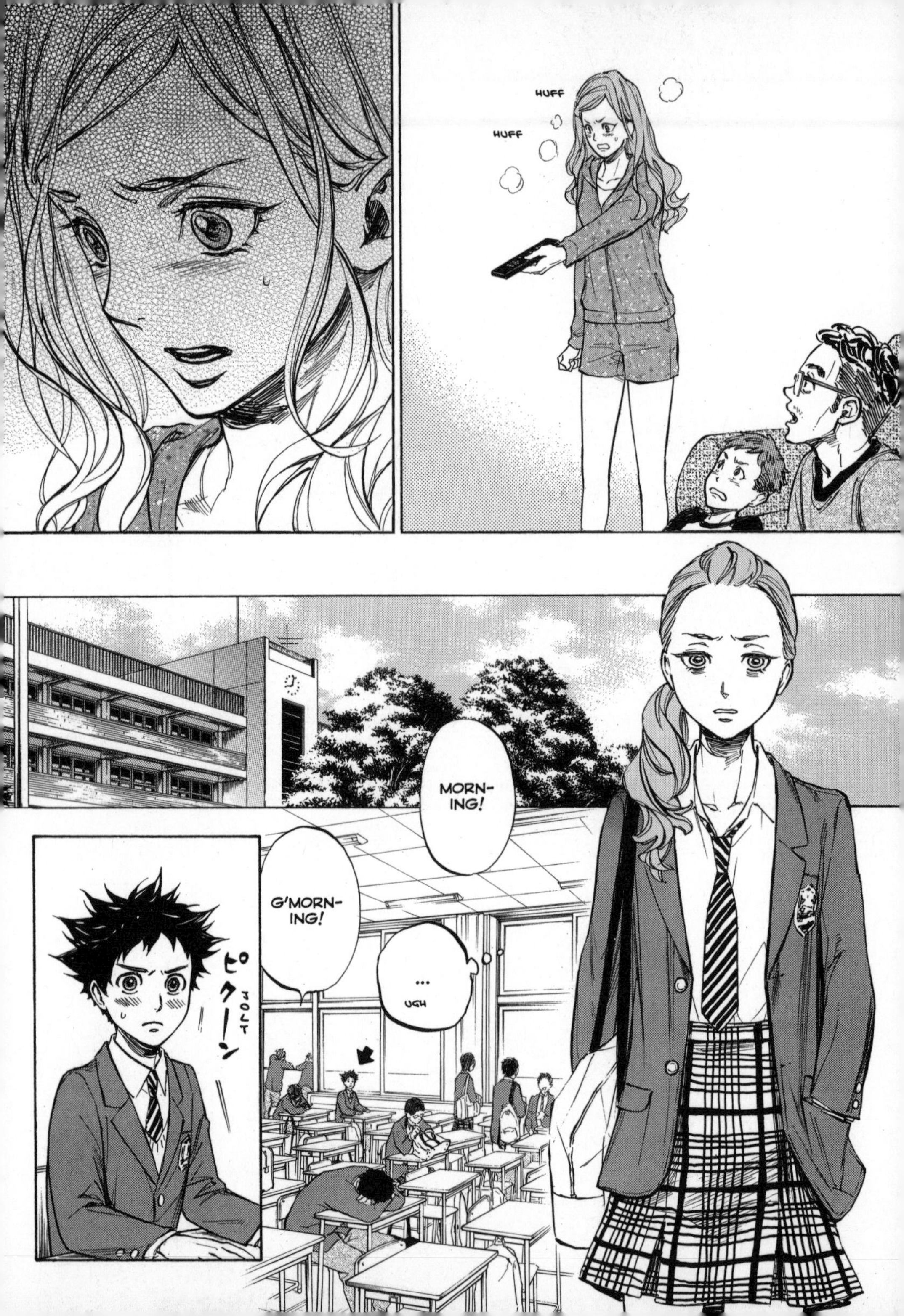
HUFF
HUFF
MORN-ING!
G'MORN-ING!
... UGH
ピクーン
JOLT

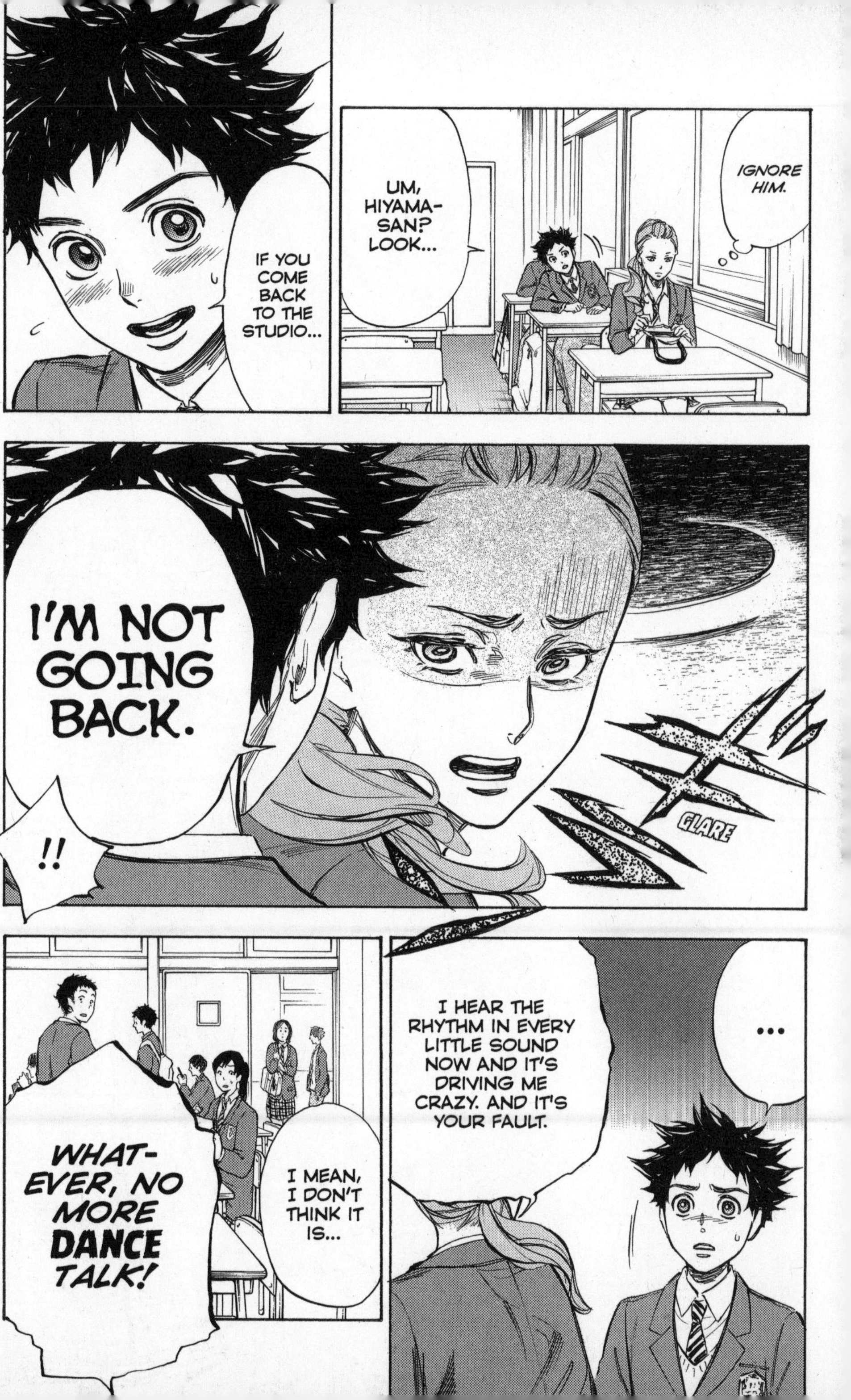
IGNORE HIM.
UM, HIYAMA-SAN? LOOK...
IF YOU COME BACK TO THE STUDIO...
I'M NOT GOING BACK.
GLARE
!!
...
I HEAR THE RHYTHM IN EVERY LITTLE SOUND NOW AND IT'S DRIVING ME CRAZY. AND IT'S YOUR FAULT.
I MEAN, I DON'T THINK IT IS...
WHAT-EVER, NO MORE DANCE TALK!

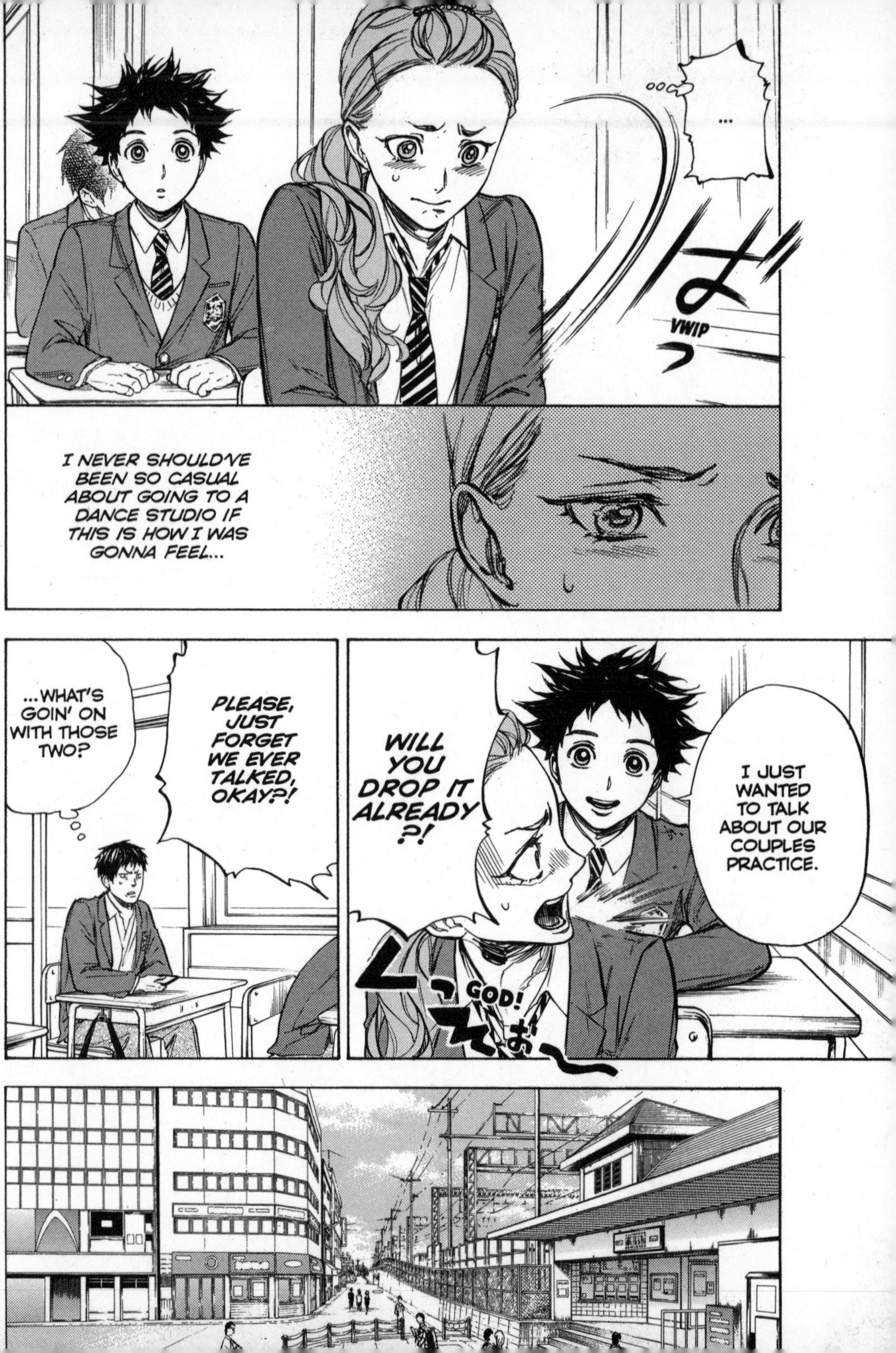
...
VWIP
I NEVER SHOULD'VE BEEN SO CASUAL ABOUT GOING TO A DANCE STUDIO IF THIS IS HOW I WAS GONNA FEEL...
I JUST WANTED TO TALK ABOUT OUR COUPLES PRACTICE.
WILL YOU DROP IT ALREADY?!
GOD!
PLEASE, JUST FORGET WE EVER TALKED, OKAY?!
...WHAT'S GOIN' ON WITH THOSE TWO?

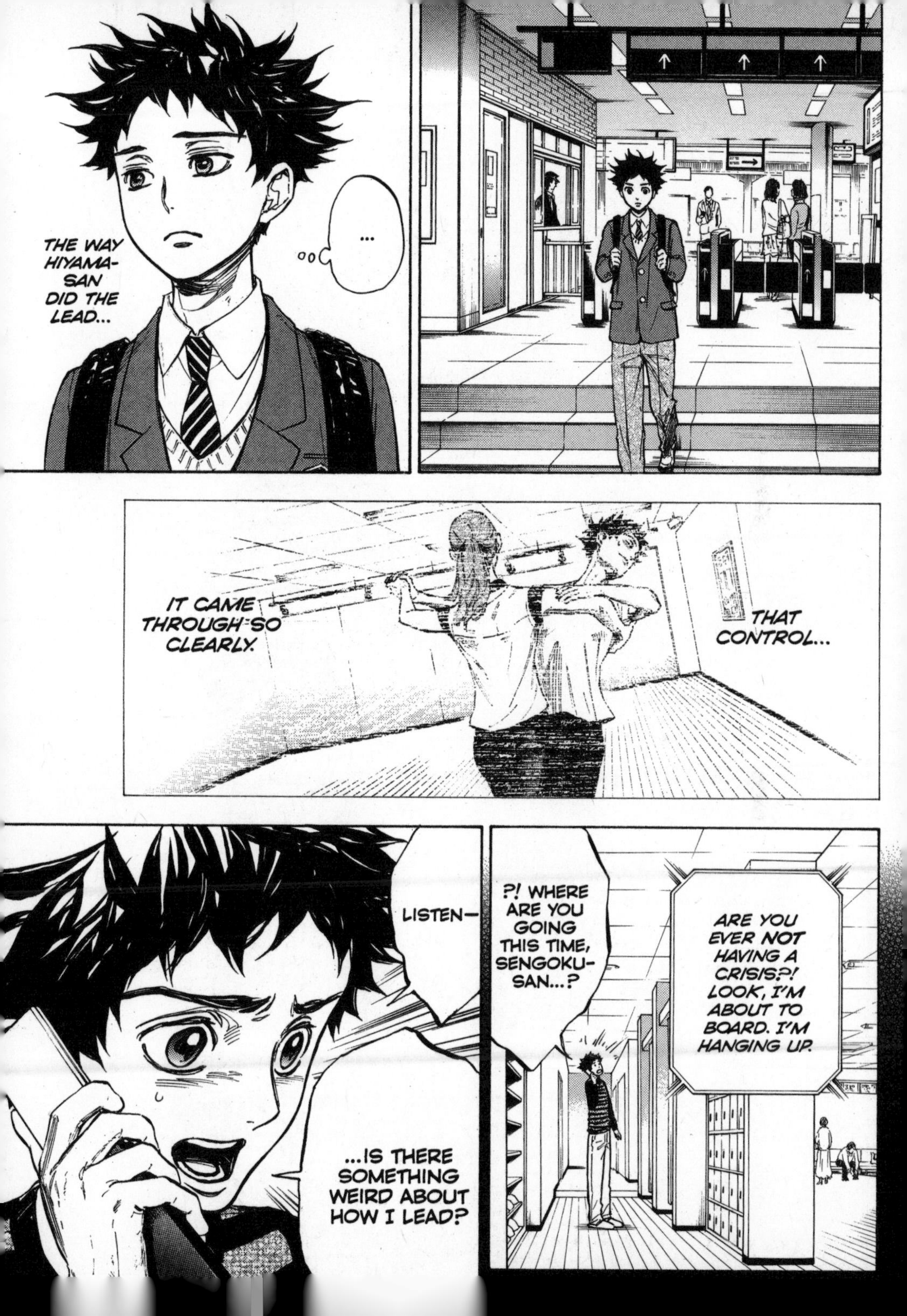
THE WAY HIYAMA-SAN DID THE LEAD...
...
THAT CONTROL...
IT CAME THROUGH SO CLEARLY.
ARE YOU EVER NOT HAVING A CRISIS?! LOOK, I'M ABOUT TO BOARD. I'M HANGING UP.
?! WHERE ARE YOU GOING THIS TIME, SENGOKU-SAN...?
LISTEN—
...IS THERE SOMETHING WEIRD ABOUT HOW I LEAD?

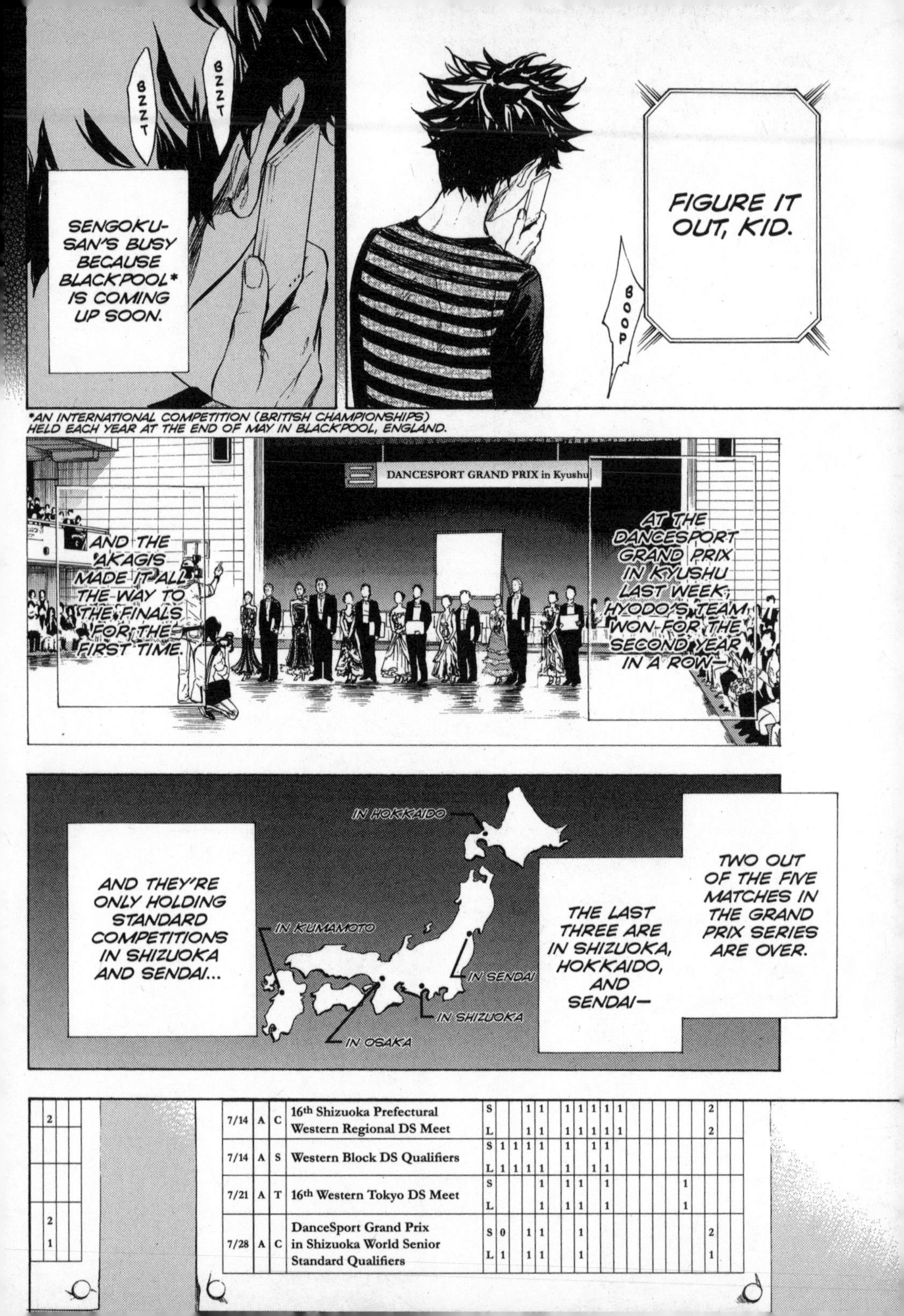
FIGURE IT OUT, KID.
BOOP
BZZT
BZZT
SENGOKU-SAN'S BUSY BECAUSE BLACKPOOL* IS COMING UP SOON.
*AN INTERNATIONAL COMPETITION (BRITISH CHAMPIONSHIPS) HELD EACH YEAR AT THE END OF MAY IN BLACKPOOL, ENGLAND.
DANCESPORT GRAND PRIX in Kyushu
AT THE DANCESPORT GRAND PRIX IN KYUSHU LAST WEEK, HYODO'S TEAM WON FOR THE SECOND YEAR IN A ROW—
AND THE AKAGIS MADE IT ALL THE WAY TO THE FINALS FOR THE FIRST TIME.
TWO OUT OF THE FIVE MATCHES IN THE GRAND PRIX SERIES ARE OVER.
THE LAST THREE ARE IN SHIZUOKA, HOKKAIDO, AND SENDAI—
IN HOKKAIDO
IN SENDAI
IN SHIZUOKA
IN OSAKA
IN KUMAMOTO
AND THEY'RE ONLY HOLDING STANDARD COMPETITIONS IN SHIZUOKA AND SENDAI...
7/14 A C 16th Shizuoka Prefectural Western Regional DS Meet
7/14 A S Western Block DS Qualifiers
7/21 A T 16th Western Tokyo DS Meet
7/28 A C DanceSport Grand Prix in Shizuoka World Senior Standard Qualifiers

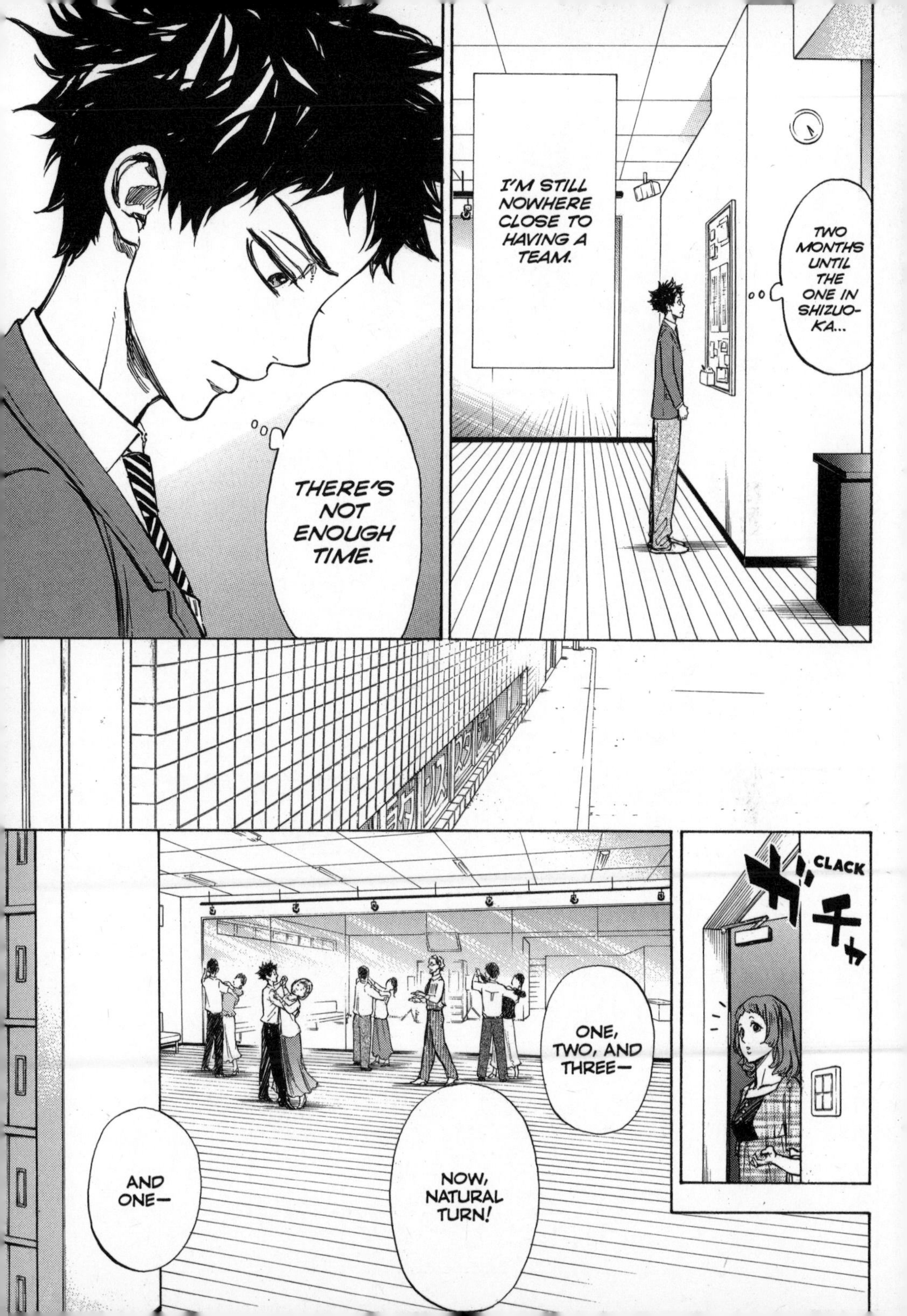
TWO MONTHS UNTIL THE ONE IN SHIZUOKA...
I'M STILL NOWHERE CLOSE TO HAVING A TEAM.
THERE'S NOT ENOUGH TIME.
ガチャ
CLACK
ONE, TWO, AND THREE—
NOW, NATURAL TURN!
AND ONE—

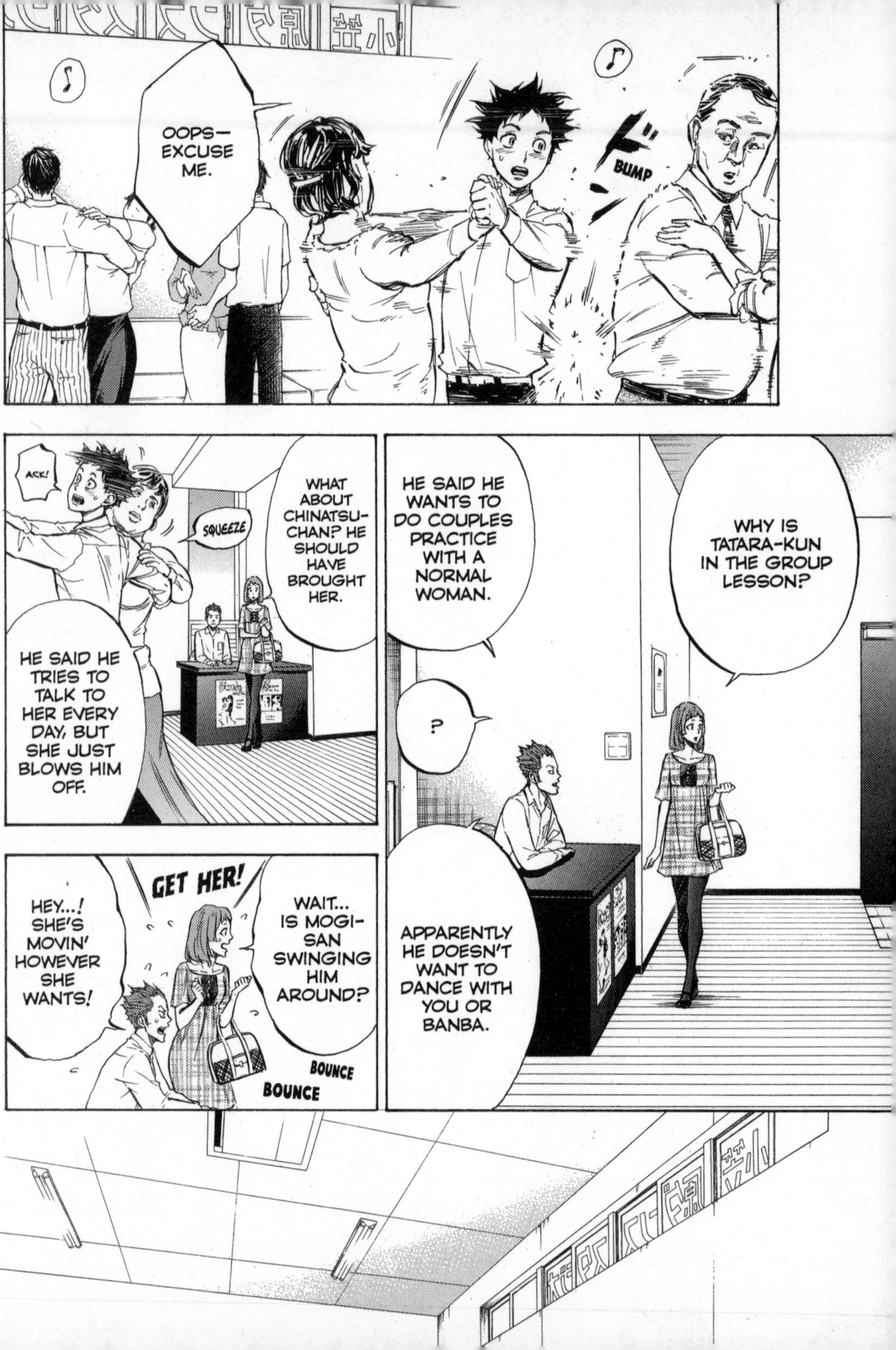
♪
BUMP
♪
OOPS— EXCUSE ME.
WHY IS TATARA-KUN IN THE GROUP LESSON?
HE SAID HE WANTS TO DO COUPLES PRACTICE WITH A NORMAL WOMAN.
?
APPARENTLY HE DOESN'T WANT TO DANCE WITH YOU OR BANBA.
WHAT ABOUT CHINATSU-CHAN? HE SHOULD HAVE BROUGHT HER.
SQUEEZE
ACK!
HE SAID HE TRIES TO TALK TO HER EVERY DAY, BUT SHE JUST BLOWS HIM OFF.
GET HER!
WAIT... IS MOGI-SAN SWINGING HIM AROUND?
HEY...! SHE'S MOVIN' HOWEVER SHE WANTS!
BOUNCE
BOUNCE

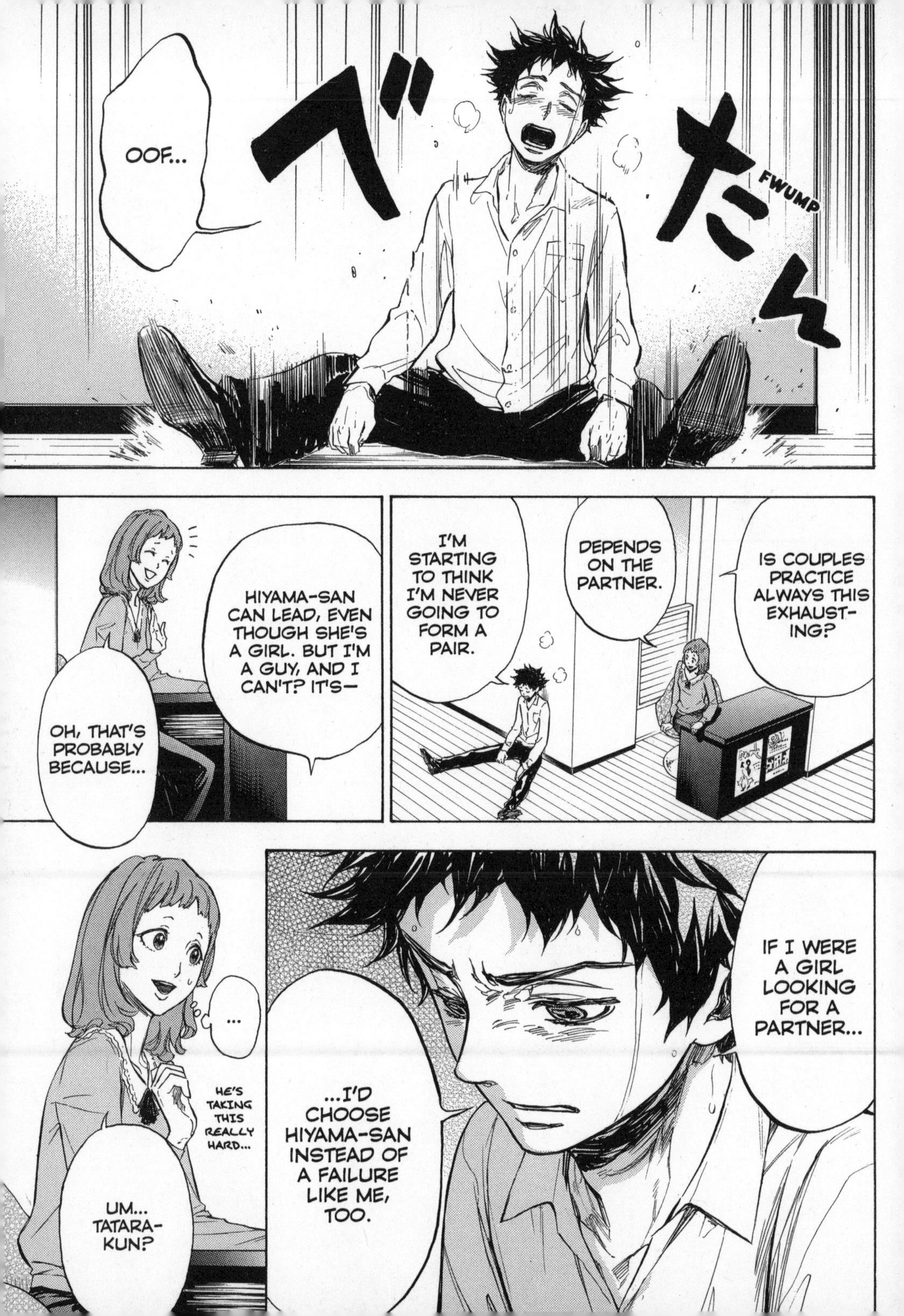
ベたん
FWUMP
OOF...
IS COUPLES PRACTICE ALWAYS THIS EXHAUST-ING?
DEPENDS ON THE PARTNER.
I'M STARTING TO THINK I'M NEVER GOING TO FORM A PAIR.
HIYAMA-SAN CAN LEAD, EVEN THOUGH SHE'S A GIRL. BUT I'M A GUY, AND I CAN'T? IT'S—
OH, THAT'S PROBABLY BECAUSE...
IF I WERE A GIRL LOOKING FOR A PARTNER...
...I'D CHOOSE HIYAMA-SAN INSTEAD OF A FAILURE LIKE ME, TOO.
...
HE'S TAKING THIS REALLY HARD...
UM... TATARA-KUN?

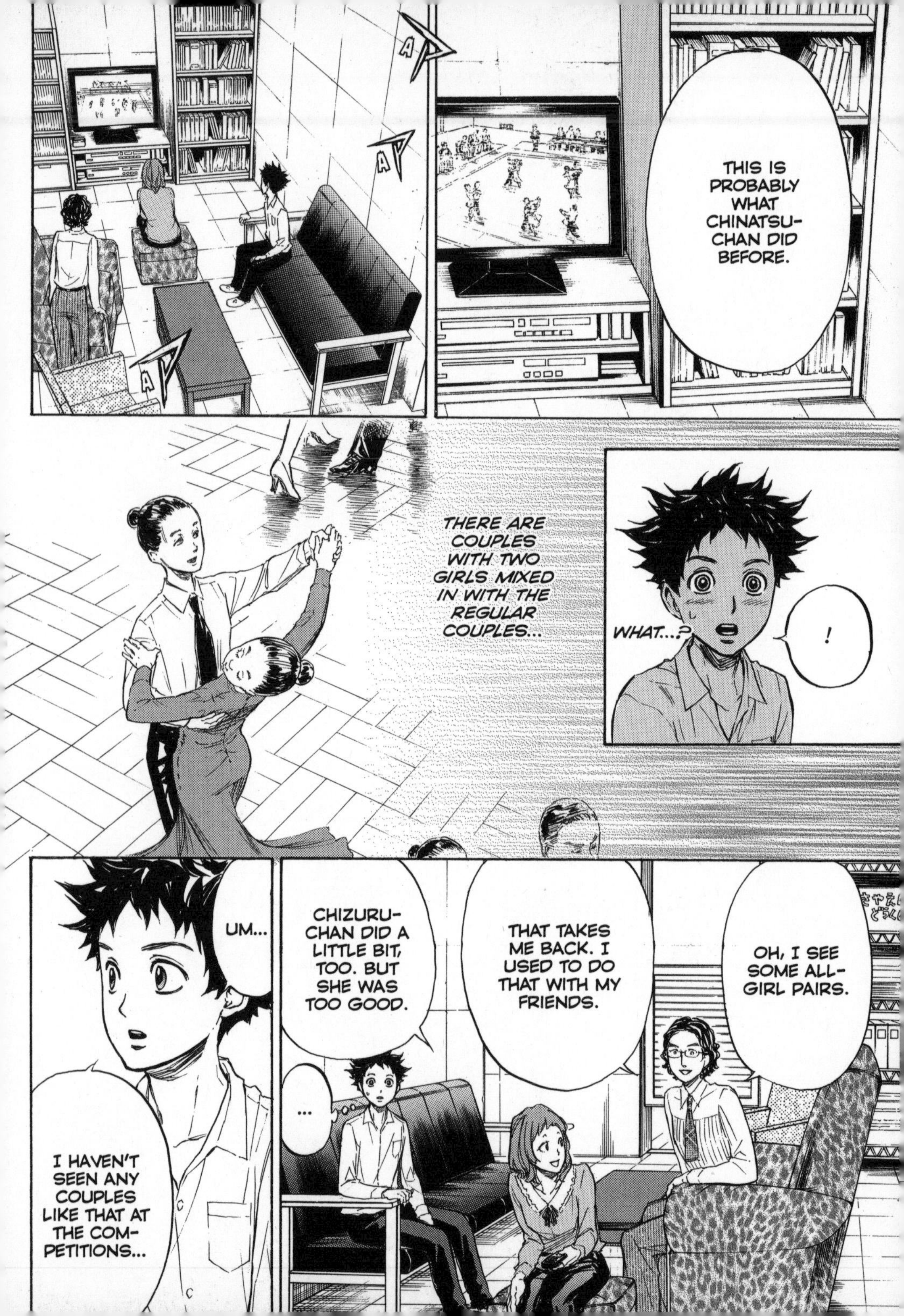
THIS IS PROBABLY WHAT CHINATSU-CHAN DID BEFORE.
!
WHAT...?
THERE ARE COUPLES WITH TWO GIRLS MIXED IN WITH THE REGULAR COUPLES...
OH, I SEE SOME ALL-GIRL PAIRS.
THAT TAKES ME BACK. I USED TO DO THAT WITH MY FRIENDS.
CHIZURU-CHAN DID A LITTLE BIT, TOO. BUT SHE WAS TOO GOOD.
...
UM...
I HAVEN'T SEEN ANY COUPLES LIKE THAT AT THE COMPETITIONS...

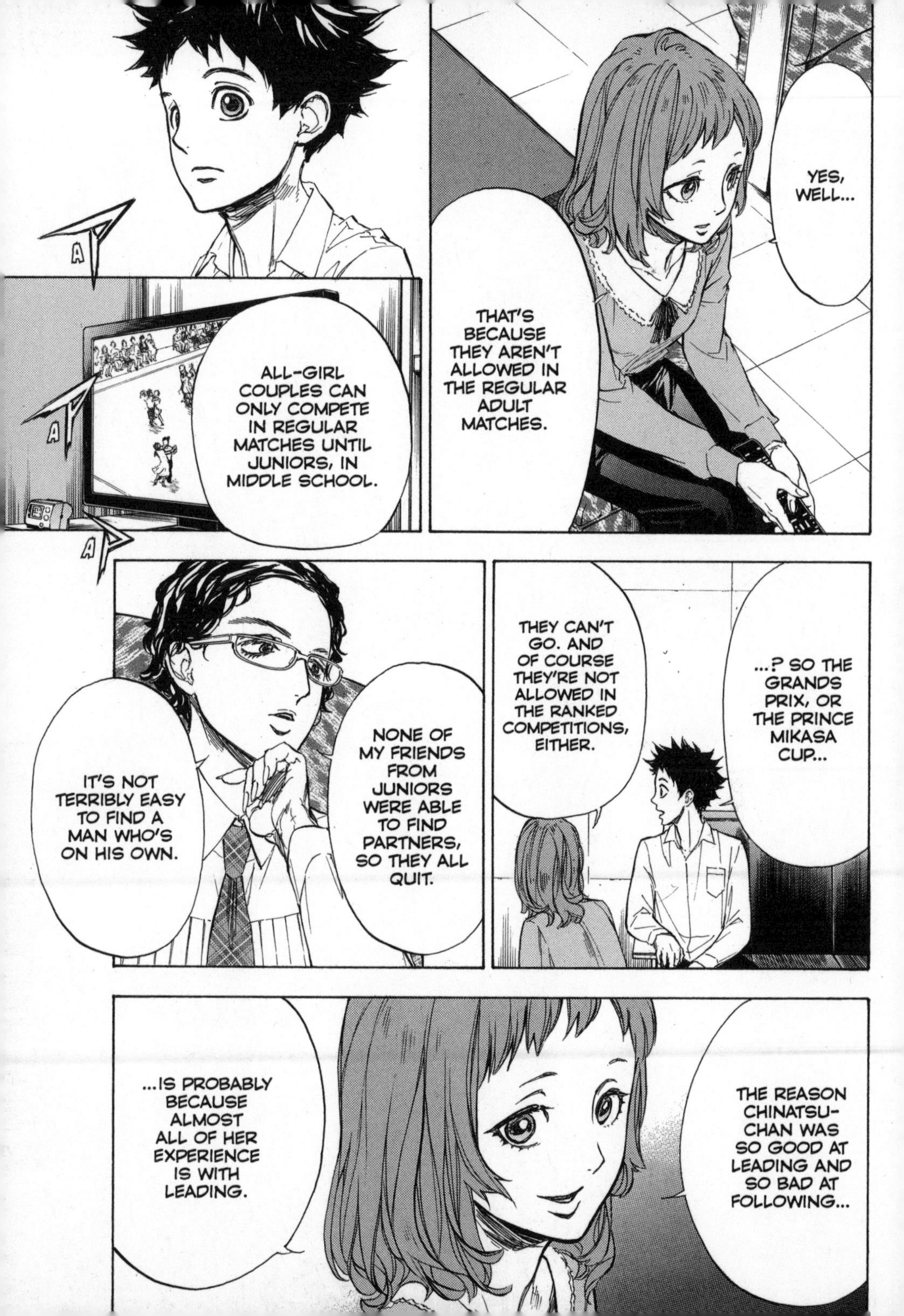
YES, WELL...
THAT'S BECAUSE THEY AREN'T ALLOWED IN THE REGULAR ADULT MATCHES.
TAP
TAP
ALL-GIRL COUPLES CAN ONLY COMPETE IN REGULAR MATCHES UNTIL JUNIORS, IN MIDDLE SCHOOL.
TAP
...? SO THE GRANDS PRIX, OR THE PRINCE MIKASA CUP...
THEY CAN'T GO. AND OF COURSE THEY'RE NOT ALLOWED IN THE RANKED COMPETITIONS, EITHER.
NONE OF MY FRIENDS FROM JUNIORS WERE ABLE TO FIND PARTNERS, SO THEY ALL QUIT.
IT'S NOT TERRIBLY EASY TO FIND A MAN WHO'S ON HIS OWN.
THE REASON CHINATSU-CHAN WAS SO GOOD AT LEADING AND SO BAD AT FOLLOWING...
...IS PROBABLY BECAUSE ALMOST ALL OF HER EXPERIENCE IS WITH LEADING.

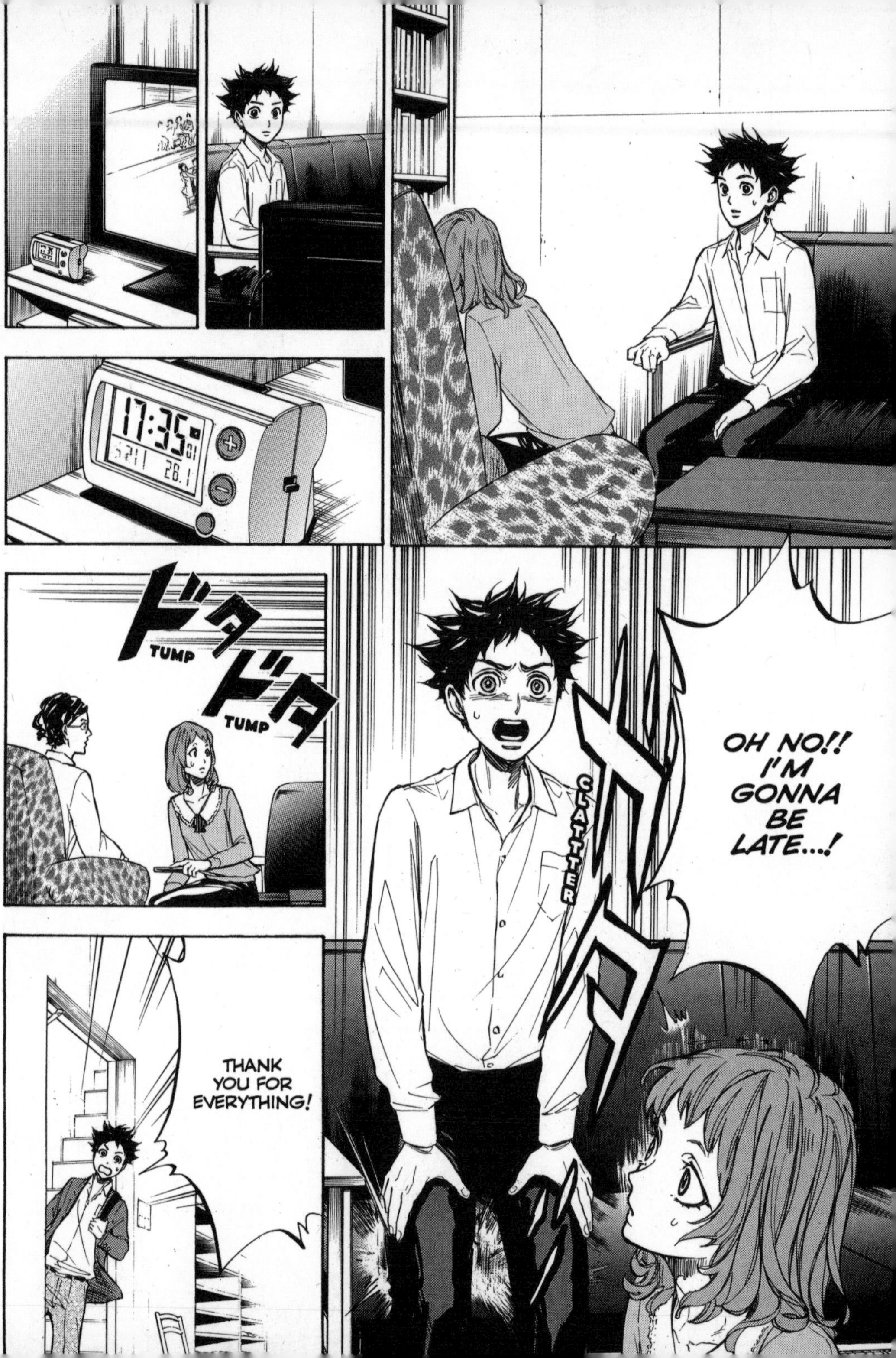
17:35
OH NO!! I'M GONNA BE LATE...!
CLATTER
ドタ TUMP
ドタ TUMP
THANK YOU FOR EVERYTHING!

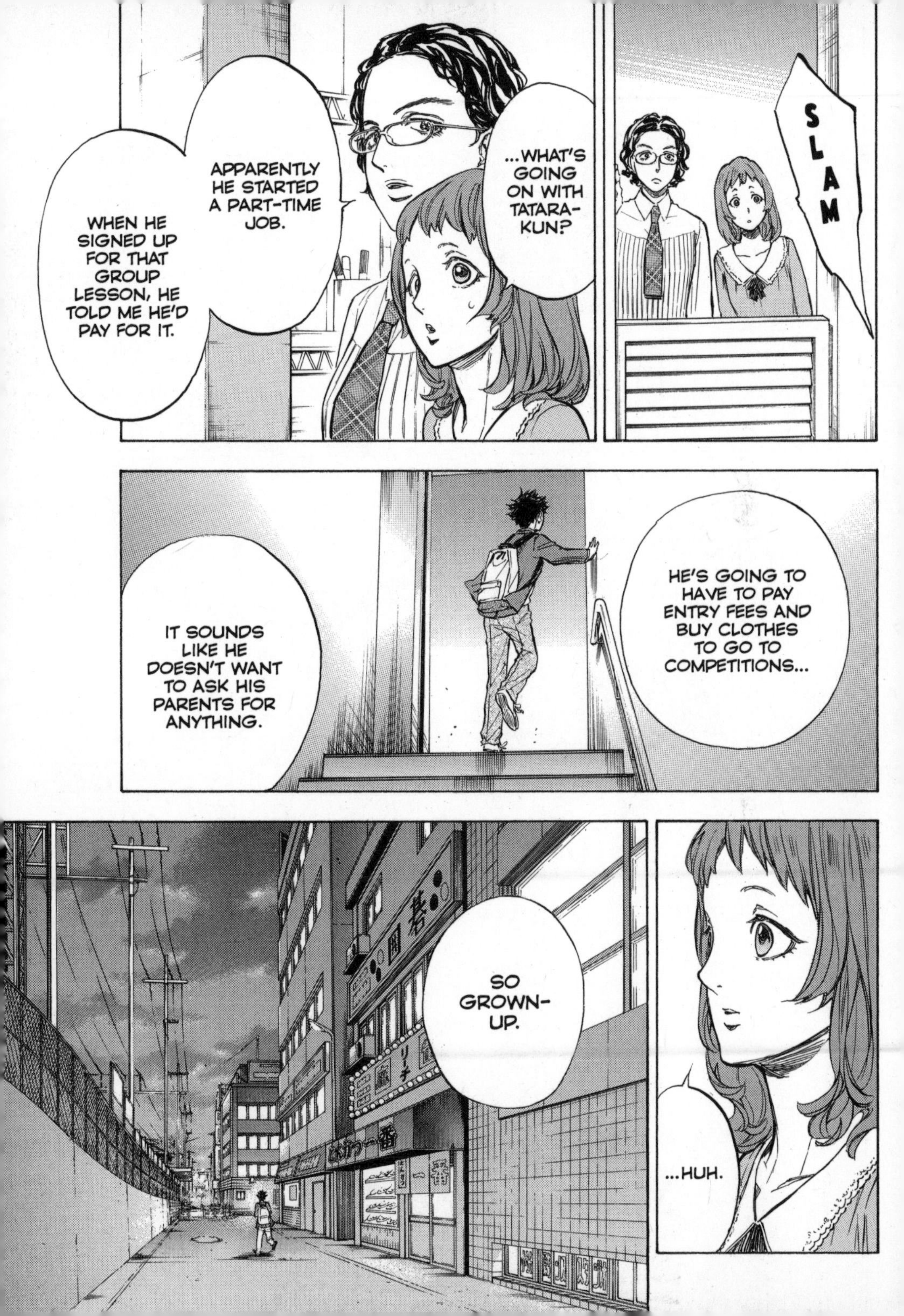
SLAM
...WHAT'S GOING ON WITH TATARA-KUN?
APPARENTLY HE STARTED A PART-TIME JOB.
WHEN HE SIGNED UP FOR THAT GROUP LESSON, HE TOLD ME HE'D PAY FOR IT.
HE'S GOING TO HAVE TO PAY ENTRY FEES AND BUY CLOTHES TO GO TO COMPETITIONS...
IT SOUNDS LIKE HE DOESN'T WANT TO ASK HIS PARENTS FOR ANYTHING.
...HUH.
SO GROWN-UP.

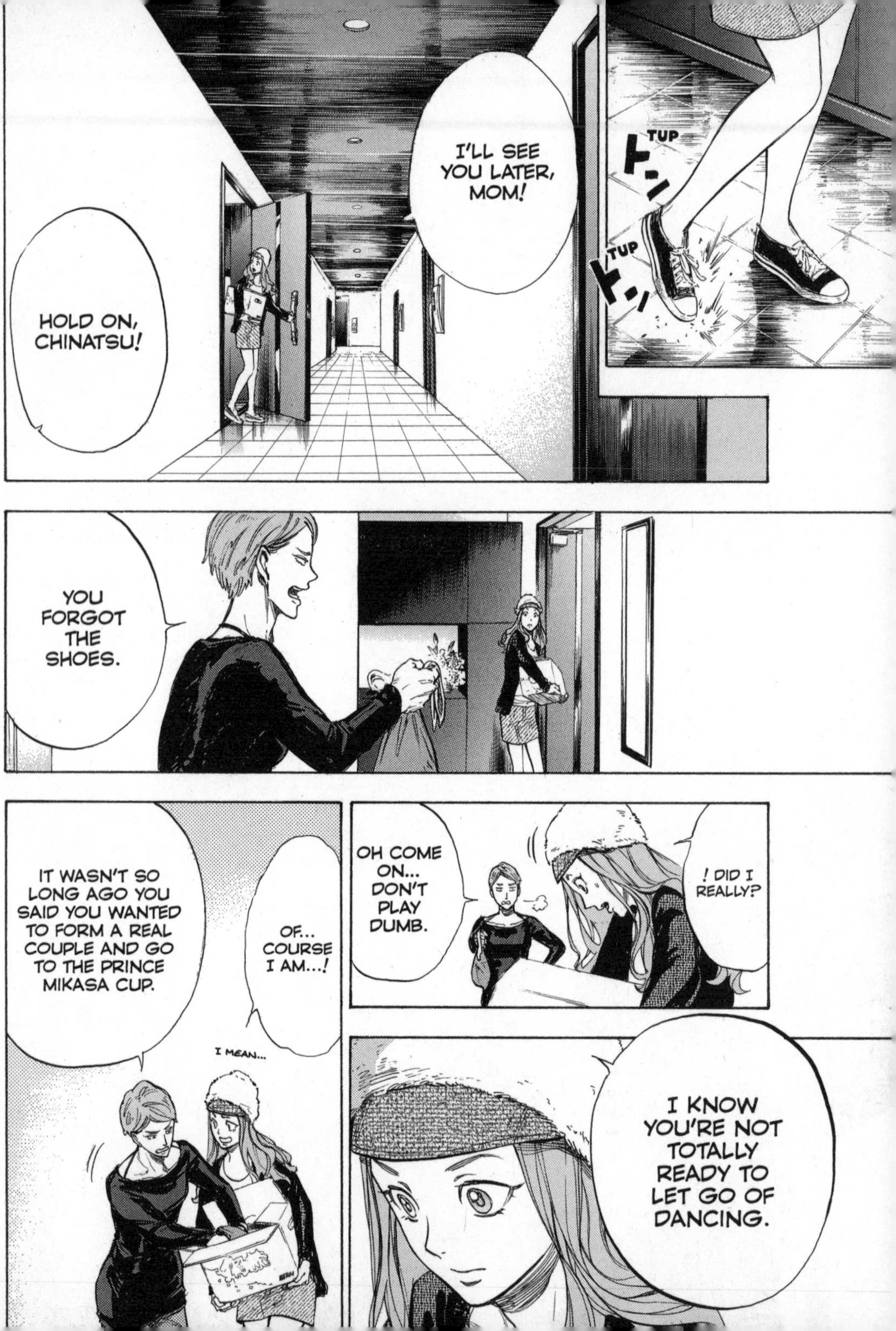
TUP
トッ
TUP
トッ
I'LL SEE YOU LATER, MOM!
HOLD ON, CHINATSU!
YOU FORGOT THE SHOES.
! DID I REALLY?
OH COME ON... DON'T PLAY DUMB.
I KNOW YOU'RE NOT TOTALLY READY TO LET GO OF DANCING.
OF... COURSE I AM...!
IT WASN'T SO LONG AGO YOU SAID YOU WANTED TO FORM A REAL COUPLE AND GO TO THE PRINCE MIKASA CUP.
I MEAN...

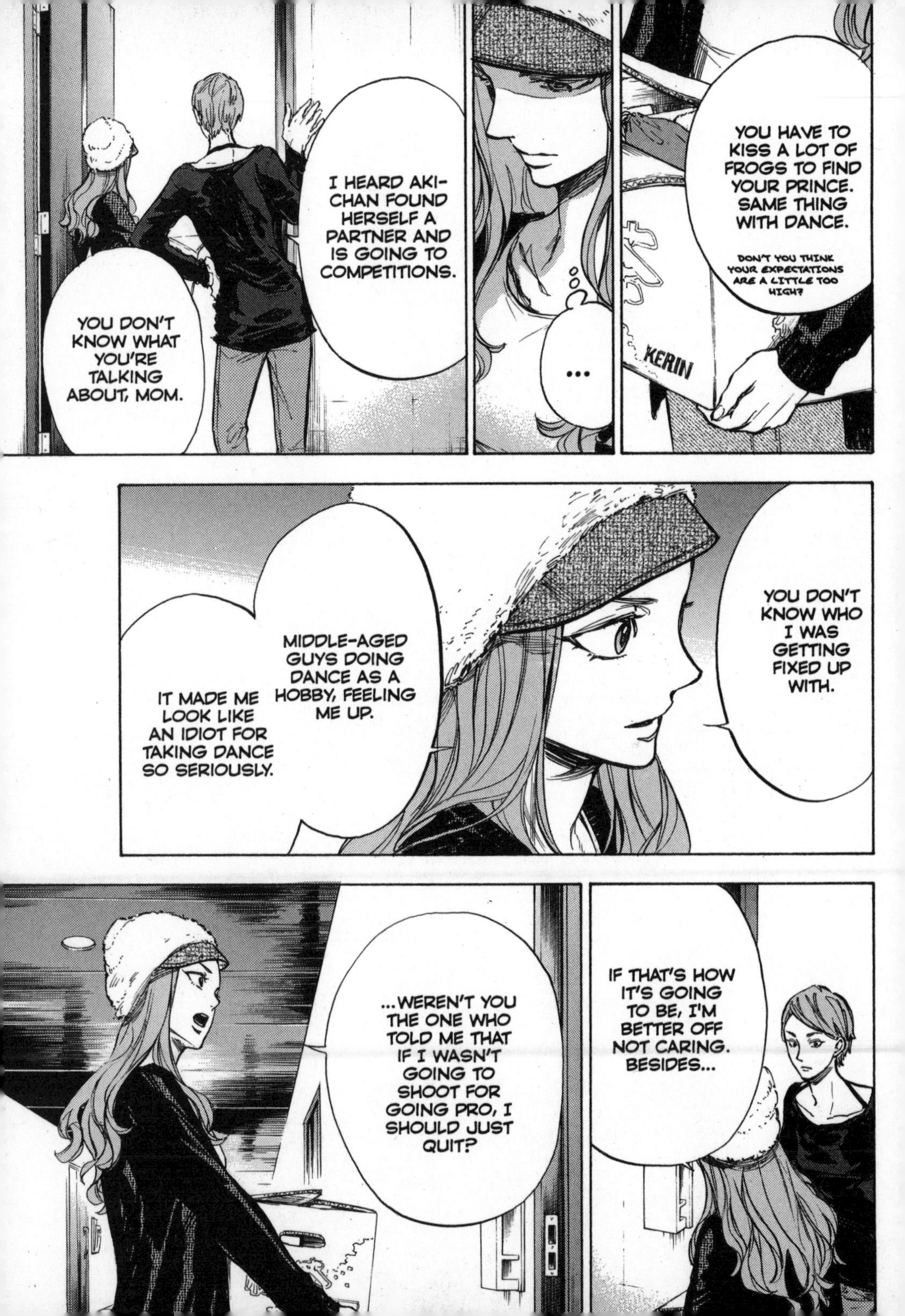
YOU HAVE TO KISS A LOT OF FROGS TO FIND YOUR PRINCE. SAME THING WITH DANCE.
DON'T YOU THINK YOUR EXPECTATIONS ARE A LITTLE TOO HIGH?
KERIN
...
I HEARD AKI-CHAN FOUND HERSELF A PARTNER AND IS GOING TO COMPETITIONS.
YOU DON'T KNOW WHAT YOU'RE TALKING ABOUT, MOM.
YOU DON'T KNOW WHO I WAS GETTING FIXED UP WITH.
MIDDLE-AGED GUYS DOING DANCE AS A HOBBY, FEELING ME UP.
IT MADE ME LOOK LIKE AN IDIOT FOR TAKING DANCE SO SERIOUSLY.
IF THAT'S HOW IT'S GOING TO BE, I'M BETTER OFF NOT CARING. BESIDES...
...WEREN'T YOU THE ONE WHO TOLD ME THAT IF I WASN'T GOING TO SHOOT FOR GOING PRO, I SHOULD JUST QUIT?

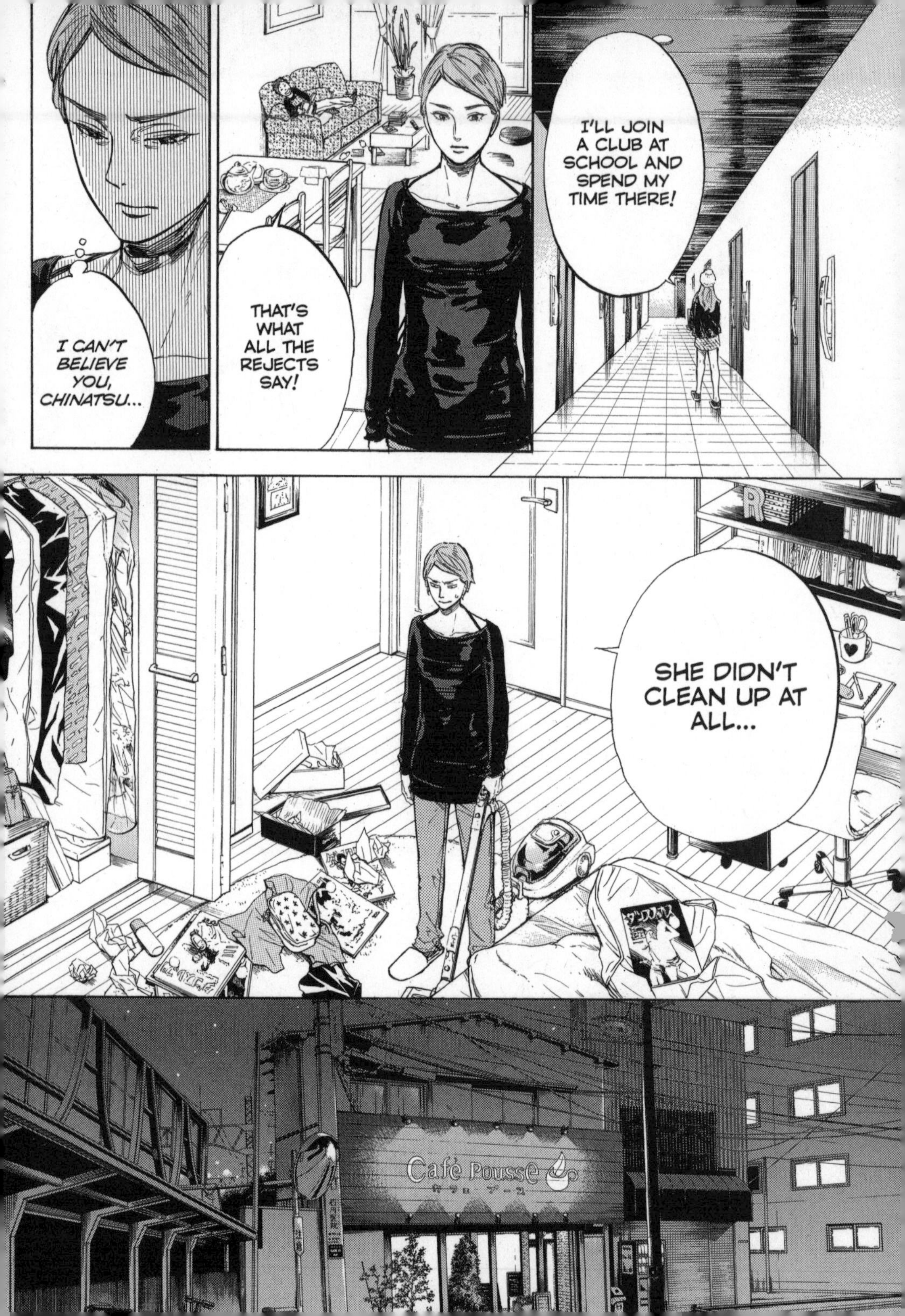
I'LL JOIN A CLUB AT SCHOOL AND SPEND MY TIME THERE!
THAT'S WHAT ALL THE REJECTS SAY!
I CAN'T BELIEVE YOU, CHINATSU...
SHE DIDN'T CLEAN UP AT ALL...
Café Pousse

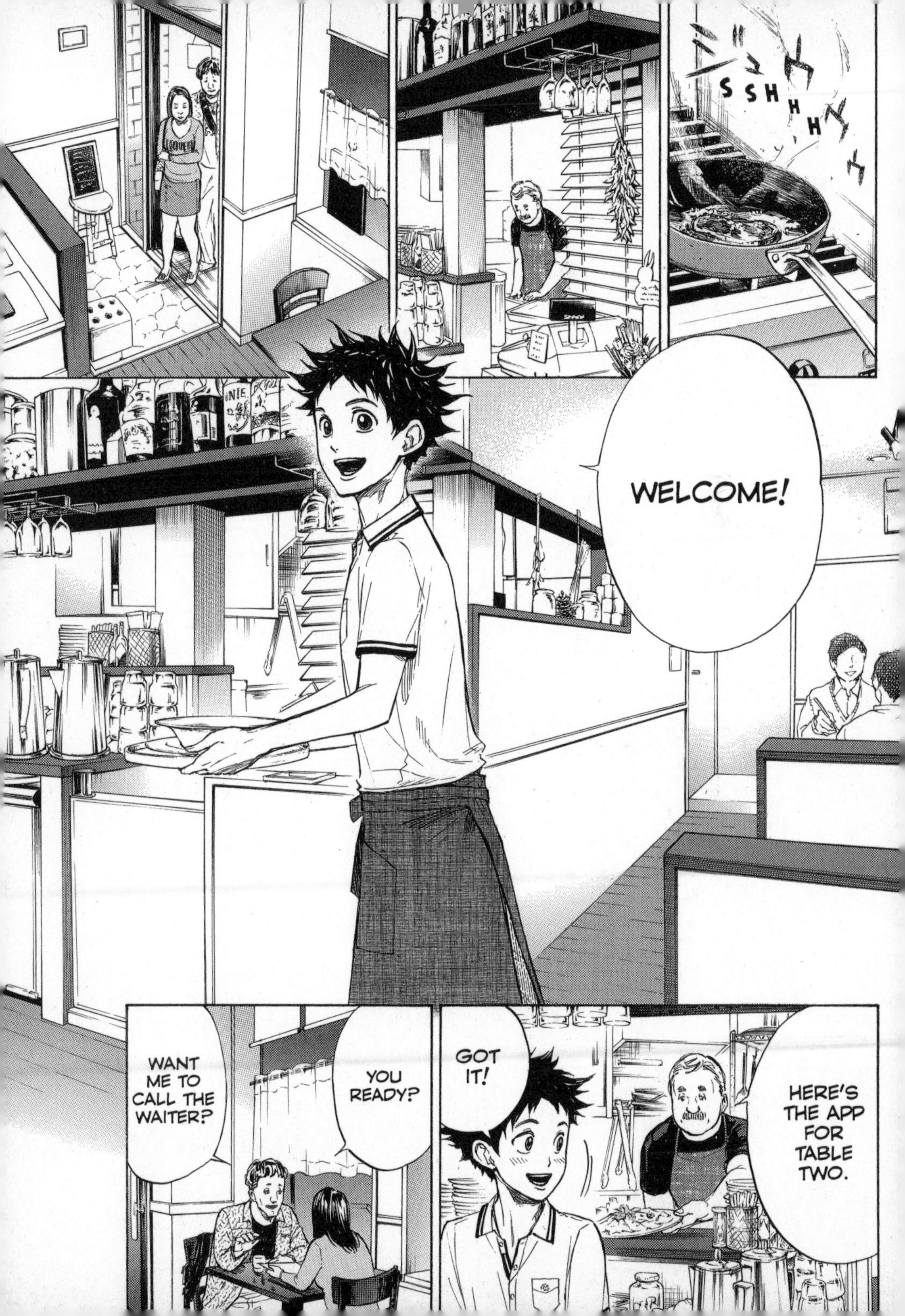
SSHHH
WELCOME!
HERE'S THE APP FOR TABLE TWO.
GOT IT!
YOU READY?
WANT ME TO CALL THE WAITER?

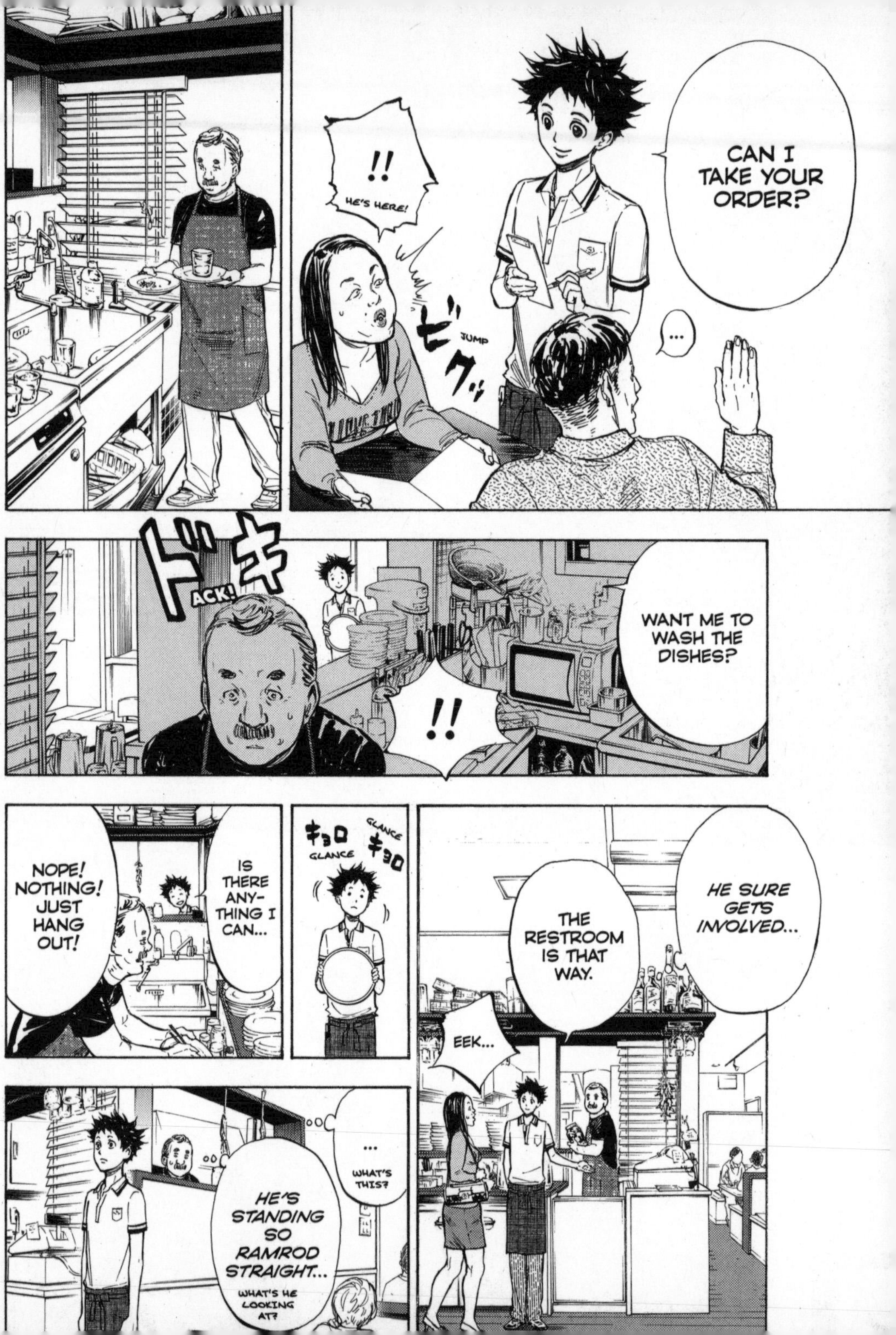
CAN I TAKE YOUR ORDER?
!!
HE'S HERE!
...
ビクッ
JUMP
WANT ME TO WASH THE DISHES?
ドキ
ACK!
!!
HE SURE GETS INVOLVED...
THE RESTROOM IS THAT WAY.
EEK...
キョロ
GLANCE
キョロ
GLANCE
IS THERE ANY-THING I CAN...
NOPE! NOTHING! JUST HANG OUT!
...
WHAT'S THIS?
HE'S STANDING SO RAMROD STRAIGHT...
WHAT'S HE LOOKING AT?

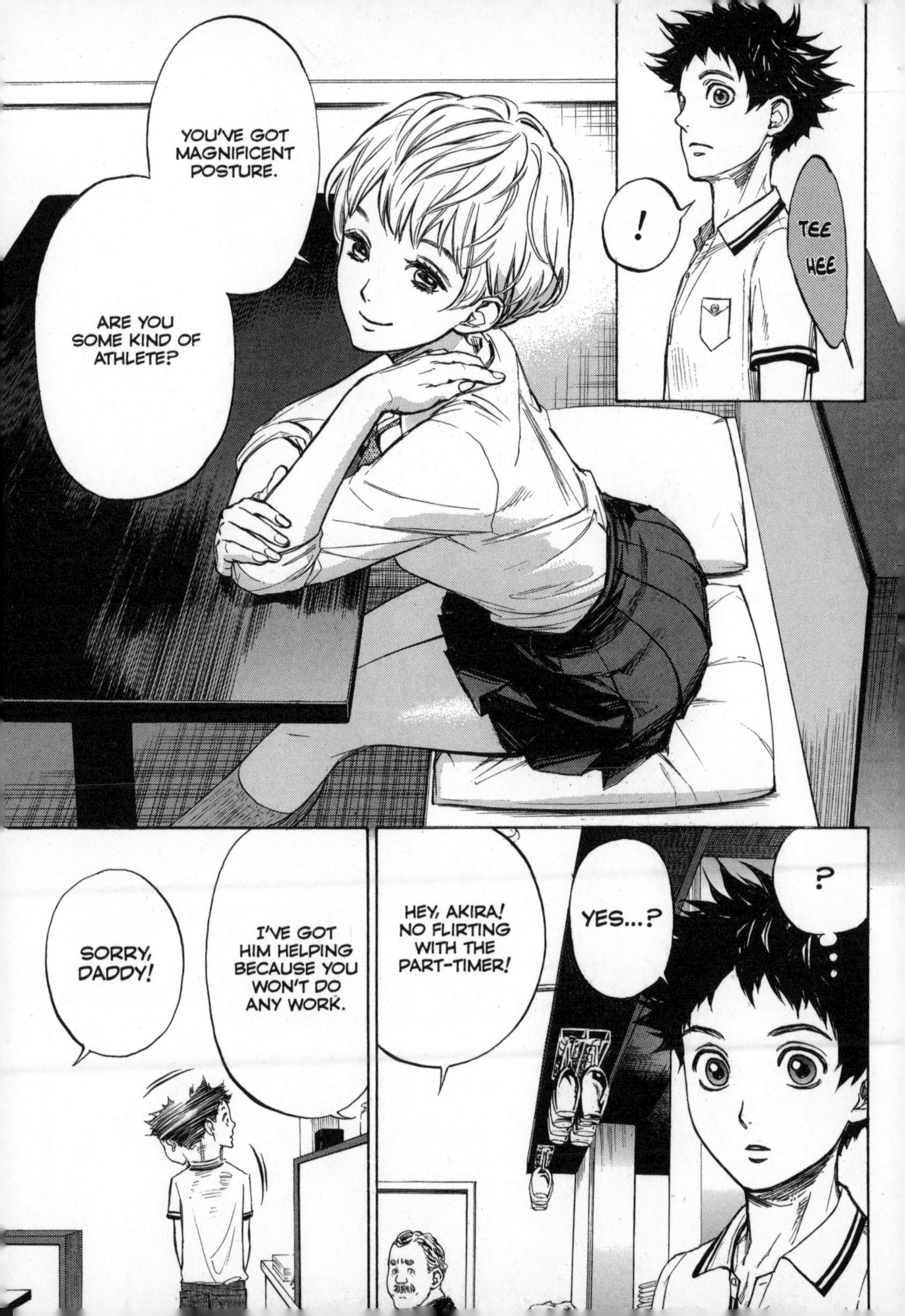
!
TEE HEE
YOU'VE GOT MAGNIFICENT POSTURE.
ARE YOU SOME KIND OF ATHLETE?
?
YES...?
HEY, AKIRA! NO FLIRTING WITH THE PART-TIMER!
I'VE GOT HIM HELPING BECAUSE YOU WON'T DO ANY WORK.
SORRY, DADDY!

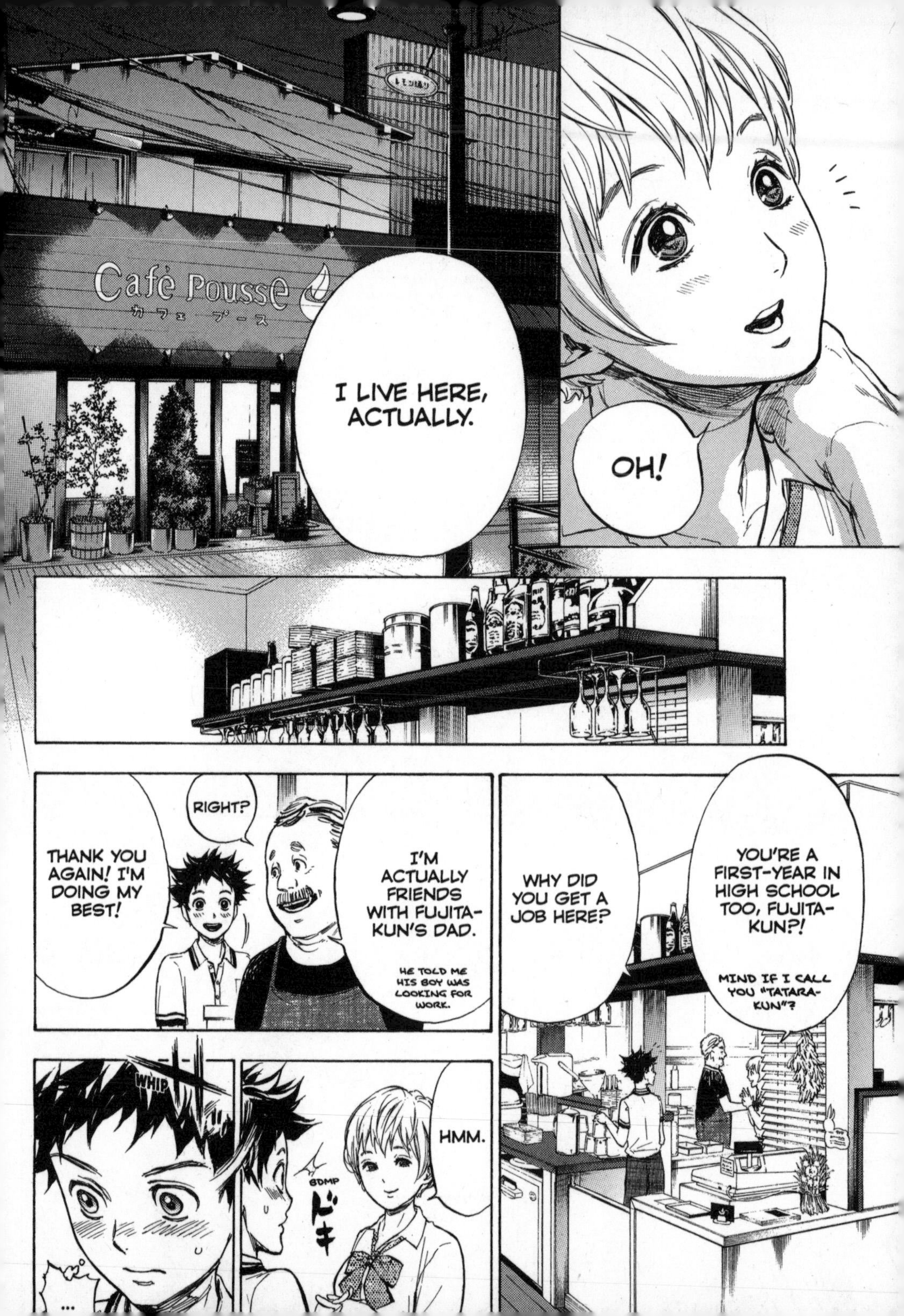
I LIVE HERE, ACTUALLY.
OH!
Café Pousse
カフェ プース
YOU'RE A FIRST-YEAR IN HIGH SCHOOL TOO, FUJITA-KUN?!
MIND IF I CALL YOU "TATARA-KUN"?
WHY DID YOU GET A JOB HERE?
I'M ACTUALLY FRIENDS WITH FUJITA-KUN'S DAD.
HE TOLD ME HIS BOY WAS LOOKING FOR WORK.
RIGHT?
THANK YOU AGAIN! I'M DOING MY BEST!
HMM.
BDMP
ドキ
WHIP
...

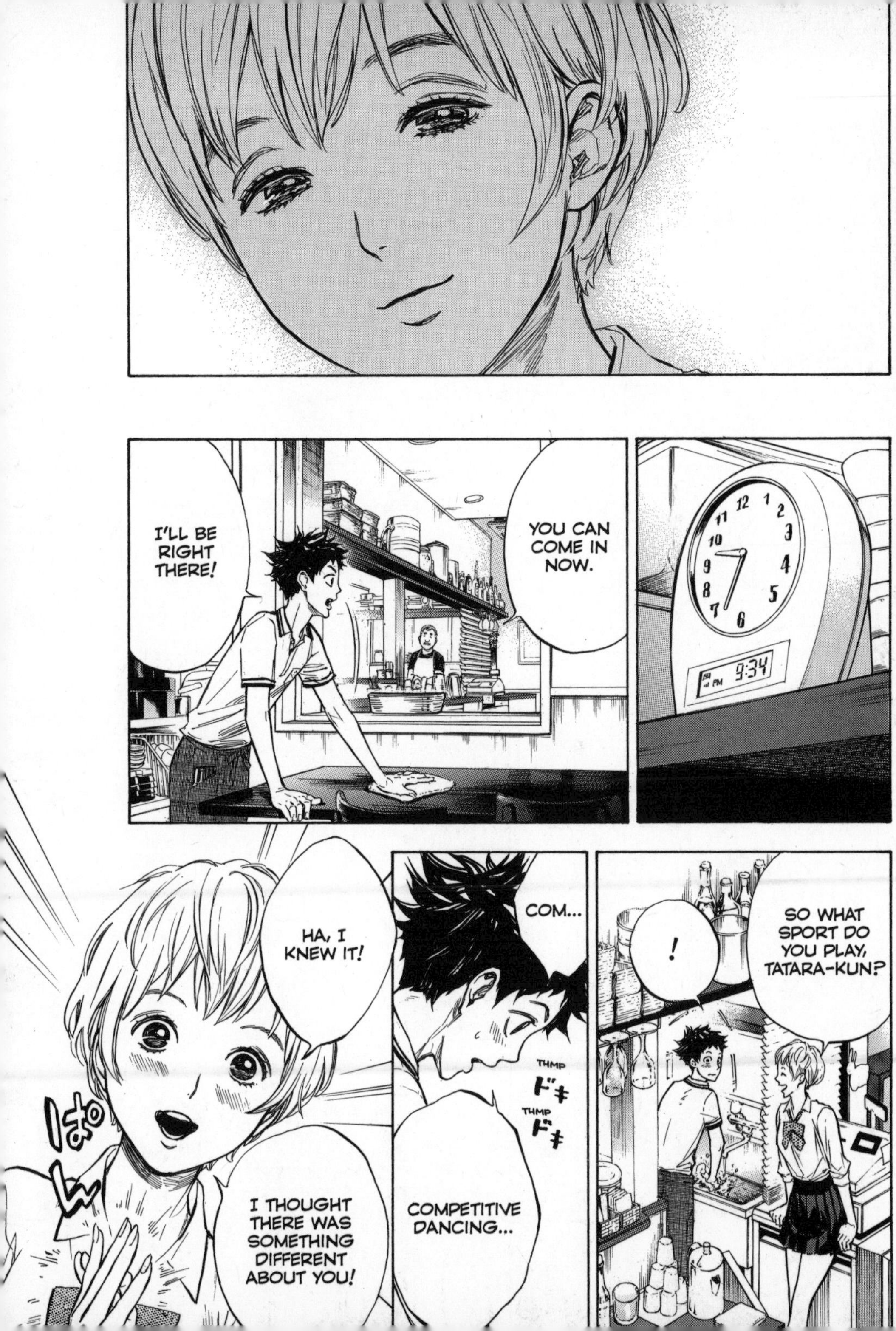
9:34
YOU CAN COME IN NOW.
I'LL BE RIGHT THERE!
SO WHAT SPORT DO YOU PLAY, TATARA-KUN?
!
COM...
THMP ドキ
THMP ドキ
COMPETITIVE DANCING...
HA, I KNEW IT!
I THOUGHT THERE WAS SOMETHING DIFFERENT ABOUT YOU!

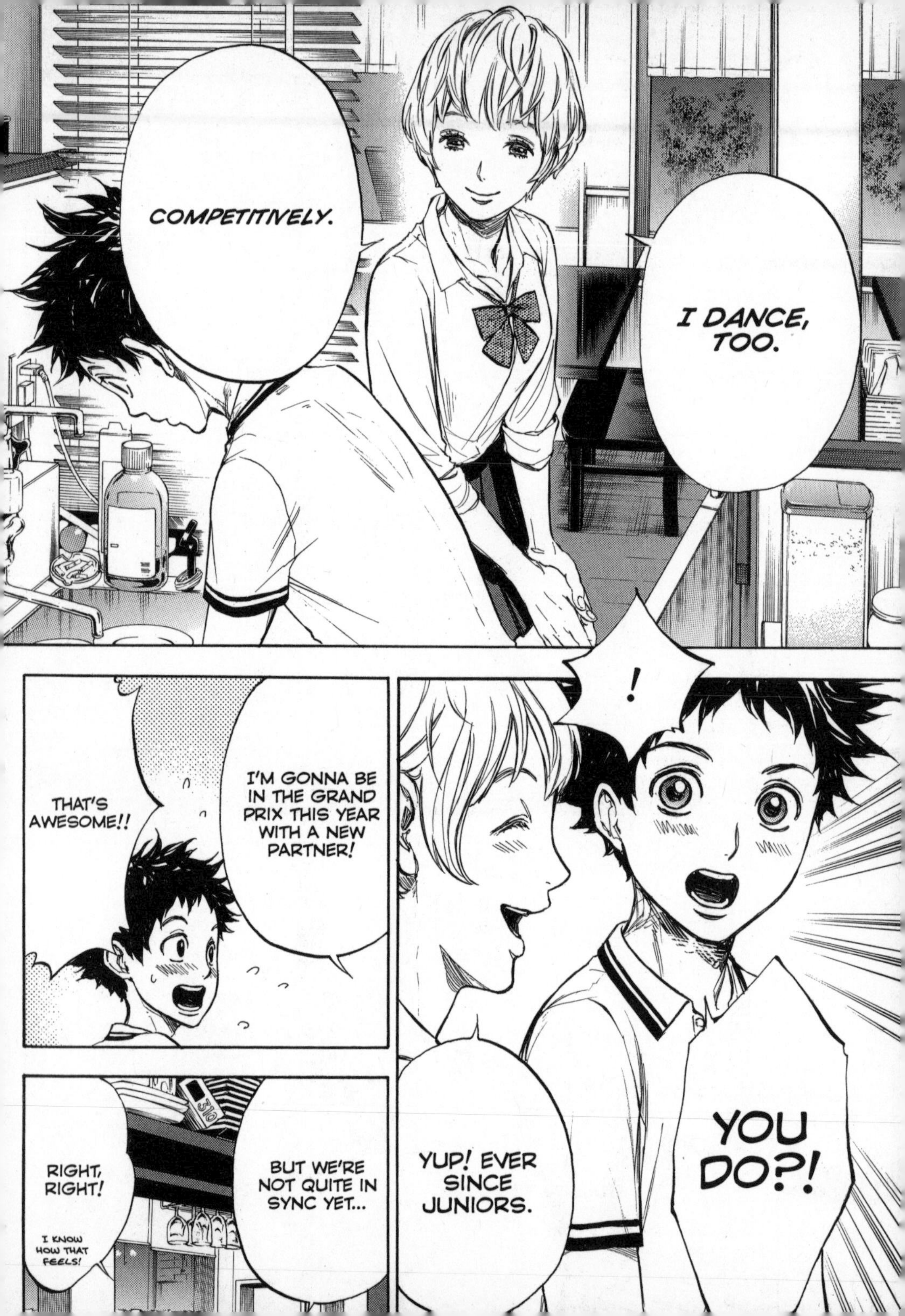
I DANCE, TOO.
COMPETITIVELY.
!
YOU DO?!
YUP! EVER SINCE JUNIORS.
I'M GONNA BE IN THE GRAND PRIX THIS YEAR WITH A NEW PARTNER!
THAT'S AWESOME!!
BUT WE'RE NOT QUITE IN SYNC YET...
RIGHT, RIGHT!
I KNOW HOW THAT FEELS!

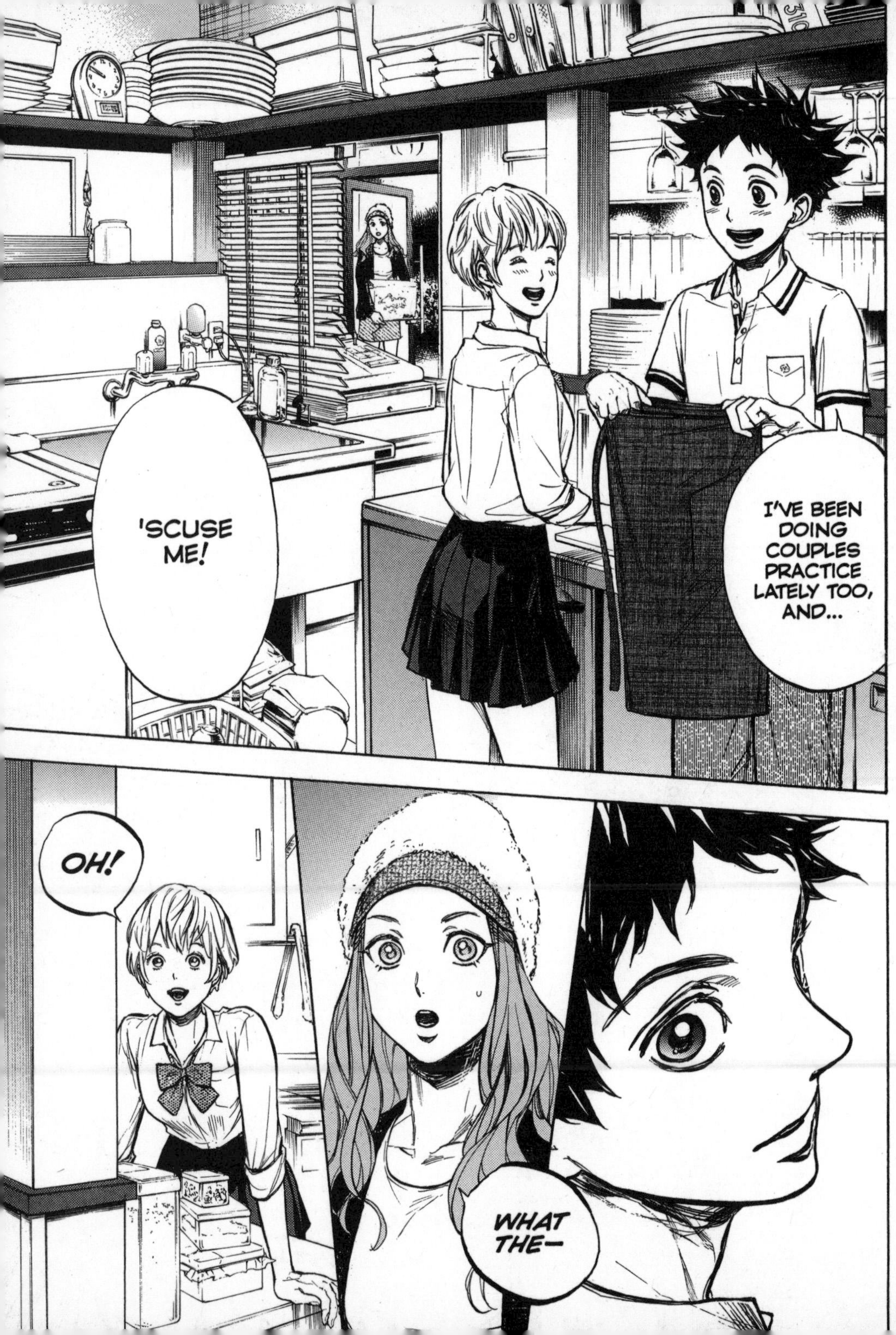
I'VE BEEN DOING COUPLES PRACTICE LATELY TOO, AND...
'SCUSE ME!
WHAT THE—
OH!

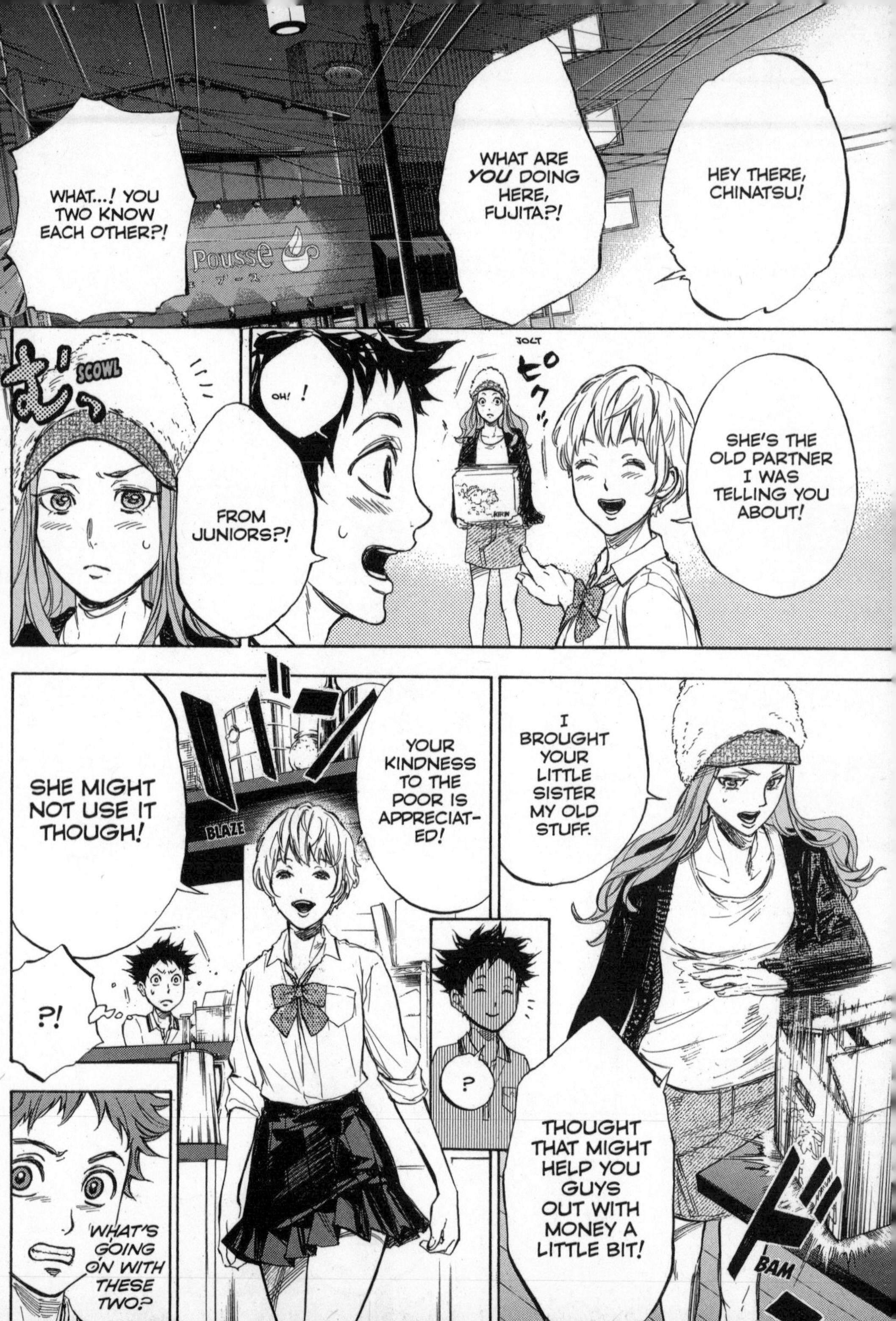
HEY THERE, CHINATSU!
WHAT ARE YOU DOING HERE, FUJITA?!
Pousse
WHAT...! YOU TWO KNOW EACH OTHER?!
JOLT
ピク
SHE'S THE OLD PARTNER I WAS TELLING YOU ABOUT!
OH! !
FROM JUNIORS?!
む
SCOWL
I BROUGHT YOUR LITTLE SISTER MY OLD STUFF.
THOUGHT THAT MIGHT HELP YOU GUYS OUT WITH MONEY A LITTLE BIT!
BAM
YOUR KINDNESS TO THE POOR IS APPRECIAT-ED!
BLAZE
SHE MIGHT NOT USE IT THOUGH!
?!
?
WHAT'S GOING ON WITH THESE TWO?

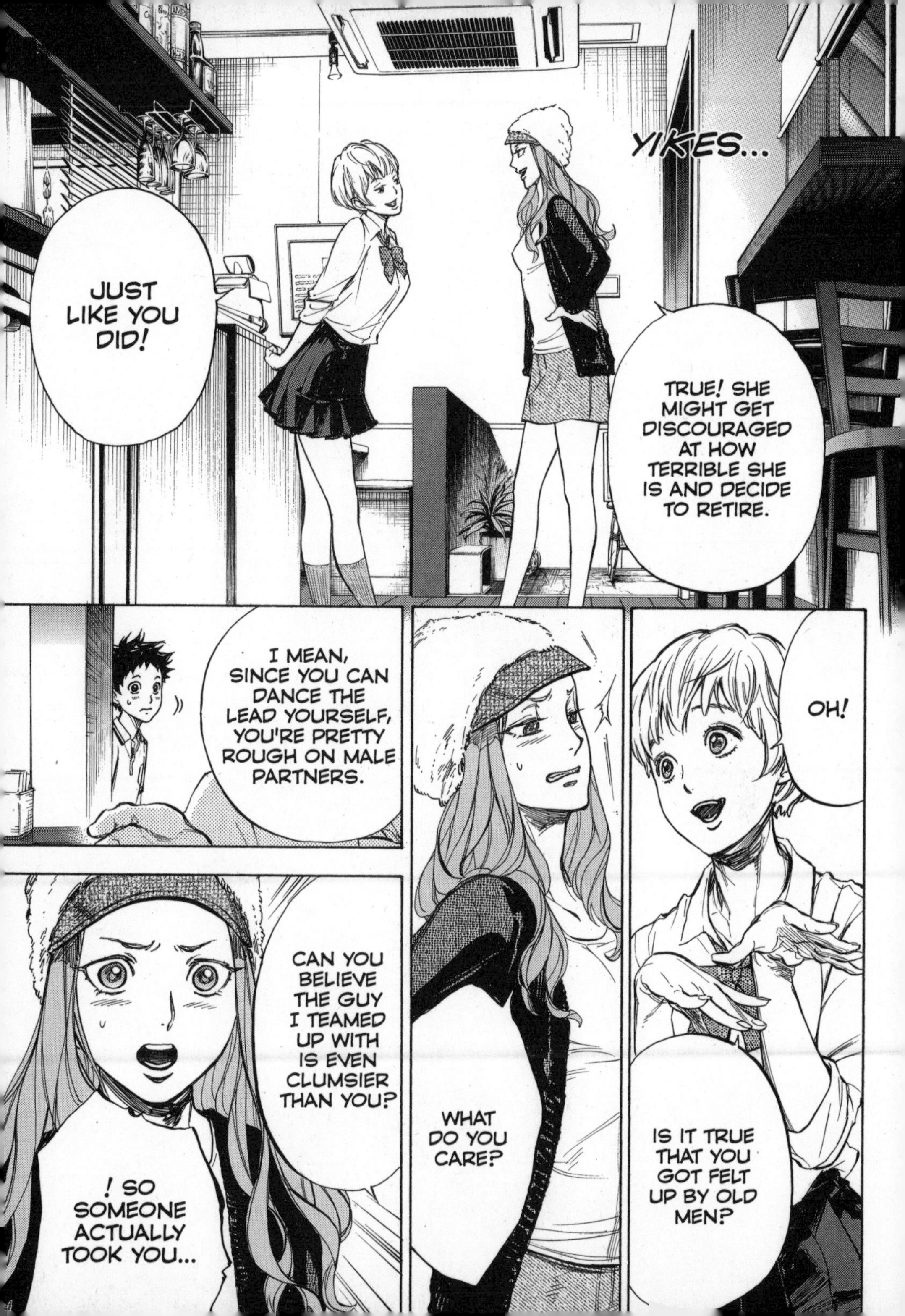
YIKES...
TRUE! SHE MIGHT GET DISCOURAGED AT HOW TERRIBLE SHE IS AND DECIDE TO RETIRE.
JUST LIKE YOU DID!
OH!
IS IT TRUE THAT YOU GOT FELT UP BY OLD MEN?
WHAT DO YOU CARE?
I MEAN, SINCE YOU CAN DANCE THE LEAD YOURSELF, YOU'RE PRETTY ROUGH ON MALE PARTNERS.
CAN YOU BELIEVE THE GUY I TEAMED UP WITH IS EVEN CLUMSIER THAN YOU?
! SO SOMEONE ACTUALLY TOOK YOU...

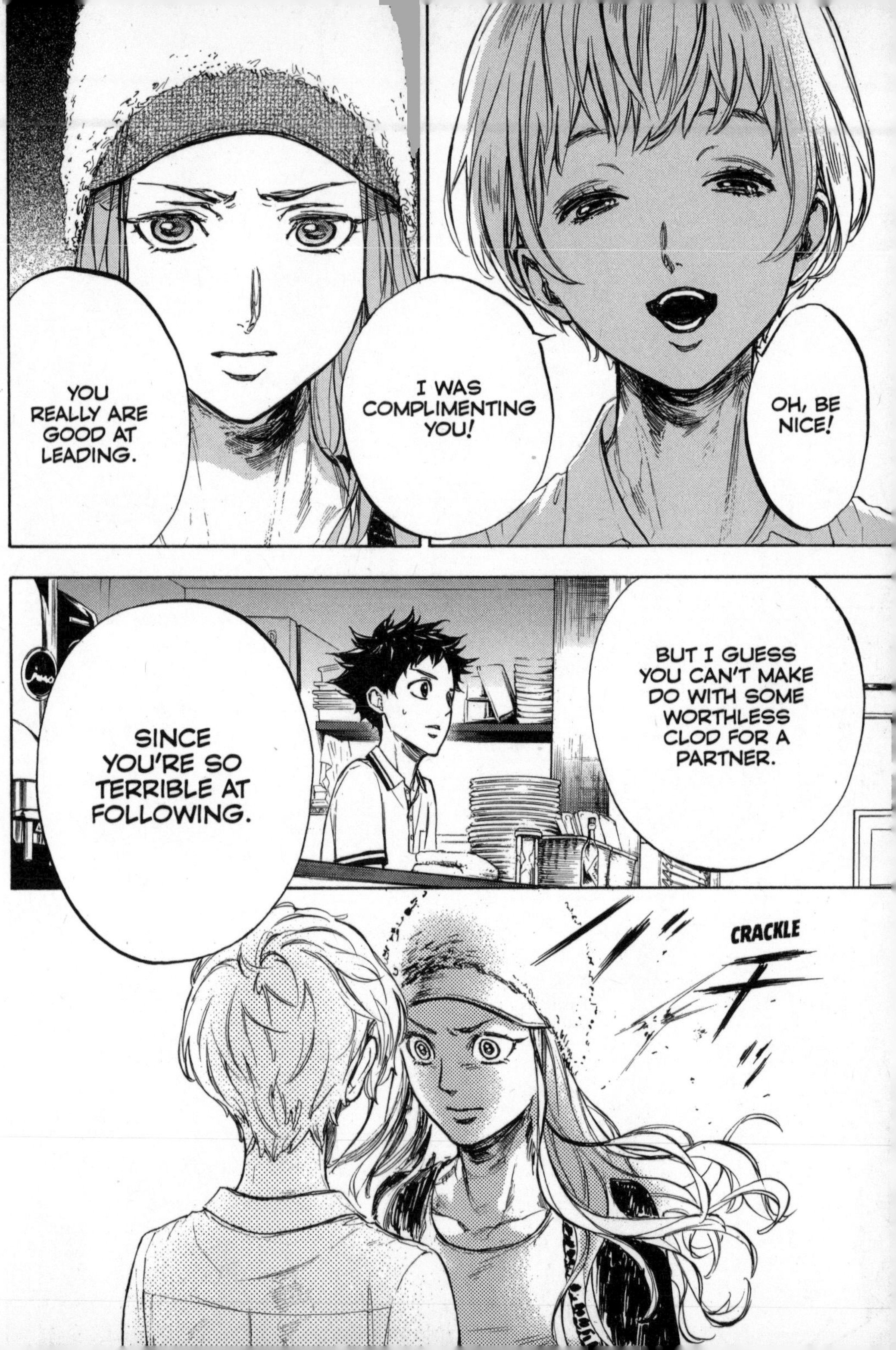
OH, BE NICE!
I WAS COMPLIMENTING YOU!
YOU REALLY ARE GOOD AT LEADING.
BUT I GUESS YOU CAN'T MAKE DO WITH SOME WORTHLESS CLOD FOR A PARTNER.
SINCE YOU'RE SO TERRIBLE AT FOLLOWING.
CRACKLE

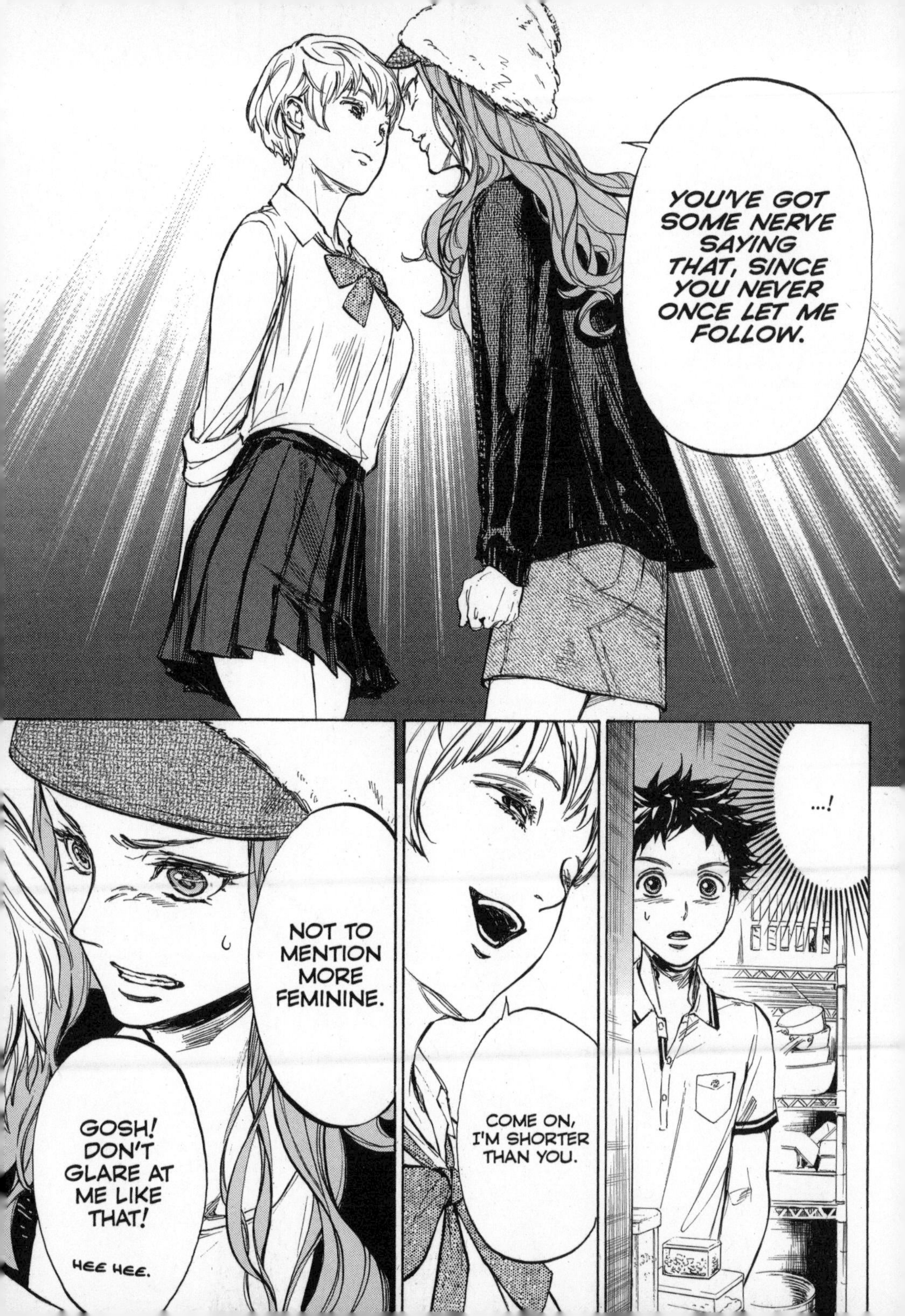
YOU'VE GOT SOME NERVE SAYING THAT, SINCE YOU NEVER ONCE LET ME FOLLOW.
...!
COME ON, I'M SHORTER THAN YOU.
NOT TO MENTION MORE FEMININE.
GOSH! DON'T GLARE AT ME LIKE THAT!
HEE HEE.

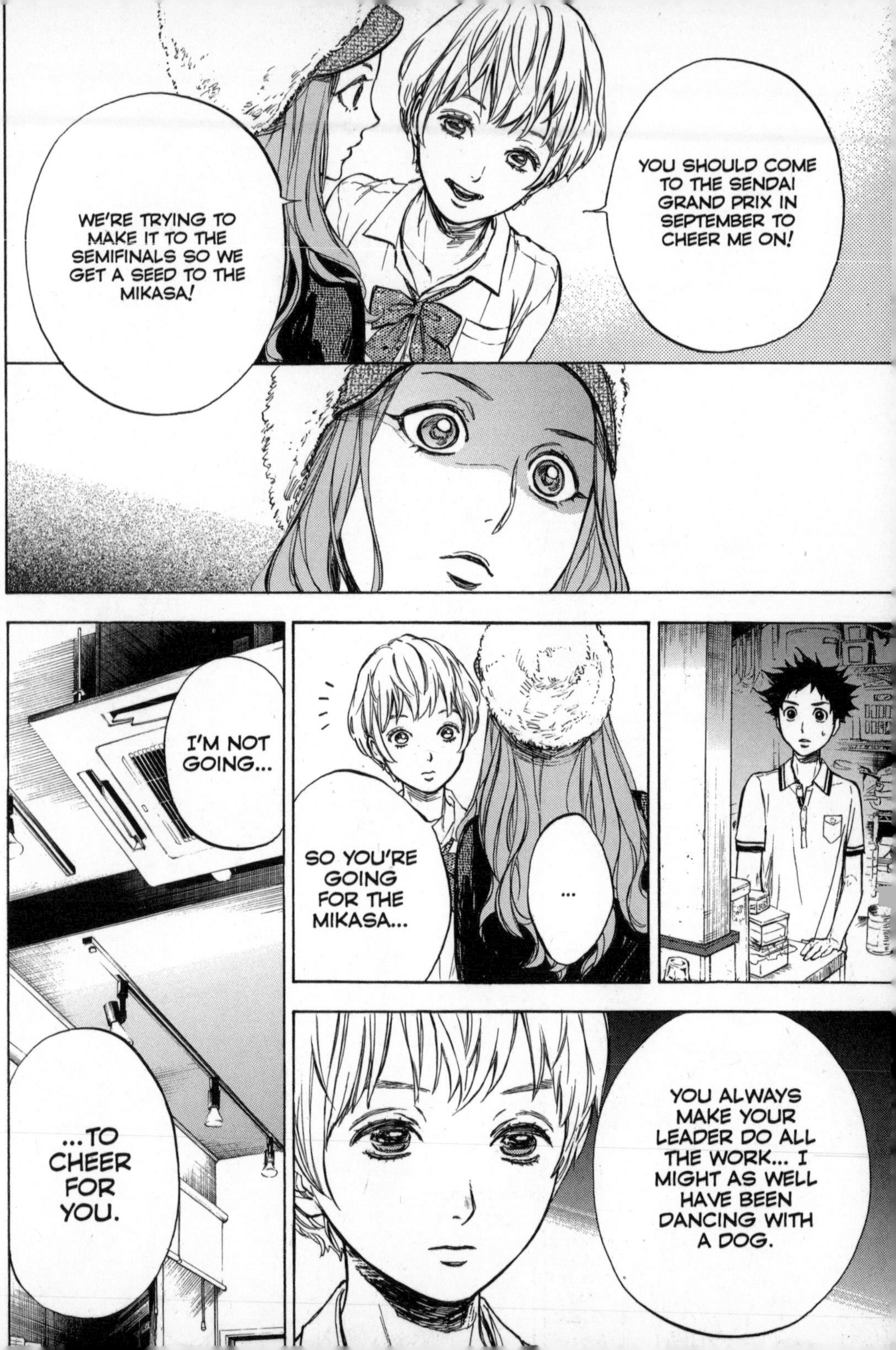

YOU SHOULD COME TO THE SENDAI GRAND PRIX IN SEPTEMBER TO CHEER ME ON!
WE'RE TRYING TO MAKE IT TO THE SEMIFINALS SO WE GET A SEED TO THE MIKASA!
...
SO YOU'RE GOING FOR THE MIKASA...
YOU ALWAYS MAKE YOUR LEADER DO ALL THE WORK... I MIGHT AS WELL HAVE BEEN DANCING WITH A DOG.
I'M NOT GOING...
...TO CHEER FOR YOU.

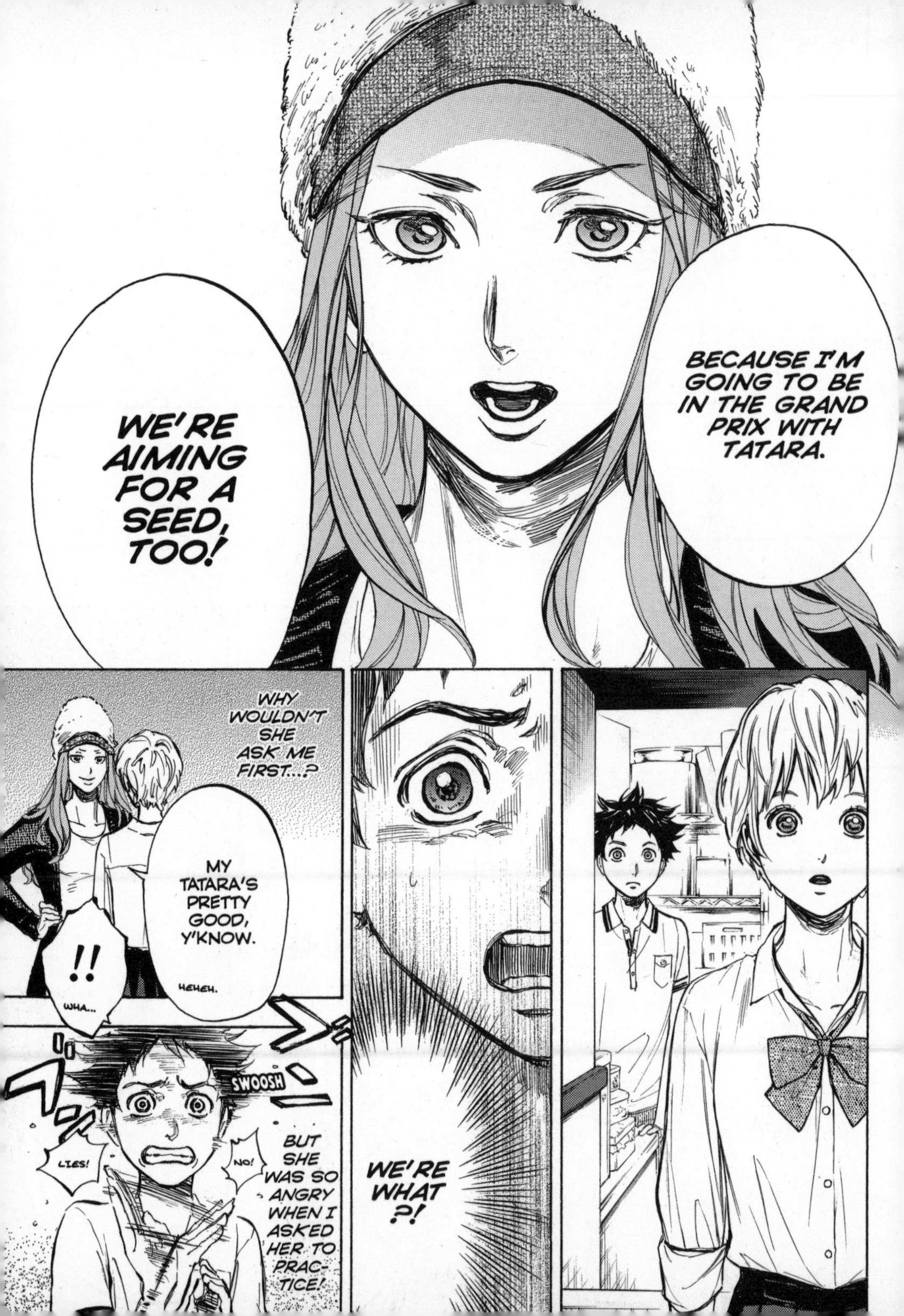
BECAUSE I'M GOING TO BE IN THE GRAND PRIX WITH TATARA.
WE'RE AIMING FOR A SEED, TOO!
WE'RE WHAT?!
WHY WOULDN'T SHE ASK ME FIRST...?
MY TATARA'S PRETTY GOOD, Y'KNOW.
HEHEH.
!!
WHA...
SWOOSH
NO!
LIES!
BUT SHE WAS SO ANGRY WHEN I ASKED HER TO PRAC-TICE!

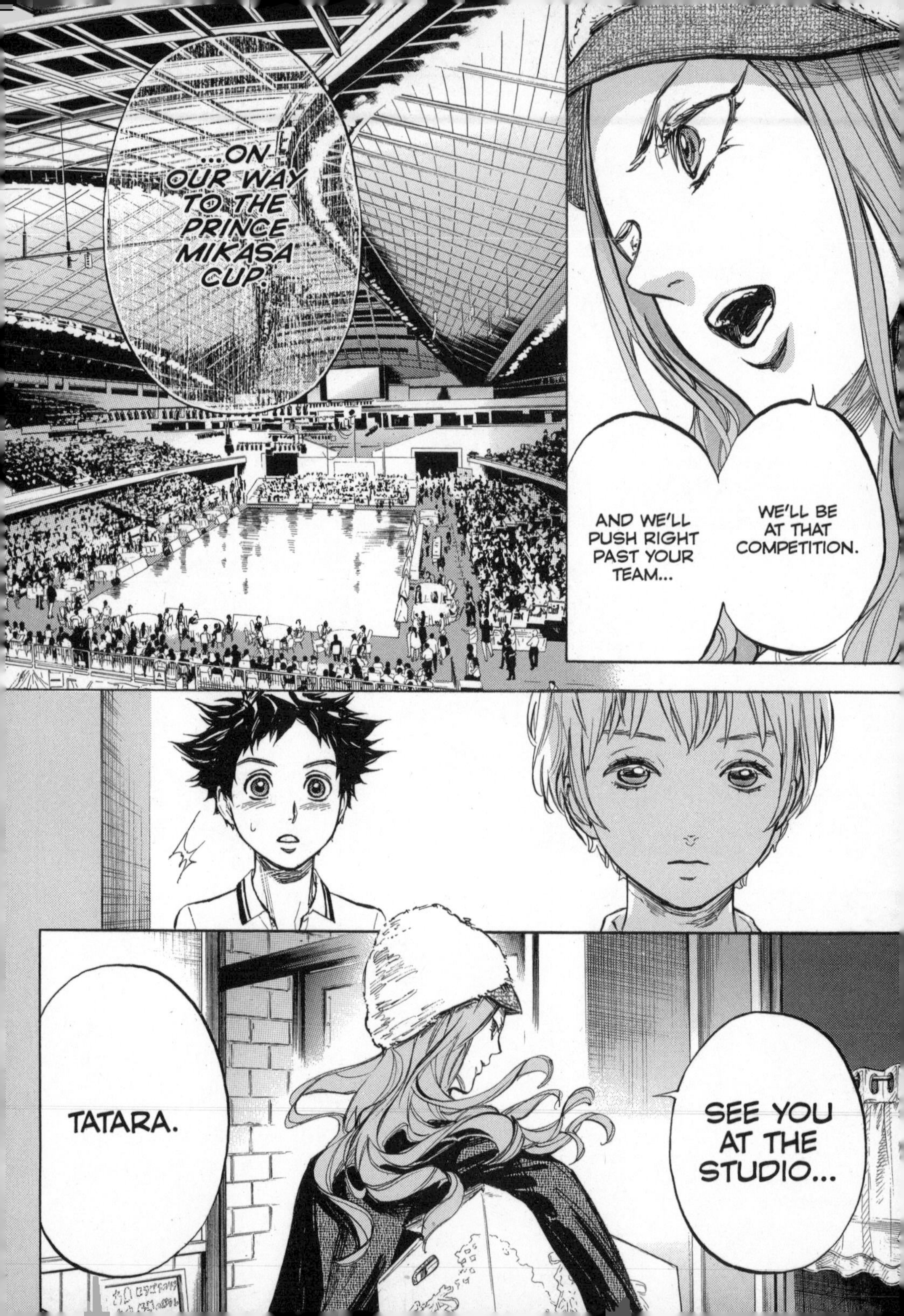
WE'LL BE AT THAT COMPETITION.
AND WE'LL PUSH RIGHT PAST YOUR TEAM...
...ON OUR WAY TO THE PRINCE MIKASA CUP.
SEE YOU AT THE STUDIO...
TATARA.

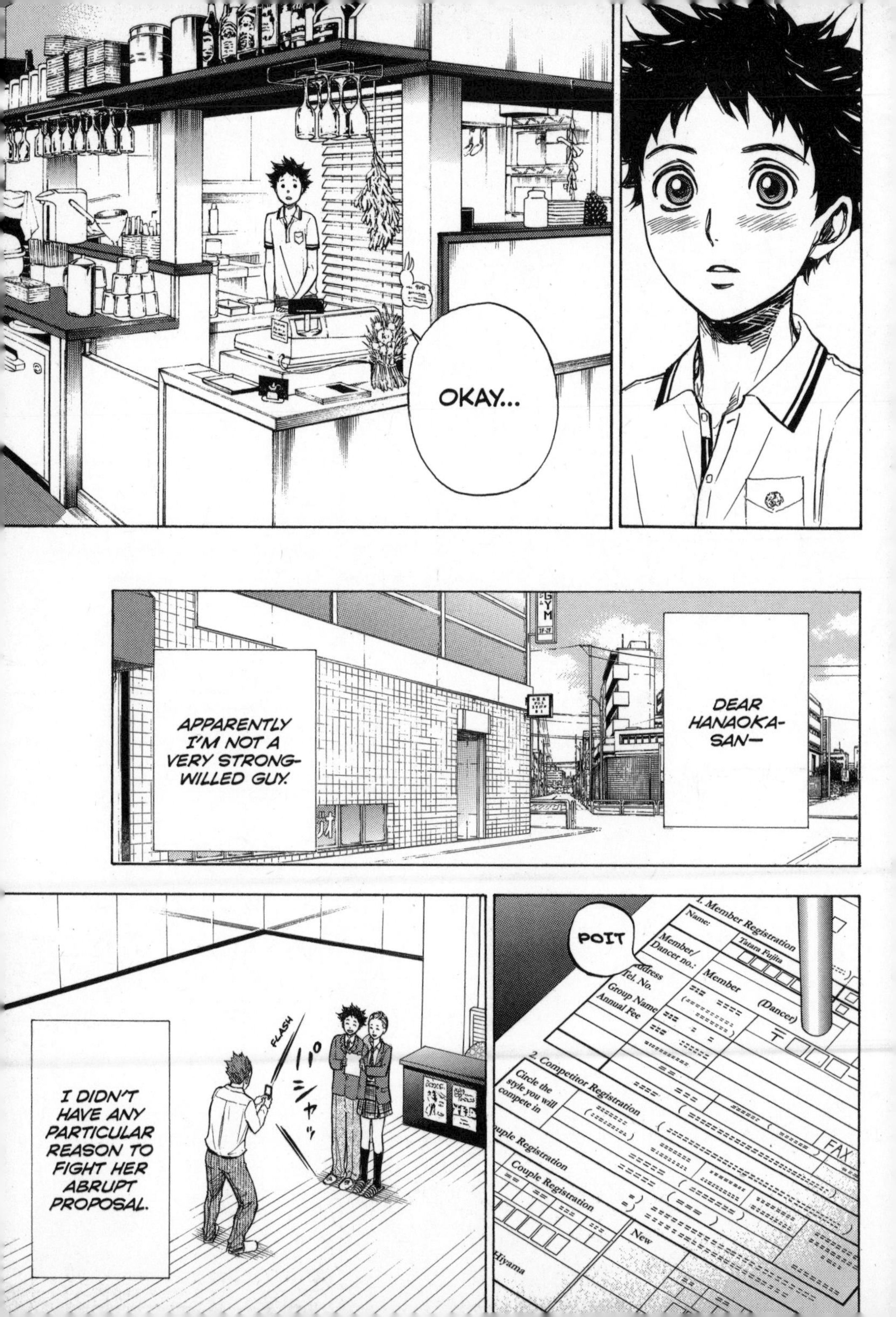
OKAY...
DEAR HANAOKA-SAN—
APPARENTLY I'M NOT A VERY STRONG-WILLED GUY.
POIT
1. Member Registration
Name:
Tatara Fujita
Member/
Dancer no.:
Address
Tel. No.
Group Name
Annual Fee
Member
(Dancer)
2. Competitor Registration
Circle the style you will compete in
FAX
Couple Registration
Couple Registration
New
Hiyama
FLASH
パシャッ
I DIDN'T HAVE ANY PARTICULAR REASON TO FIGHT HER ABRUPT PROPOSAL.

SO I TEAMED UP WITH HIYAMA-SAN.
TO SENGOKU-SAN
SUB JUST MARRIED
TEXT
size
OKAY, SENDIN' TO SENGOKU-SAN!
NOW WE GET ALONG SO WELL THAT I CALL HER "CHII-CHAN" AND SHE CALLS ME "TATARA."
OHO!
GUESS THEY'RE A PAIR NOW.
Heat 23: END
IN TWO WEEKS, WE'LL BE IN THE NOVICE MATCH.
A B C D N 1 2
S 1 1 2 2 1
L 1 1 2 2 1
S 2 2 1 1
L 2 2 1 1
S 1 1 1
L 1 1 1
S 1 1 1 1
L 1 1 1 1
THAT'S US!!
Sumida DS Contest S 1 1 1 1
L 1 1 1 1
22nd Chofu City DS Contest S 1 1
L 1 1
All-Kyushu Dance Championships S 1 1 2 2 1 1

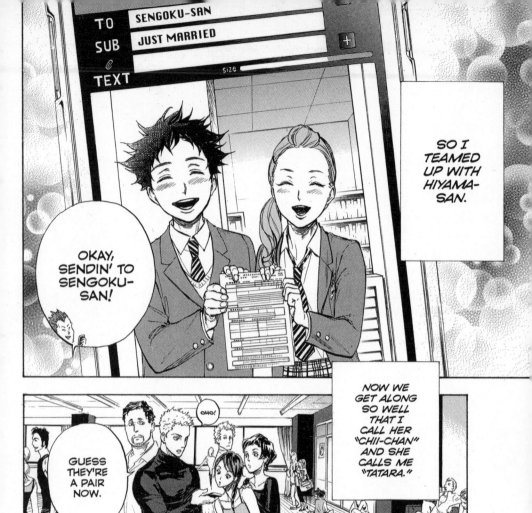

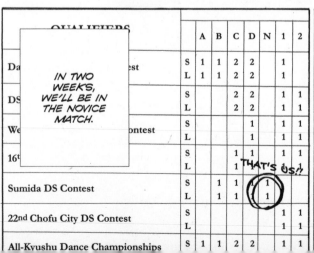

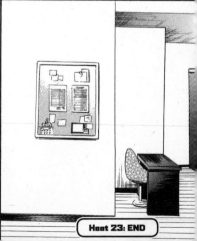

# WELCOME TO THE BALLROOM

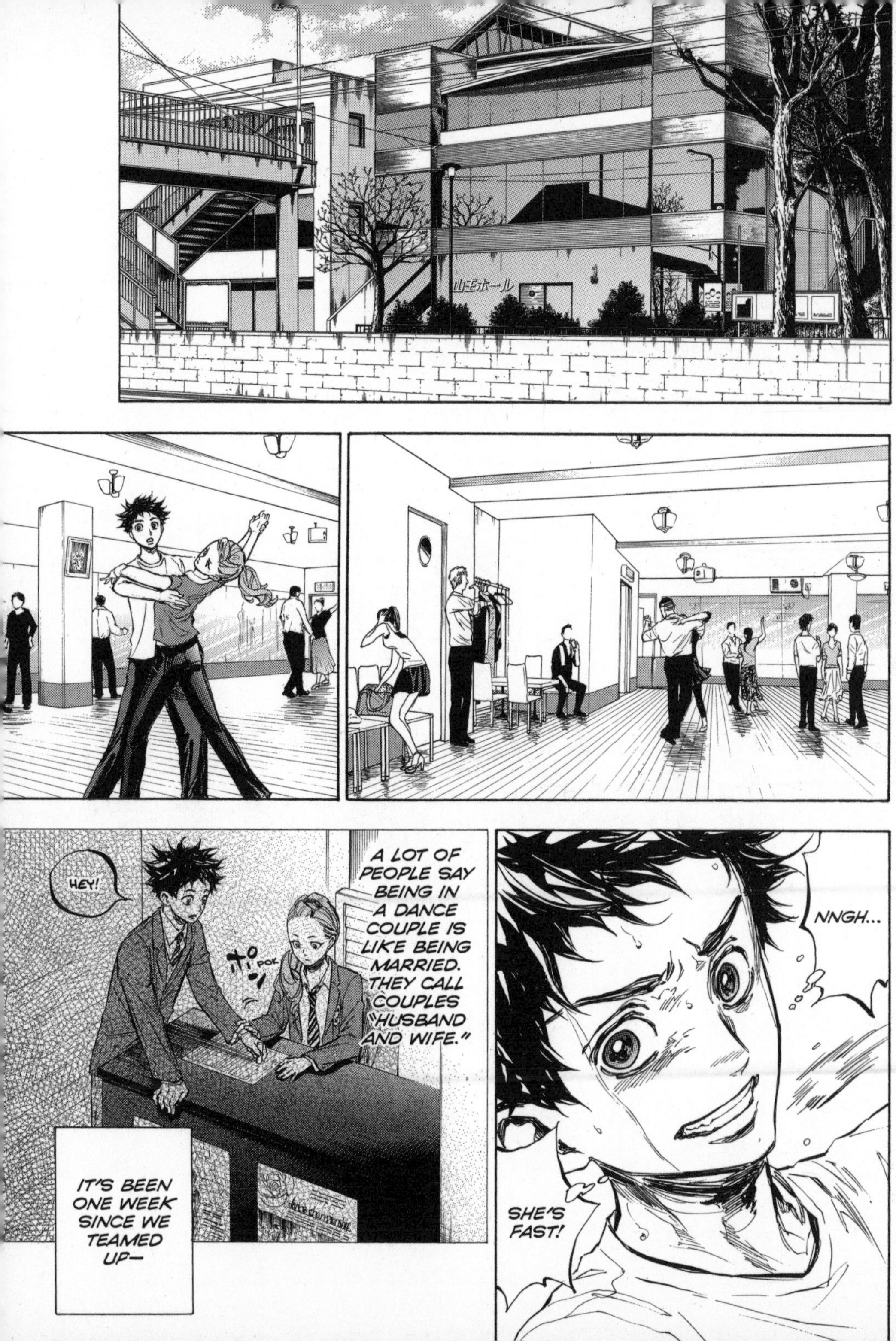
NNGH...
SHE'S FAST!
A LOT OF PEOPLE SAY BEING IN A DANCE COUPLE IS LIKE BEING MARRIED. THEY CALL COUPLES "HUSBAND AND WIFE."
HEY!
POK
IT'S BEEN ONE WEEK SINCE WE TEAMED UP—

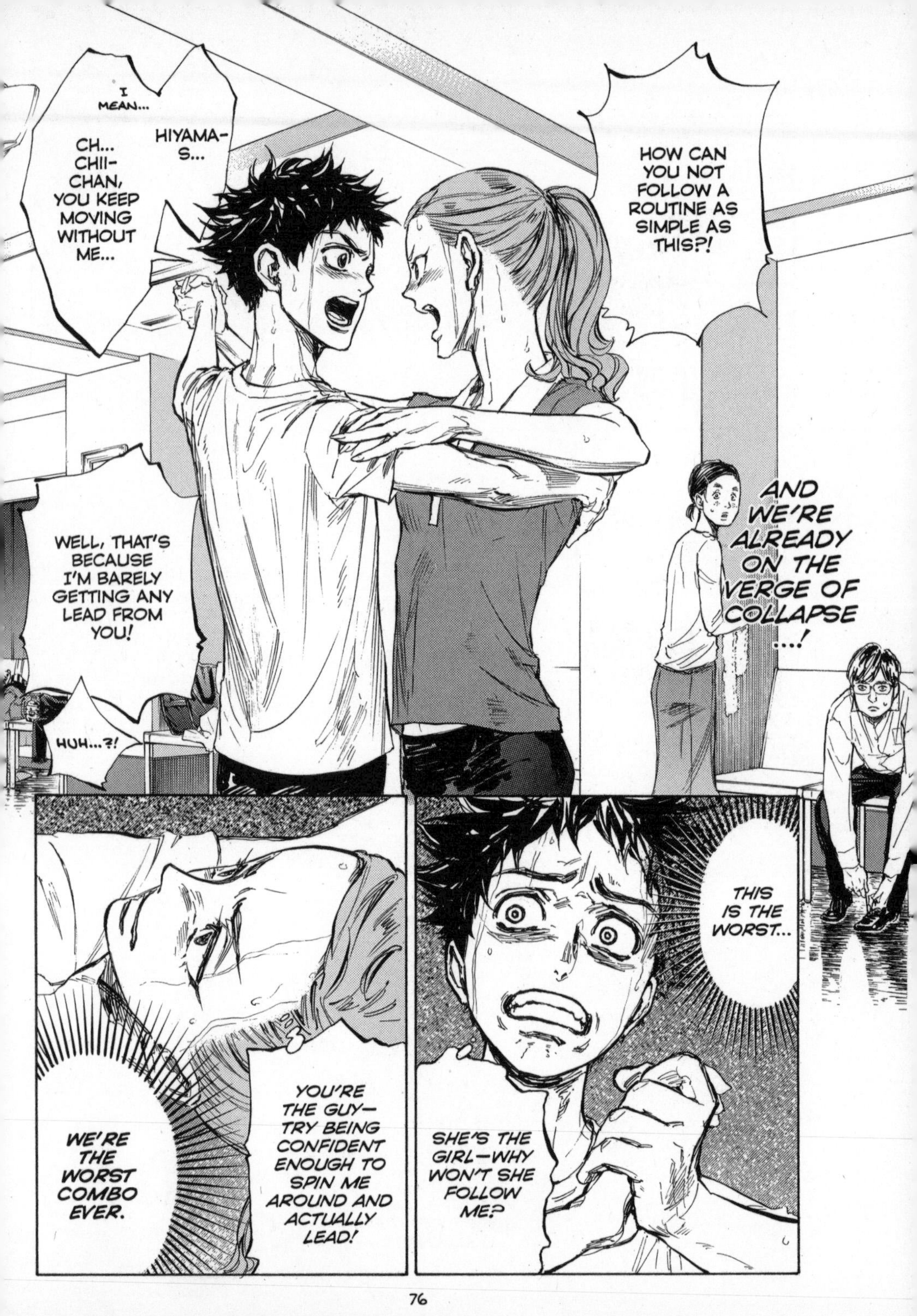
HOW CAN YOU NOT FOLLOW A ROUTINE AS SIMPLE AS THIS?!
I MEAN... HIYAMA-S... CH... CHII-CHAN, YOU KEEP MOVING WITHOUT ME...
AND WE'RE ALREADY ON THE VERGE OF COLLAPSE ...!
WELL, THAT'S BECAUSE I'M BARELY GETTING ANY LEAD FROM YOU!
HUH...?!
THIS IS THE WORST...
SHE'S THE GIRL—WHY WON'T SHE FOLLOW ME?
YOU'RE THE GUY—TRY BEING CONFIDENT ENOUGH TO SPIN ME AROUND AND ACTUALLY LEAD!
WE'RE THE WORST COMBO EVER.

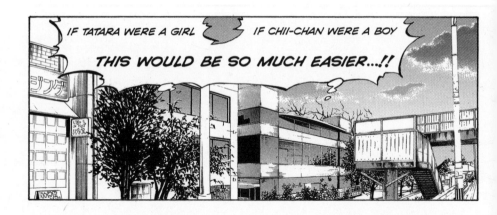

IF CHII-CHAN WERE A BOY
IF TATARA WERE A GIRL
THIS WOULD BE SO MUCH EASIER...!!

# Heat 24 Give and Take

"NOVICE" REFERS TO AN UNRANKED BEGINNER IN COMPETITION.

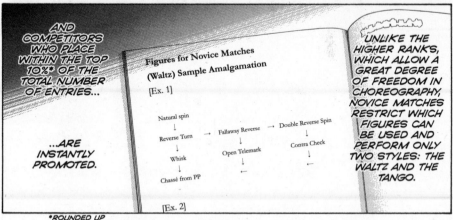

UNLIKE THE HIGHER RANKS, WHICH ALLOW A GREAT DEGREE OF FREEDOM IN CHOREOGRAPHY, NOVICE MATCHES RESTRICT WHICH FIGURES CAN BE USED AND PERFORM ONLY TWO STYLES: THE WALTZ AND THE TANGO.
Figures for Novice Matches
(Waltz) Sample Amalgamation
[Ex. 1]
Natural spin ↓ Reverse Turn ↓ Whisk ↓ Chassé from PP
Reverse Turn → Fallaway Reverse → Double Reverse Spin
Fallaway Reverse ↓ Open Telemark ↓ ←
Double Reverse Spin ↓ Contra Check ↓ ←
[Ex. 2]
AND COMPETITORS WHO PLACE WITHIN THE TOP 10%* OF THE TOTAL NUMBER OF ENTRIES...
...ARE INSTANTLY PROMOTED.

*ROUNDED UP

THEY'RE REGISTERED AS LEVEL D COMPETITORS, AND ARE THEN ALLOWED TO ENTER OFFICIAL COMPETITIONS.

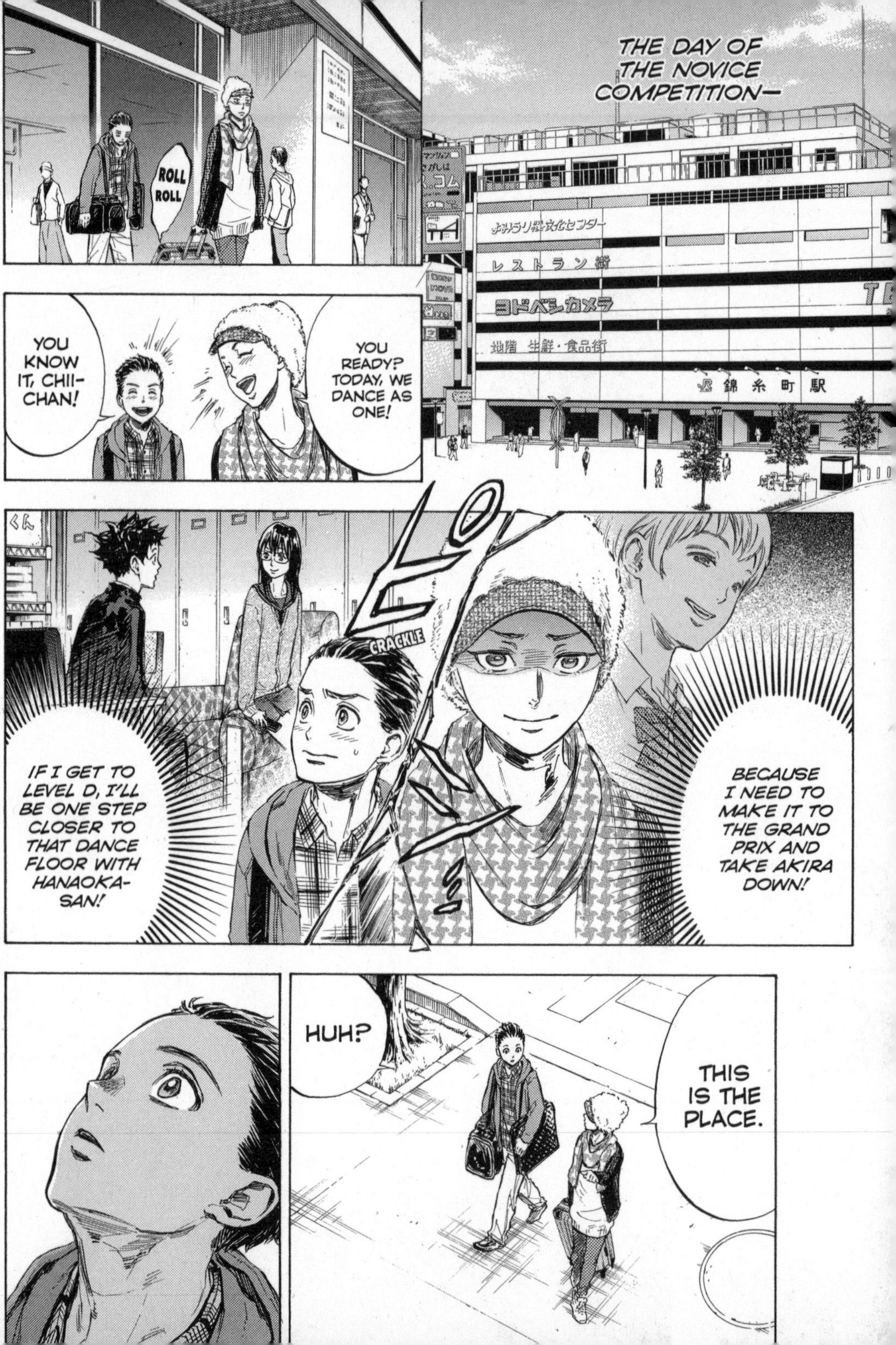
THE DAY OF THE NOVICE COMPETITION—
レストラン街
ヨドバシカメラ
地階 生鮮・食品街
錦糸町駅
ROLL ROLL
YOU READY? TODAY, WE DANCE AS ONE!
YOU KNOW IT, CHII-CHAN!
BECAUSE I NEED TO MAKE IT TO THE GRAND PRIX AND TAKE AKIRA DOWN!
CRACKLE
IF I GET TO LEVEL D, I'LL BE ONE STEP CLOSER TO THAT DANCE FLOOR WITH HANAOKA-SAN!
THIS IS THE PLACE.
HUH?

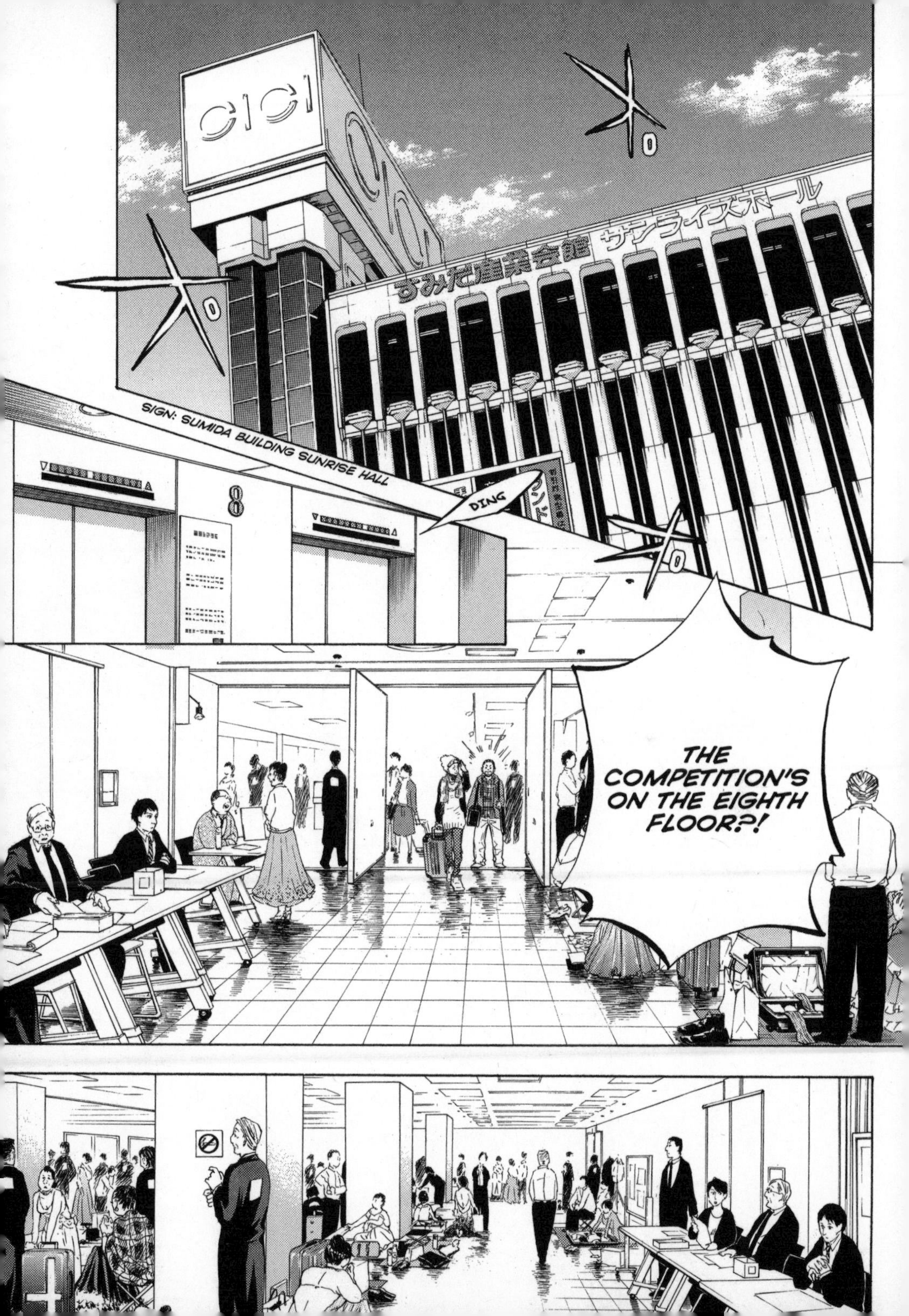
すみだ産業会館 サンライズホール
SIGN: SUMIDA BUILDING SUNRISE HALL
DING
THE COMPETITION'S ON THE EIGHTH FLOOR?!

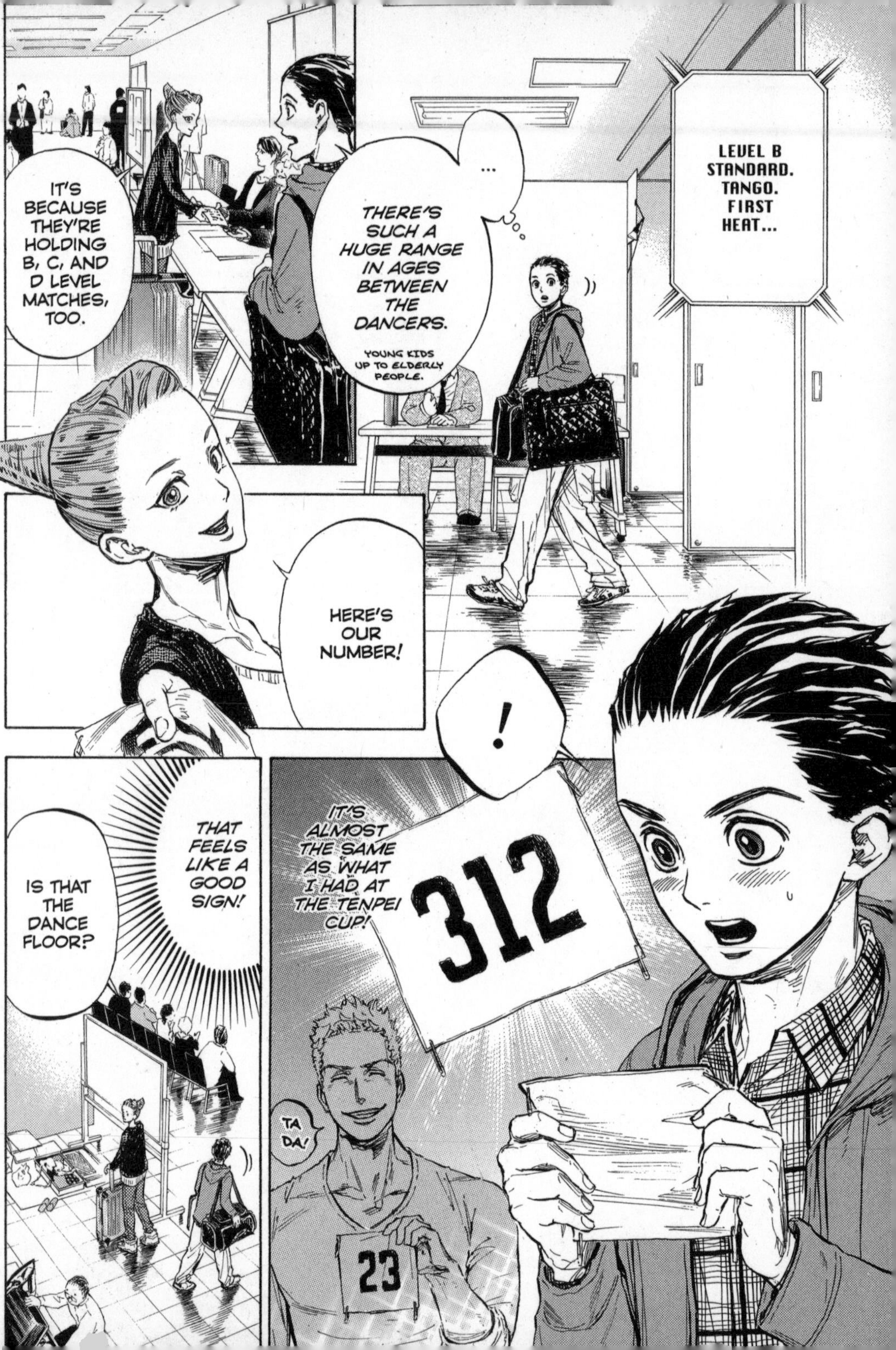
LEVEL B STANDARD. TANGO. FIRST HEAT...
...
THERE'S SUCH A HUGE RANGE IN AGES BETWEEN THE DANCERS.
YOUNG KIDS UP TO ELDERLY PEOPLE.
IT'S BECAUSE THEY'RE HOLDING B, C, AND D LEVEL MATCHES, TOO.
HERE'S OUR NUMBER!
!
IT'S ALMOST THE SAME AS WHAT I HAD AT THE TENPEI CUP!
312
TA DA!
23
THAT FEELS LIKE A GOOD SIGN!
IS THAT THE DANCE FLOOR?

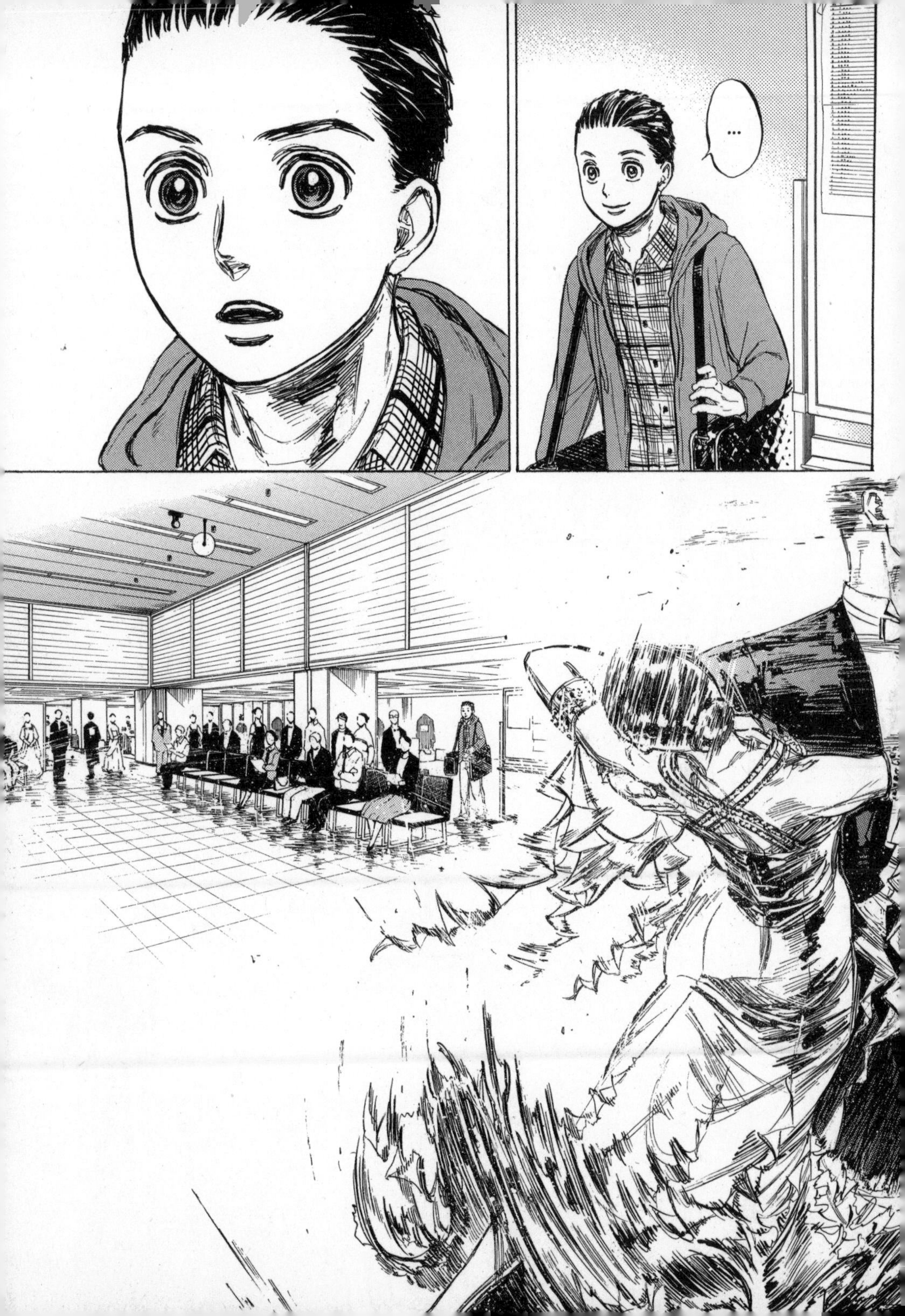
...

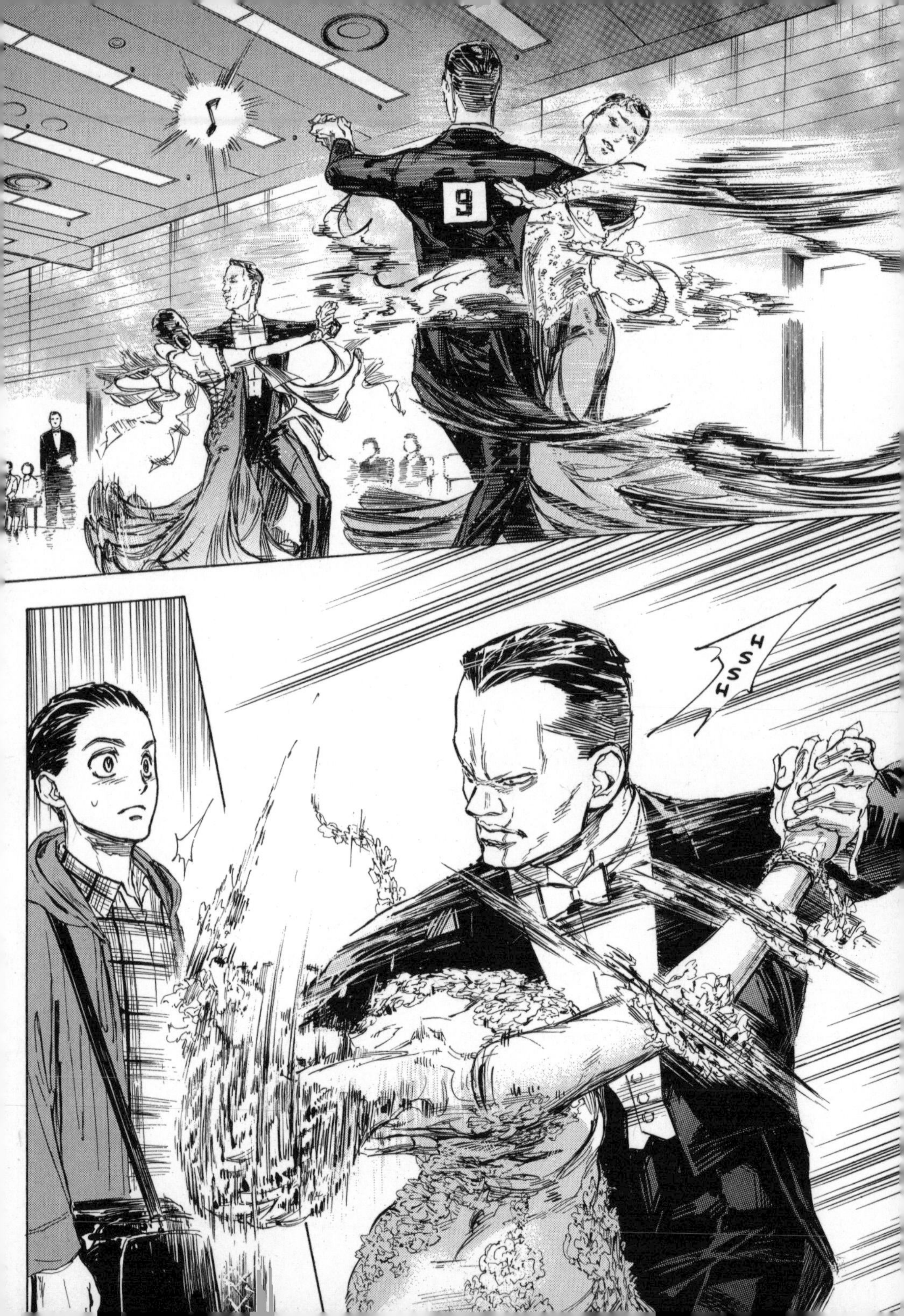
9
HSSH

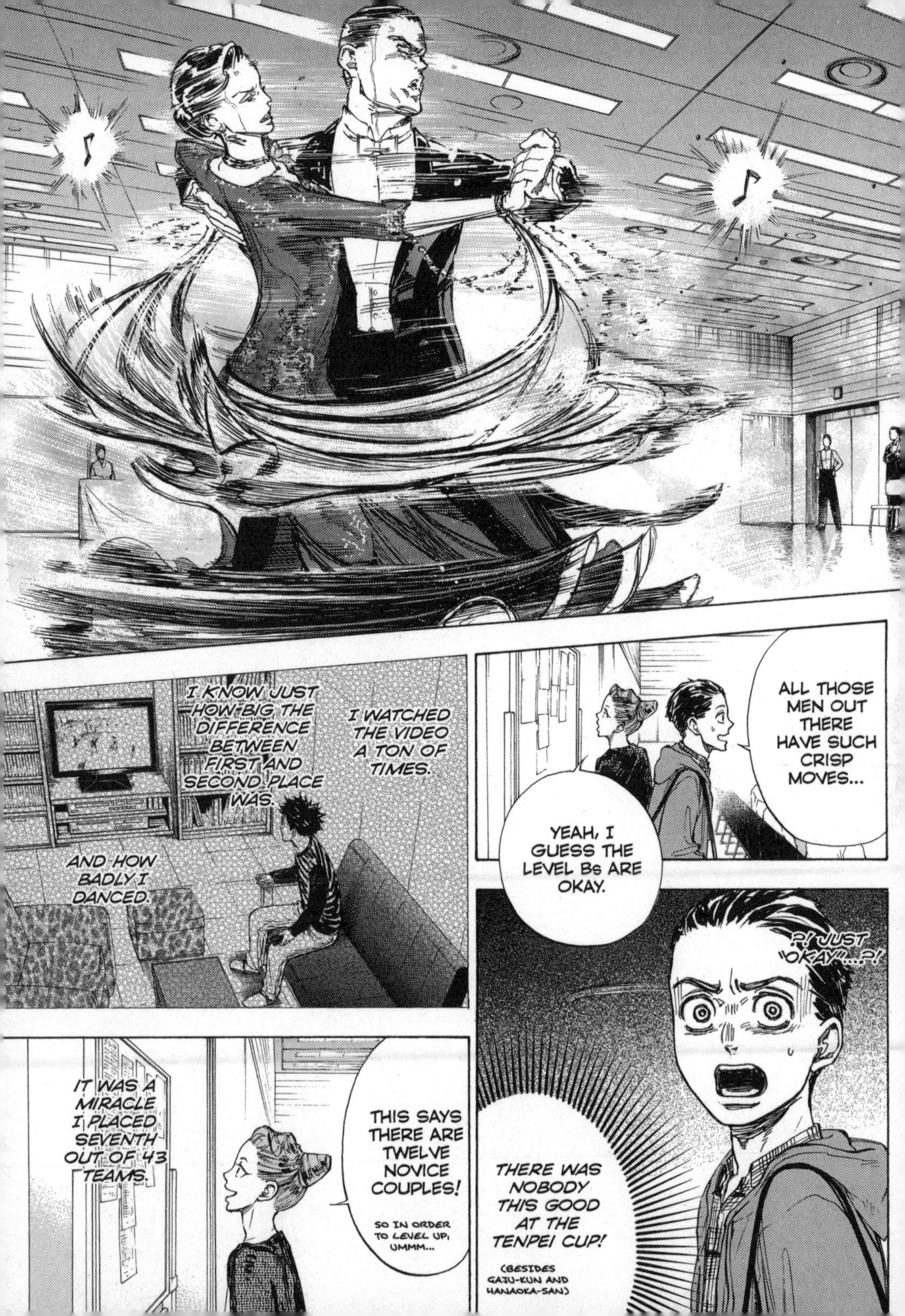
ALL THOSE MEN OUT THERE HAVE SUCH CRISP MOVES...
YEAH, I GUESS THE LEVEL Bs ARE OKAY.
?! JUST "OKAY"...?!
THERE WAS NOBODY THIS GOOD AT THE TENPEI CUP!
(BESIDES GAJU-KUN AND HANAOKA-SAN)
I WATCHED THE VIDEO A TON OF TIMES.
I KNOW JUST HOW BIG THE DIFFERENCE BETWEEN FIRST AND SECOND PLACE WAS.
AND HOW BADLY I DANCED.
THIS SAYS THERE ARE TWELVE NOVICE COUPLES!
SO IN ORDER TO LEVEL UP, UMMM...
IT WAS A MIRACLE I PLACED SEVENTH OUT OF 43 TEAMS.

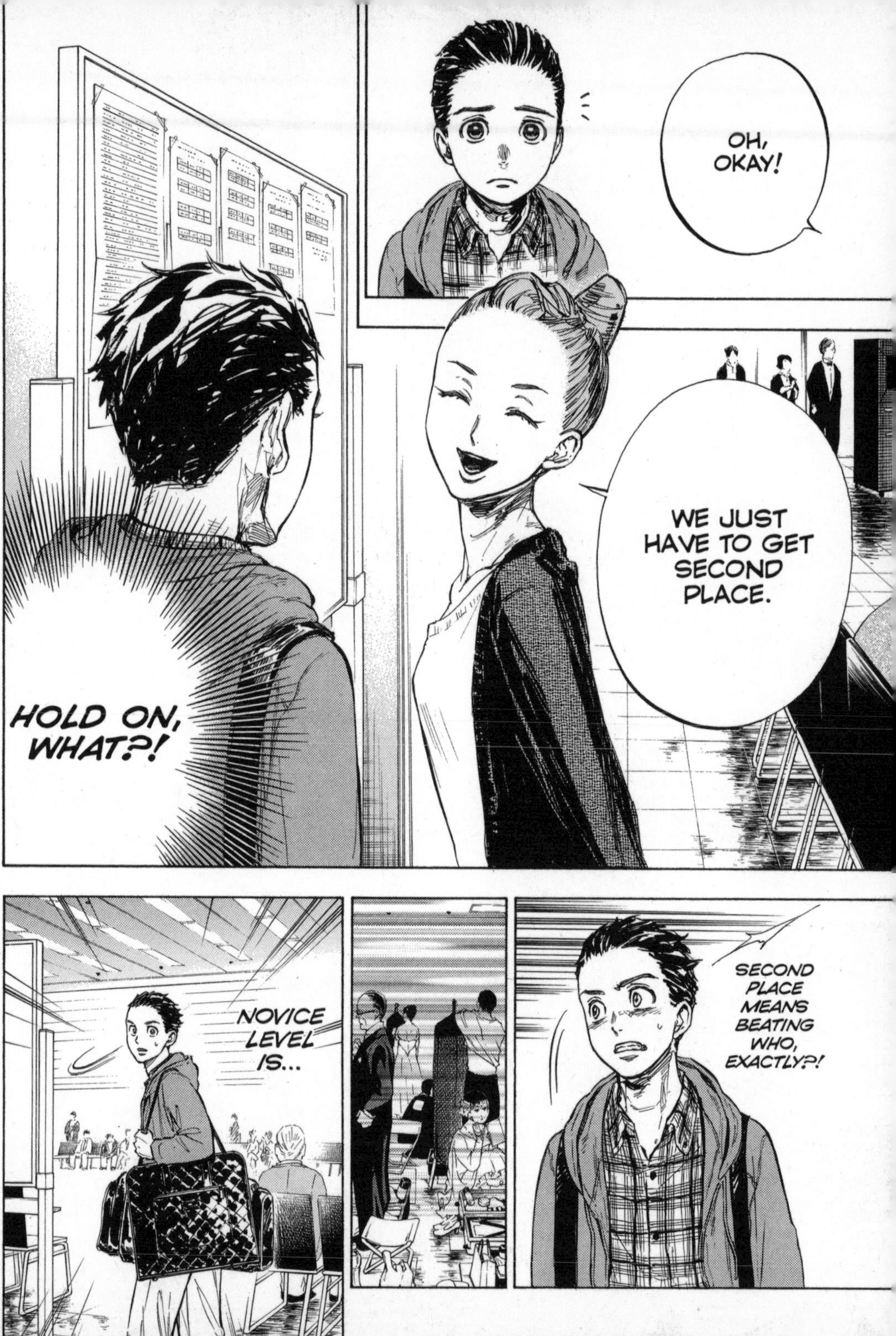
OH, OKAY!
WE JUST HAVE TO GET SECOND PLACE.
HOLD ON, WHAT?!
SECOND PLACE MEANS BEATING WHO, EXACTLY?!
NOVICE LEVEL IS...

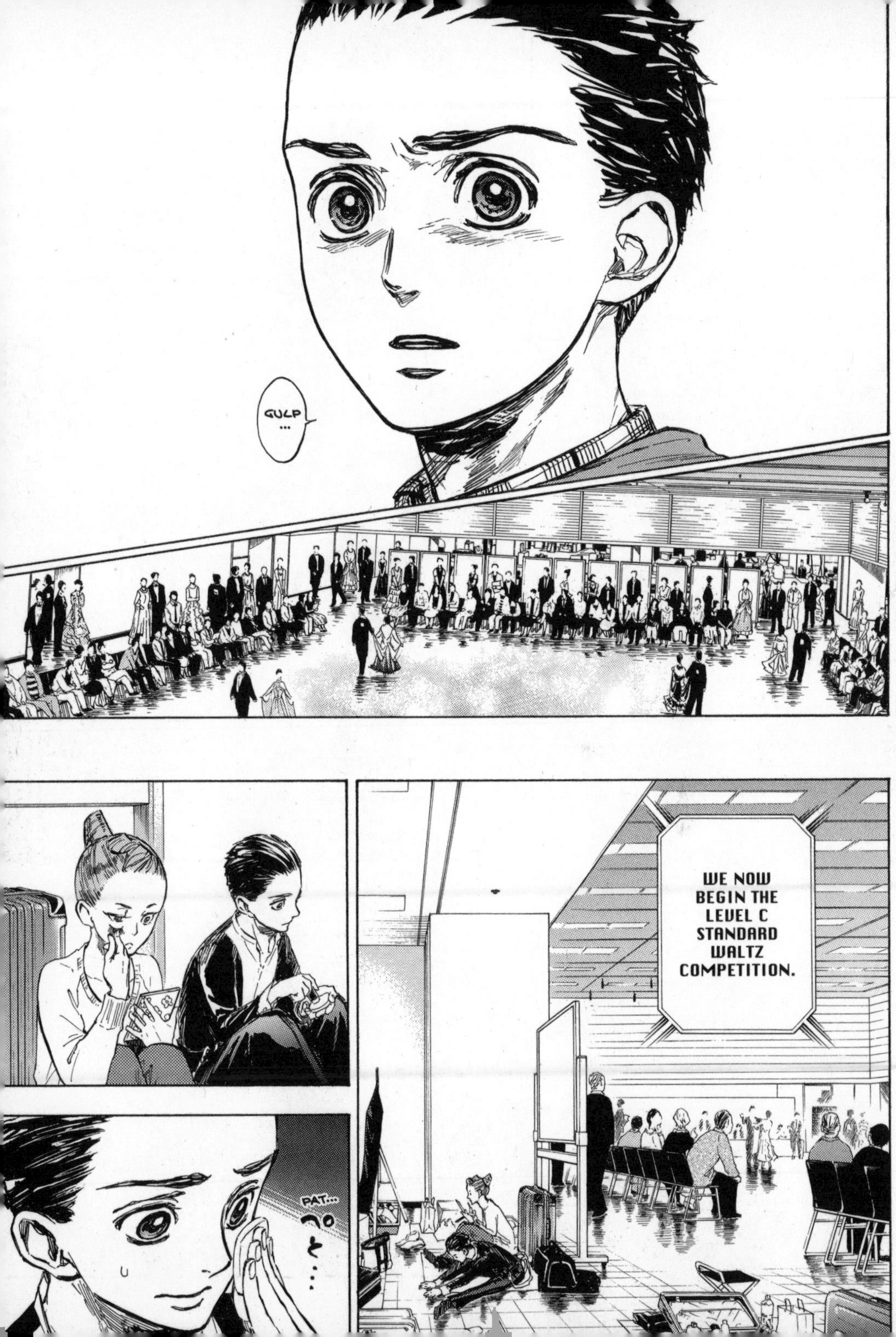
GULP ...
WE NOW BEGIN THE LEVEL C STANDARD WALTZ COMPETITION.
PAT...

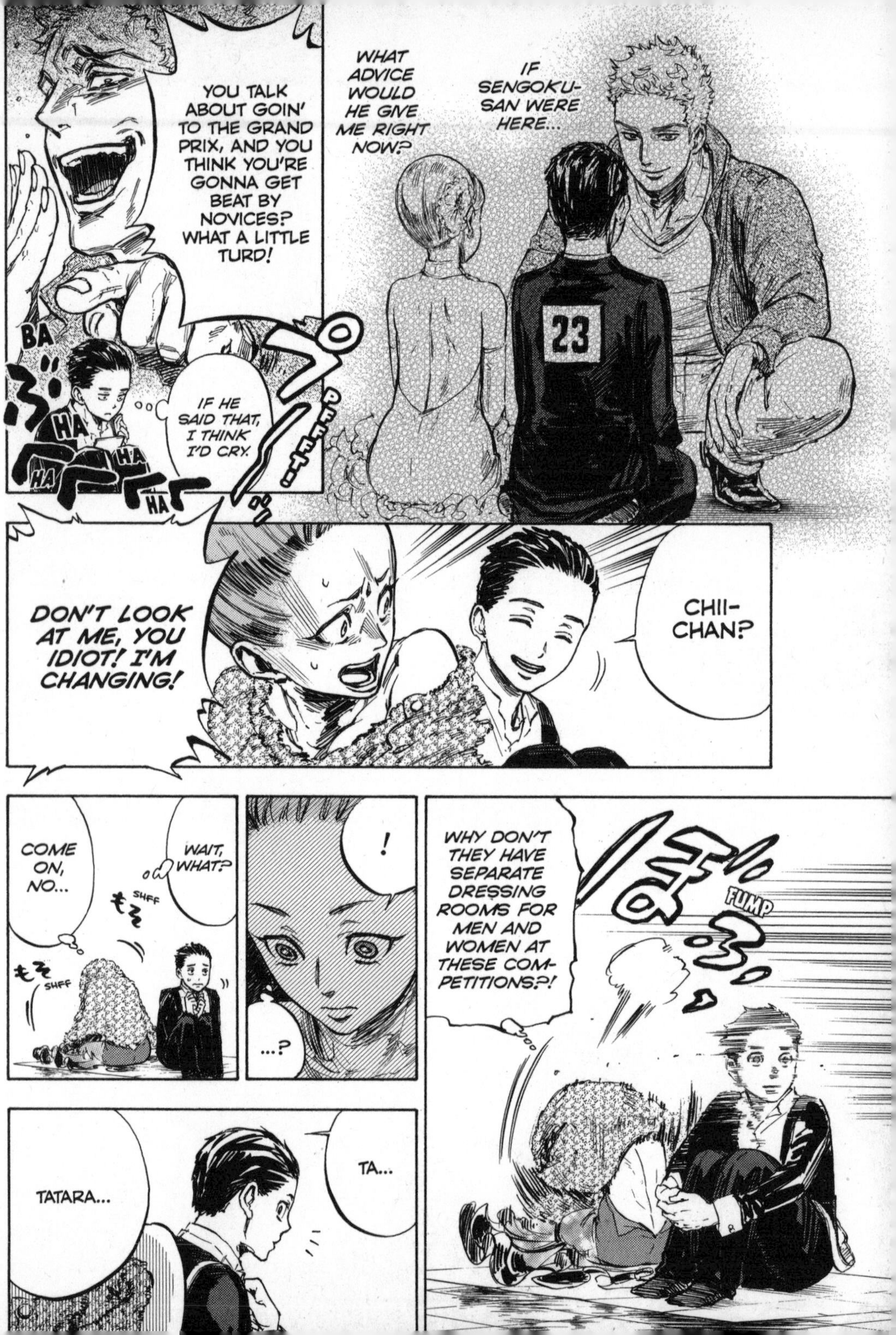
IF SENGOKU-SAN WERE HERE...
WHAT ADVICE WOULD HE GIVE ME RIGHT NOW?
23
YOU TALK ABOUT GOIN' TO THE GRAND PRIX, AND YOU THINK YOU'RE GONNA GET BEAT BY NOVICES? WHAT A LITTLE TURD!
BA HA HA HA HA
PFFFT!!
IF HE SAID THAT, I THINK I'D CRY.
CHII-CHAN?
DON'T LOOK AT ME, YOU IDIOT! I'M CHANGING!
FUMP
WHY DON'T THEY HAVE SEPARATE DRESSING ROOMS FOR MEN AND WOMEN AT THESE COMPETITIONS?!
!
...?
WAIT, WHAT?
SHFF
COME ON, NO...
SHFF
TA...
TATARA...

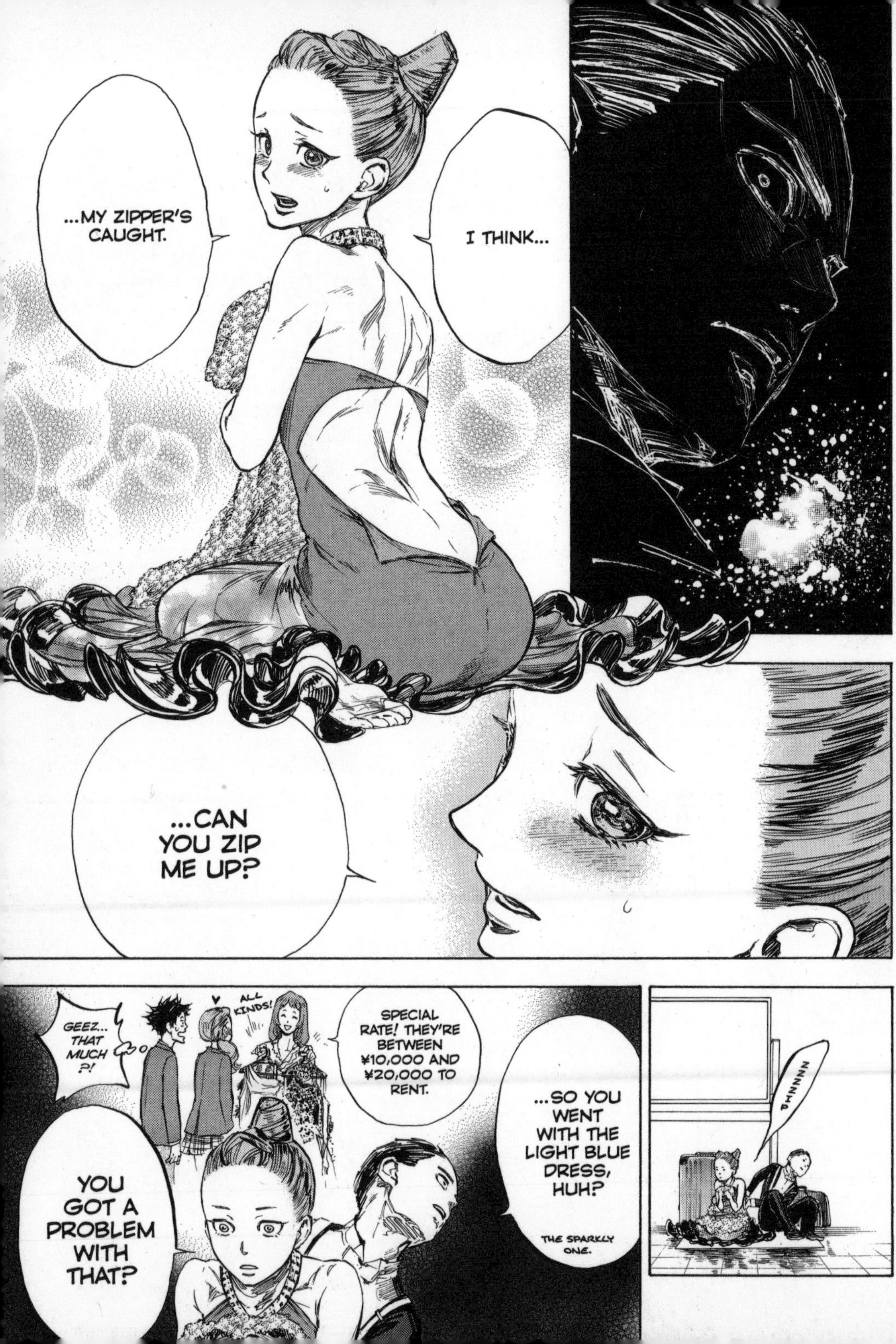
I THINK...
...MY ZIPPER'S CAUGHT.
...CAN YOU ZIP ME UP?
ZZZZZIP
...SO YOU WENT WITH THE LIGHT BLUE DRESS, HUH?
THE SPARKLY ONE.
SPECIAL RATE! THEY'RE BETWEEN ¥10,000 AND ¥20,000 TO RENT.
ALL KINDS!
GEEZ... THAT MUCH?!
YOU GOT A PROBLEM WITH THAT?

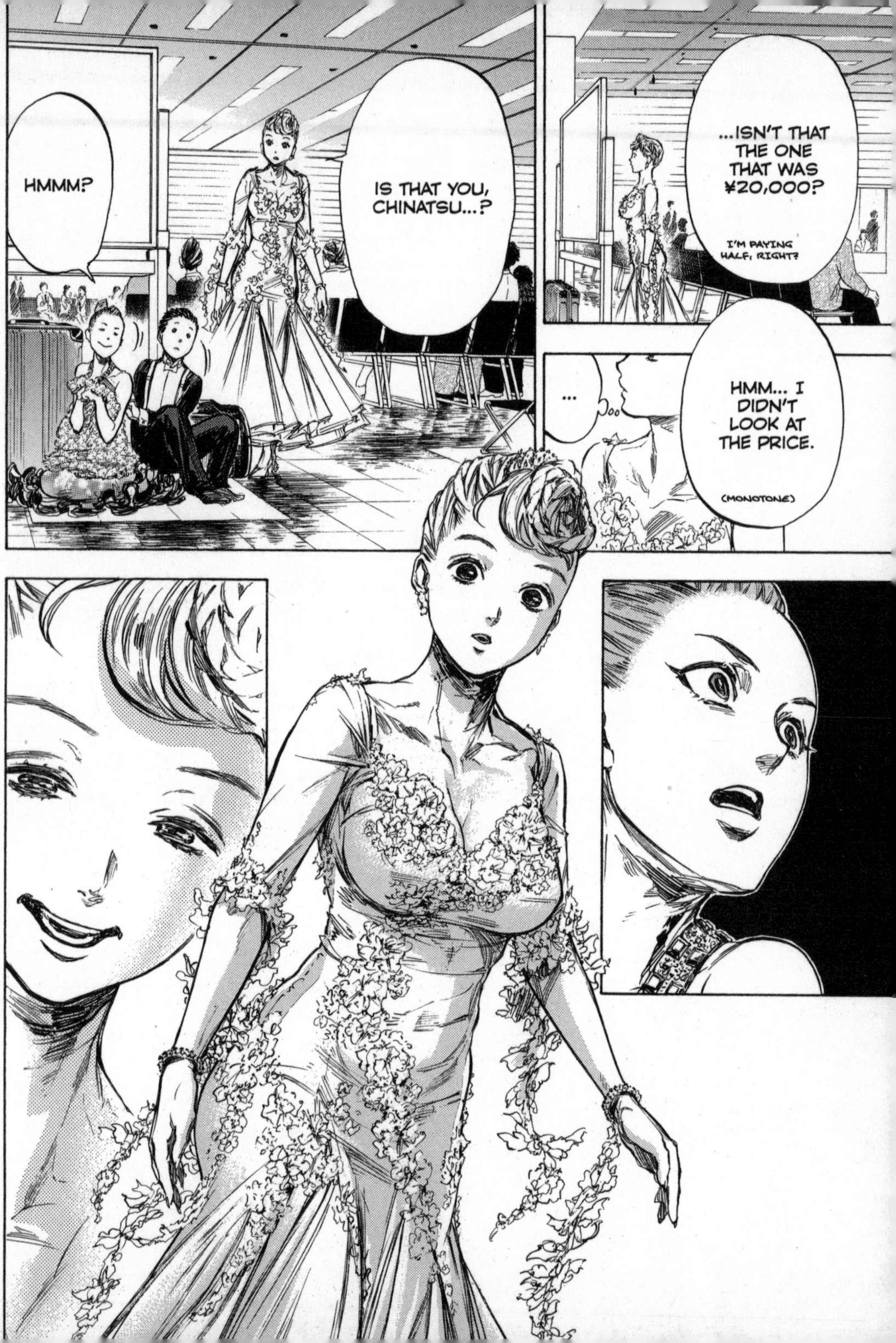
...ISN'T THAT THE ONE THAT WAS ¥20,000?
I'M PAYING HALF, RIGHT?
HMM... I DIDN'T LOOK AT THE PRICE.
(MONOTONE)
...
IS THAT YOU, CHINATSU...?
HMMM?

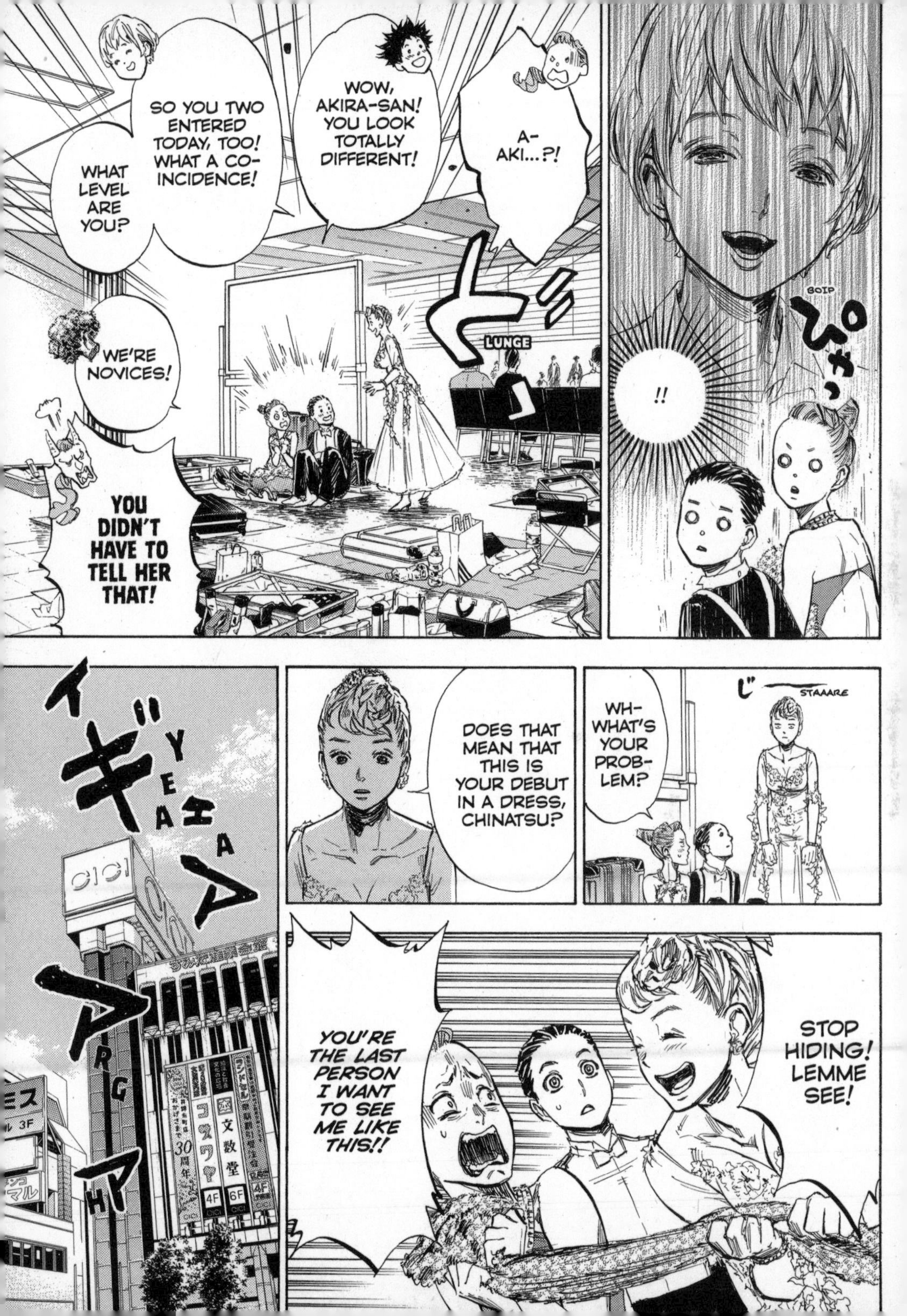
BOIP
!!
A- AKI...?!
WOW, AKIRA-SAN! YOU LOOK TOTALLY DIFFERENT!
SO YOU TWO ENTERED TODAY, TOO! WHAT A CO-INCIDENCE!
WHAT LEVEL ARE YOU?
LUNGE
WE'RE NOVICES!
YOU DIDN'T HAVE TO TELL HER THAT!
STAAARE
WH- WHAT'S YOUR PROB-LEM?
DOES THAT MEAN THAT THIS IS YOUR DEBUT IN A DRESS, CHINATSU?
STOP HIDING! LEMME SEE!
YOU'RE THE LAST PERSON I WANT TO SEE ME LIKE THIS!!
YEAAARGH

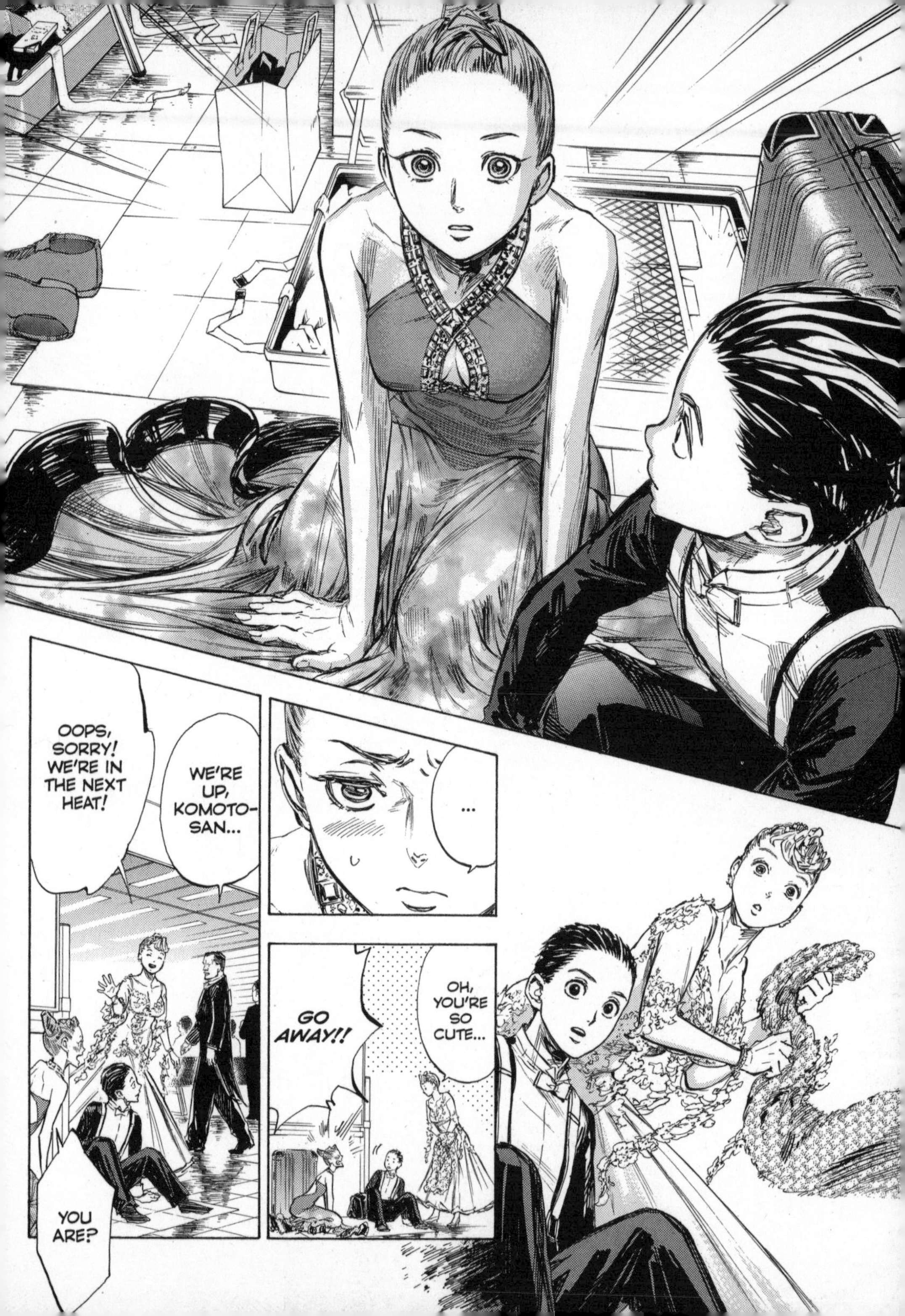
...
OH, YOU'RE SO CUTE...
GO AWAY!!
WE'RE UP, KOMOTO-SAN...
OOPS, SORRY! WE'RE IN THE NEXT HEAT!
YOU ARE?

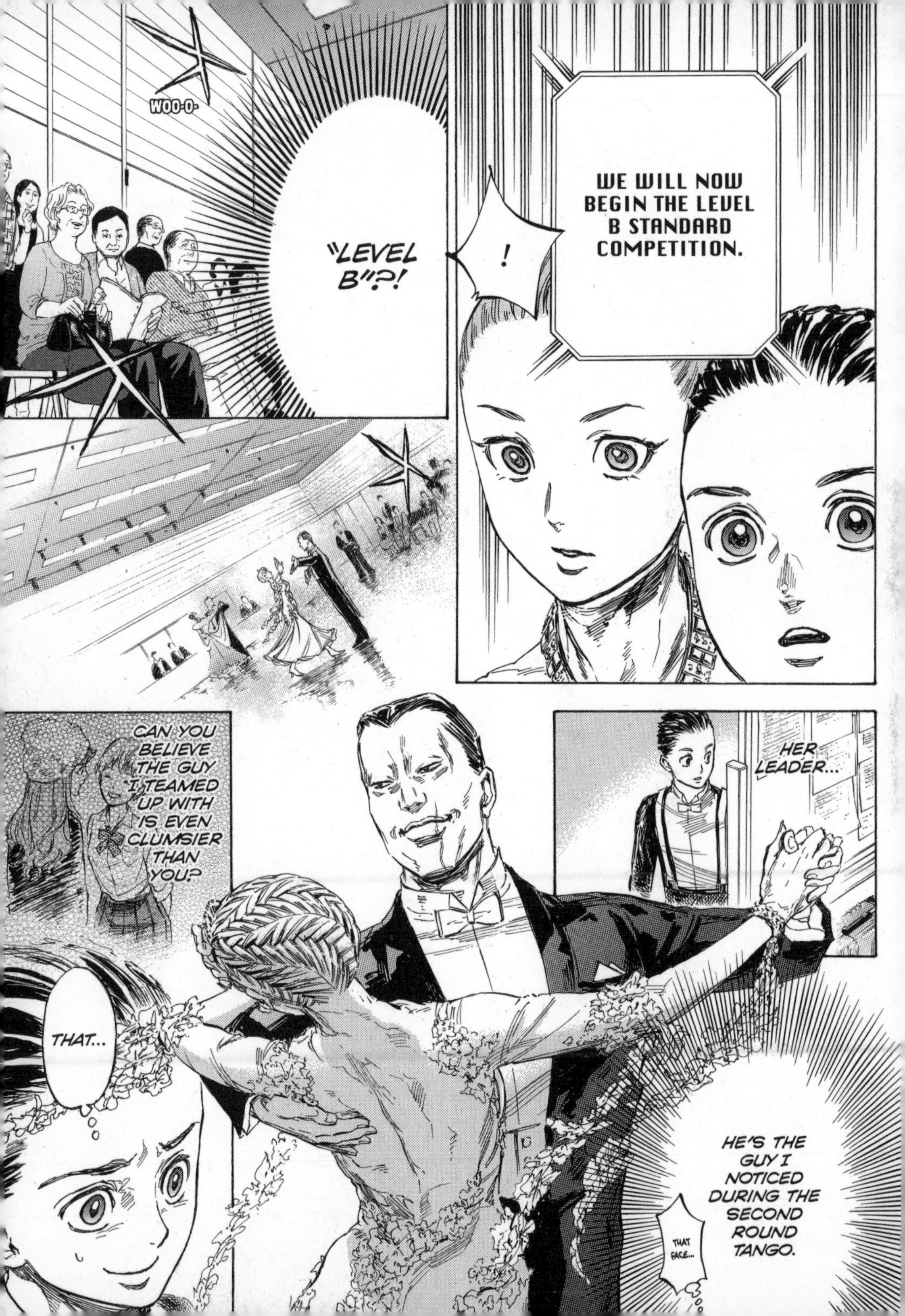
WE WILL NOW BEGIN THE LEVEL B STANDARD COMPETITION.
!
WOO-O-
"LEVEL B"?!
HER LEADER...
HE'S THE GUY I NOTICED DURING THE SECOND ROUND TANGO.
THAT FACE...
CAN YOU BELIEVE THE GUY I TEAMED UP WITH IS EVEN CLUMSIER THAN YOU?
THAT...

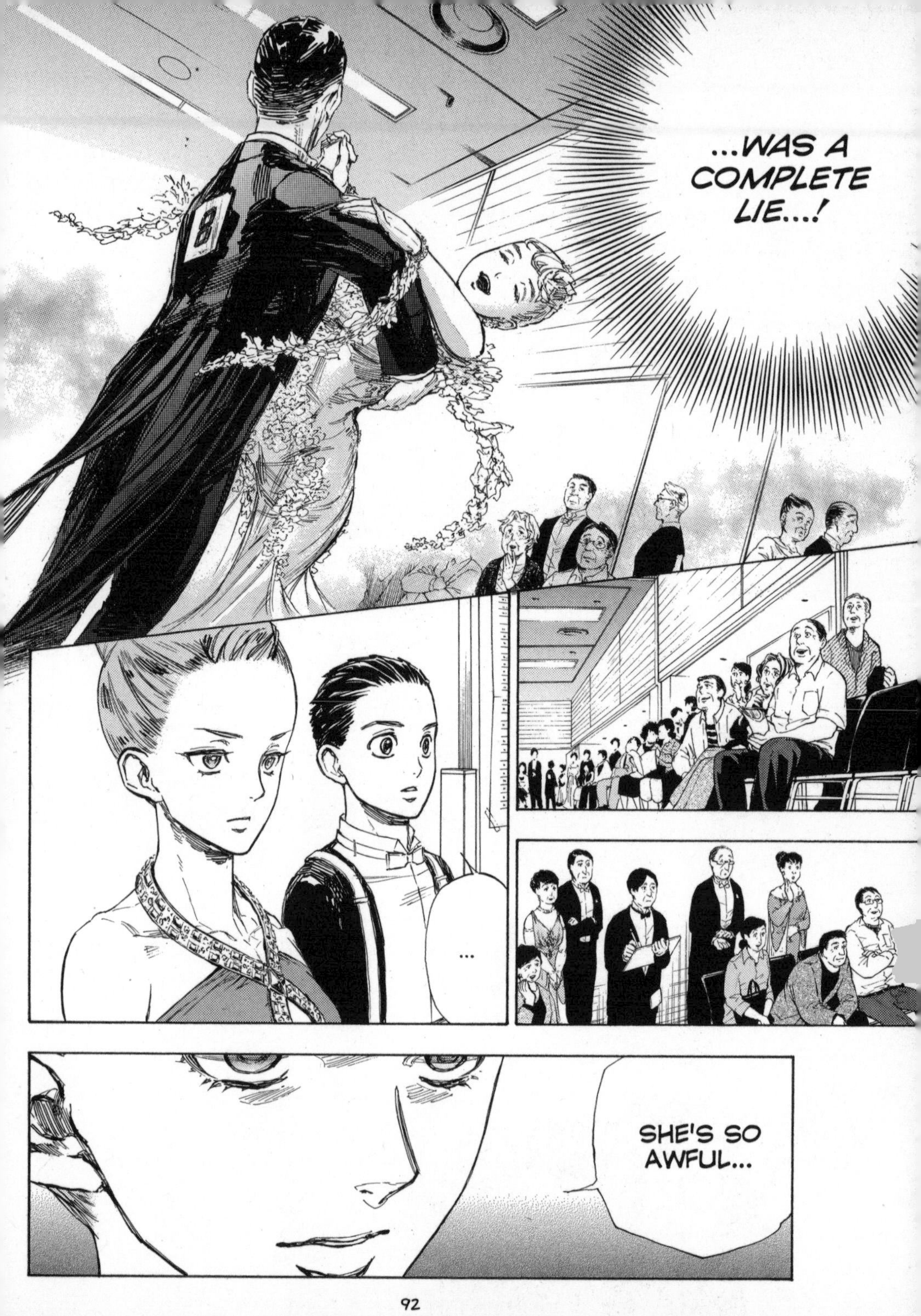
...WAS A COMPLETE LIE...!
...
SHE'S SO AWFUL...

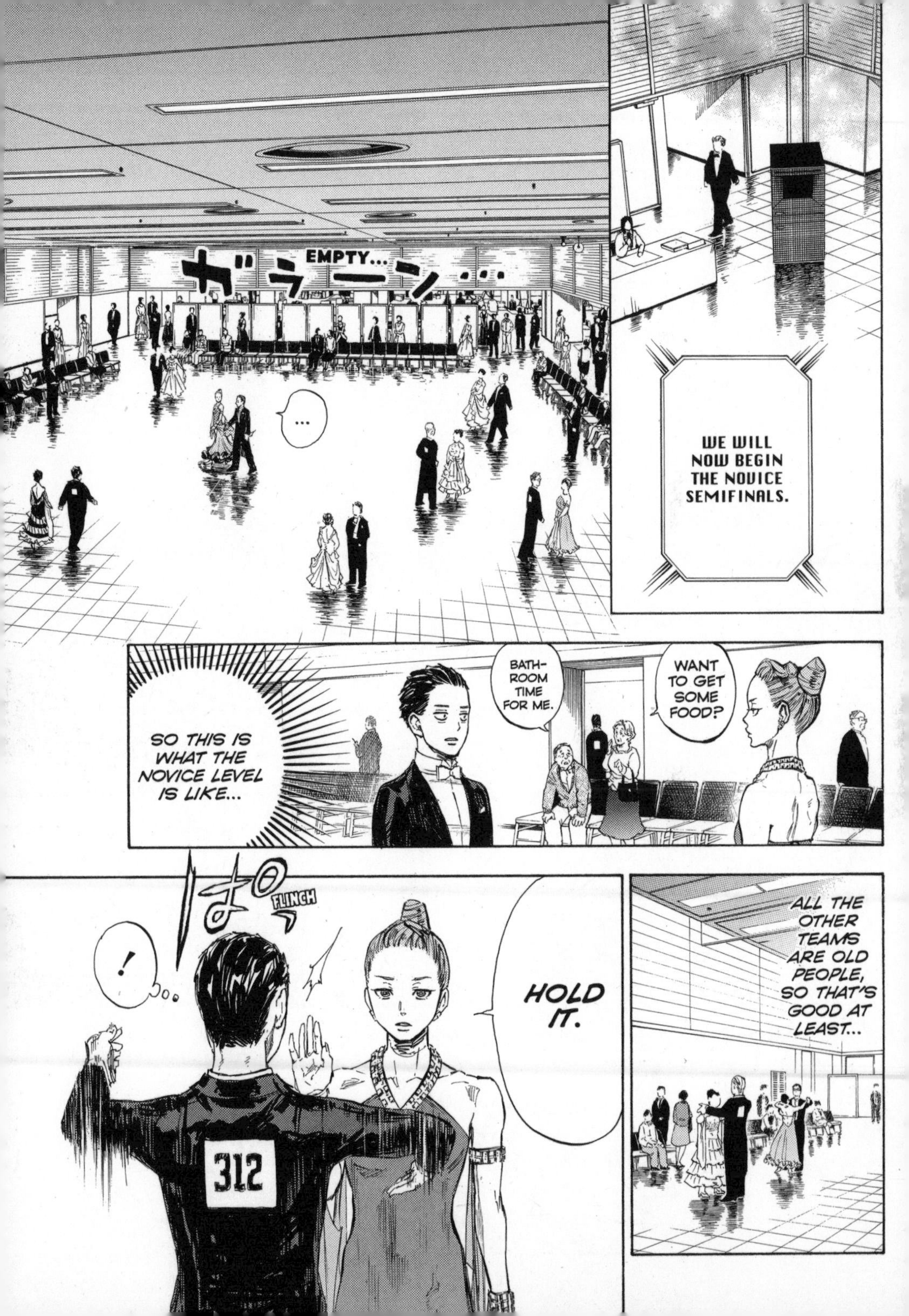
WE WILL NOW BEGIN THE NOVICE SEMIFINALS.
EMPTY...
ガラーン...
...
WANT TO GET SOME FOOD?
BATH-ROOM TIME FOR ME.
SO THIS IS WHAT THE NOVICE LEVEL IS LIKE...
ALL THE OTHER TEAMS ARE OLD PEOPLE, SO THAT'S GOOD AT LEAST...
HOLD IT.
はっ
FLINCH
!
312

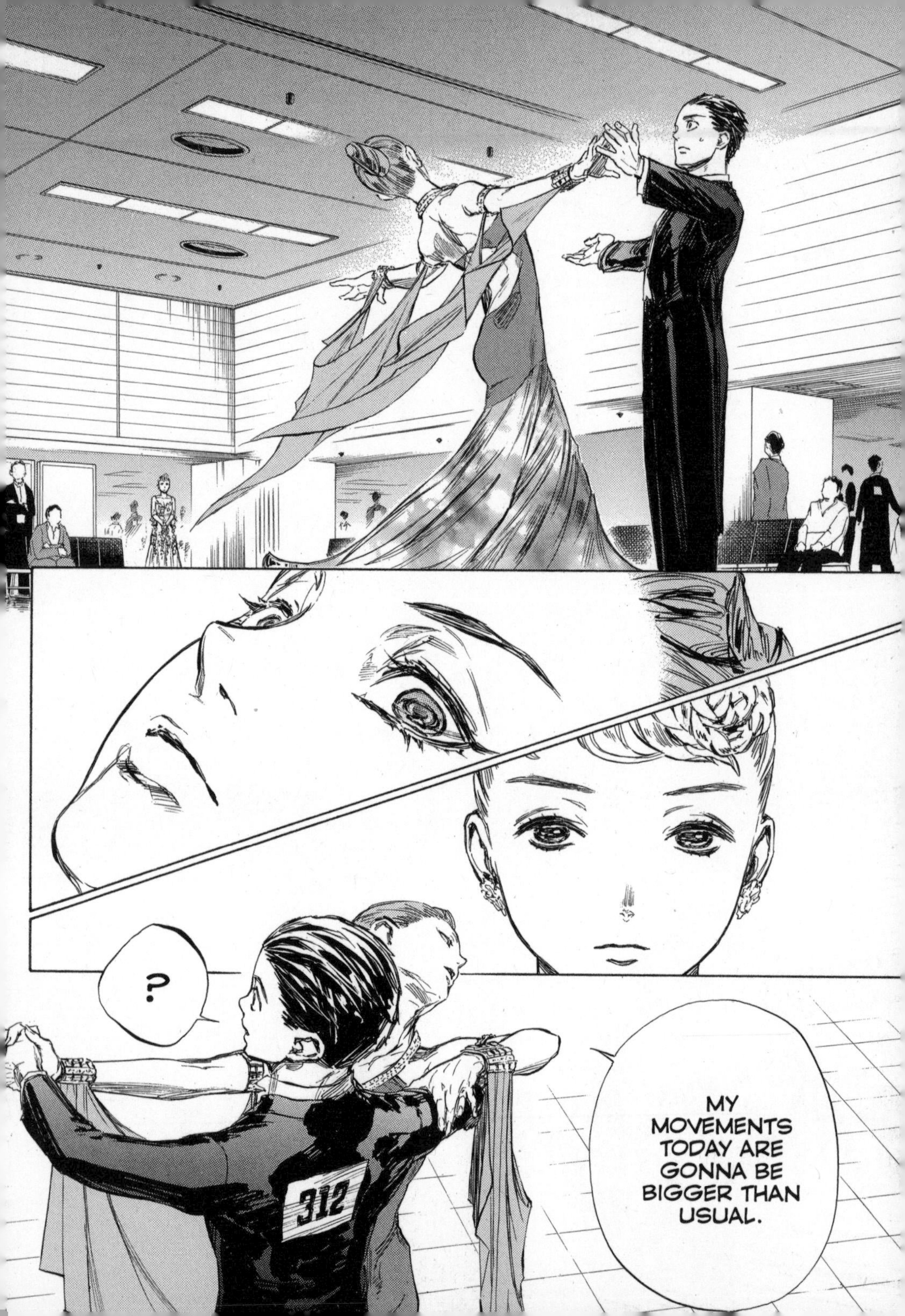
?
MY MOVEMENTS TODAY ARE GONNA BE BIGGER THAN USUAL.
312

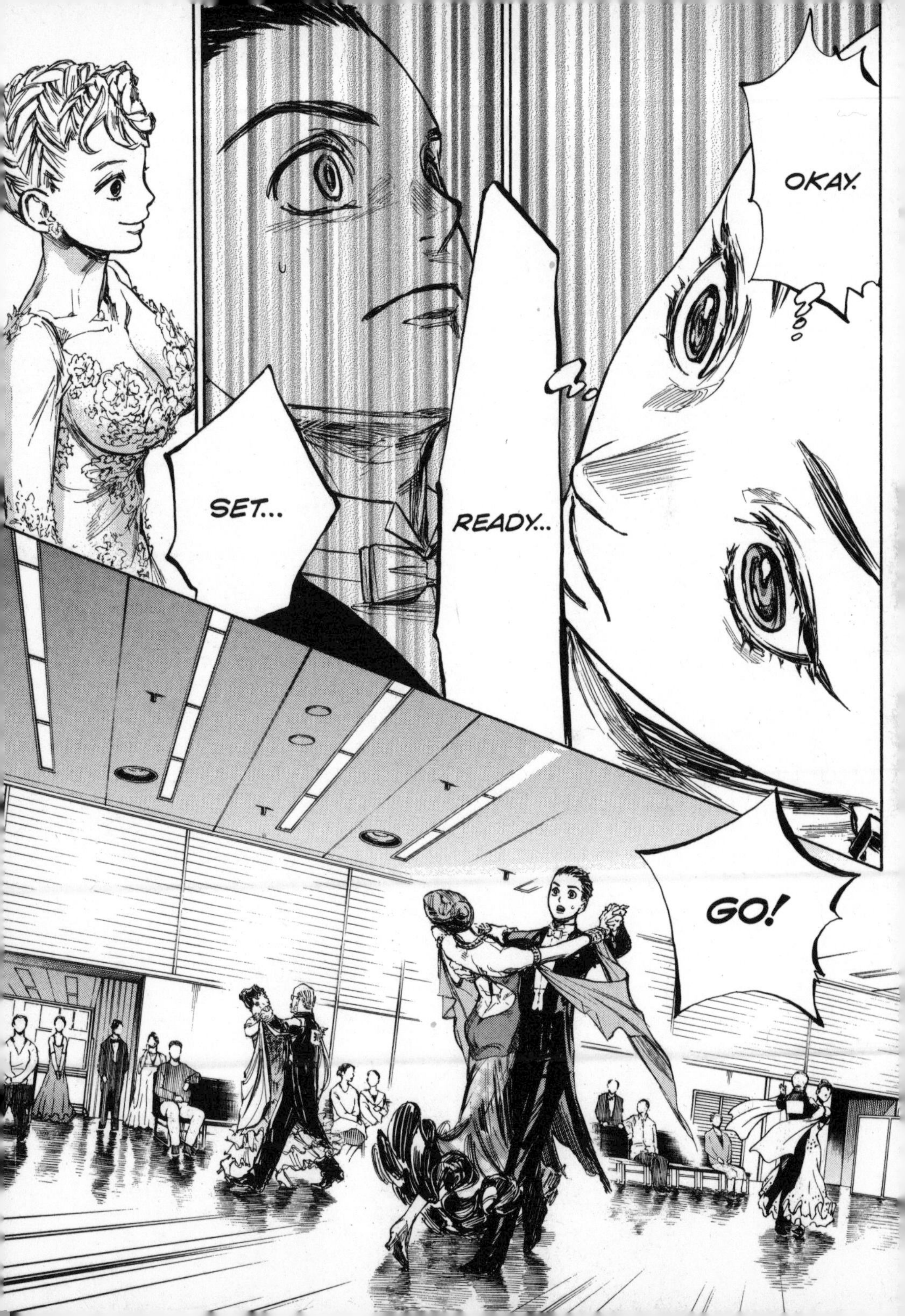
OKAY.
READY...
SET...
GO!

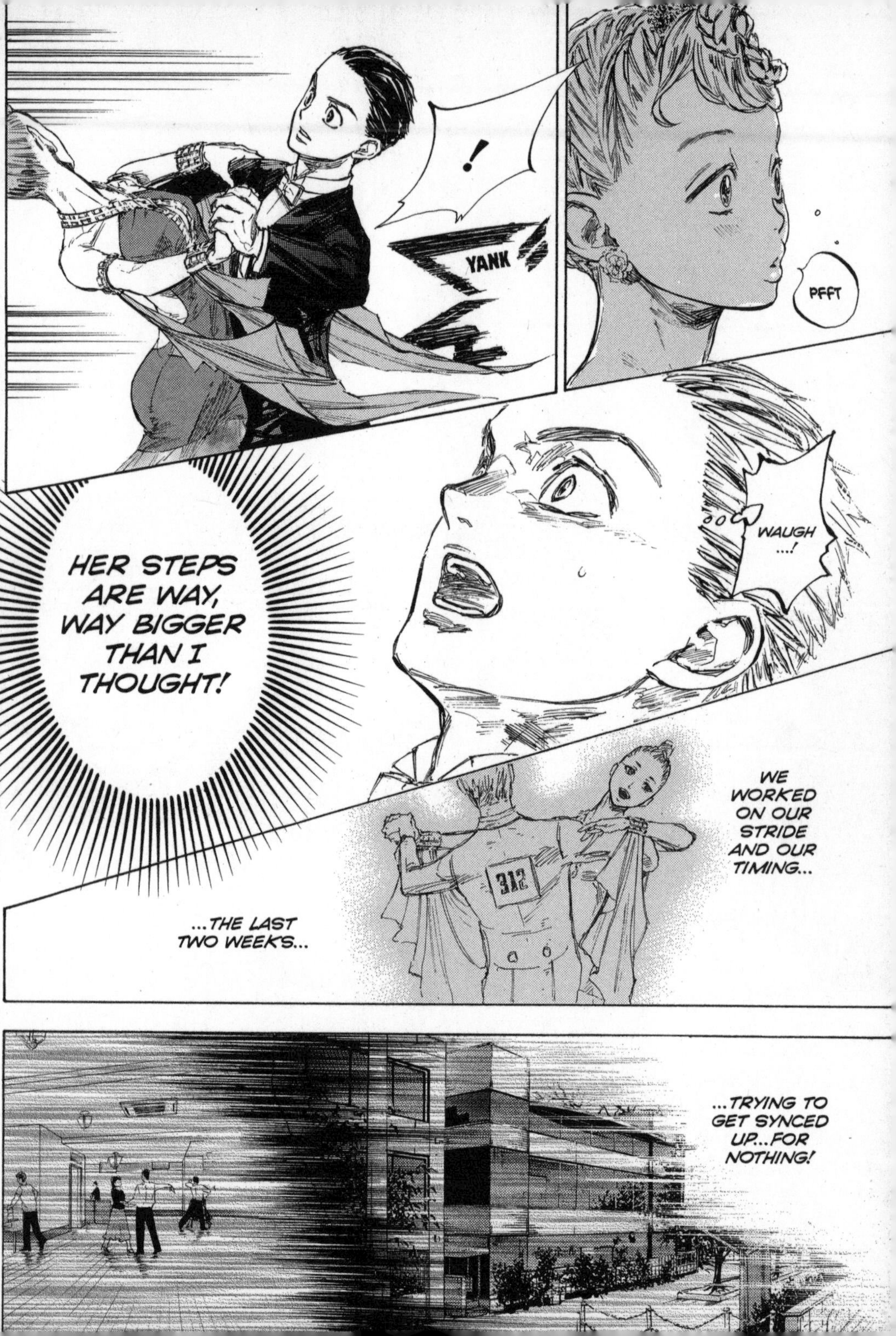
PFFT
!
YANK
WAUGH ...!
HER STEPS ARE WAY, WAY BIGGER THAN I THOUGHT!
WE WORKED ON OUR STRIDE AND OUR TIMING...
...THE LAST TWO WEEKS...
312
...TRYING TO GET SYNCED UP...FOR NOTHING!

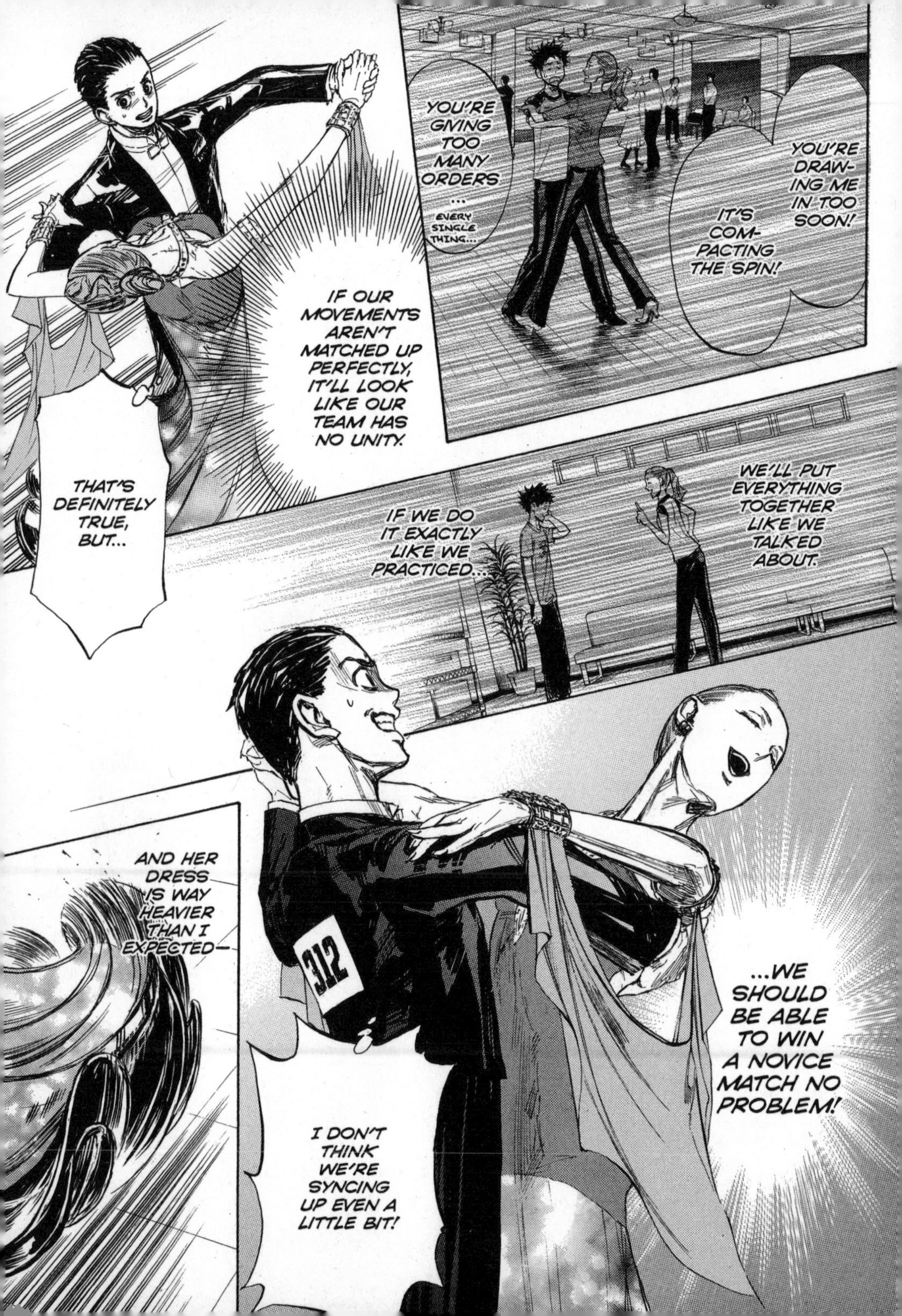
YOU'RE DRAWING ME IN TOO SOON!
IT'S COMPACTING THE SPIN!
YOU'RE GIVING TOO MANY ORDERS ... EVERY SINGLE THING...
IF OUR MOVEMENTS AREN'T MATCHED UP PERFECTLY, IT'LL LOOK LIKE OUR TEAM HAS NO UNITY.
THAT'S DEFINITELY TRUE, BUT...
WE'LL PUT EVERYTHING TOGETHER LIKE WE TALKED ABOUT.
IF WE DO IT EXACTLY LIKE WE PRACTICED...
...WE SHOULD BE ABLE TO WIN A NOVICE MATCH NO PROBLEM!
312
AND HER DRESS IS WAY HEAVIER THAN I EXPECTED—
I DON'T THINK WE'RE SYNCING UP EVEN A LITTLE BIT!

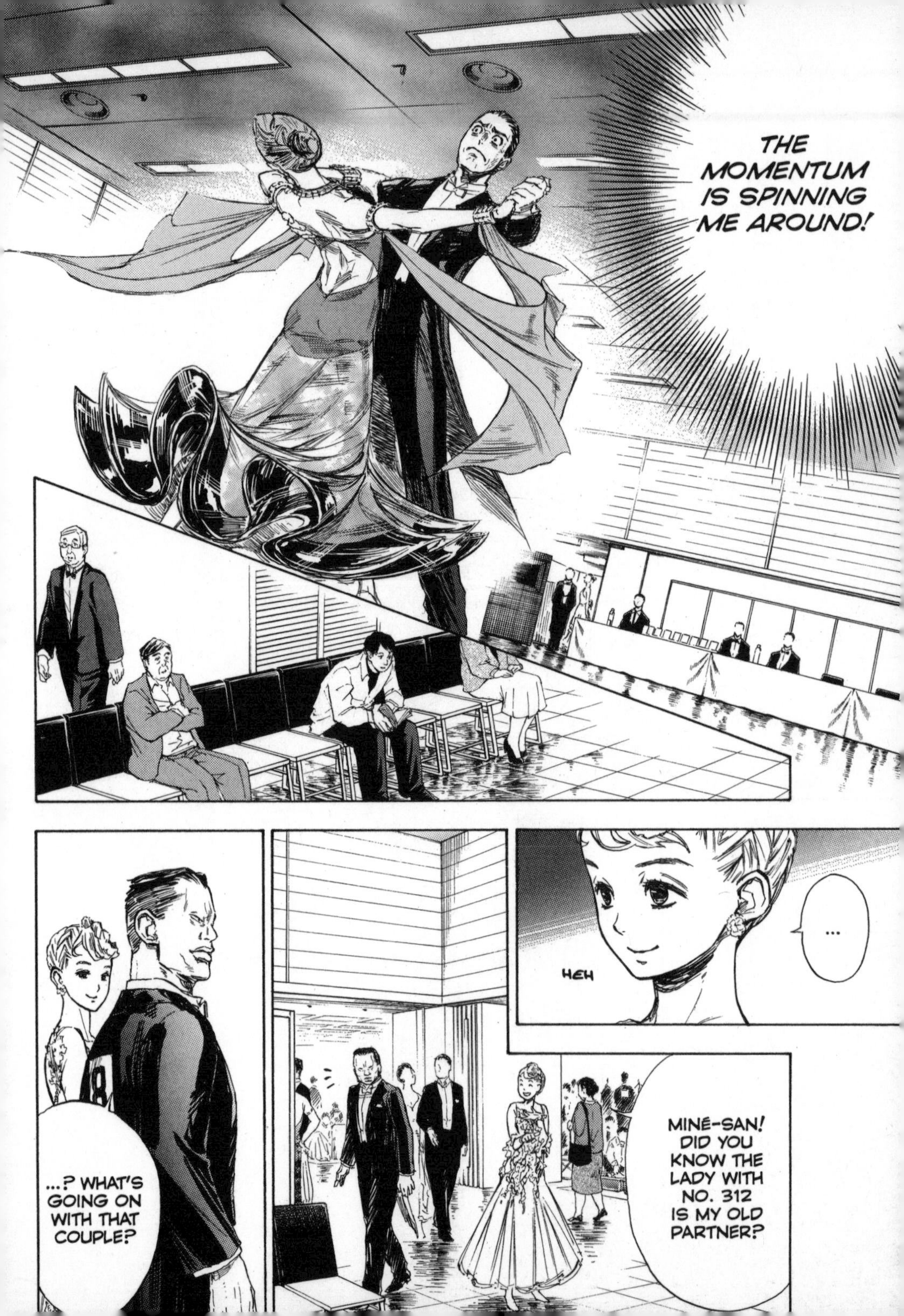
THE MOMENTUM IS SPINNING ME AROUND!
...
HEH
MINÉ-SAN! DID YOU KNOW THE LADY WITH NO. 312 IS MY OLD PARTNER?
...? WHAT'S GOING ON WITH THAT COUPLE?

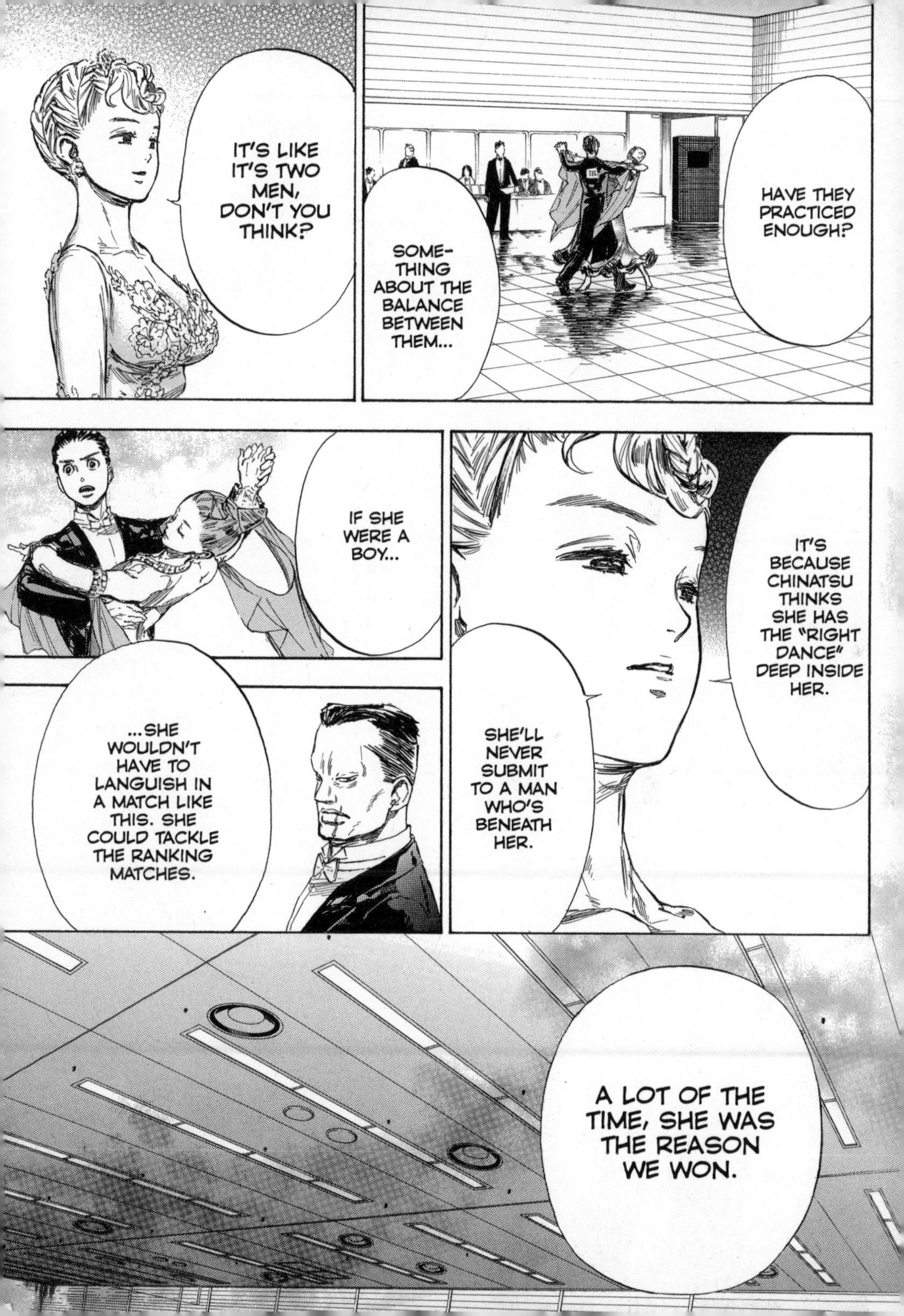
HAVE THEY PRACTICED ENOUGH?
SOME-THING ABOUT THE BALANCE BETWEEN THEM...
IT'S LIKE IT'S TWO MEN, DON'T YOU THINK?
IT'S BECAUSE CHINATSU THINKS SHE HAS THE "RIGHT DANCE" DEEP INSIDE HER.
SHE'LL NEVER SUBMIT TO A MAN WHO'S BENEATH HER.
IF SHE WERE A BOY...
...SHE WOULDN'T HAVE TO LANGUISH IN A MATCH LIKE THIS. SHE COULD TACKLE THE RANKING MATCHES.
A LOT OF THE TIME, SHE WAS THE REASON WE WON.

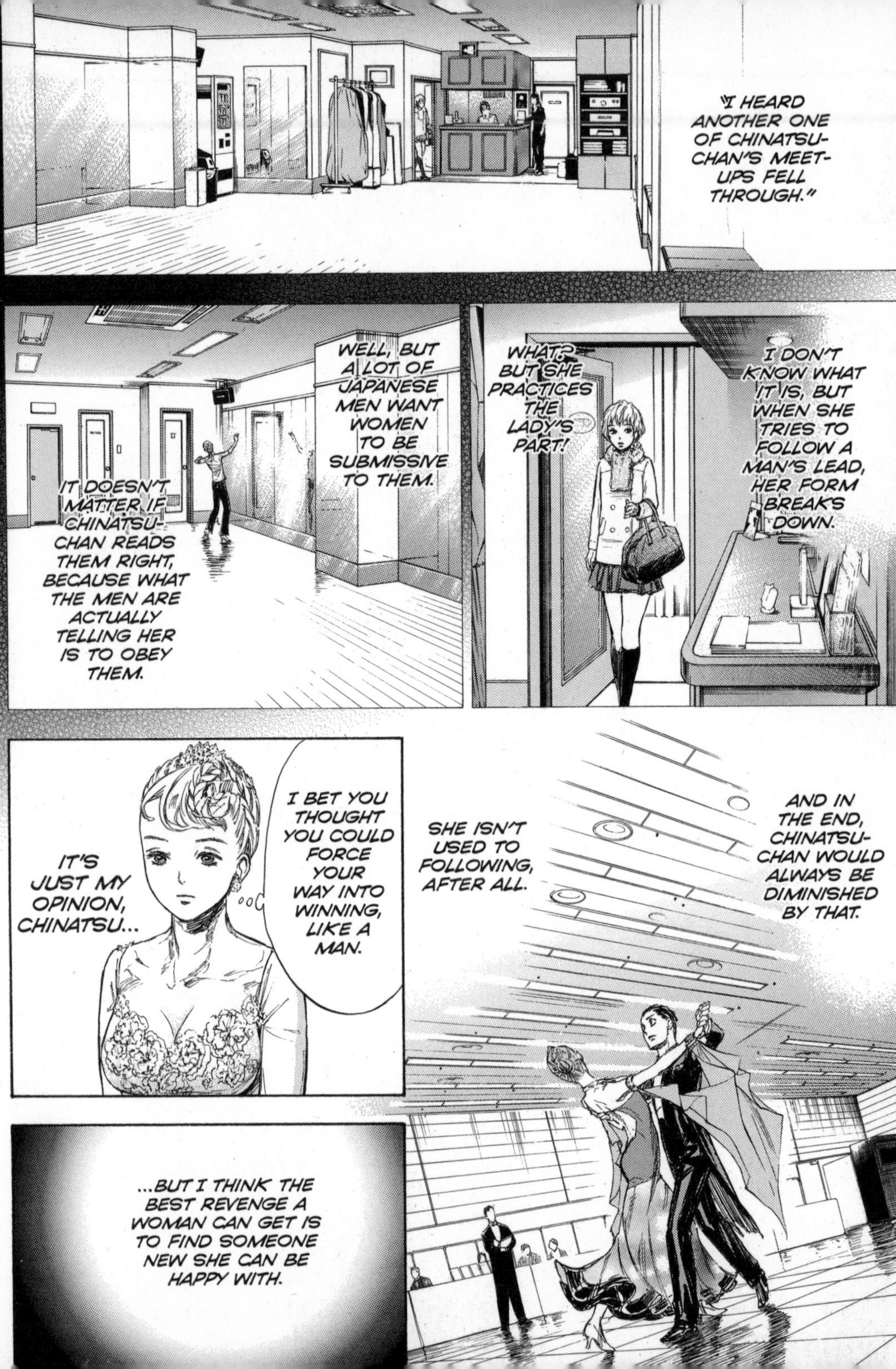
"I HEARD ANOTHER ONE OF CHINATSU-CHAN'S MEET-UPS FELL THROUGH."
I DON'T KNOW WHAT IT IS, BUT WHEN SHE TRIES TO FOLLOW A MAN'S LEAD, HER FORM BREAKS DOWN.
WHAT? BUT SHE PRACTICES THE LADY'S PART!
WELL, BUT A LOT OF JAPANESE MEN WANT WOMEN TO BE SUBMISSIVE TO THEM.
IT DOESN'T MATTER IF CHINATSU-CHAN READS THEM RIGHT, BECAUSE WHAT THE MEN ARE ACTUALLY TELLING HER IS TO OBEY THEM.
AND IN THE END, CHINATSU-CHAN WOULD ALWAYS BE DIMINISHED BY THAT.
SHE ISN'T USED TO FOLLOWING, AFTER ALL.
I BET YOU THOUGHT YOU COULD FORCE YOUR WAY INTO WINNING, LIKE A MAN.
IT'S JUST MY OPINION, CHINATSU...
...BUT I THINK THE BEST REVENGE A WOMAN CAN GET IS TO FIND SOMEONE NEW SHE CAN BE HAPPY WITH.

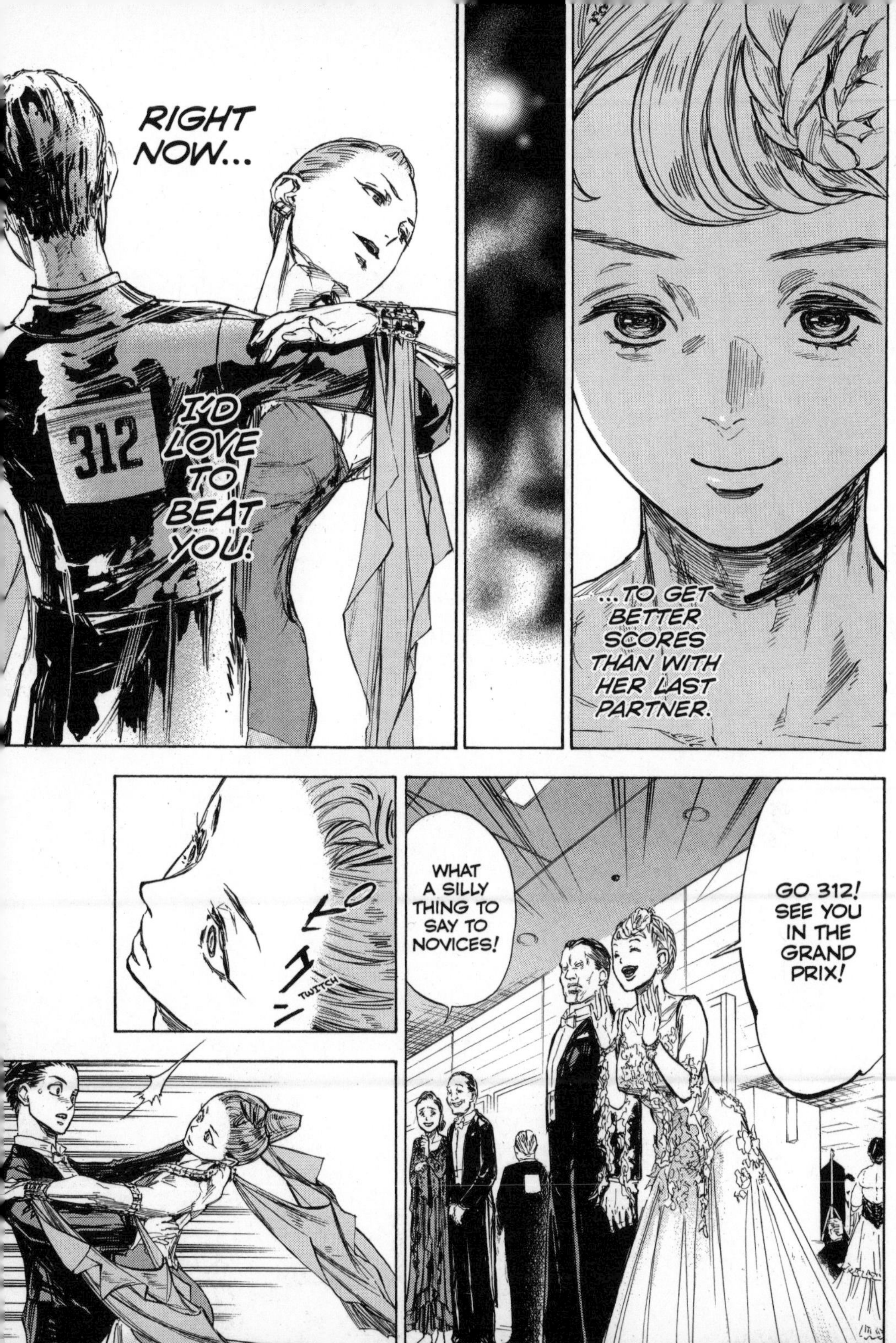
...TO GET BETTER SCORES THAN WITH HER LAST PARTNER.
RIGHT NOW...
312
I'D LOVE TO BEAT YOU.
GO 312! SEE YOU IN THE GRAND PRIX!
WHAT A SILLY THING TO SAY TO NOVICES!
TWITCH

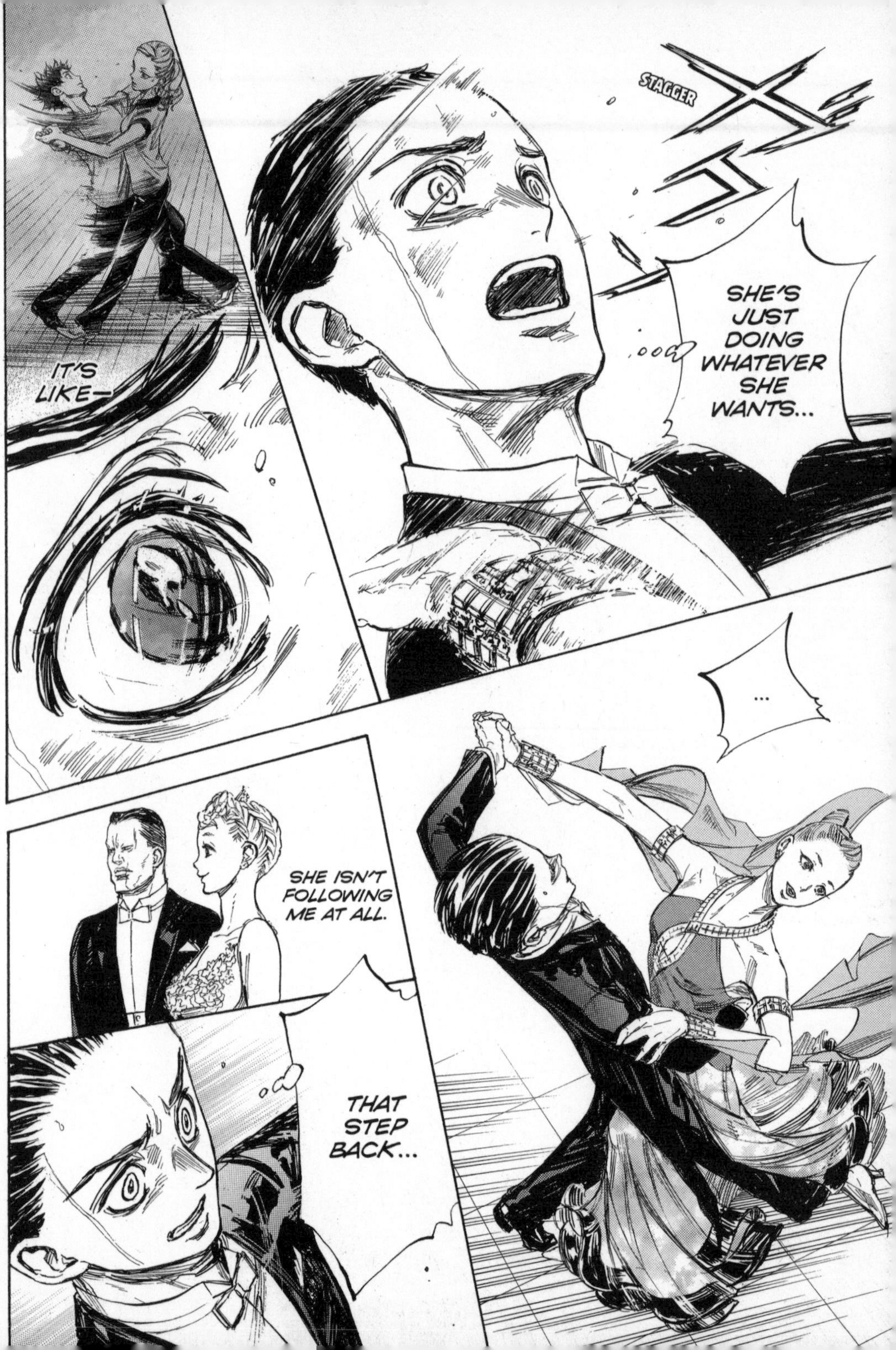
STAGGER
SHE'S JUST DOING WHATEVER SHE WANTS...
IT'S LIKE—
...
SHE ISN'T FOLLOWING ME AT ALL.
THAT STEP BACK...

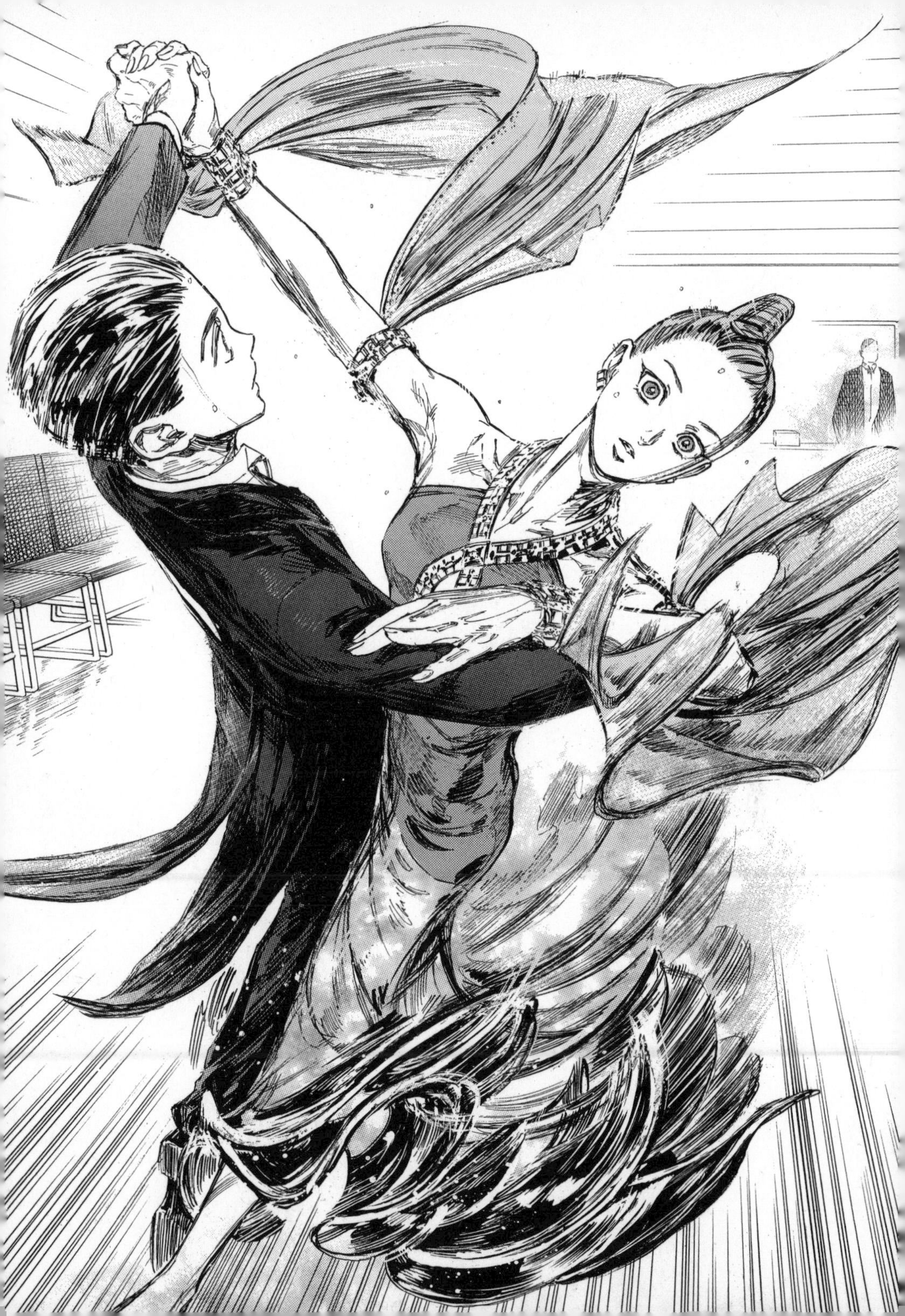

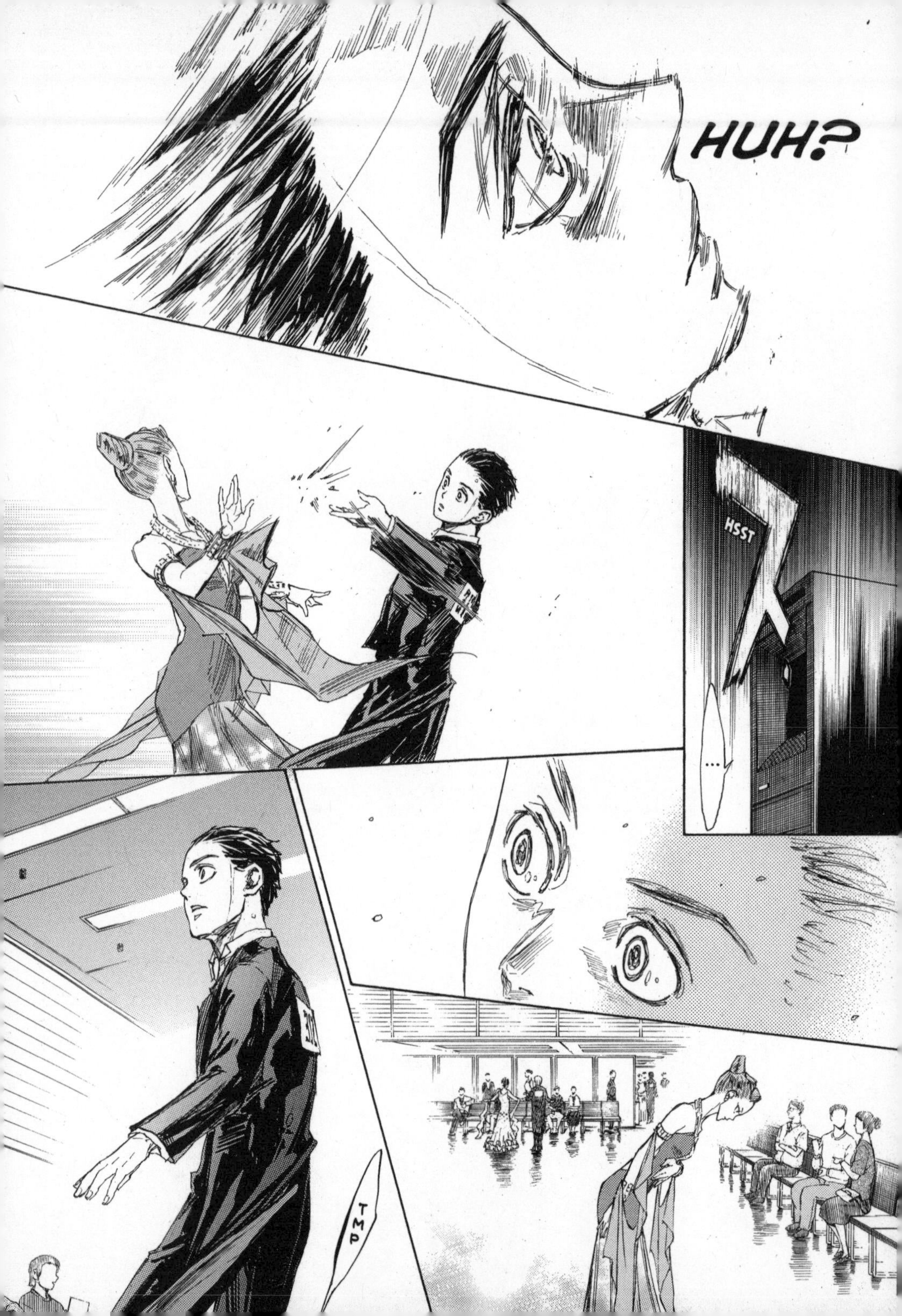
HUH?
HSST
...
TMP

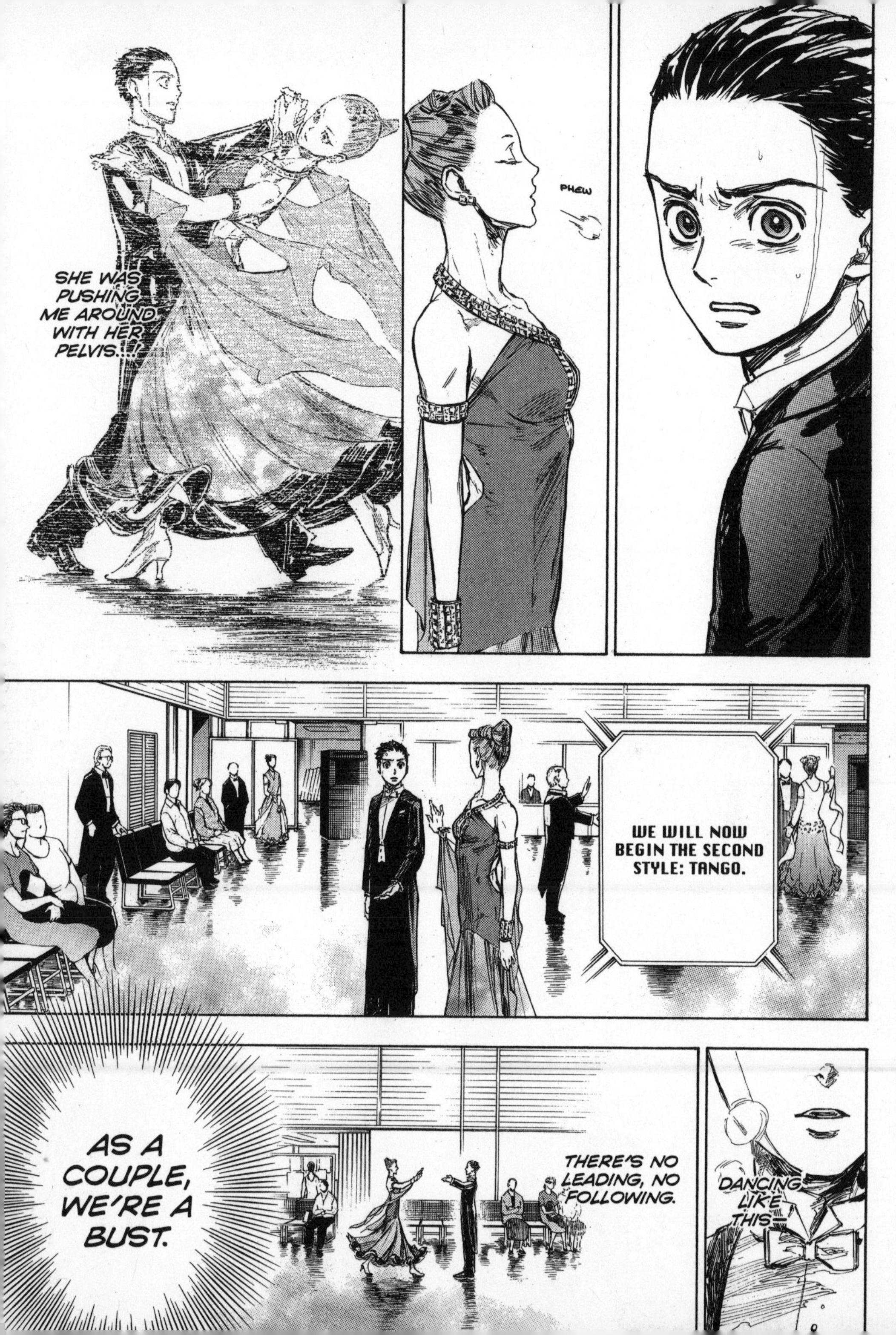
PHEW
SHE WAS PUSHING ME AROUND WITH HER PELVIS...!
WE WILL NOW BEGIN THE SECOND STYLE: TANGO.
DANCING LIKE THIS—
THERE'S NO LEADING, NO FOLLOWING.
AS A COUPLE, WE'RE A BUST.

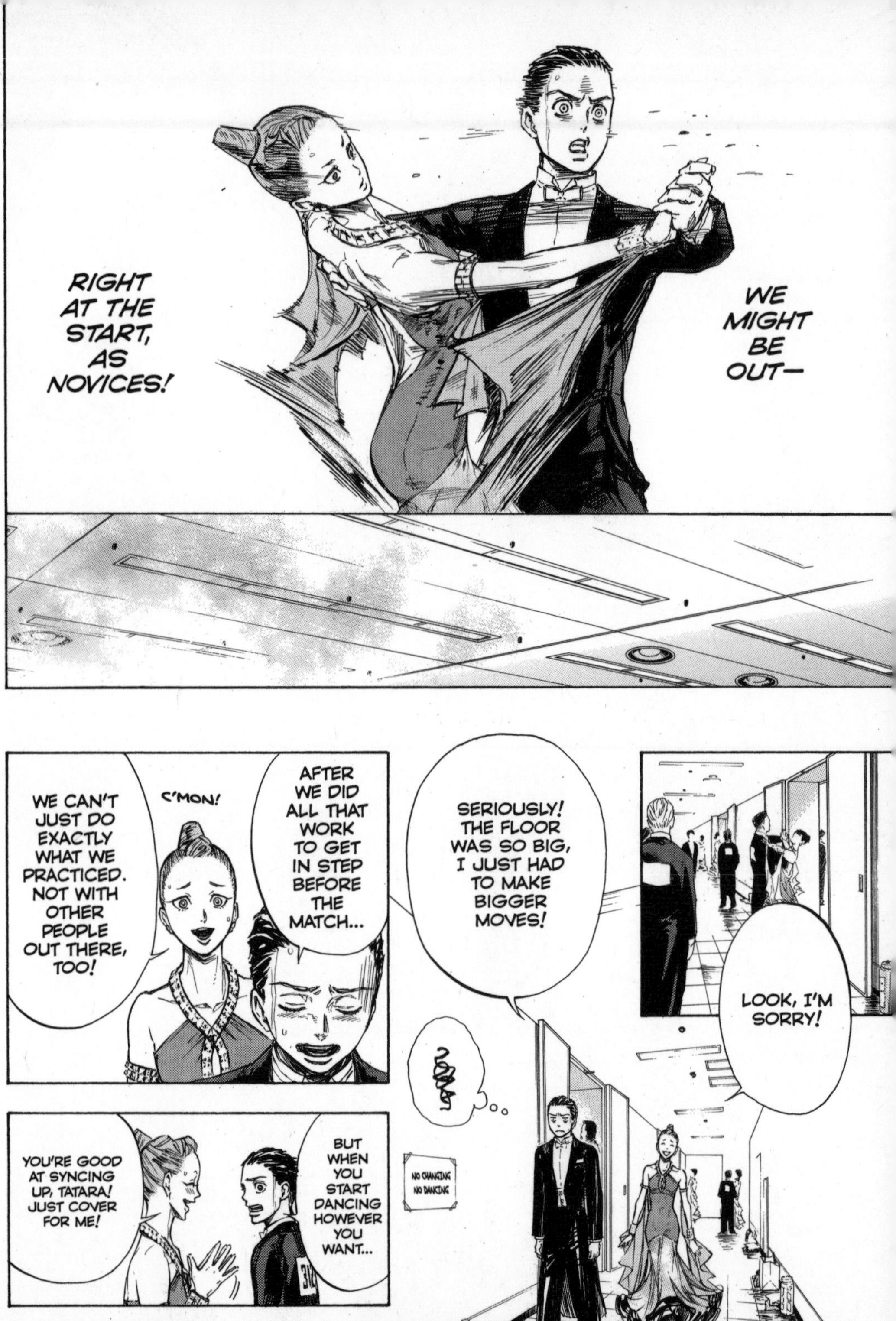
WE MIGHT BE OUT—
RIGHT AT THE START, AS NOVICES!
SERIOUSLY! THE FLOOR WAS SO BIG, I JUST HAD TO MAKE BIGGER MOVES!
LOOK, I'M SORRY!
NO CHANGING
NO DANCING
AFTER WE DID ALL THAT WORK TO GET IN STEP BEFORE THE MATCH...
C'MON!
WE CAN'T JUST DO EXACTLY WHAT WE PRACTICED. NOT WITH OTHER PEOPLE OUT THERE, TOO!
BUT WHEN YOU START DANCING HOWEVER YOU WANT...
YOU'RE GOOD AT SYNCING UP, TATARA! JUST COVER FOR ME!

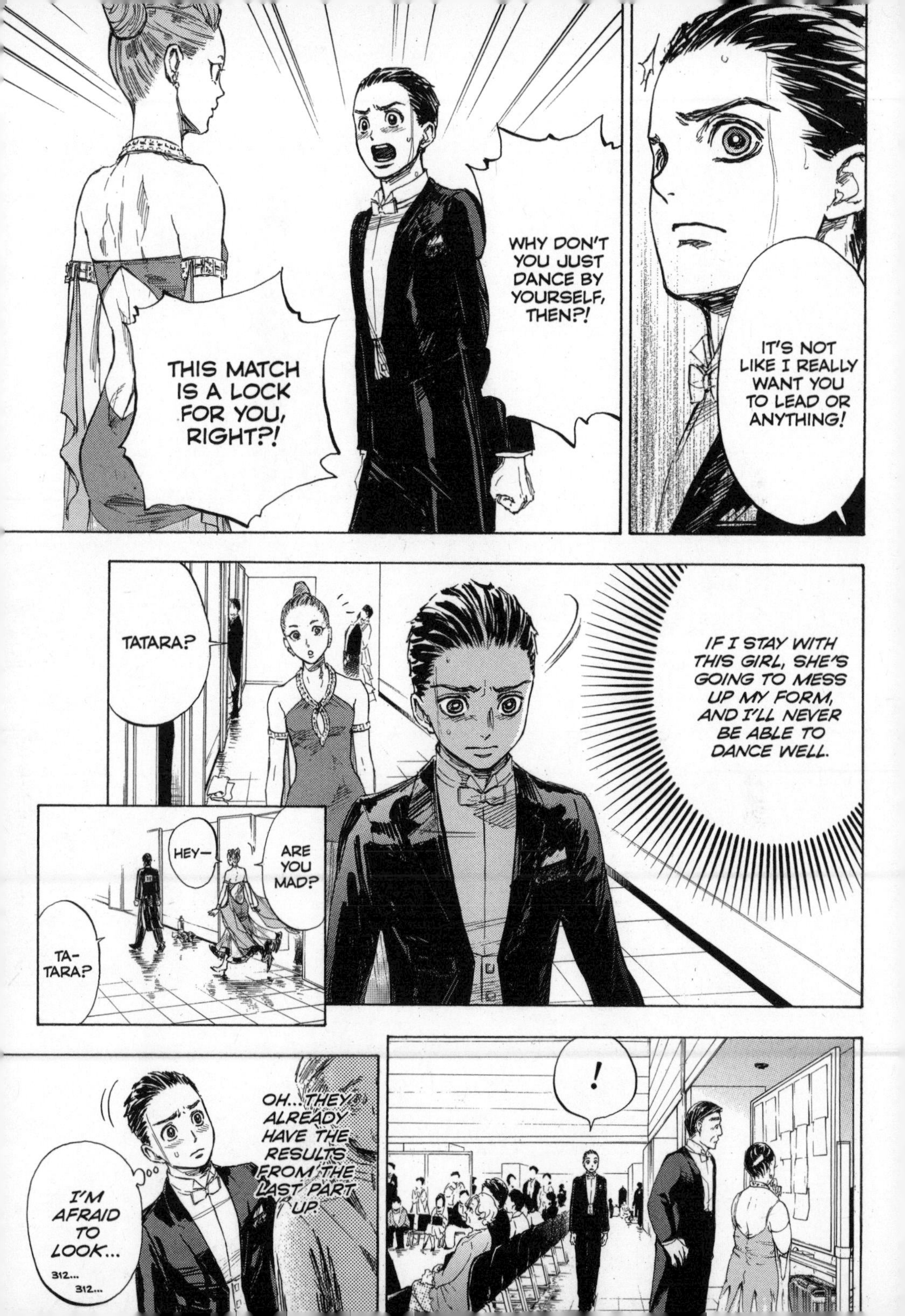
IT'S NOT LIKE I REALLY WANT YOU TO LEAD OR ANYTHING!
WHY DON'T YOU JUST DANCE BY YOURSELF, THEN?!
THIS MATCH IS A LOCK FOR YOU, RIGHT?!
IF I STAY WITH THIS GIRL, SHE'S GOING TO MESS UP MY FORM, AND I'LL NEVER BE ABLE TO DANCE WELL.
TATARA?
ARE YOU MAD?
HEY—
TA-TARA?
!
OH... THEY ALREADY HAVE THE RESULTS FROM THE LAST PART UP.
I'M AFRAID TO LOOK...
312...
312...

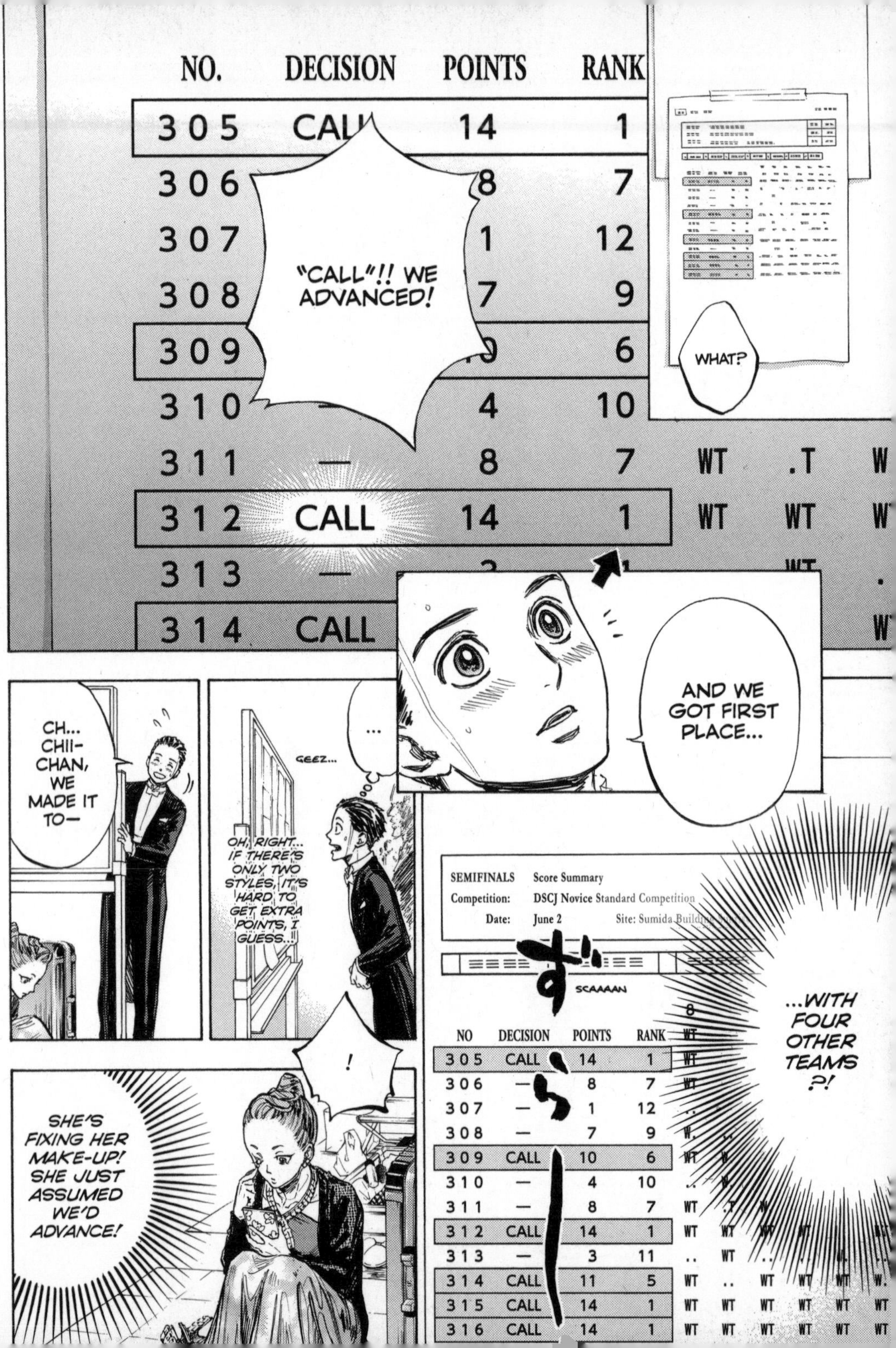
WHAT?
NO. DECISION POINTS RANK
"CALL"!! WE ADVANCED!
AND WE GOT FIRST PLACE...
SEMIFINALS Score Summary
Competition: DSCJ Novice Standard Competition
Date: June 2
SCAAAAN
NO DECISION POINTS RANK
305 CALL 14 1
306 — 8 7
307 — 1 12
308 — 7 9
309 CALL 10 6
310 — 4 10
311 — 8 7
312 CALL 14 1
313 — 3 11
314 CALL 11 5
315 CALL 14 1
316 CALL 14 1
...WITH FOUR OTHER TEAMS?!
...
GEEZ...
OH, RIGHT... IF THERE'S ONLY TWO STYLES, IT'S HARD TO GET EXTRA POINTS, I GUESS...!
CH... CHII-CHAN, WE MADE IT TO—
!
SHE'S FIXING HER MAKE-UP! SHE JUST ASSUMED WE'D ADVANCE!

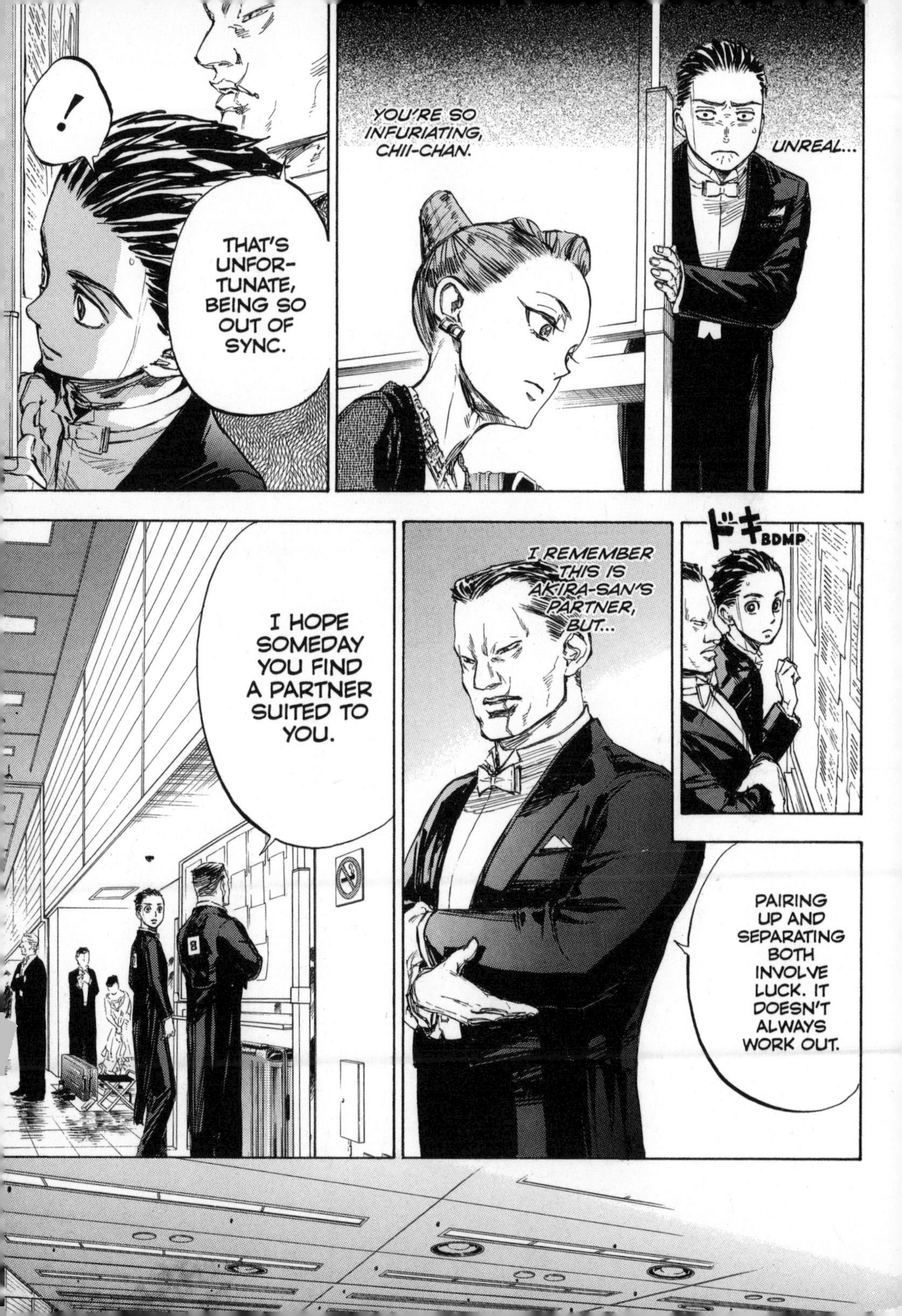
UNREAL...
YOU'RE SO INFURIATING, CHII-CHAN.
!
THAT'S UNFOR-TUNATE, BEING SO OUT OF SYNC.
ドキ BDMP
PAIRING UP AND SEPARATING BOTH INVOLVE LUCK. IT DOESN'T ALWAYS WORK OUT.
I REMEMBER THIS IS AKIRA-SAN'S PARTNER, BUT...
I HOPE SOMEDAY YOU FIND A PARTNER SUITED TO YOU.

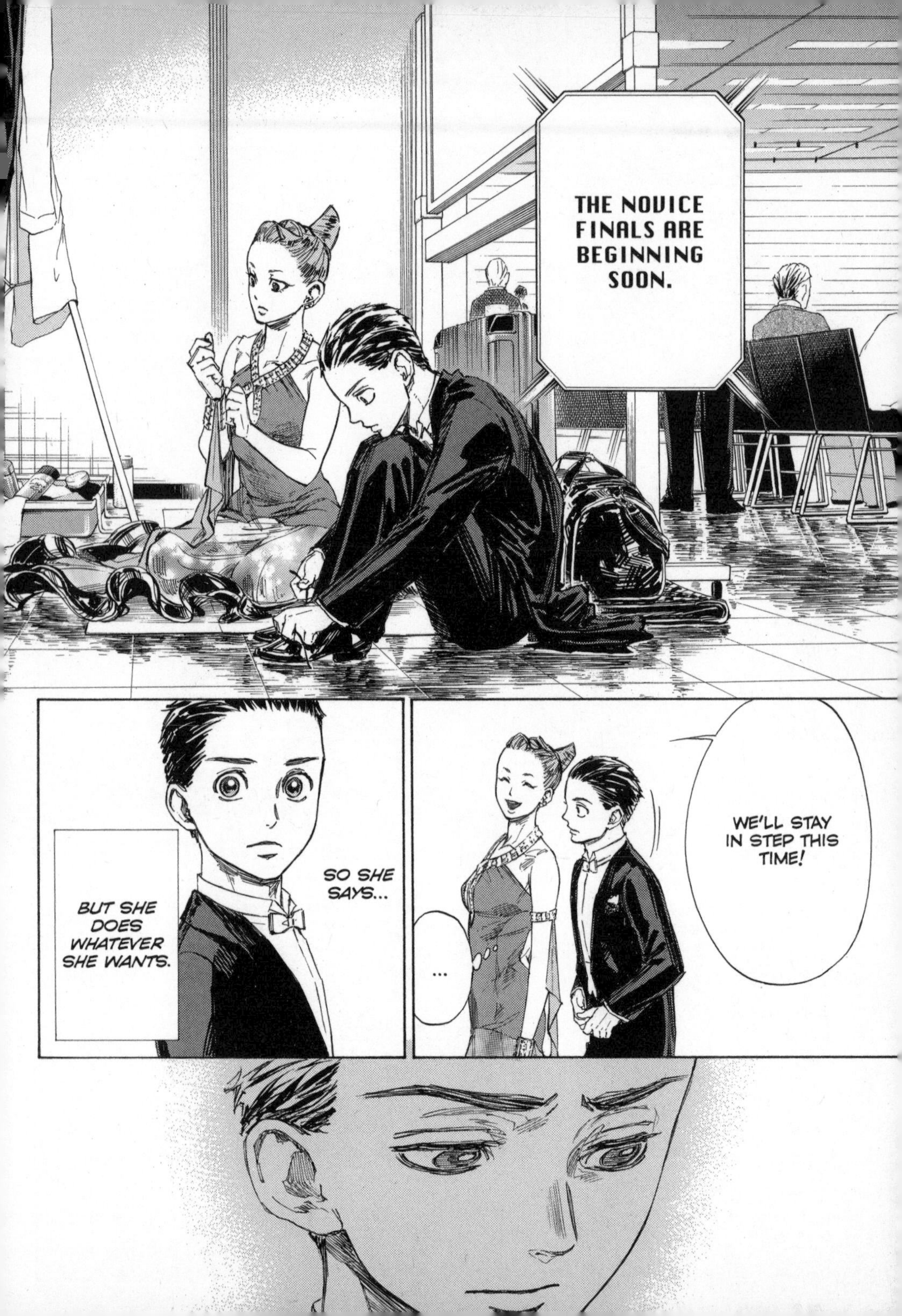
THE NOVICE FINALS ARE BEGINNING SOON.
WE'LL STAY IN STEP THIS TIME!
...
SO SHE SAYS...
BUT SHE DOES WHATEVER SHE WANTS.

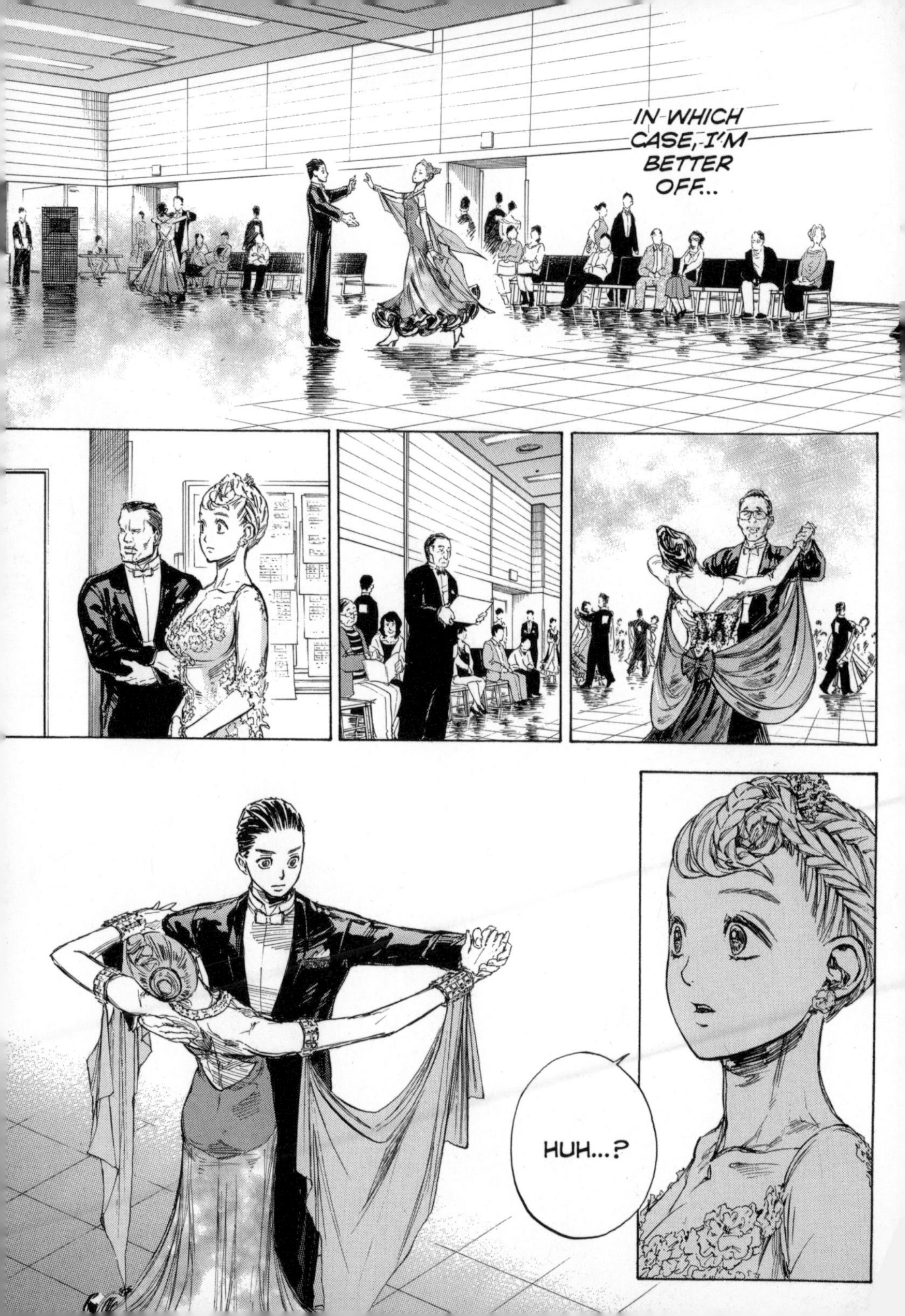
IN-WHICH CASE, I'M BETTER OFF...
HUH...?

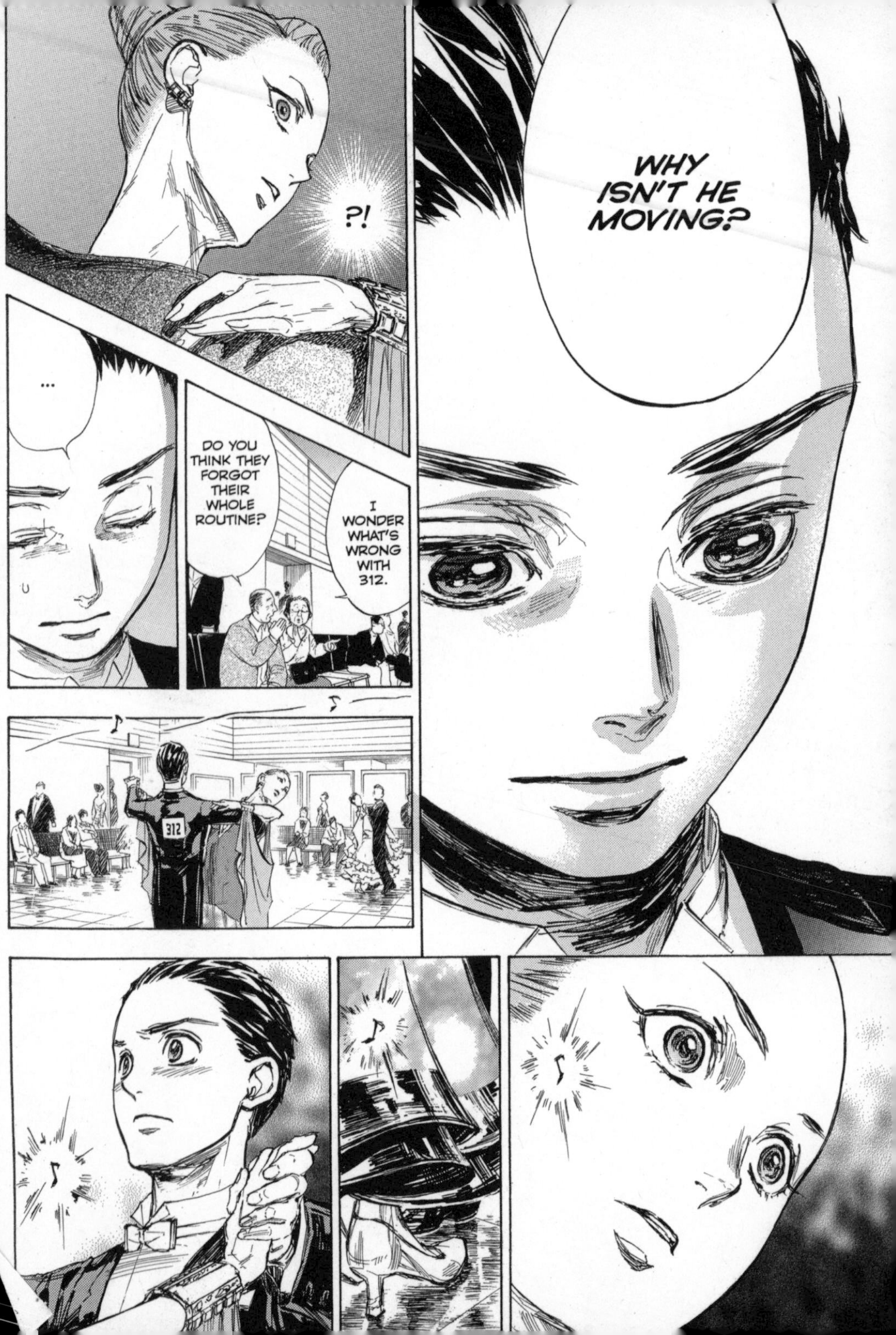
WHY ISN'T HE MOVING?
?!
I WONDER WHAT'S WRONG WITH 312.
DO YOU THINK THEY FORGOT THEIR WHOLE ROUTINE?
...
312

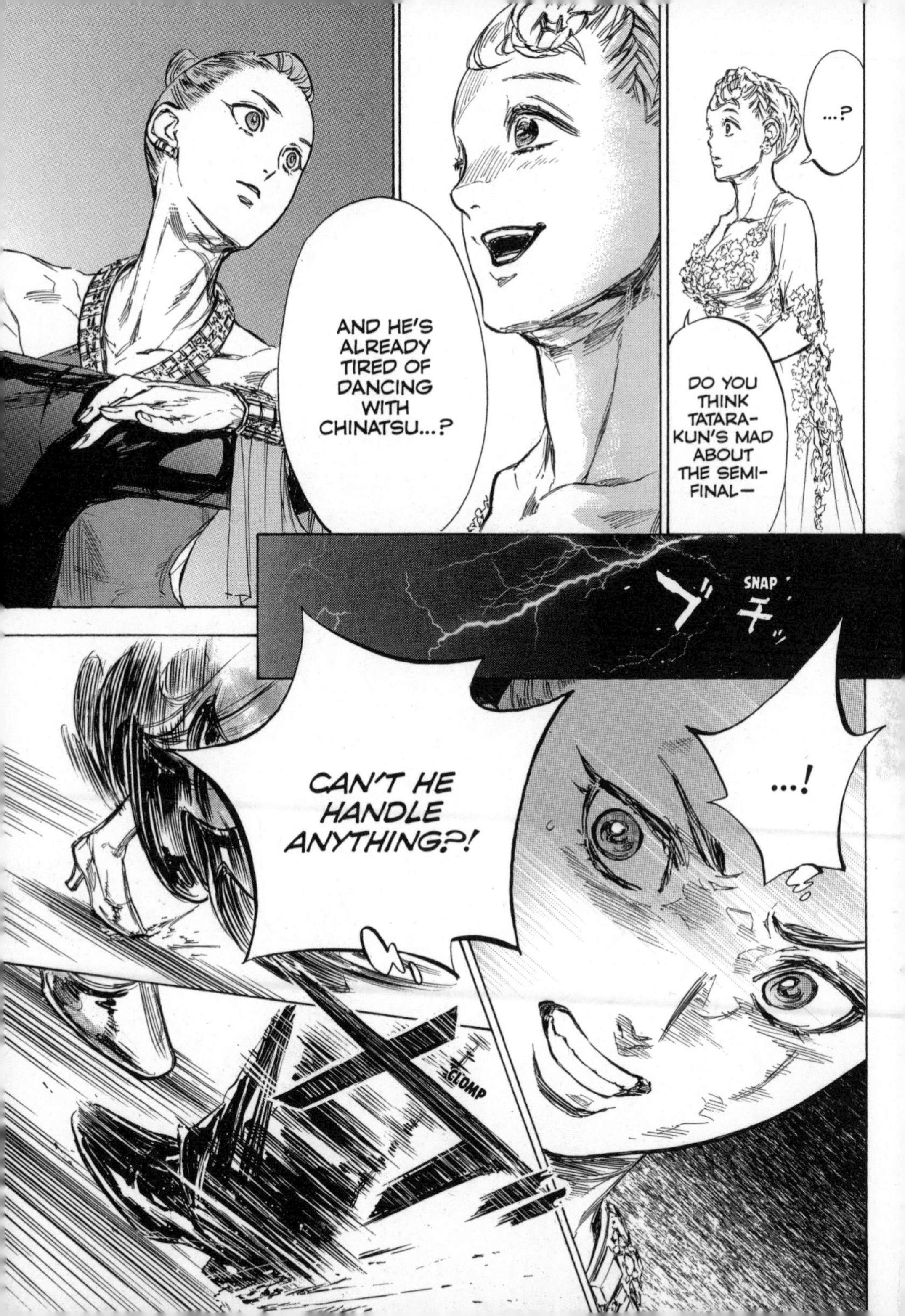
...?
DO YOU THINK TATARA-KUN'S MAD ABOUT THE SEMI-FINAL—
AND HE'S ALREADY TIRED OF DANCING WITH CHINATSU...?
SNAP
ブチッ
...!
CAN'T HE HANDLE ANYTHING?!
CLOMP

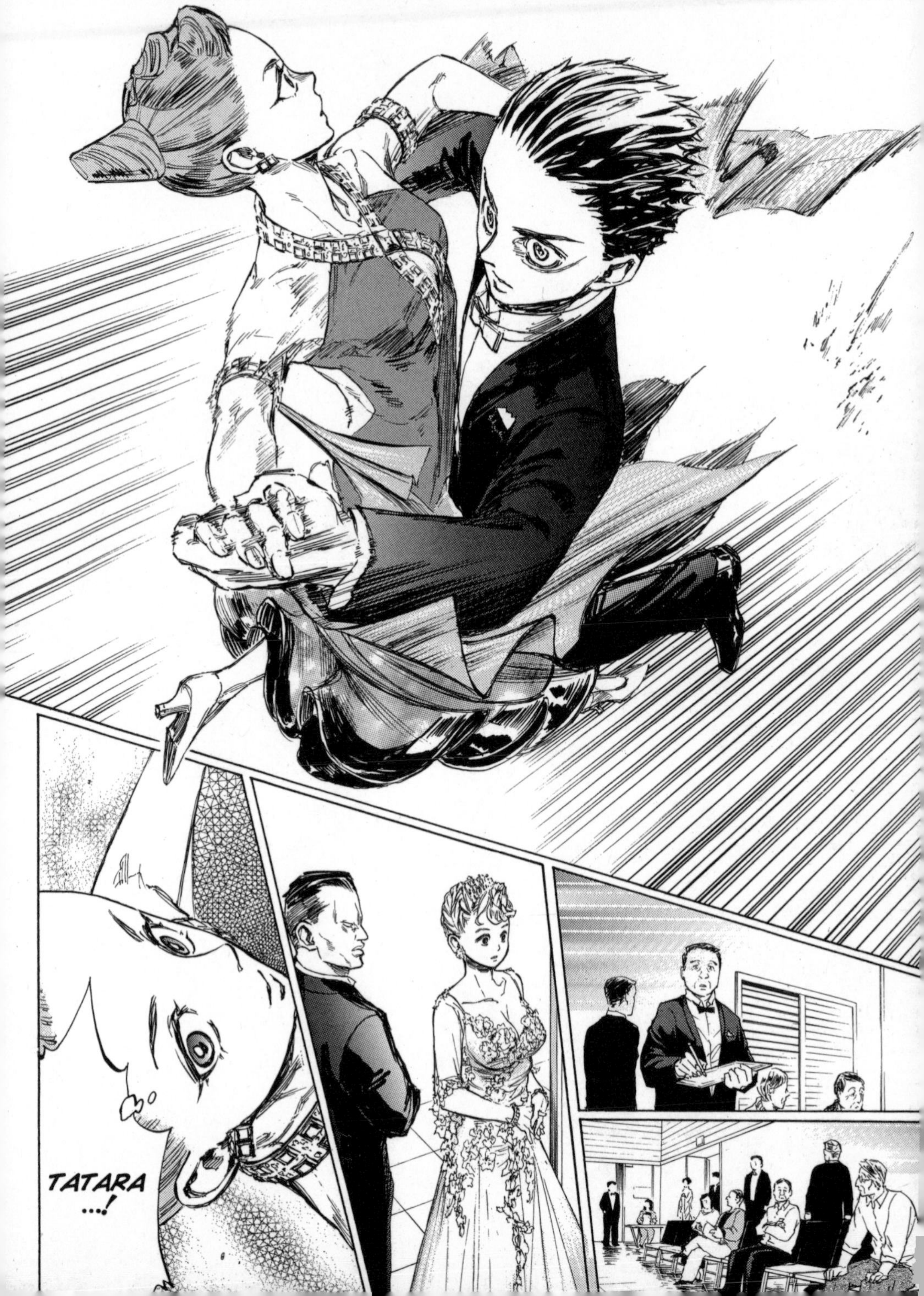
TATARA ...!

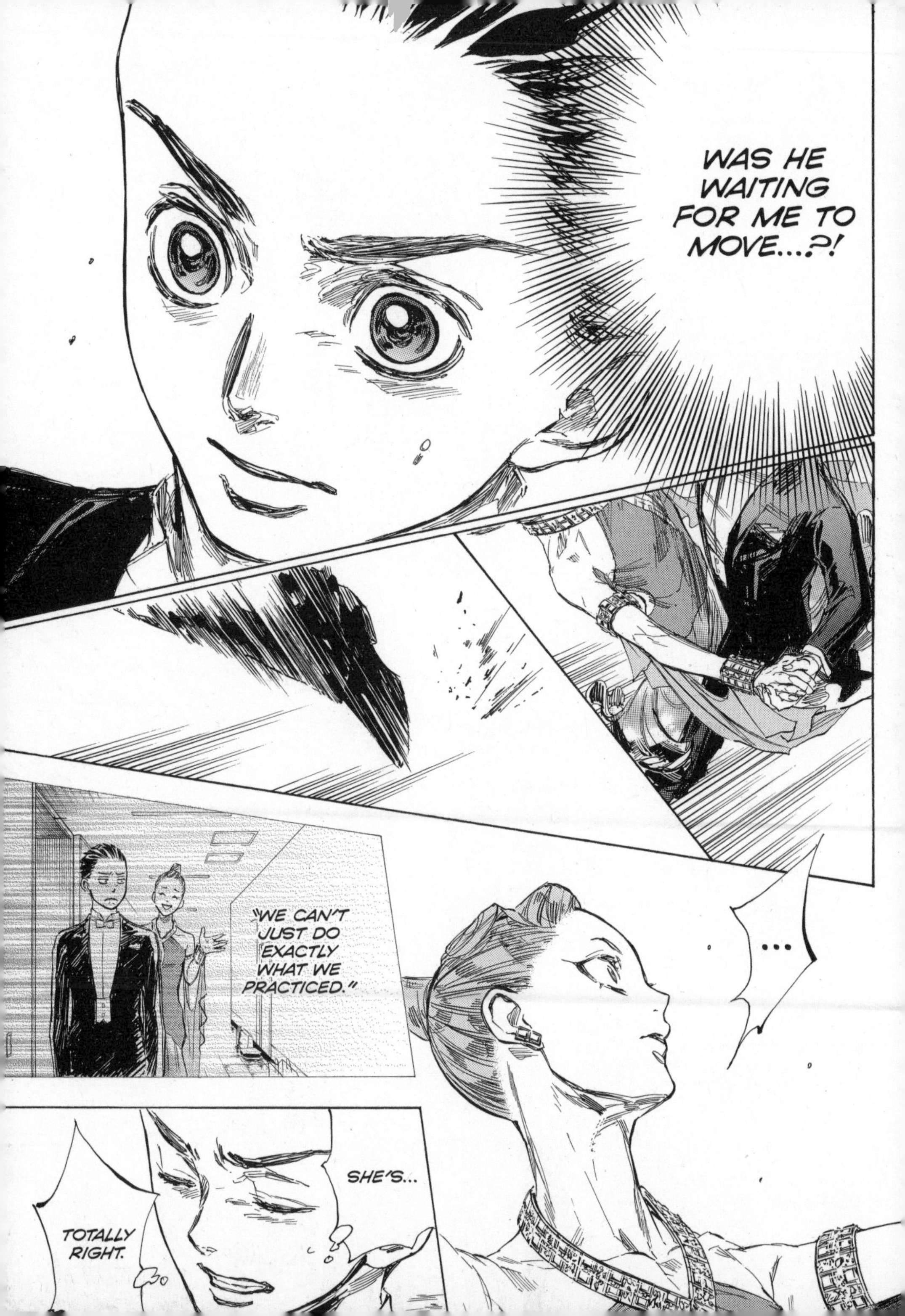
WAS HE WAITING FOR ME TO MOVE...?!
...
"WE CAN'T JUST DO EXACTLY WHAT WE PRACTICED."
SHE'S...
TOTALLY RIGHT.

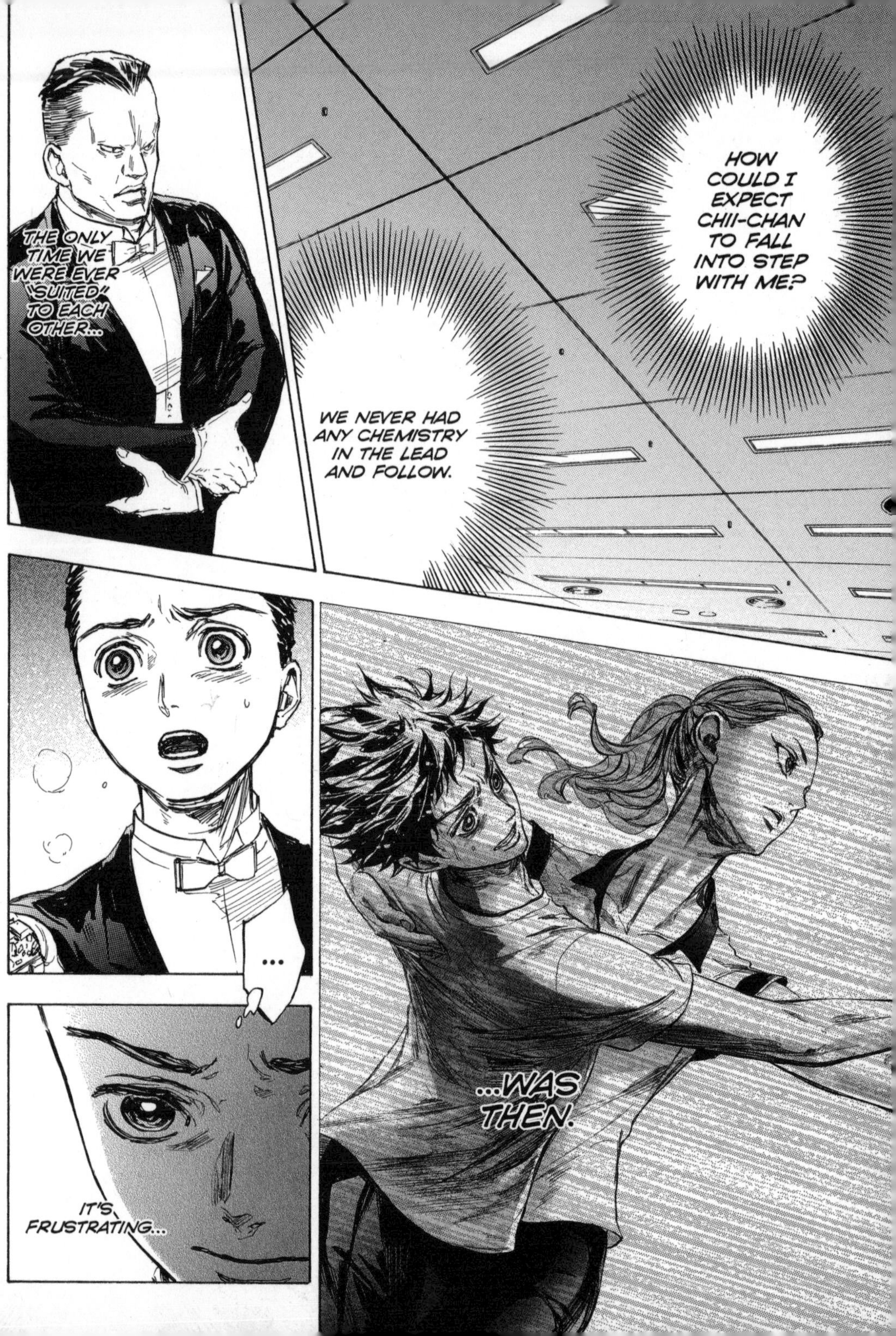
HOW COULD I EXPECT CHII-CHAN TO FALL INTO STEP WITH ME?
WE NEVER HAD ANY CHEMISTRY IN THE LEAD AND FOLLOW.
THE ONLY TIME WE WERE EVER "SUITED" TO EACH OTHER...
...WAS THEN.
...
IT'S FRUSTRATING...

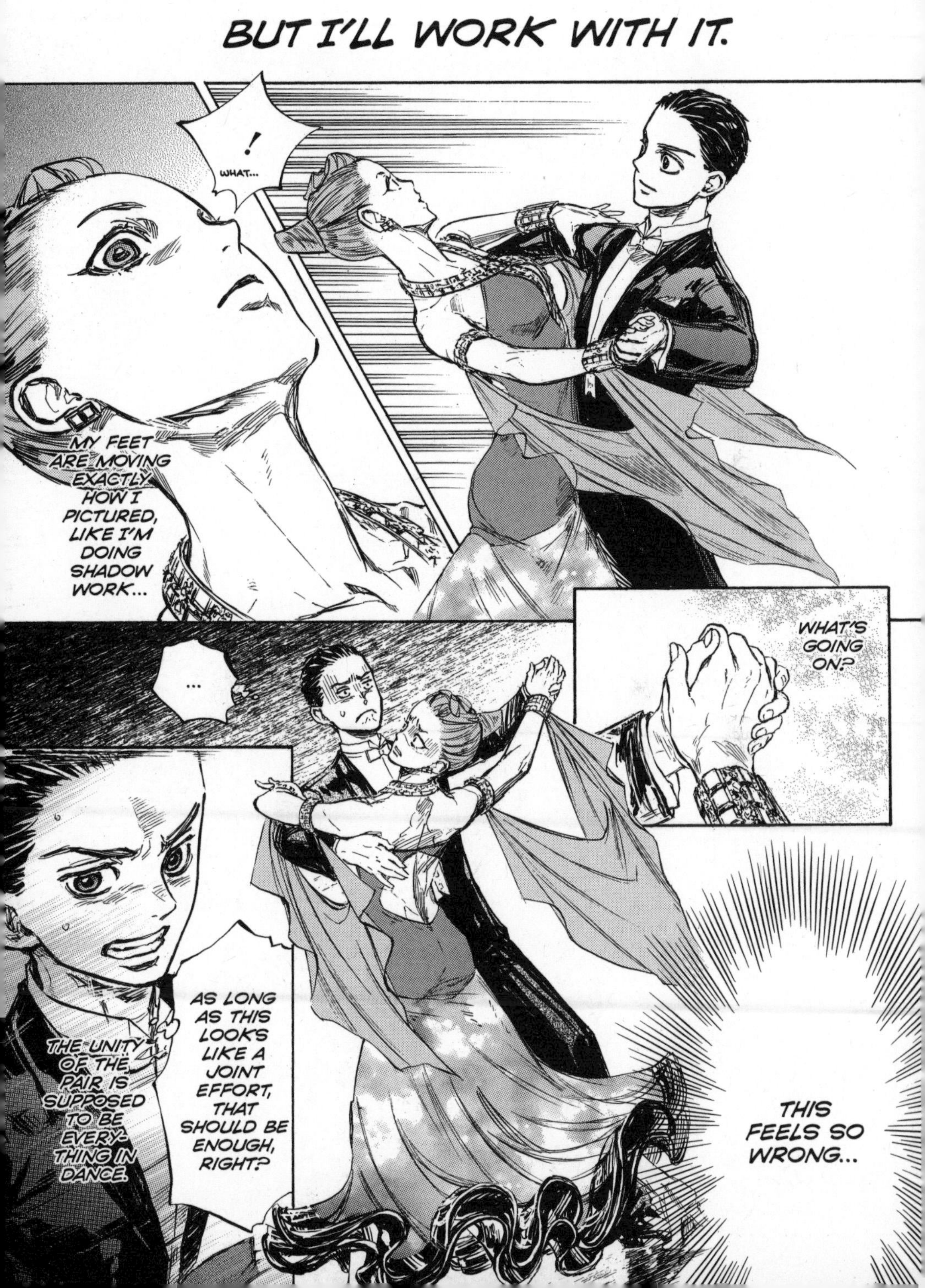

BUT I'LL WORK WITH IT.
!
WHAT...
MY FEET ARE MOVING EXACTLY HOW I PICTURED, LIKE I'M DOING SHADOW WORK...
WHAT'S GOING ON?
...
THIS FEELS SO WRONG...
AS LONG AS THIS LOOKS LIKE A JOINT EFFORT, THAT SHOULD BE ENOUGH, RIGHT?
THE UNITY OF THE PAIR IS SUPPOSED TO BE EVERYTHING IN DANCE.

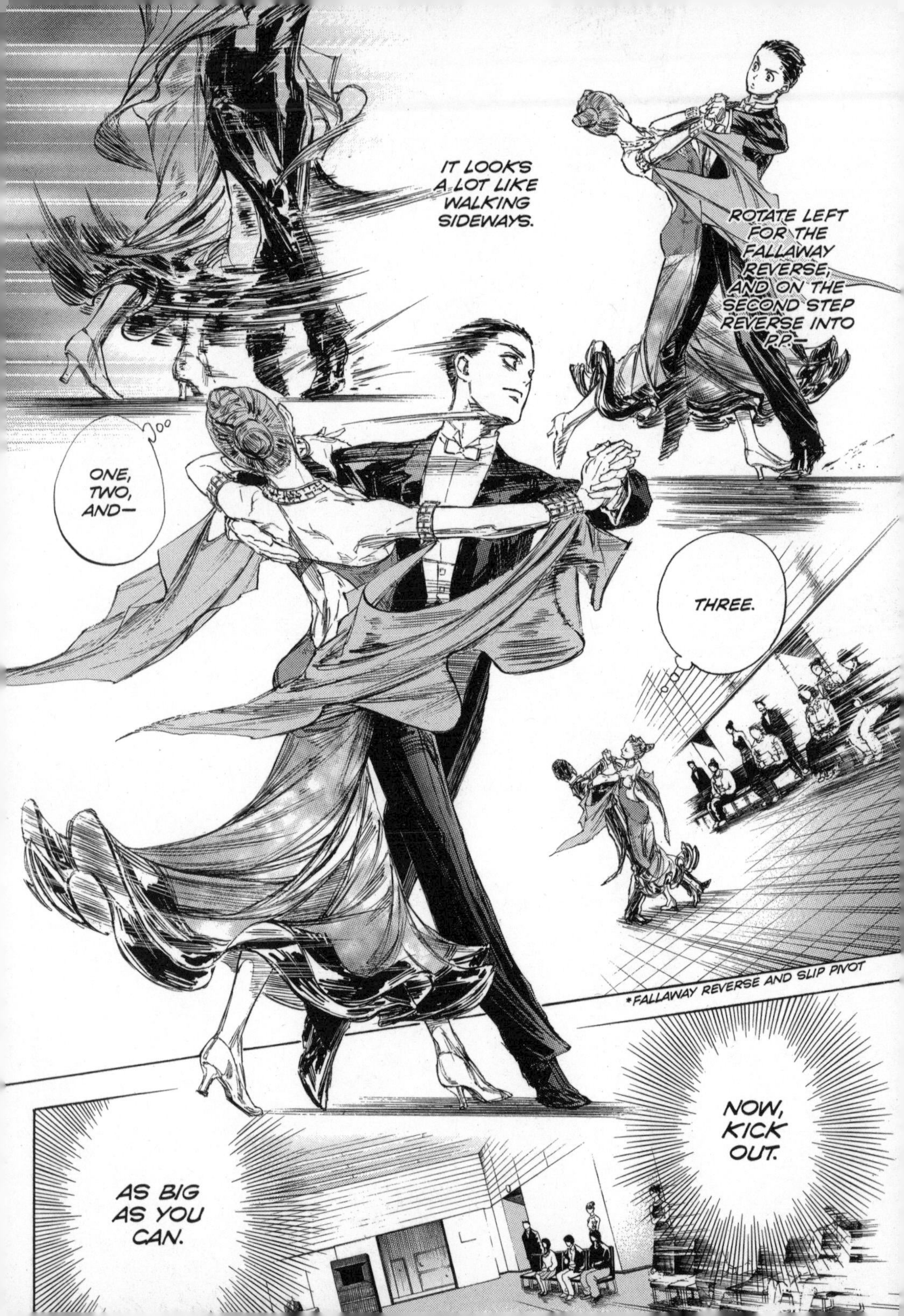
ROTATE LEFT FOR THE FALLAWAY REVERSE, AND ON THE SECOND STEP REVERSE INTO P.P.—
IT LOOKS A LOT LIKE WALKING SIDEWAYS.
ONE, TWO, AND—
THREE.
*FALLAWAY REVERSE AND SLIP PIVOT
NOW, KICK OUT.
AS BIG AS YOU CAN.

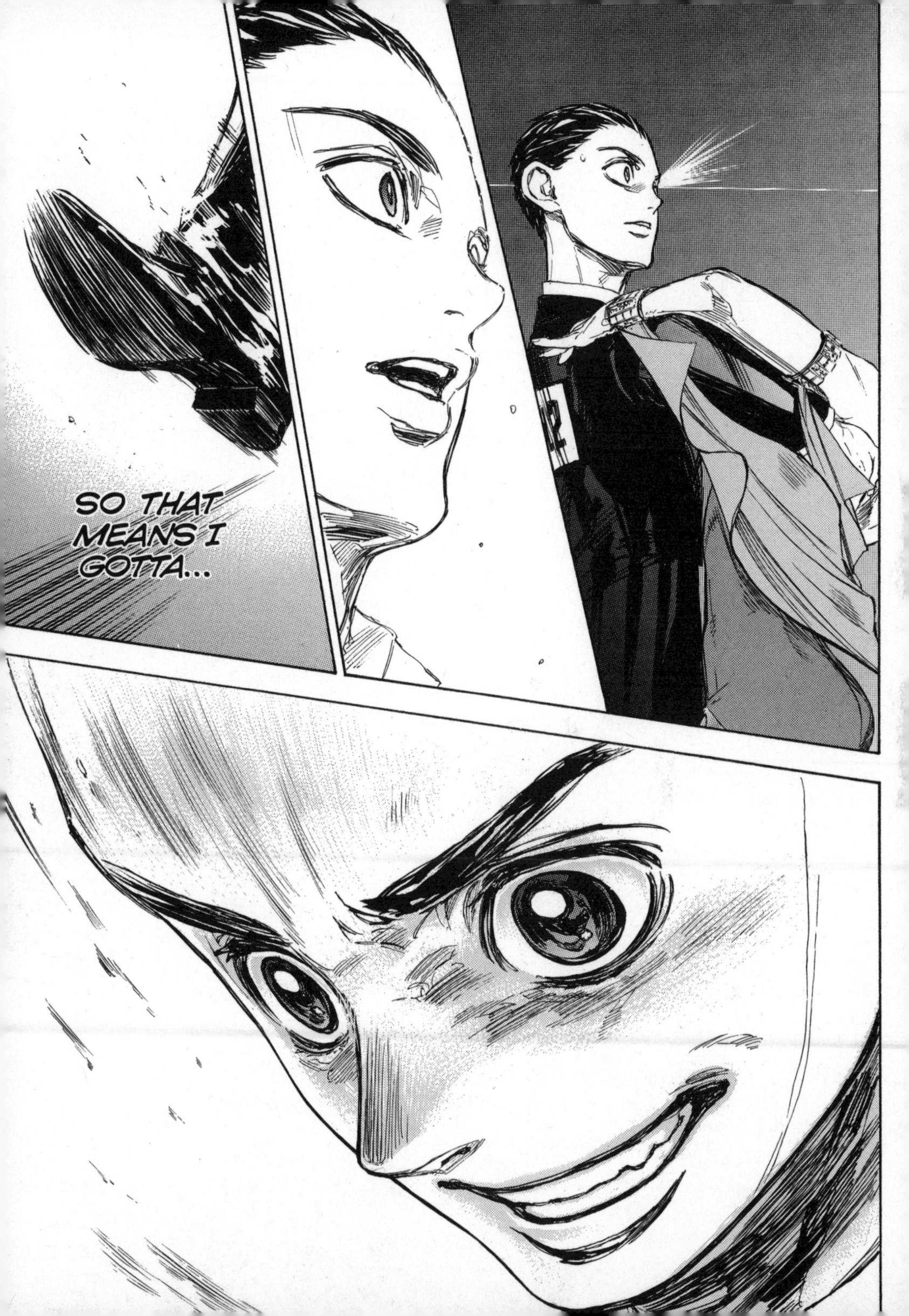
SO THAT MEANS I GOTTA...

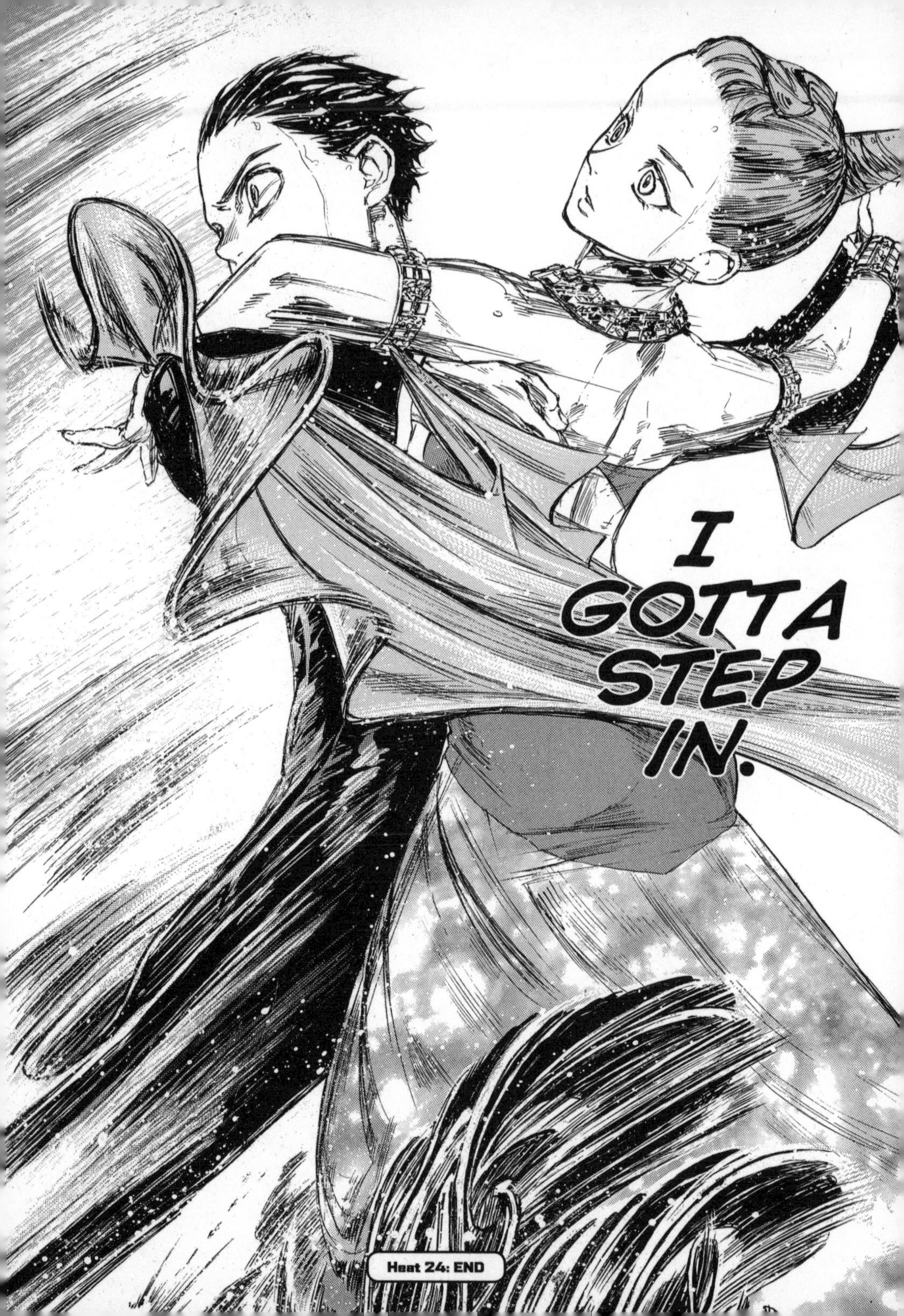
I GOTTA STEP IN.
Heat 24: END

# WELCOME TO THE BALLROOM

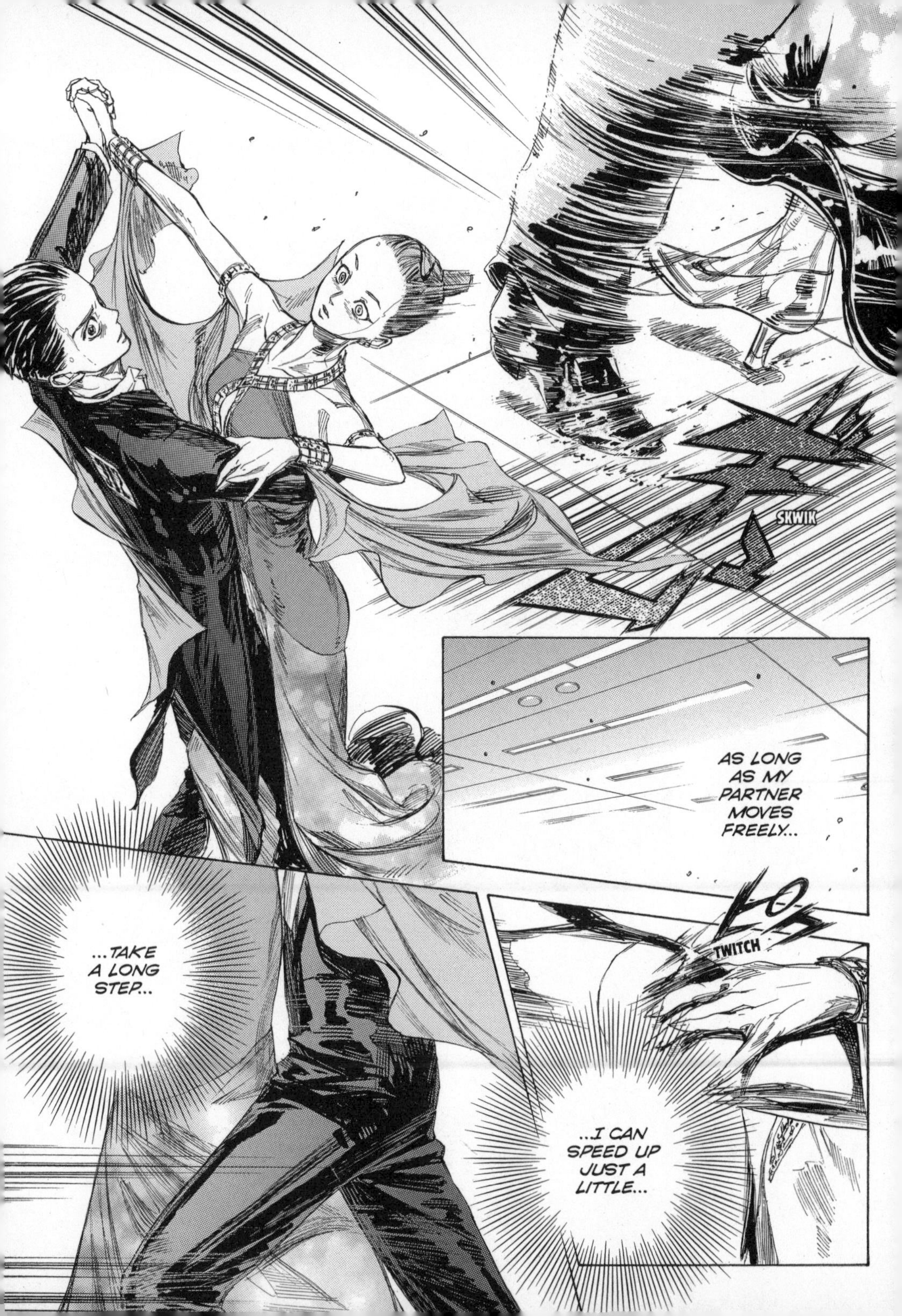
SKWIK
AS LONG AS MY PARTNER MOVES FREELY...
TWITCH
...I CAN SPEED UP JUST A LITTLE...
...TAKE A LONG STEP...

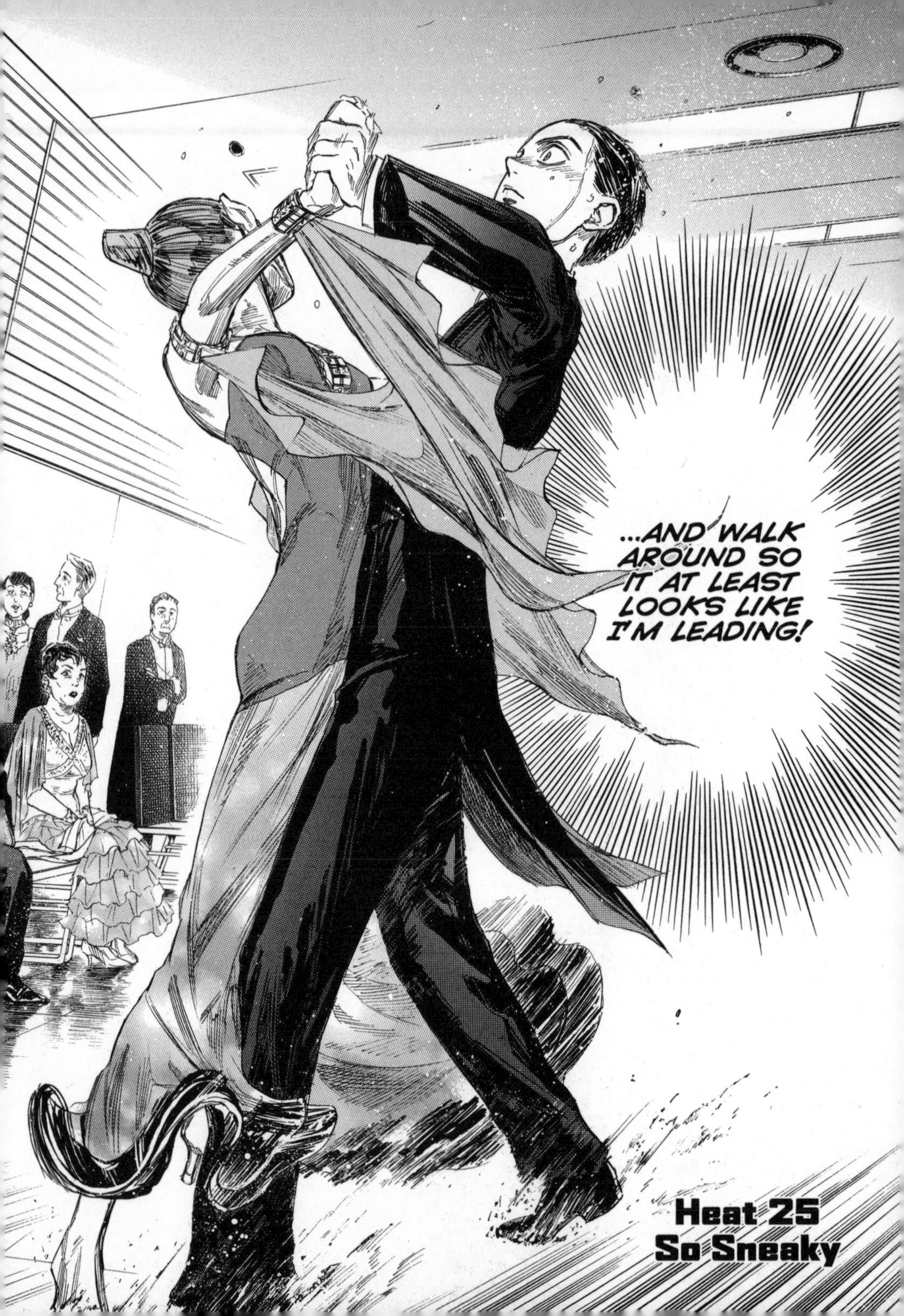
...AND WALK AROUND SO IT AT LEAST LOOKS LIKE I'M LEADING!
Heat 25
So Sneaky

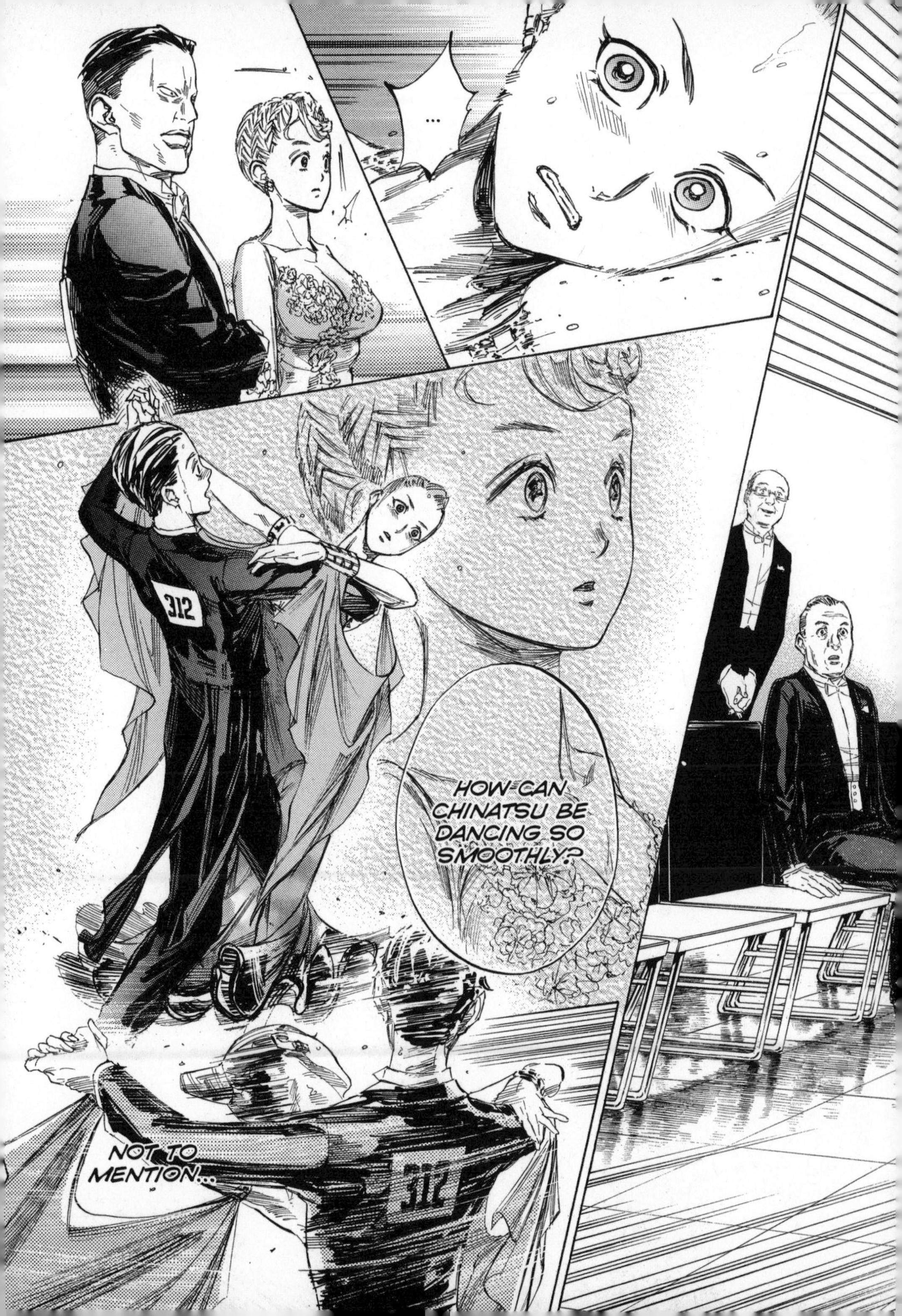
...
HOW CAN CHINATSU BE DANCING SO SMOOTHLY?
NOT TO MENTION...

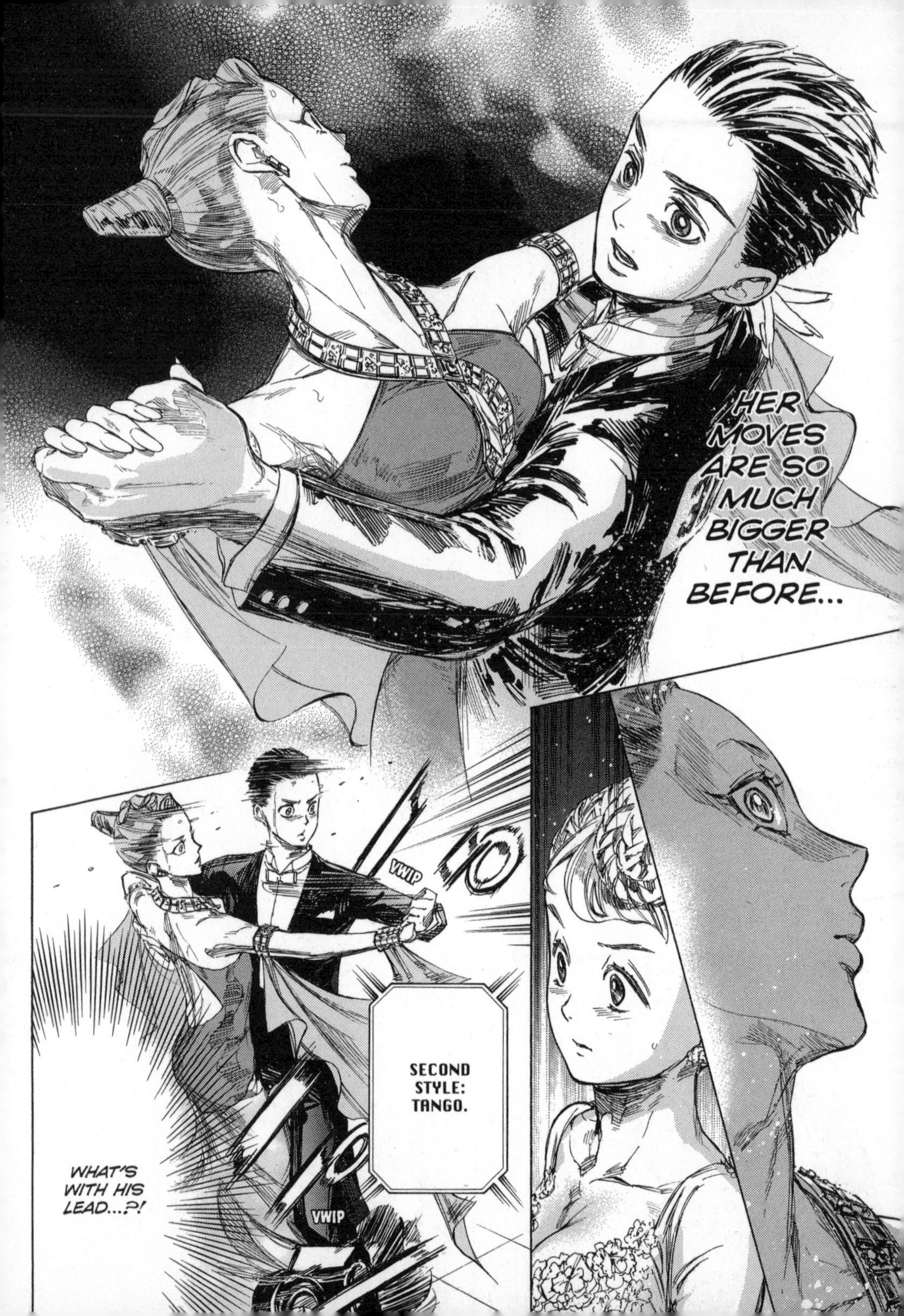
HER MOVES ARE SO MUCH BIGGER THAN BEFORE...
VWIP
SECOND STYLE: TANGO.
WHAT'S WITH HIS LEAD...?!
VWIP

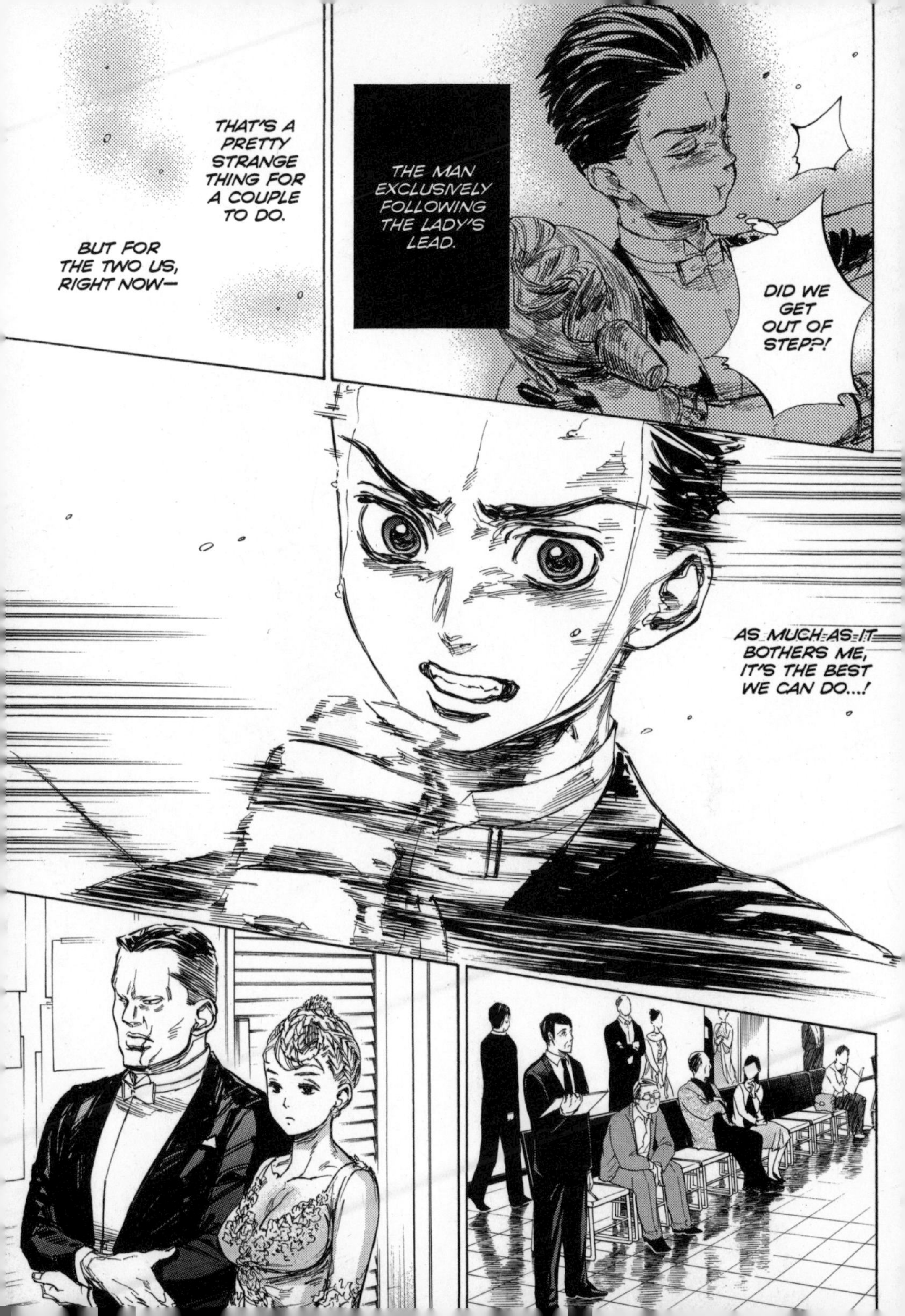
DID WE GET OUT OF STEP?!
THE MAN EXCLUSIVELY FOLLOWING THE LADY'S LEAD.
THAT'S A PRETTY STRANGE THING FOR A COUPLE TO DO.
BUT FOR THE TWO US, RIGHT NOW—
AS MUCH AS IT BOTHERS ME, IT'S THE BEST WE CAN DO...!

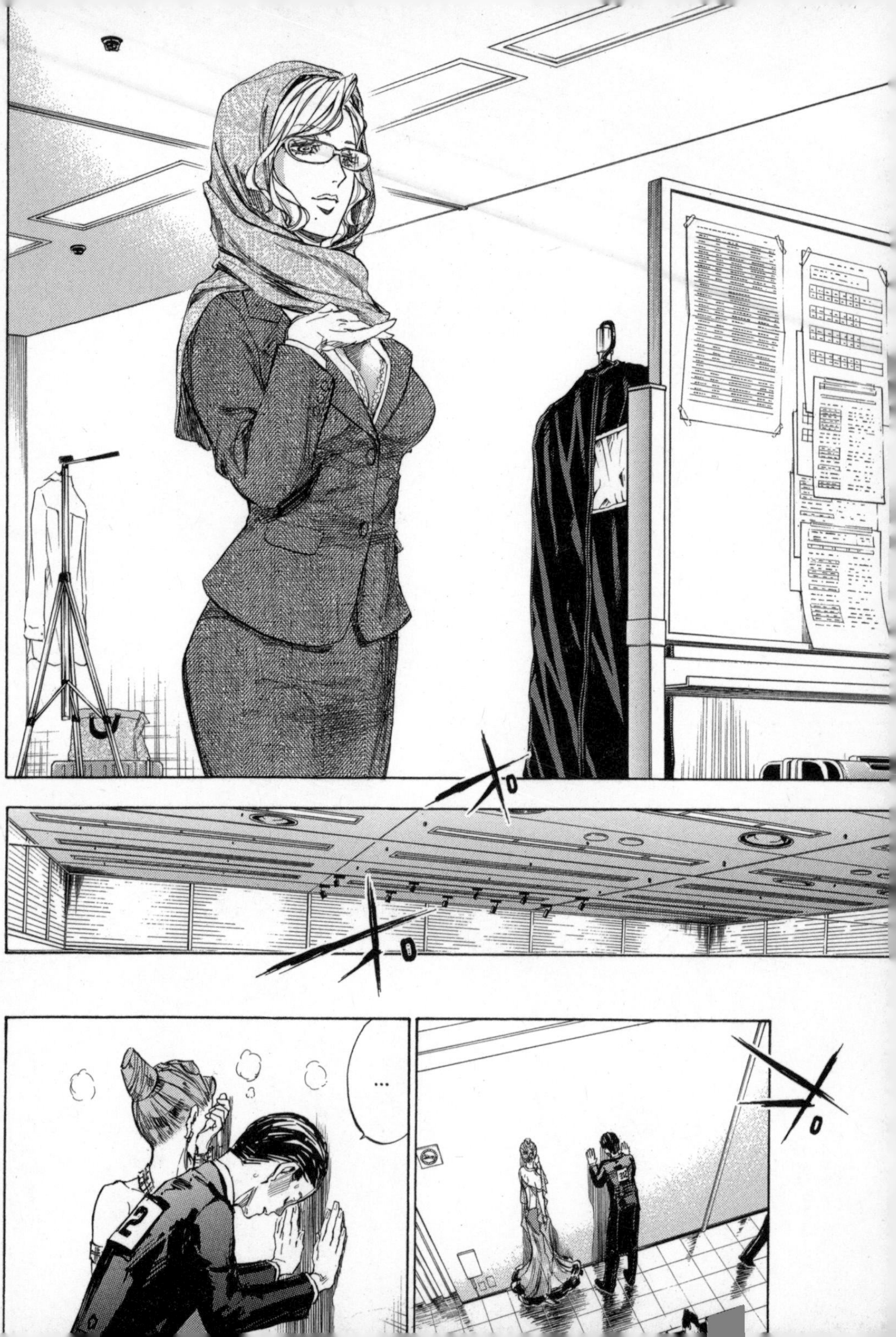
...

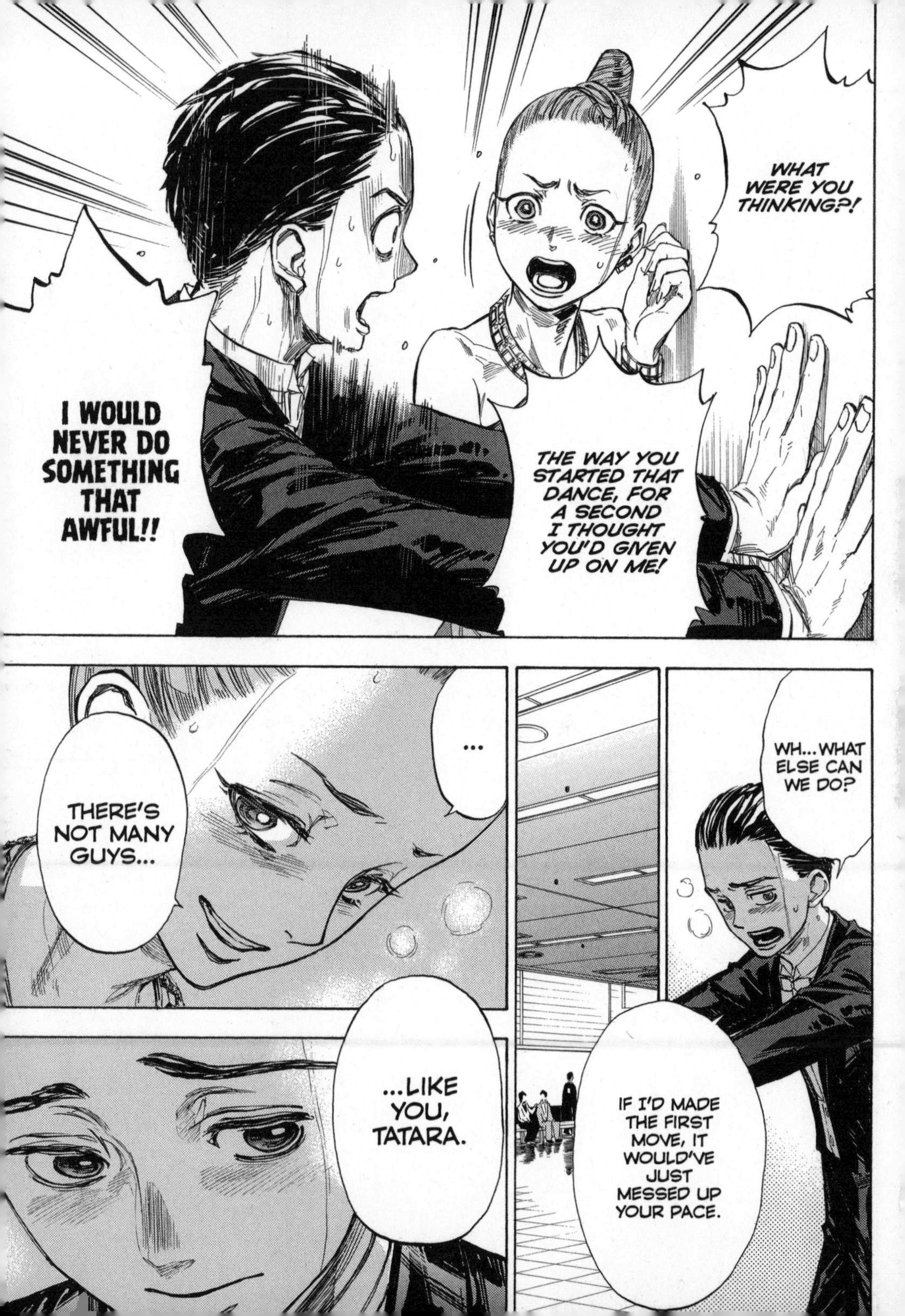
WHAT WERE YOU THINKING?!
THE WAY YOU STARTED THAT DANCE, FOR A SECOND I THOUGHT YOU'D GIVEN UP ON ME!
I WOULD NEVER DO SOMETHING THAT AWFUL!!
WH...WHAT ELSE CAN WE DO?
IF I'D MADE THE FIRST MOVE, IT WOULD'VE JUST MESSED UP YOUR PACE.
...
THERE'S NOT MANY GUYS...
...LIKE YOU, TATARA.

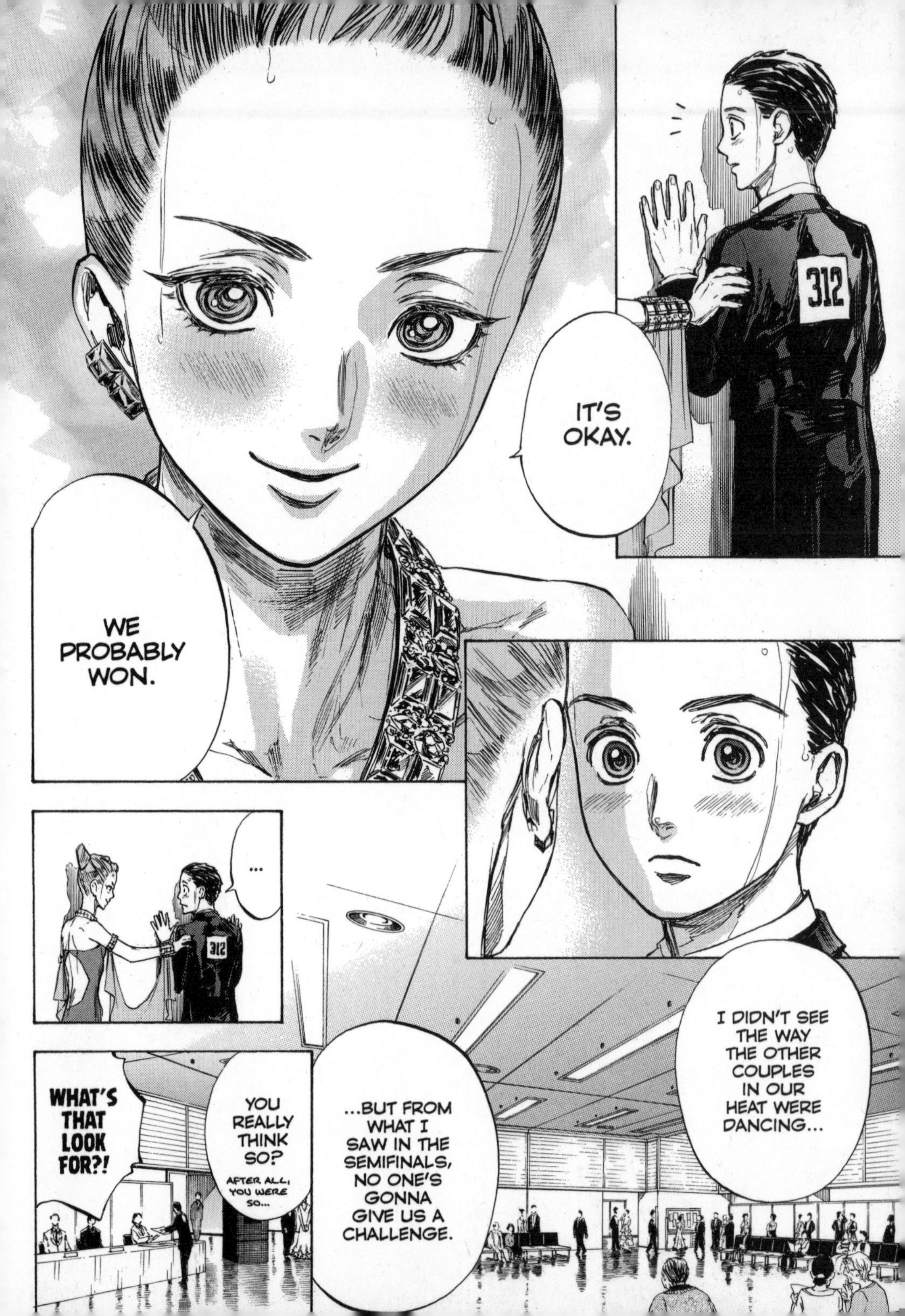
IT'S OKAY.
WE PROBABLY WON.
...
I DIDN'T SEE THE WAY THE OTHER COUPLES IN OUR HEAT WERE DANCING...
...BUT FROM WHAT I SAW IN THE SEMIFINALS, NO ONE'S GONNA GIVE US A CHALLENGE.
YOU REALLY THINK SO?
AFTER ALL, YOU WERE SO...
WHAT'S THAT LOOK FOR?!

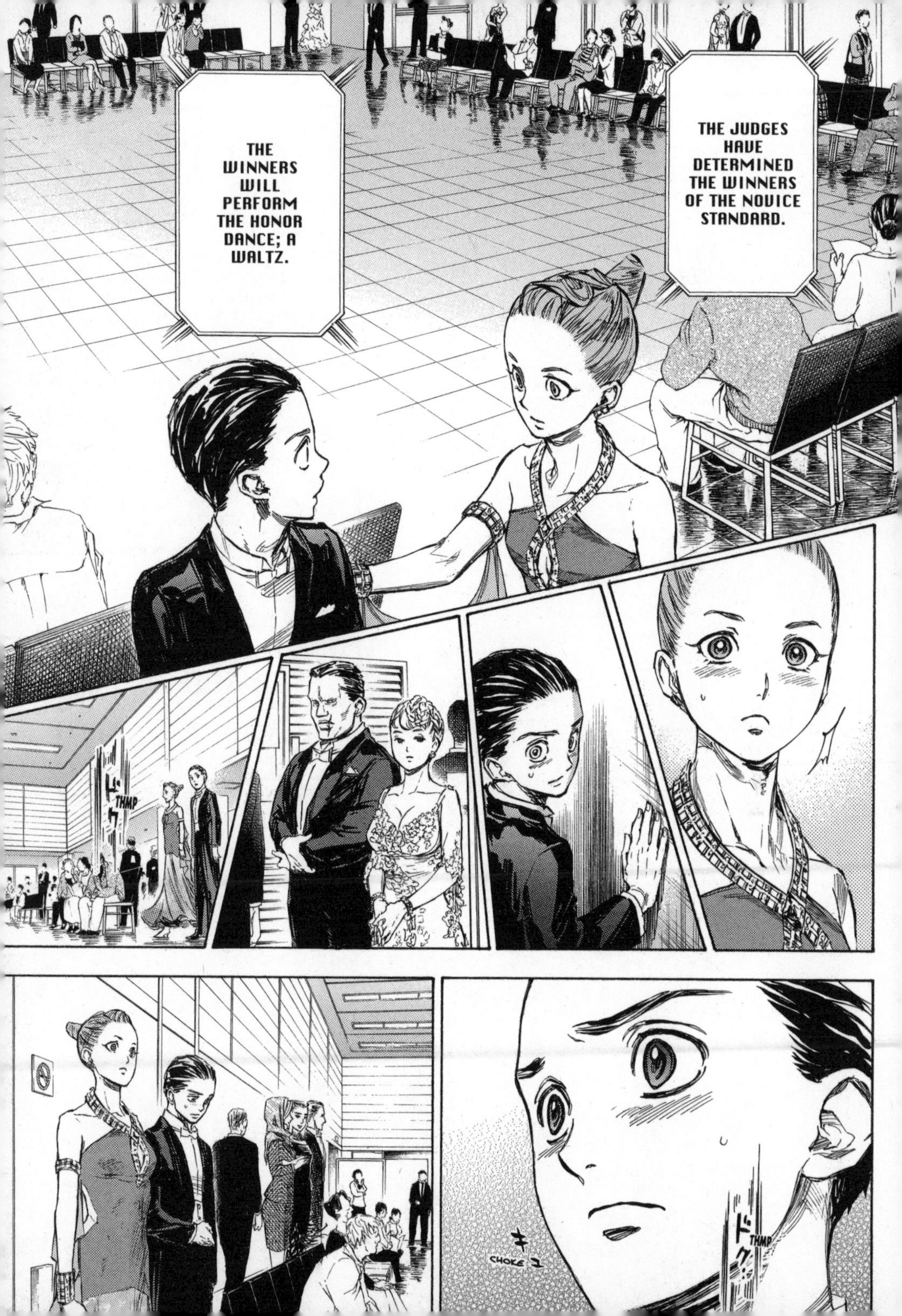
THE JUDGES HAVE DETERMINED THE WINNERS OF THE NOVICE STANDARD.
THE WINNERS WILL PERFORM THE HONOR DANCE; A WALTZ.
THMP
THMP
CHOKE

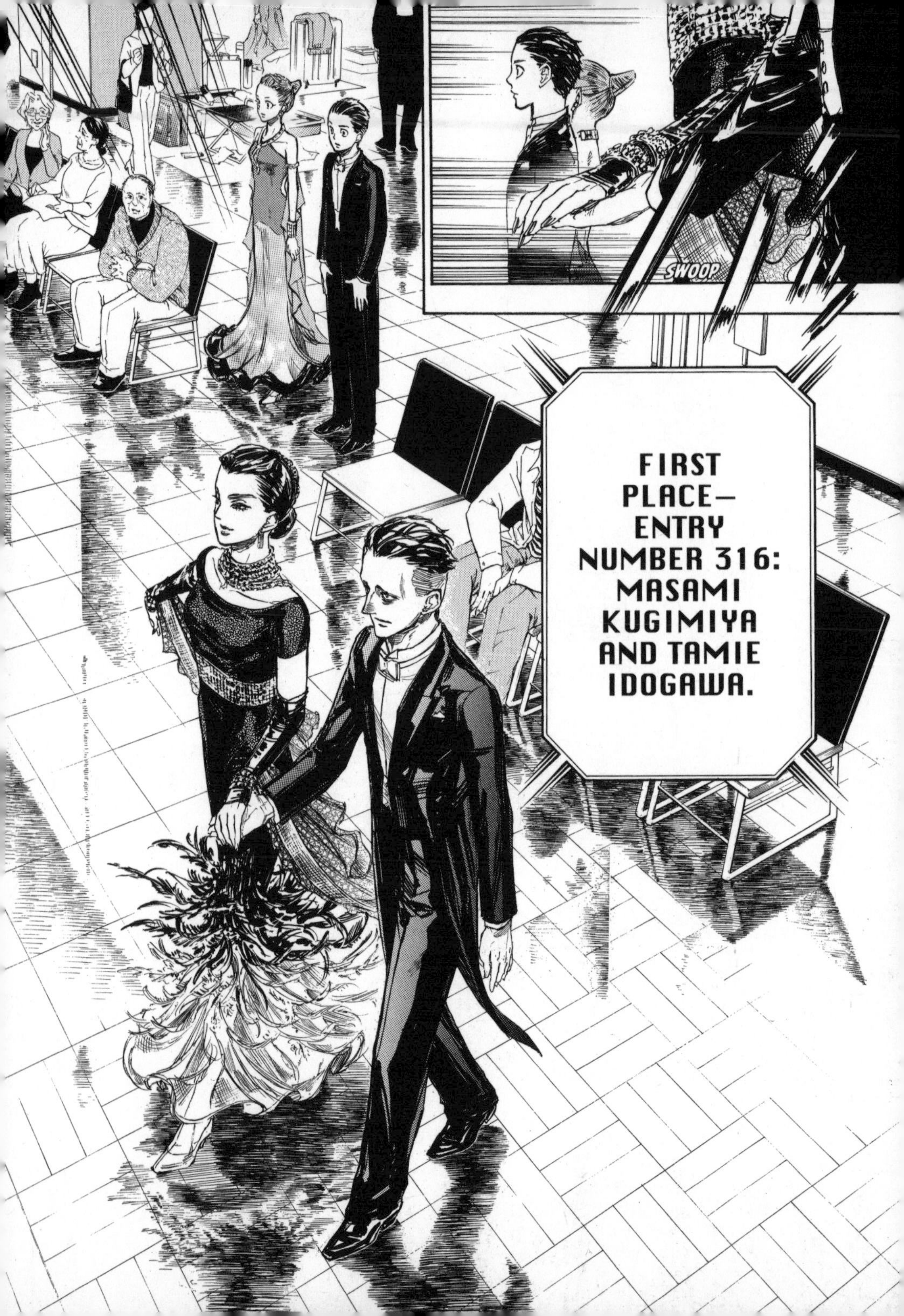
SWOOP
FIRST PLACE—ENTRY NUMBER 316: MASAMI KUGIMIYA AND TAMIE IDOGAWA.

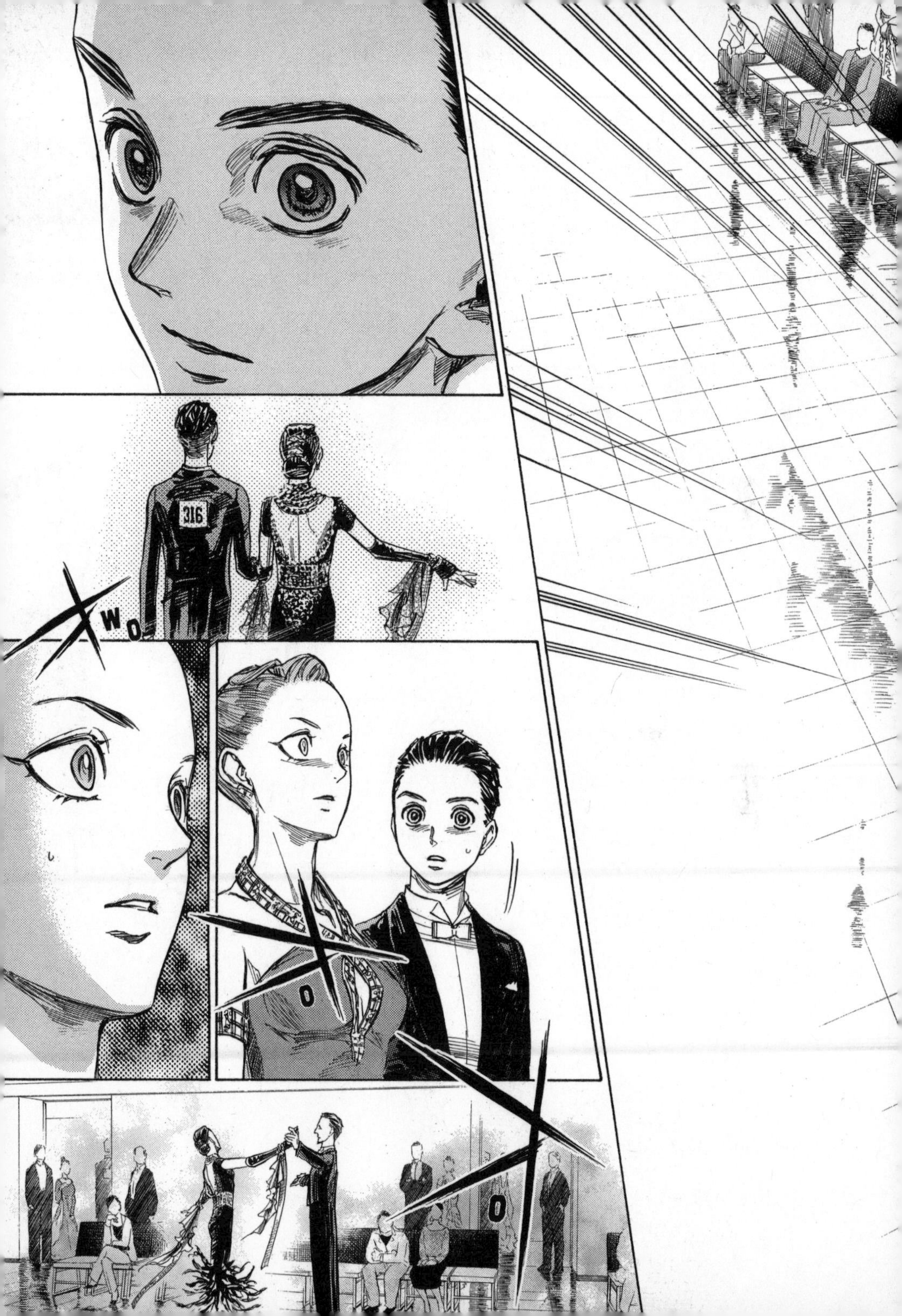
WO
O
O
O

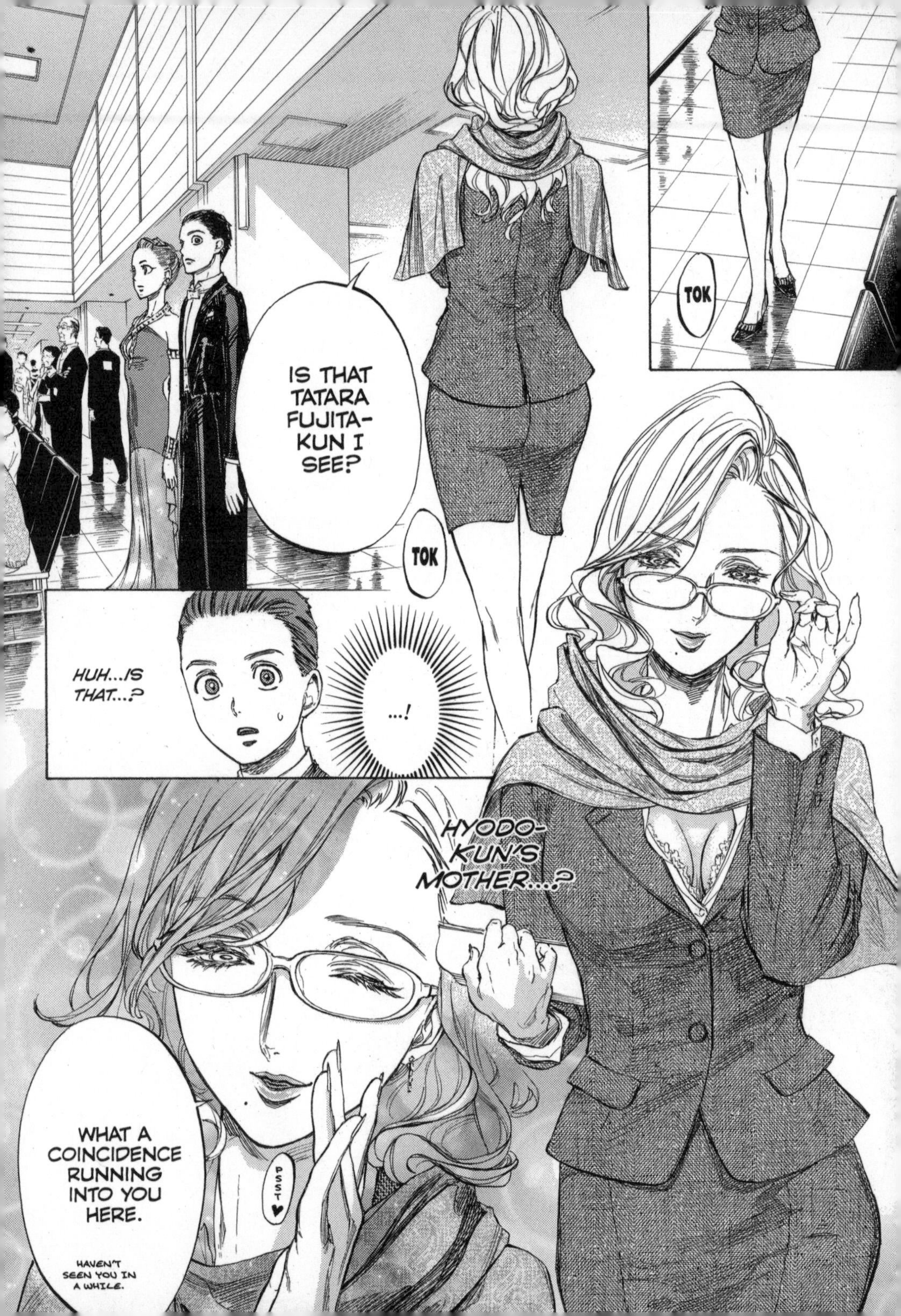

TOK
IS THAT TATARA FUJITA-KUN I SEE?
TOK
...!
HUH...IS THAT...?
HYODO-KUN'S MOTHER...?
PSST♥
WHAT A COINCIDENCE RUNNING INTO YOU HERE.
HAVEN'T SEEN YOU IN A WHILE.

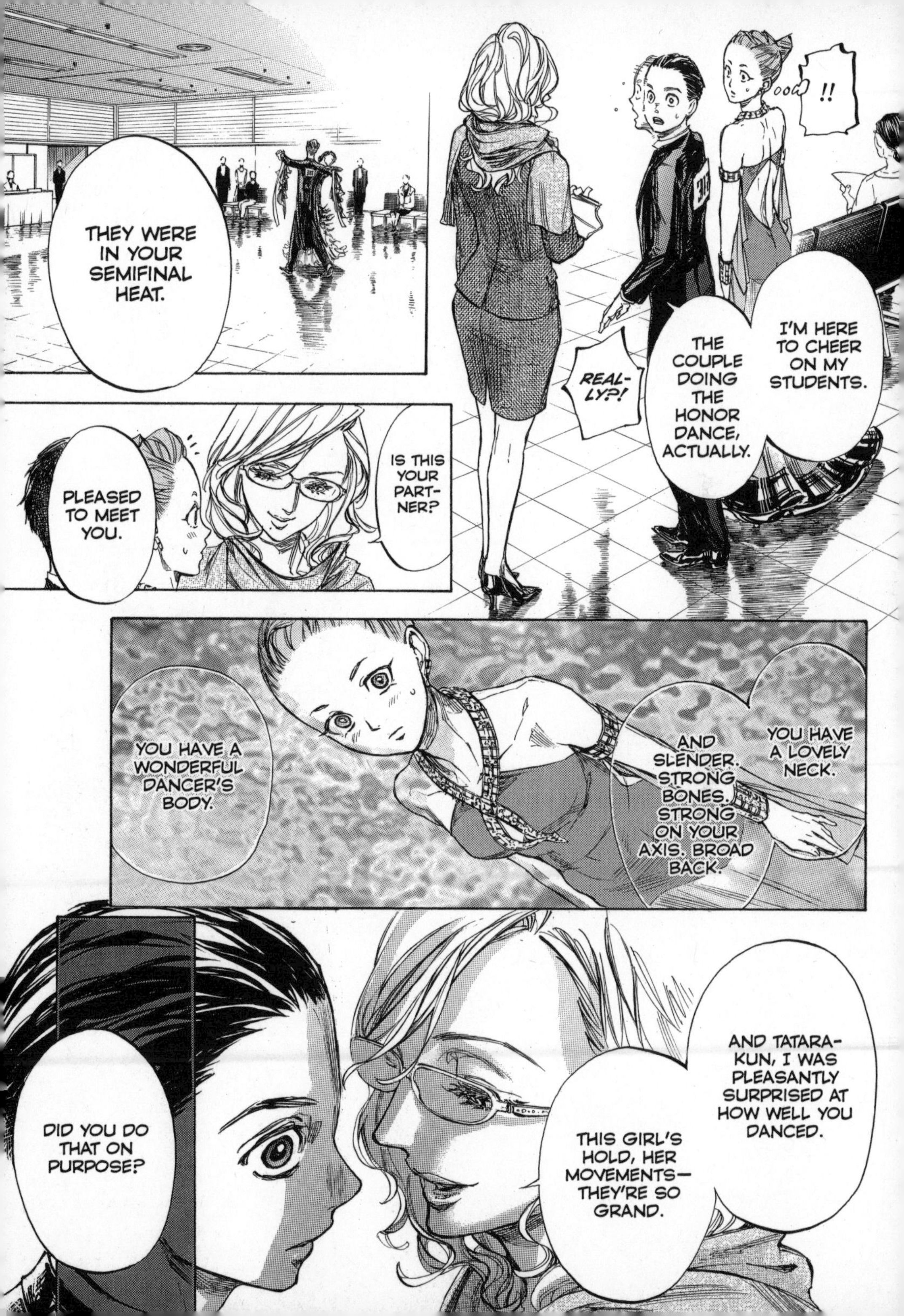
!!
I'M HERE TO CHEER ON MY STUDENTS.
THE COUPLE DOING THE HONOR DANCE, ACTUALLY.
REAL-LY?!
THEY WERE IN YOUR SEMIFINAL HEAT.
IS THIS YOUR PART-NER?
PLEASED TO MEET YOU.
YOU HAVE A LOVELY NECK.
AND SLENDER. STRONG BONES. STRONG ON YOUR AXIS. BROAD BACK.
YOU HAVE A WONDERFUL DANCER'S BODY.
AND TATARA-KUN, I WAS PLEASANTLY SURPRISED AT HOW WELL YOU DANCED.
THIS GIRL'S HOLD, HER MOVEMENTS—THEY'RE SO GRAND.
DID YOU DO THAT ON PURPOSE?

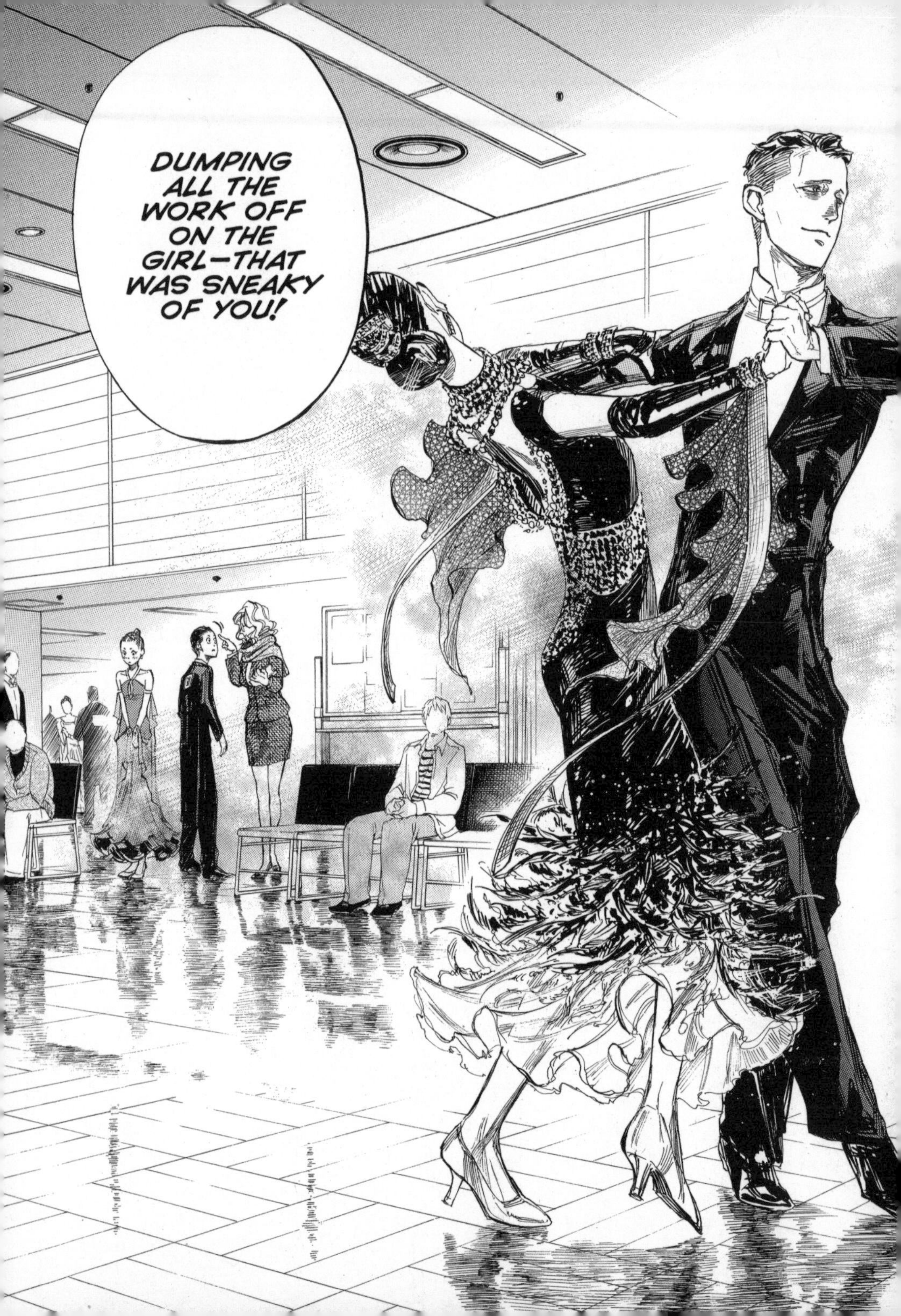
DUMPING ALL THE WORK OFF ON THE GIRL—THAT WAS SNEAKY OF YOU!

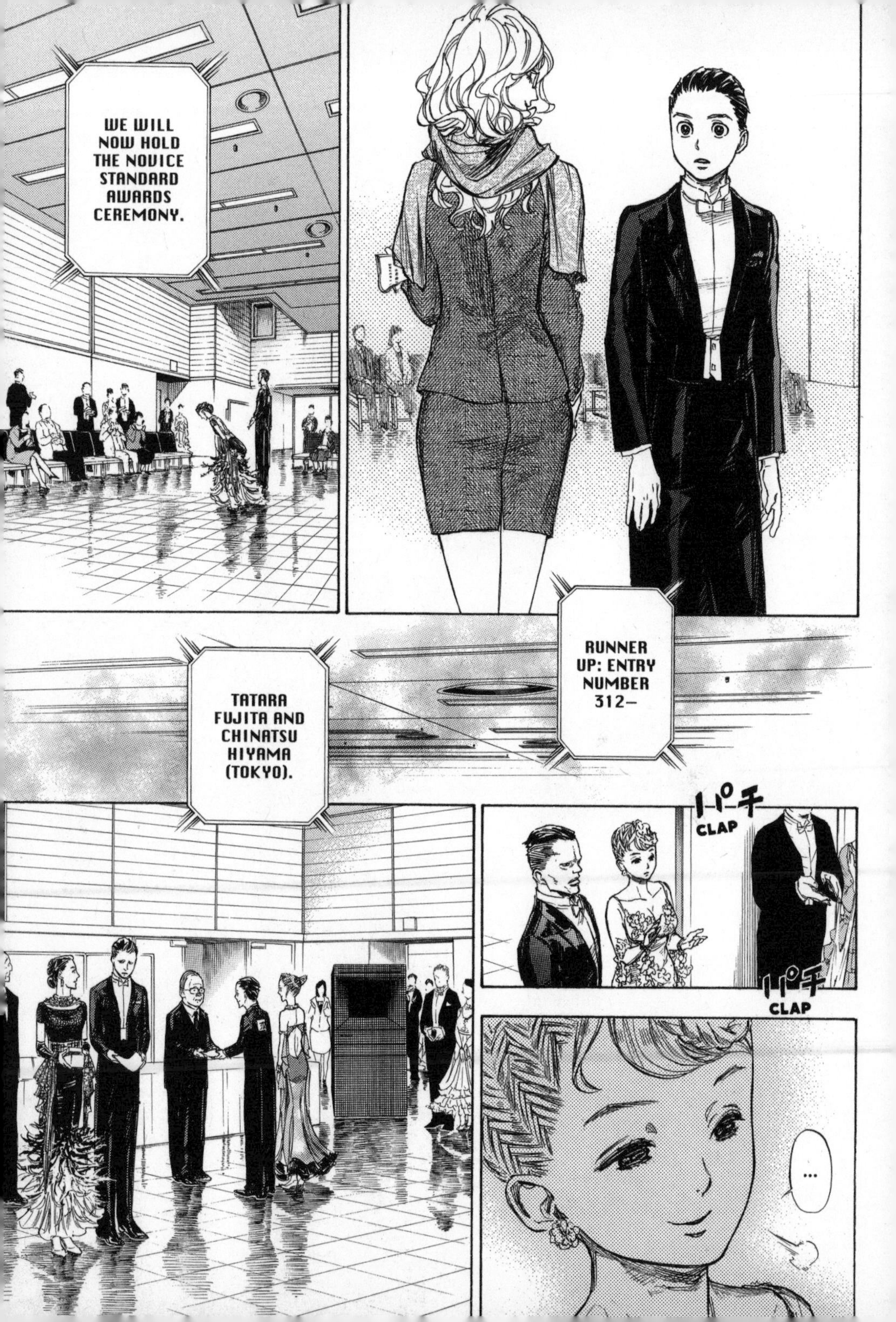
WE WILL NOW HOLD THE NOVICE STANDARD AWARDS CEREMONY.
RUNNER UP: ENTRY NUMBER 312—
TATARA FUJITA AND CHINATSU HIYAMA (TOKYO).
パチ
CLAP
パチ
CLAP
...

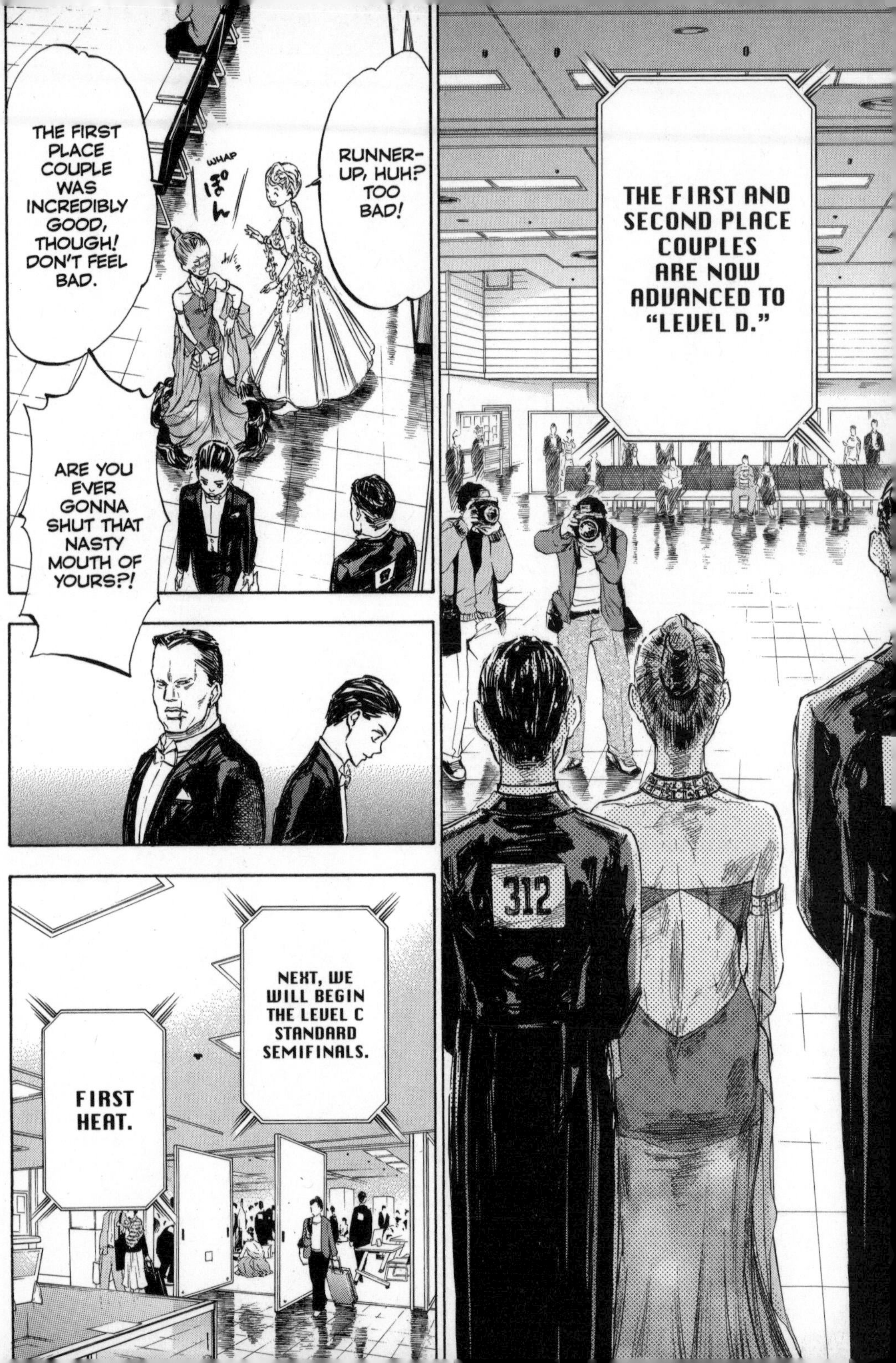
THE FIRST AND SECOND PLACE COUPLES ARE NOW ADVANCED TO "LEVEL D."
312
RUNNER-UP, HUH? TOO BAD!
WHAP
ぽん
THE FIRST PLACE COUPLE WAS INCREDIBLY GOOD, THOUGH! DON'T FEEL BAD.
ARE YOU EVER GONNA SHUT THAT NASTY MOUTH OF YOURS?!
NEXT, WE WILL BEGIN THE LEVEL C STANDARD SEMIFINALS.
FIRST HEAT.

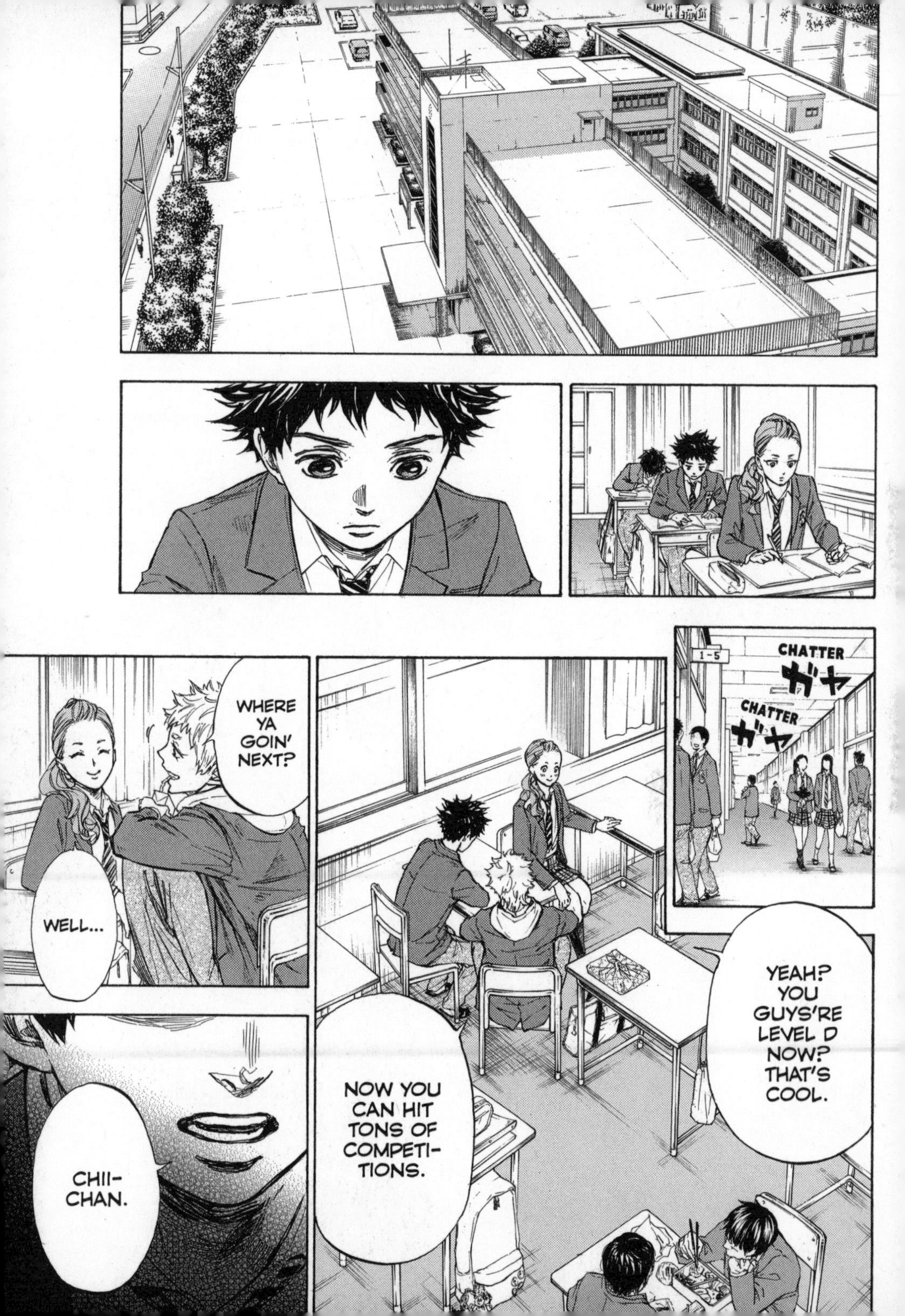
1-5
CHATTER ガヤ
CHATTER ガヤ
YEAH? YOU GUYS'RE LEVEL D NOW? THAT'S COOL.
NOW YOU CAN HIT TONS OF COMPETITIONS.
WHERE YA GOIN' NEXT?
WELL...
CHII-CHAN.

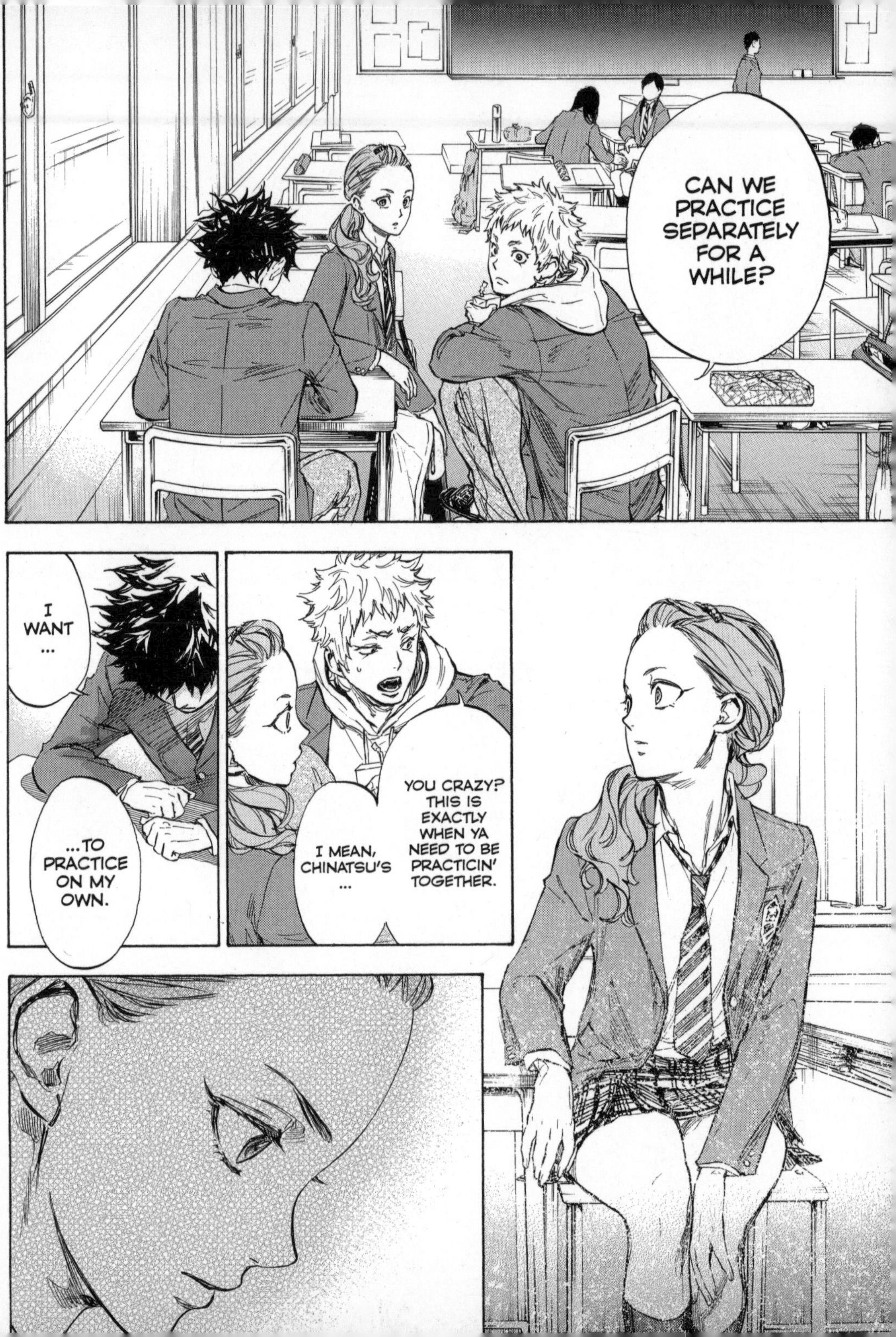
CAN WE PRACTICE SEPARATELY FOR A WHILE?
YOU CRAZY? THIS IS EXACTLY WHEN YA NEED TO BE PRACTICIN' TOGETHER.
I MEAN, CHINATSU'S ...
I WANT ...
...TO PRACTICE ON MY OWN.

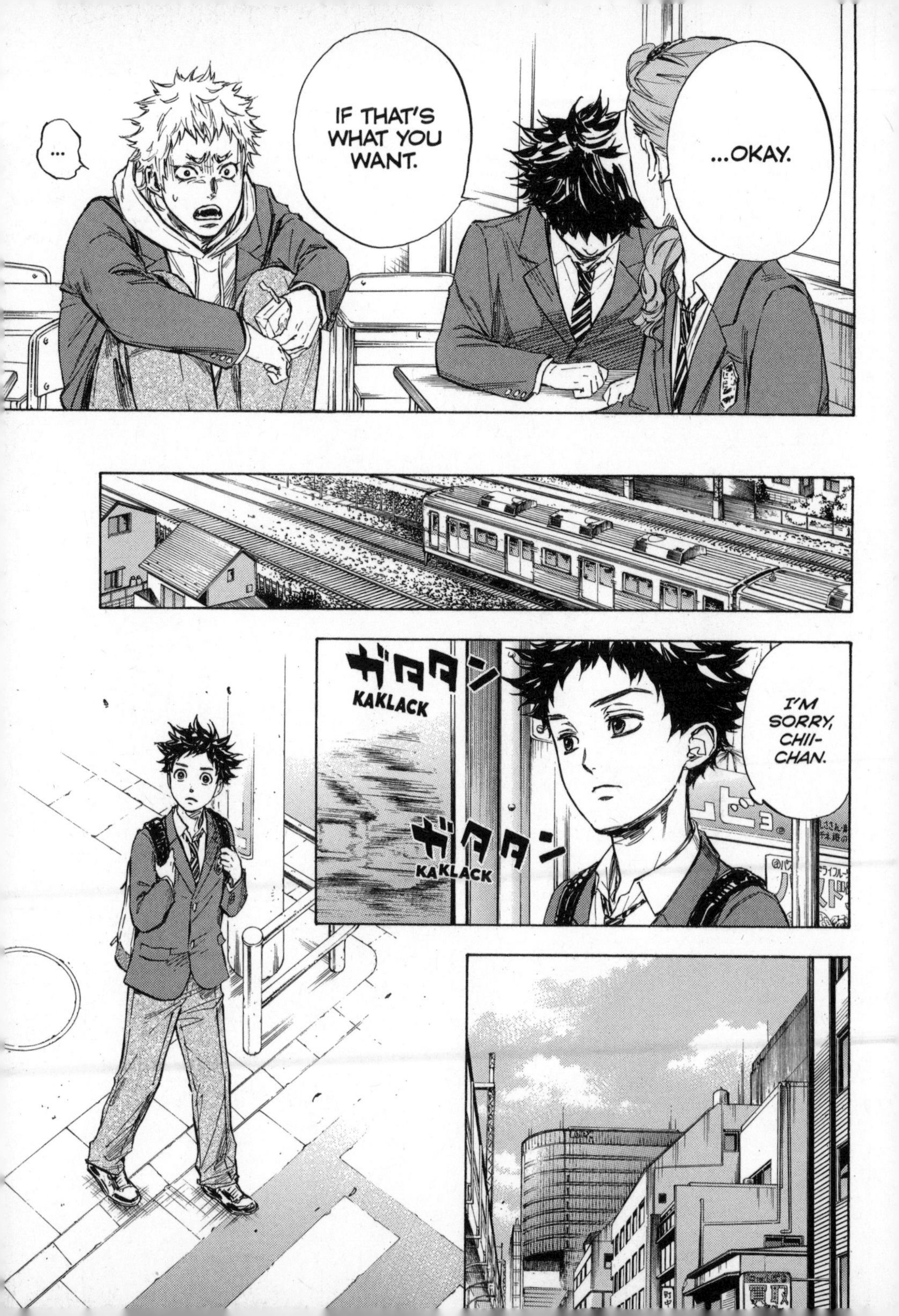
...OKAY.
IF THAT'S WHAT YOU WANT.
...
I'M SORRY, CHII-CHAN.
ガタタン
KAKLACK
ガタタン
KAKLACK

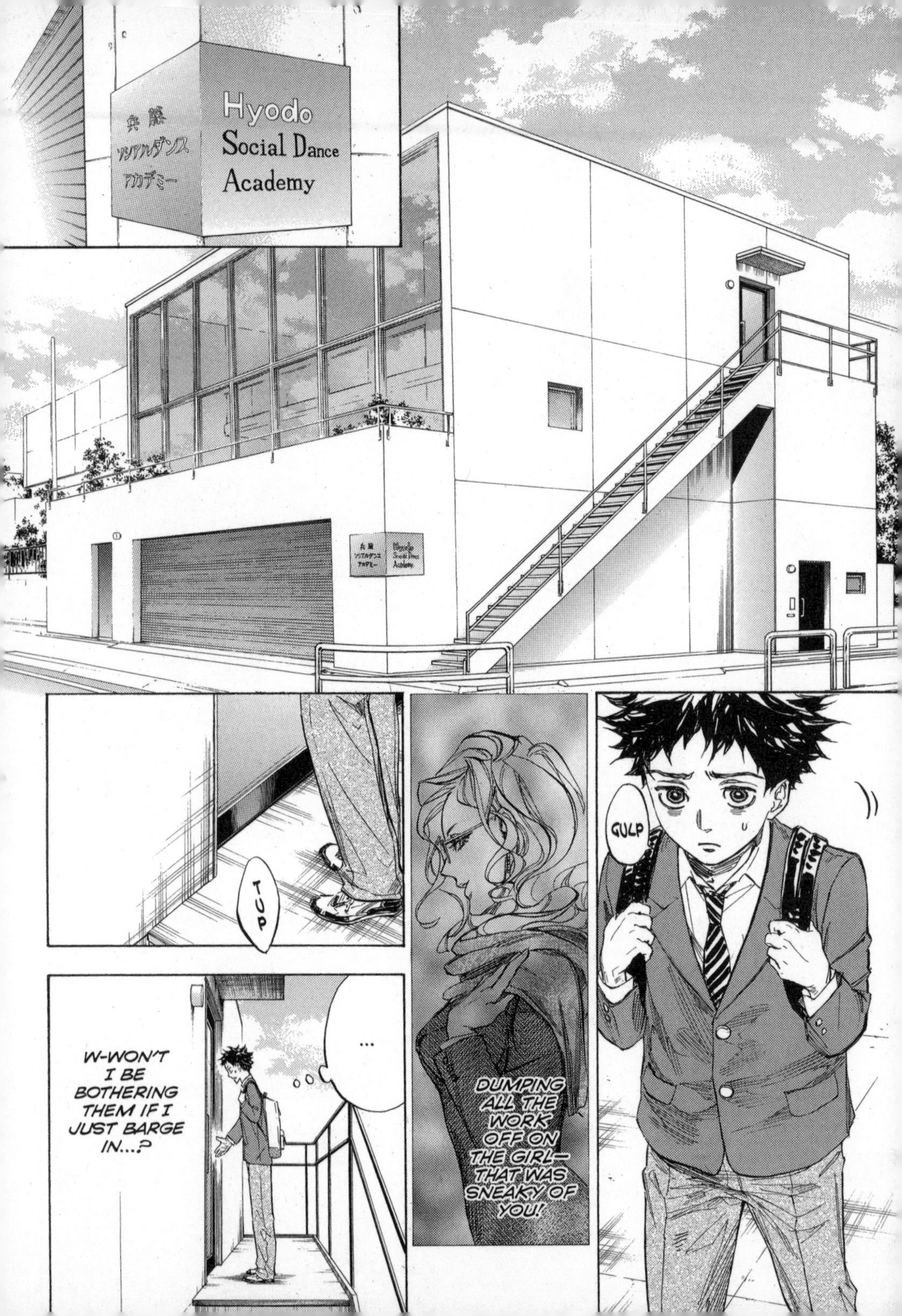
兵藤 ソシアルダンス アカデミー
Hyodo Social Dance Academy
GULP
DUMPING ALL THE WORK OFF ON THE GIRL— THAT WAS SNEAKY OF YOU!
TUP
...
W-WON'T I BE BOTHERING THEM IF I JUST BARGE IN...?

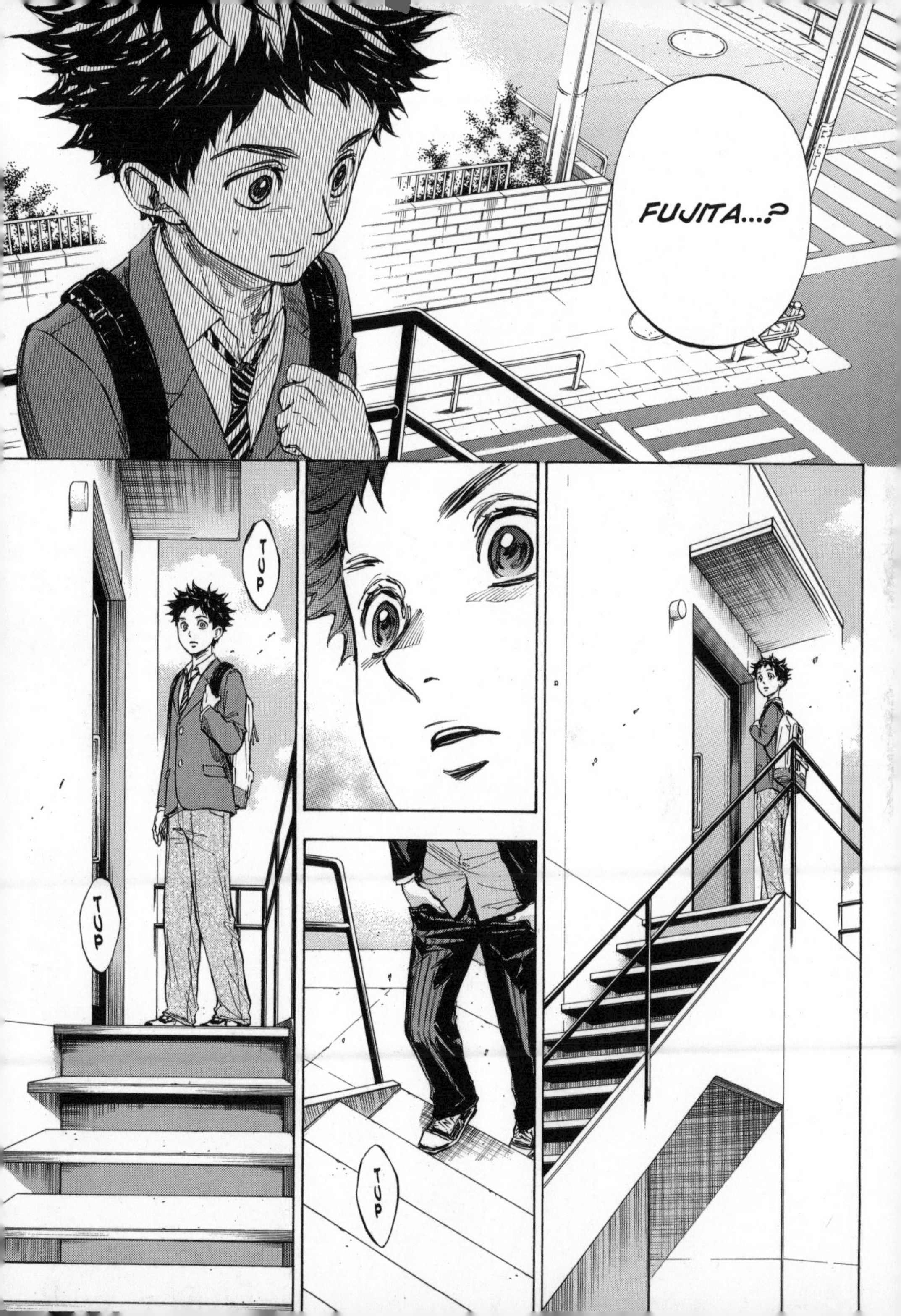
FUJITA...?
TUP
TUP
TUP

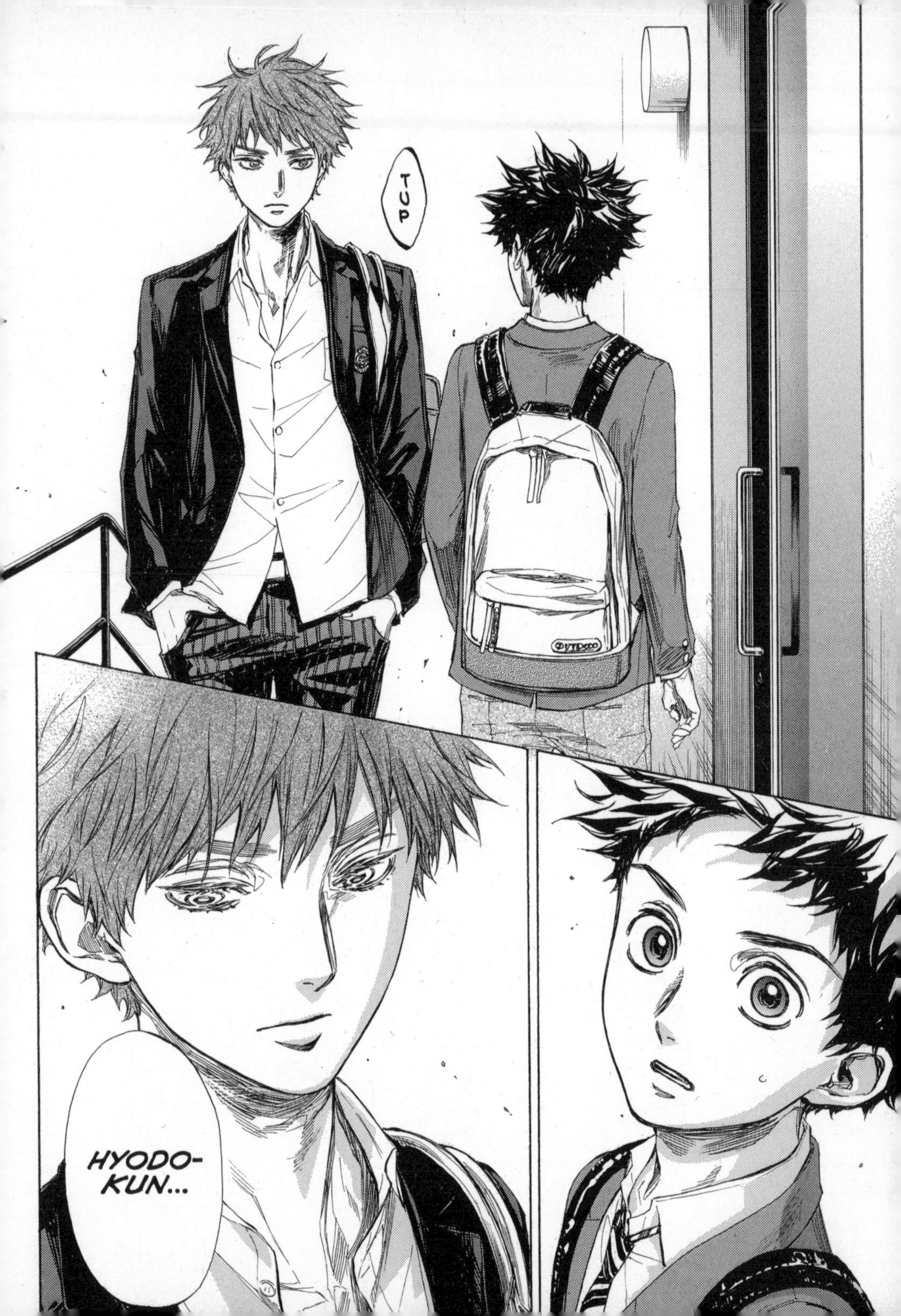
TUP
HYODO-KUN...

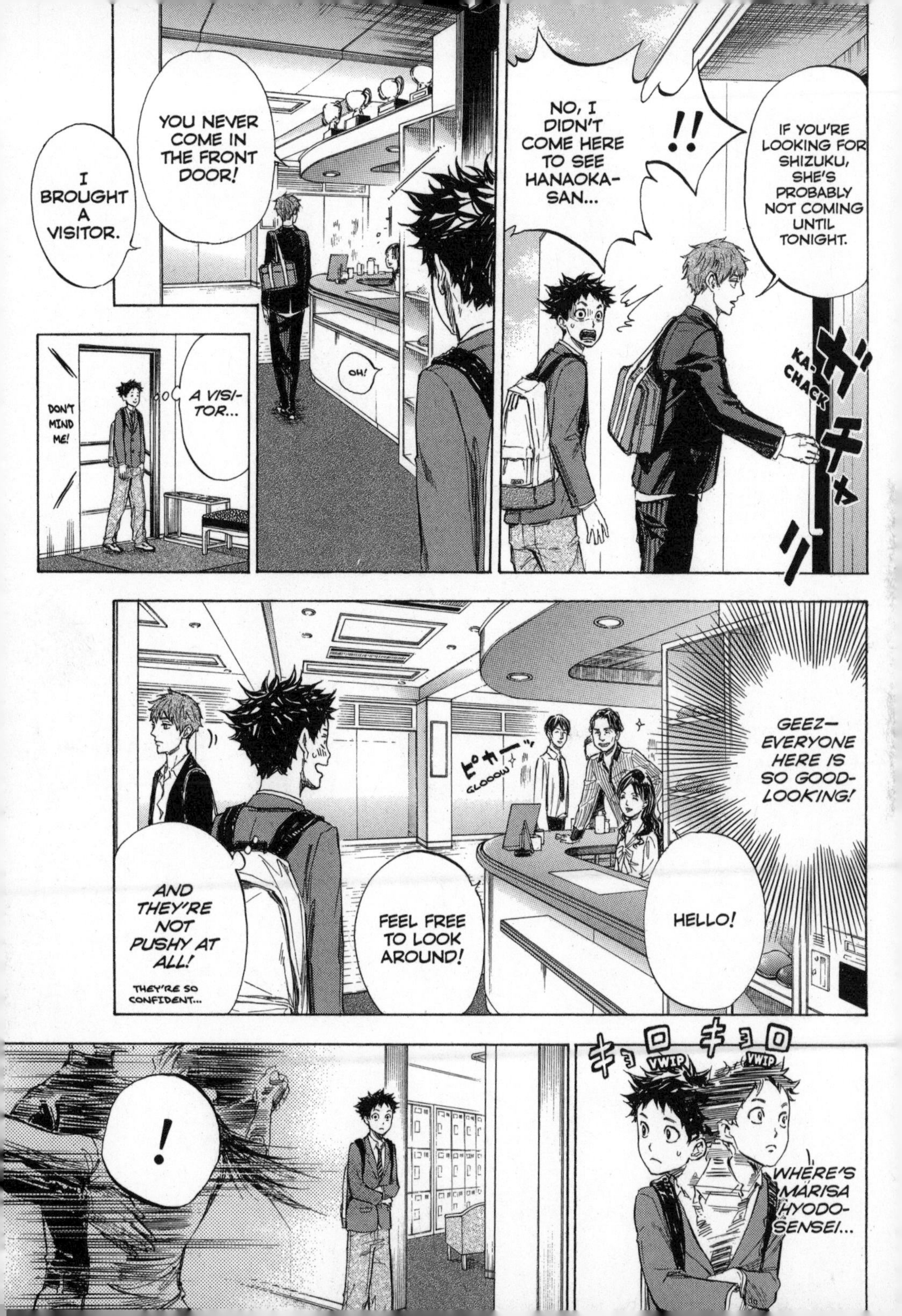
IF YOU'RE LOOKING FOR SHIZUKU, SHE'S PROBABLY NOT COMING UNTIL TONIGHT.
!!
NO, I DIDN'T COME HERE TO SEE HANAOKA-SAN...
ガチャリ
KA-CHACK
YOU NEVER COME IN THE FRONT DOOR!
I BROUGHT A VISITOR.
OH!
A VISI-TOR...
DON'T MIND ME!
GEEZ— EVERYONE HERE IS SO GOOD-LOOKING!
ピカーッ
GLOOOW
HELLO!
FEEL FREE TO LOOK AROUND!
AND THEY'RE NOT PUSHY AT ALL!
THEY'RE SO CONFIDENT...
キョロ キョロ
VWIP VWIP
WHERE'S MARISA HYODO-SENSEI...
!

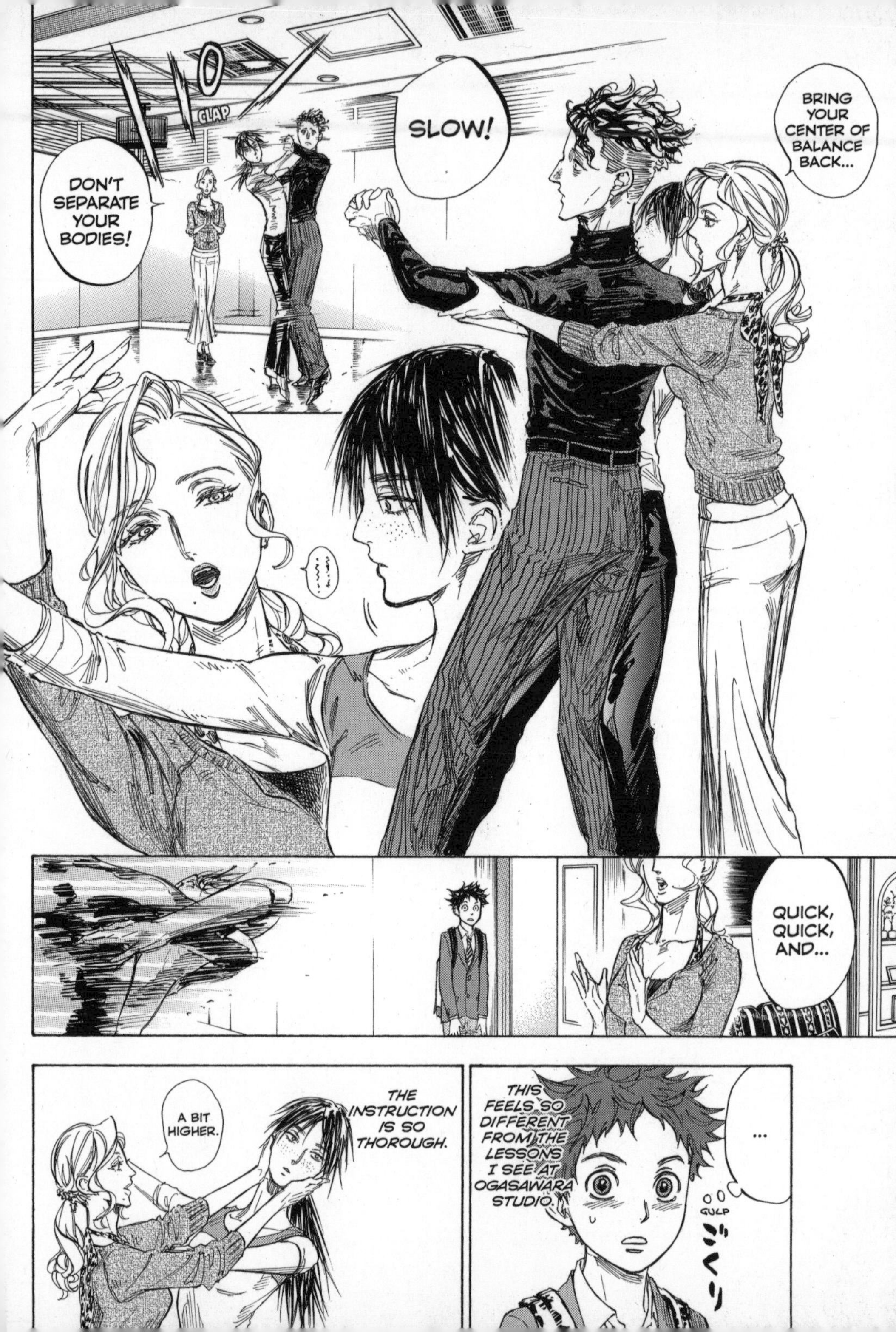
BRING YOUR CENTER OF BALANCE BACK...
SLOW!
CLAP
DON'T SEPARATE YOUR BODIES!
QUICK, QUICK, AND...
...
THIS FEELS SO DIFFERENT FROM THE LESSONS I SEE AT OGASAWARA STUDIO.
GULP
THE INSTRUCTION IS SO THOROUGH.
A BIT HIGHER.

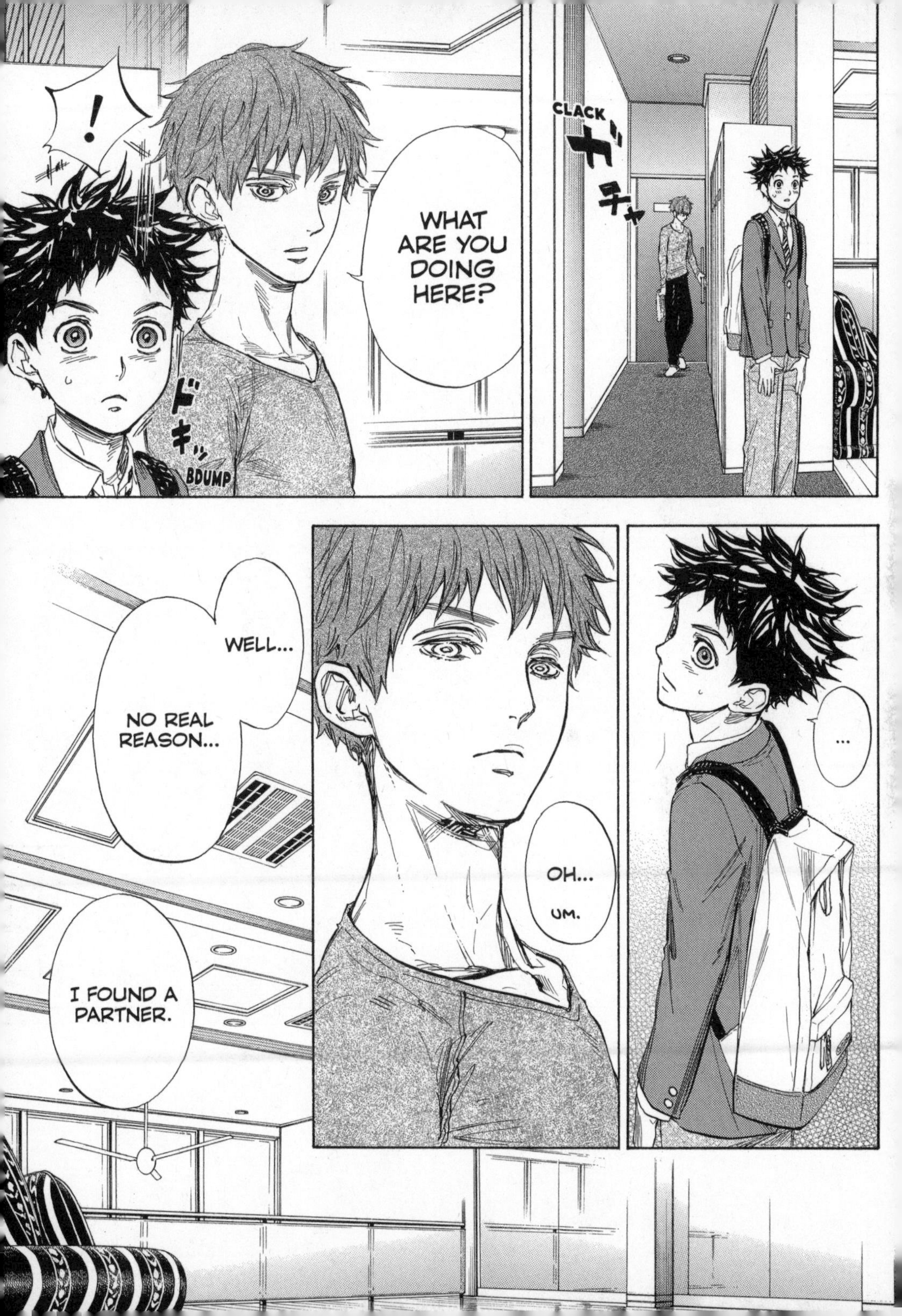
CLACK
ガチャ
WHAT ARE YOU DOING HERE?
!
ドキッ
BDUMP
...
OH...
UM.
WELL...
NO REAL REASON...
I FOUND A PARTNER.

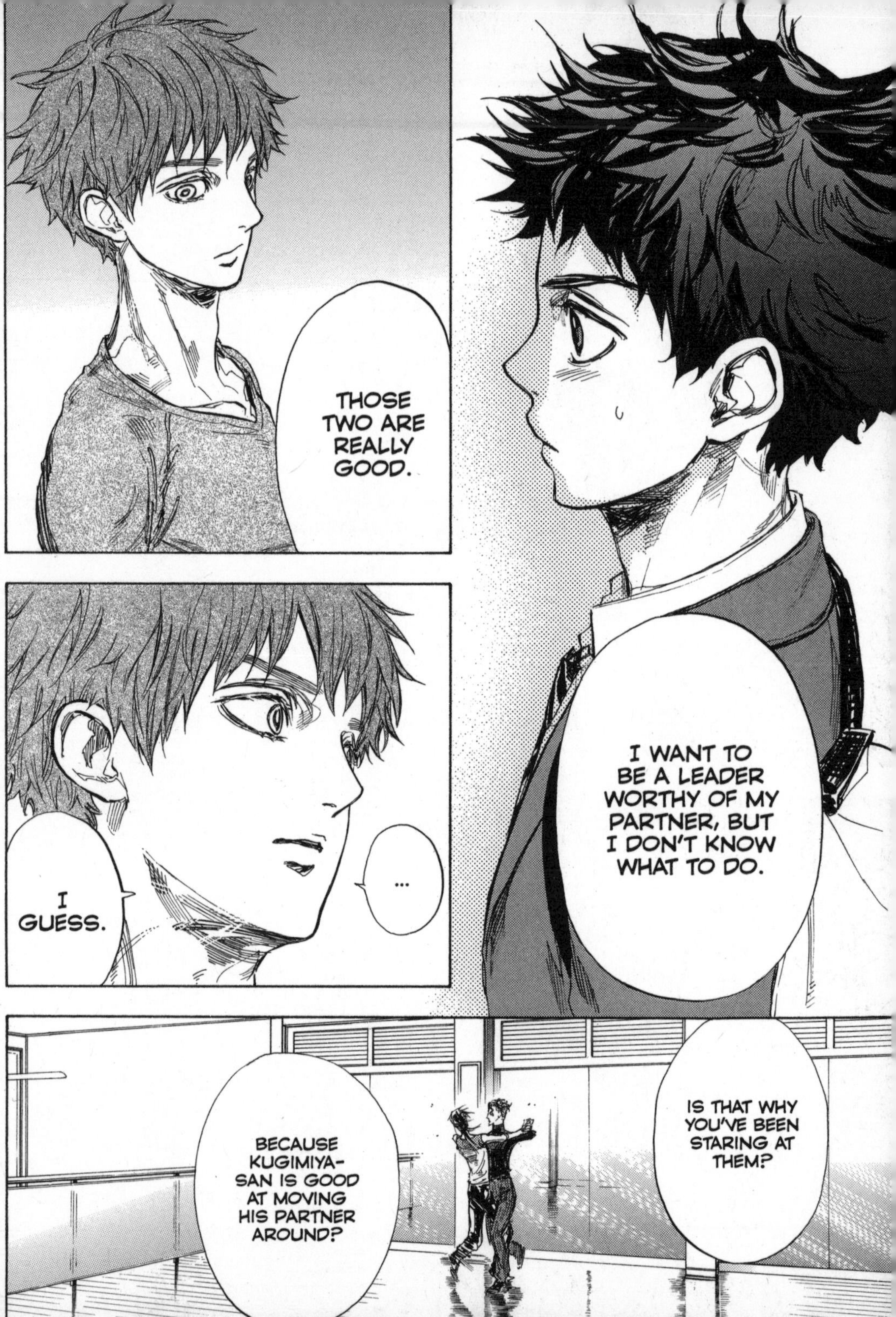
I WANT TO BE A LEADER WORTHY OF MY PARTNER, BUT I DON'T KNOW WHAT TO DO.
THOSE TWO ARE REALLY GOOD.
...
I GUESS.
IS THAT WHY YOU'VE BEEN STARING AT THEM?
BECAUSE KUGIMIYA-SAN IS GOOD AT MOVING HIS PARTNER AROUND?

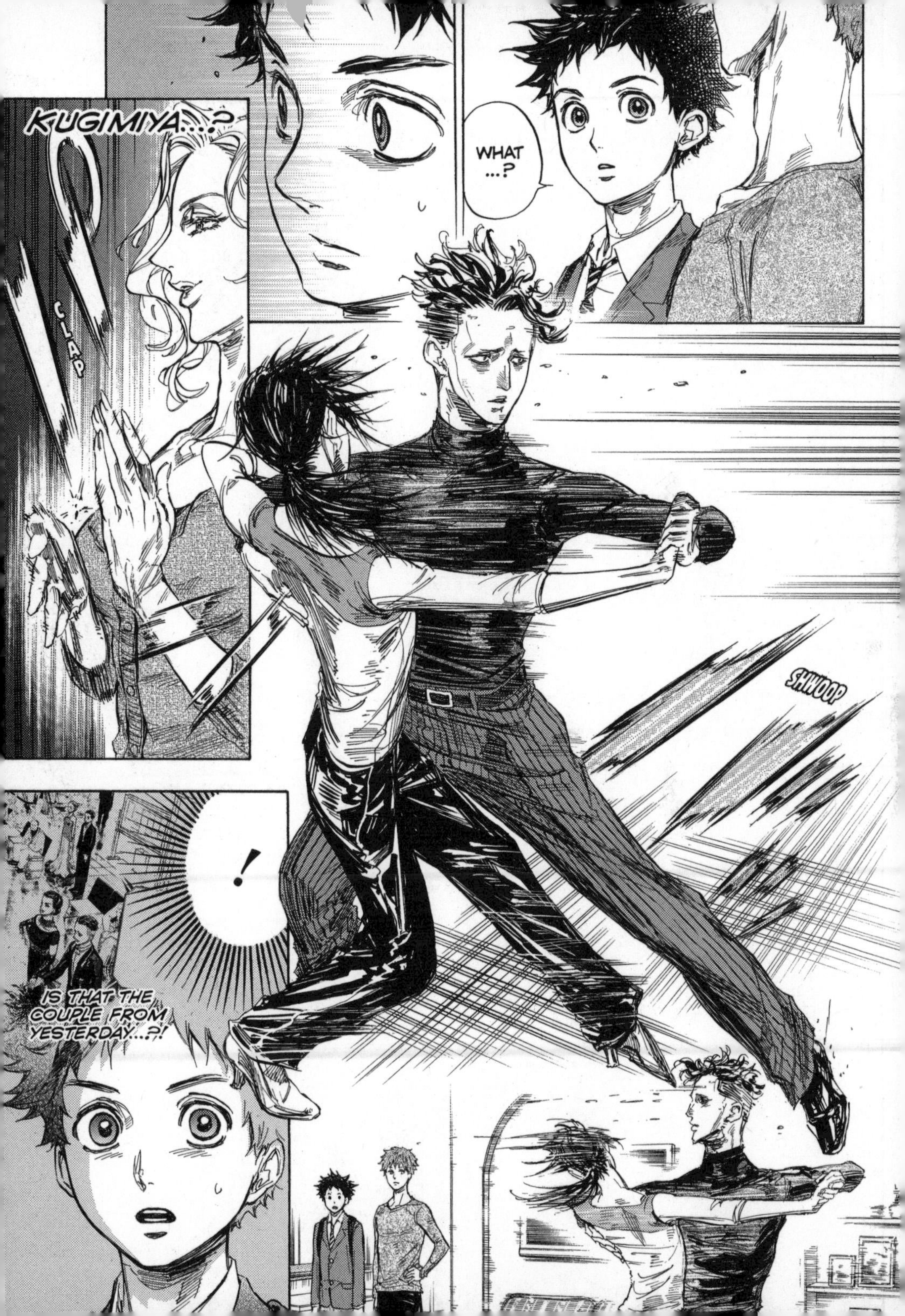
WHAT ...?
KUGIMIYA...?
CLAP
SHWOOP
!
IS THAT THE COUPLE FROM YESTERDAY...?!

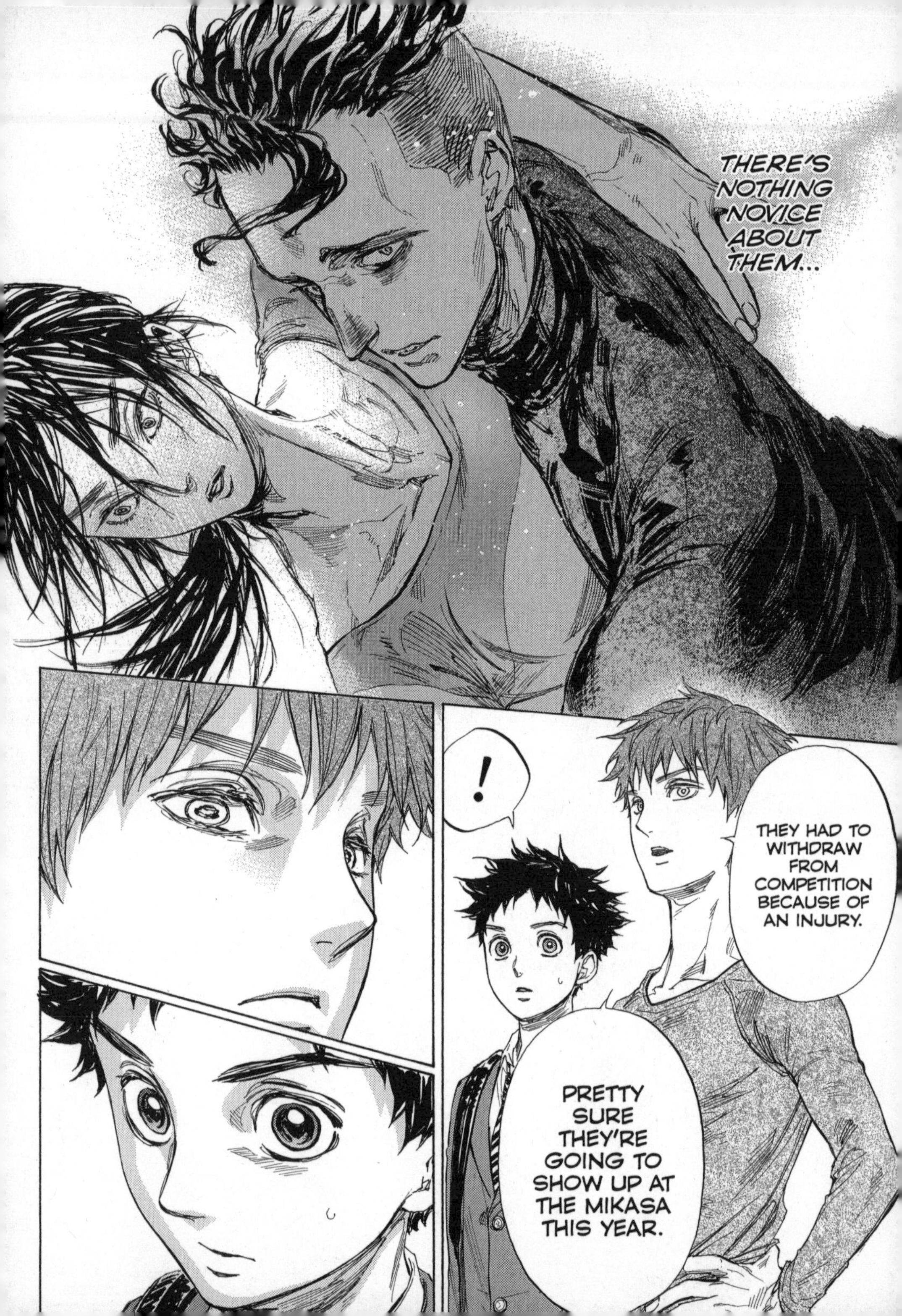
THERE'S NOTHING NOVICE ABOUT THEM...
!
THEY HAD TO WITHDRAW FROM COMPETITION BECAUSE OF AN INJURY.
PRETTY SURE THEY'RE GOING TO SHOW UP AT THE MIKASA THIS YEAR.

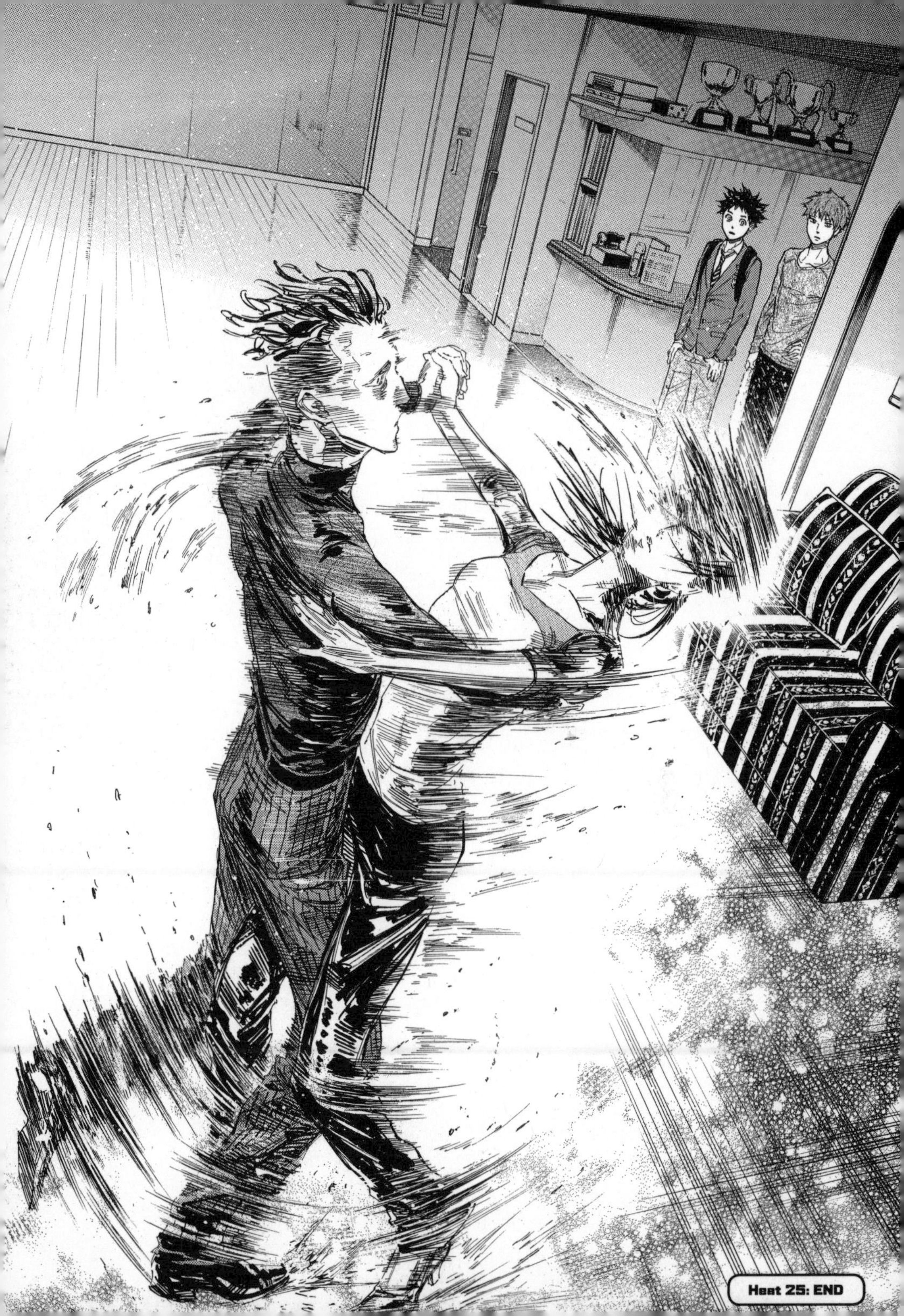
Heat 25: END

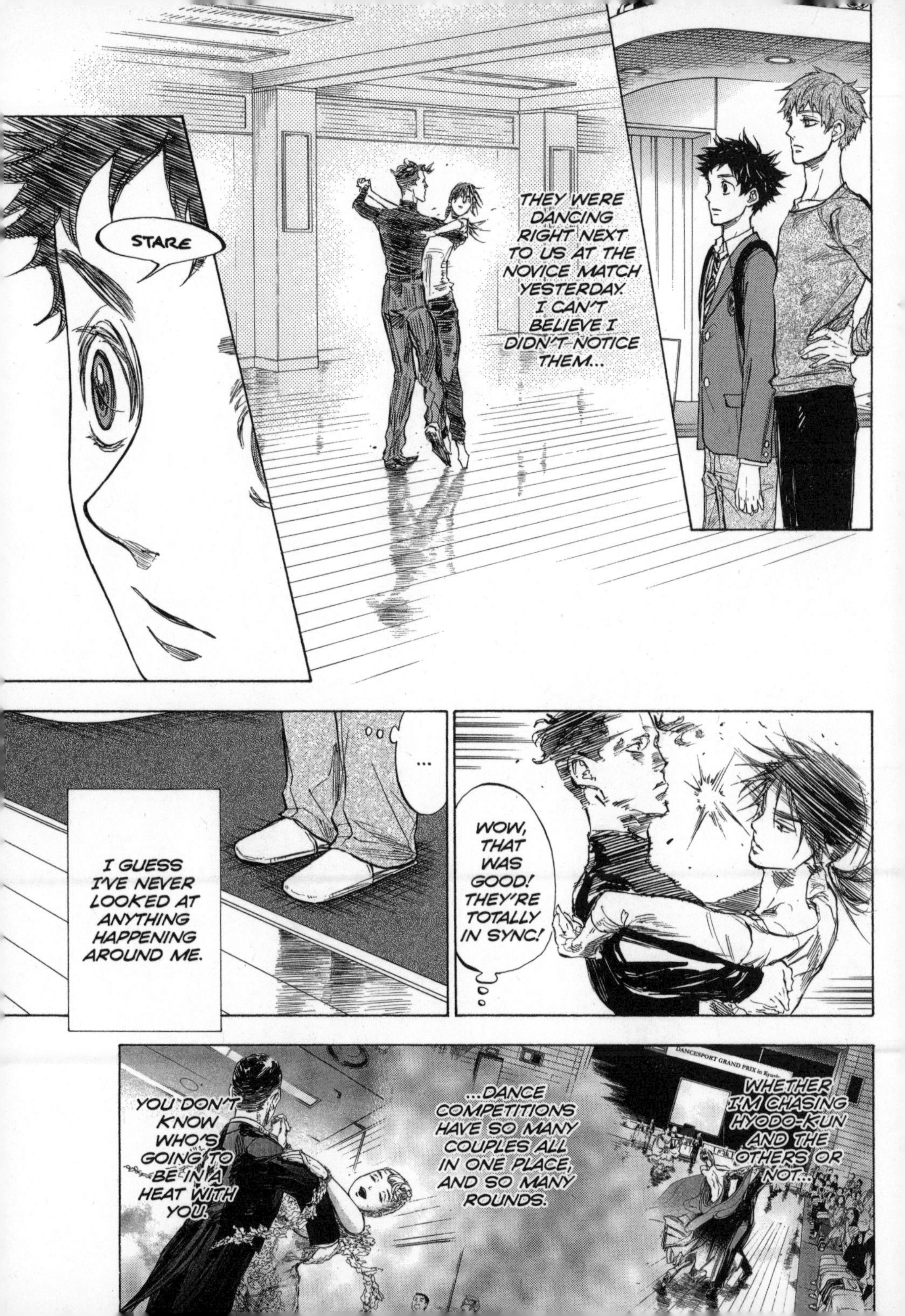
THEY WERE DANCING RIGHT NEXT TO US AT THE NOVICE MATCH YESTERDAY. I CAN'T BELIEVE I DIDN'T NOTICE THEM...
STARE
WOW, THAT WAS GOOD! THEY'RE TOTALLY IN SYNC!
...
I GUESS I'VE NEVER LOOKED AT ANYTHING HAPPENING AROUND ME.
WHETHER I'M CHASING HYODO-KUN AND THE OTHERS OR NOT...
...DANCE COMPETITIONS HAVE SO MANY COUPLES ALL IN ONE PLACE, AND SO MANY ROUNDS.
YOU DON'T KNOW WHO'S GOING TO BE IN A HEAT WITH YOU.

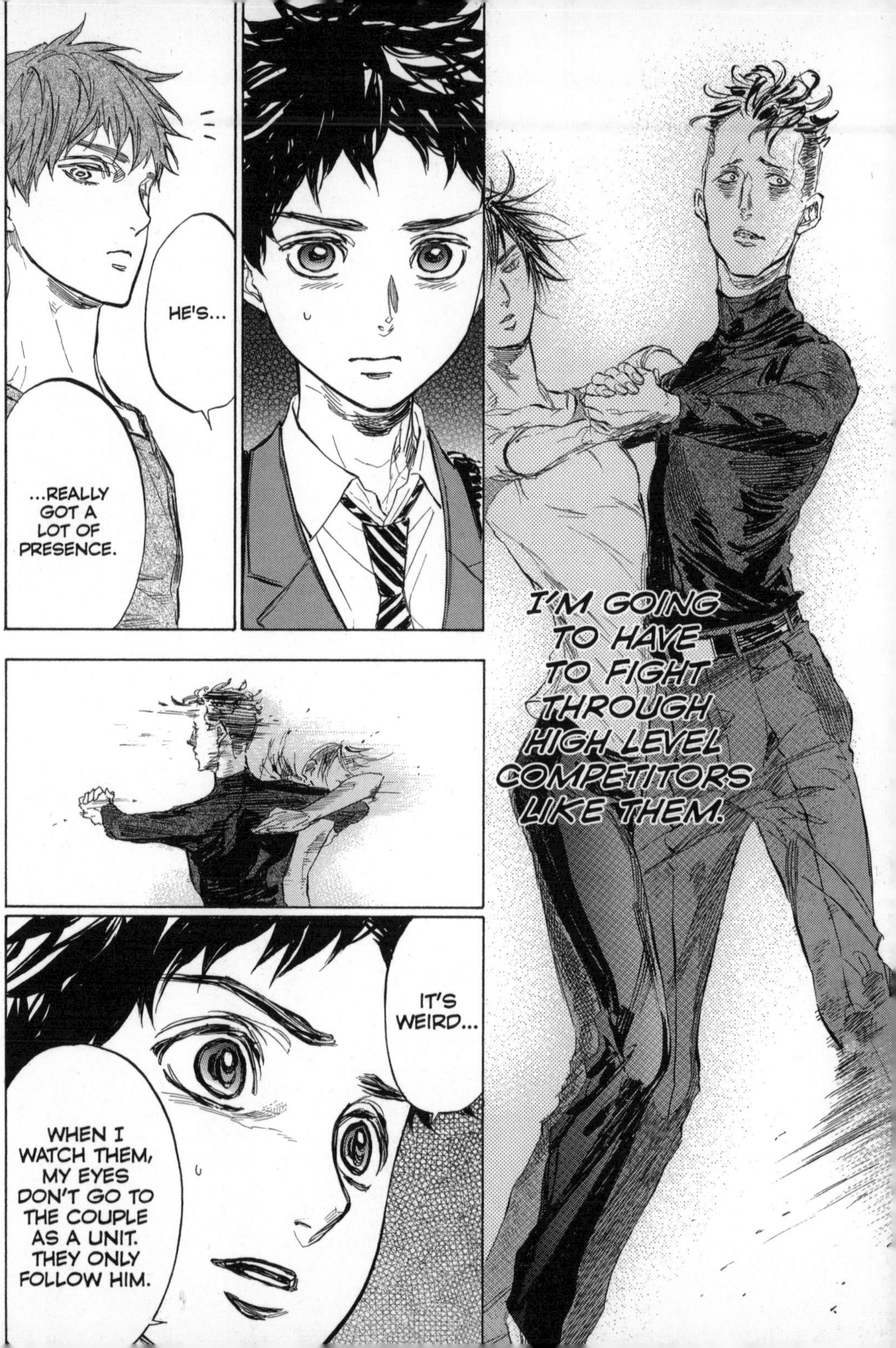
I'M GOING TO HAVE TO FIGHT THROUGH HIGH LEVEL COMPETITORS LIKE THEM.
HE'S...
...REALLY GOT A LOT OF PRESENCE.
IT'S WEIRD...
WHEN I WATCH THEM, MY EYES DON'T GO TO THE COUPLE AS A UNIT. THEY ONLY FOLLOW HIM.

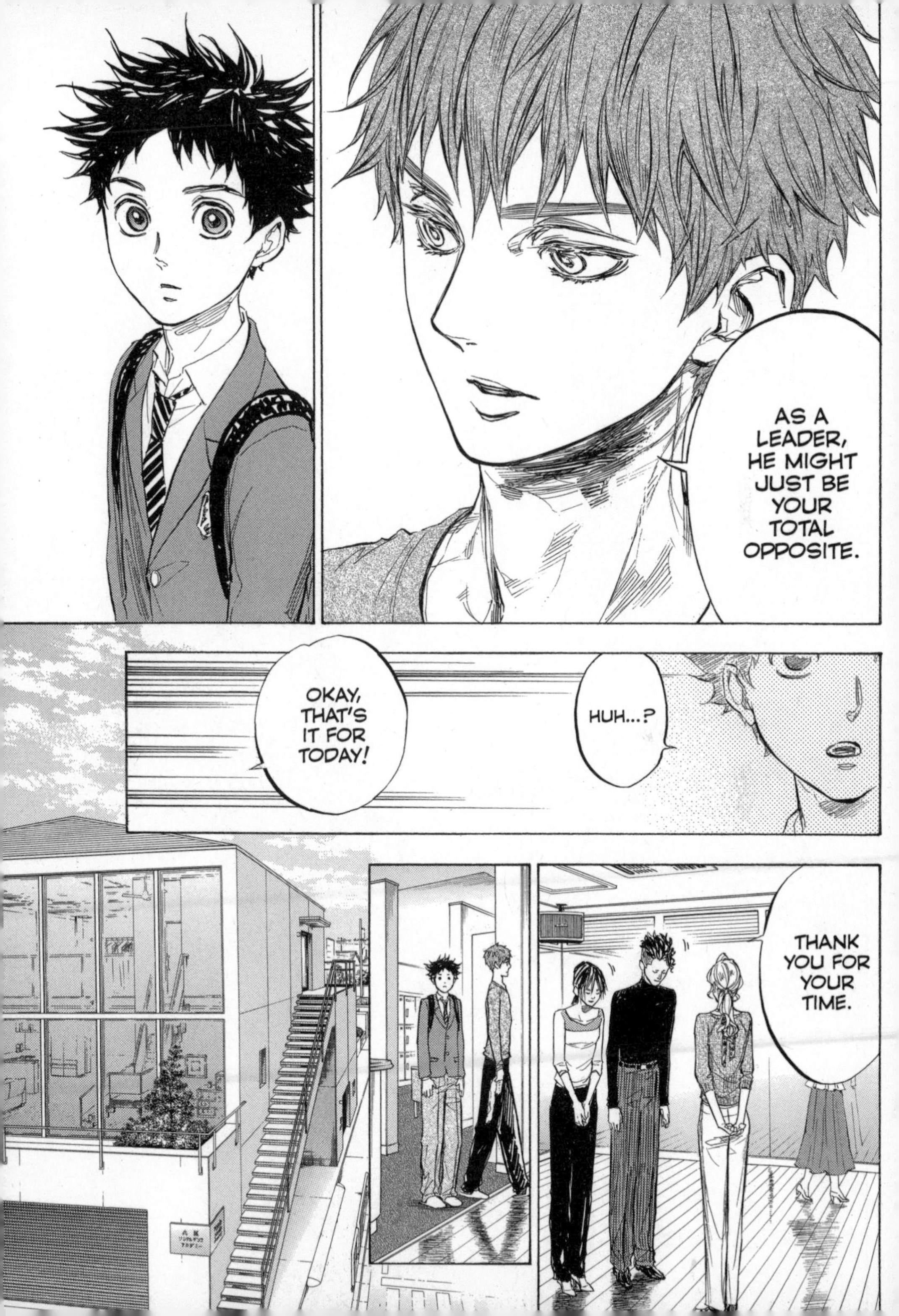
AS A LEADER, HE MIGHT JUST BE YOUR TOTAL OPPOSITE.
HUH...?
OKAY, THAT'S IT FOR TODAY!
THANK YOU FOR YOUR TIME.

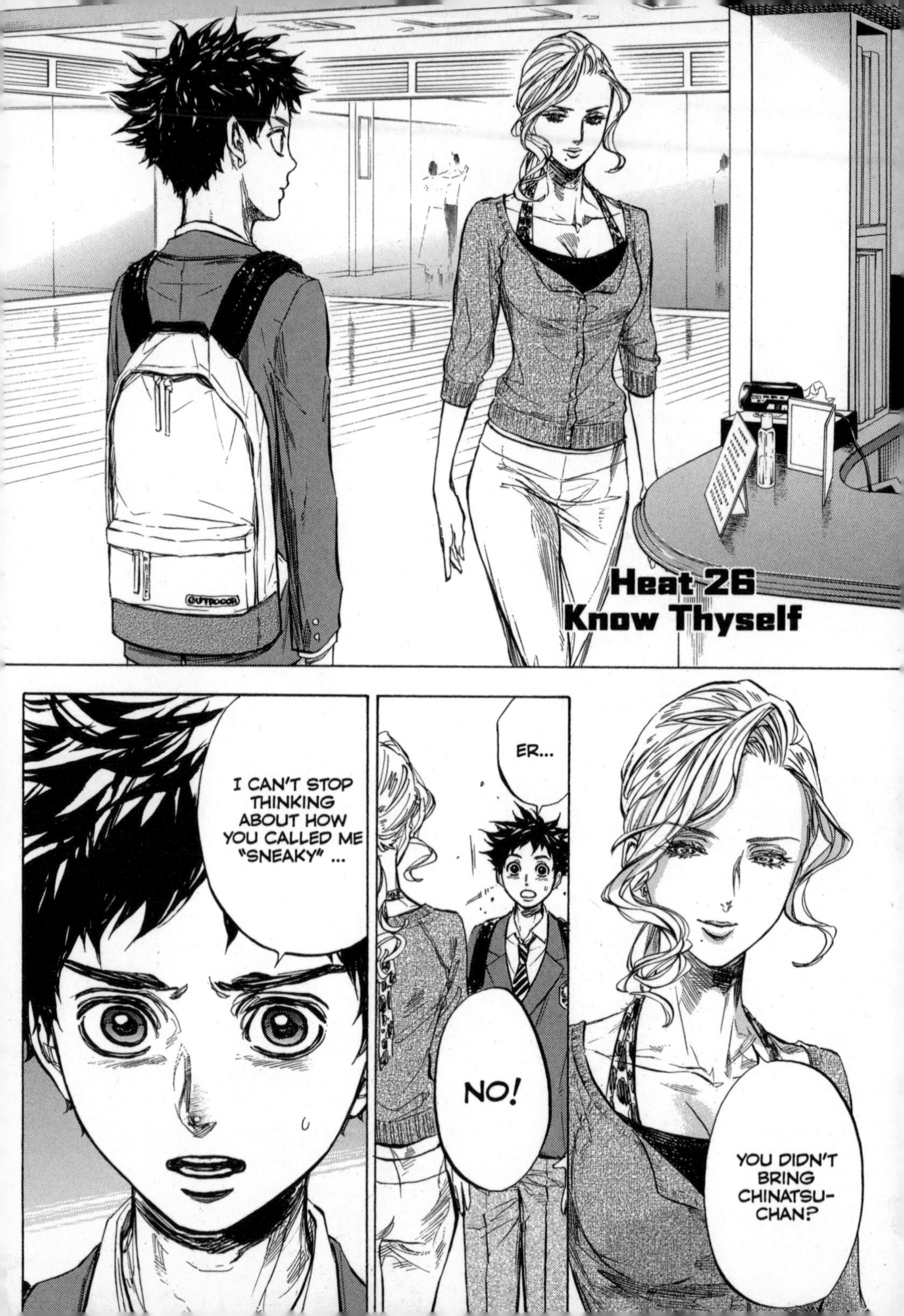
Heat 26
Know Thyself
YOU DIDN'T BRING CHINATSU-CHAN?
ER...
NO!
I CAN'T STOP THINKING ABOUT HOW YOU CALLED ME "SNEAKY" ...

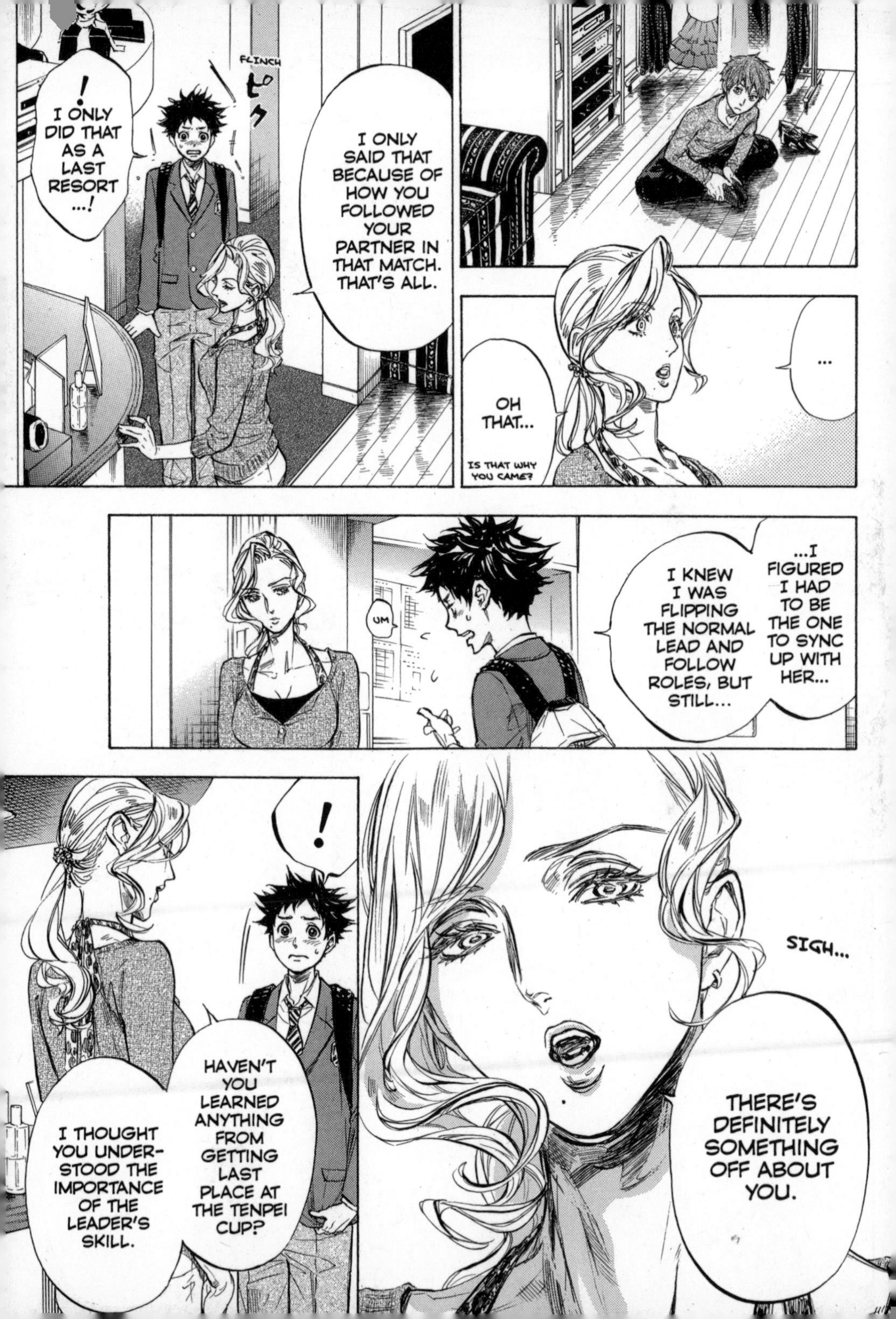
...
OH THAT...
IS THAT WHY YOU CAME?
I ONLY SAID THAT BECAUSE OF HOW YOU FOLLOWED YOUR PARTNER IN THAT MATCH. THAT'S ALL.
FLINCH
I ONLY DID THAT AS A LAST RESORT ...!
...I FIGURED I HAD TO BE THE ONE TO SYNC UP WITH HER...
I KNEW I WAS FLIPPING THE NORMAL LEAD AND FOLLOW ROLES, BUT STILL...
UM
SIGH...
THERE'S DEFINITELY SOMETHING OFF ABOUT YOU.
!
HAVEN'T YOU LEARNED ANYTHING FROM GETTING LAST PLACE AT THE TENPEI CUP?
I THOUGHT YOU UNDER-STOOD THE IMPORTANCE OF THE LEADER'S SKILL.

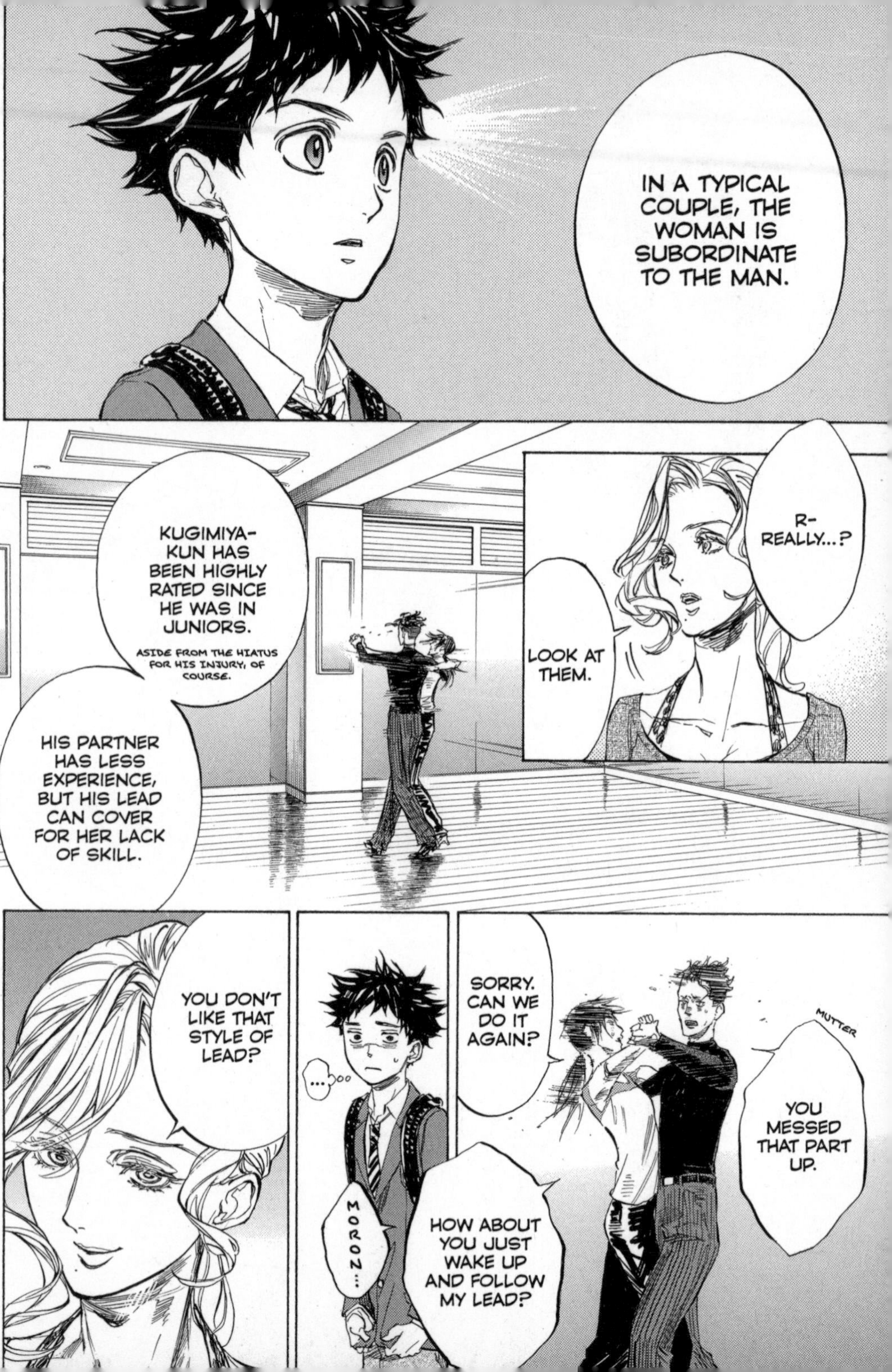
IN A TYPICAL COUPLE, THE WOMAN IS SUBORDINATE TO THE MAN.
R-REALLY...?
LOOK AT THEM.
KUGIMIYA-KUN HAS BEEN HIGHLY RATED SINCE HE WAS IN JUNIORS.
ASIDE FROM THE HIATUS FOR HIS INJURY, OF COURSE.
HIS PARTNER HAS LESS EXPERIENCE, BUT HIS LEAD CAN COVER FOR HER LACK OF SKILL.
MUTTER
YOU MESSED THAT PART UP.
SORRY. CAN WE DO IT AGAIN?
HOW ABOUT YOU JUST WAKE UP AND FOLLOW MY LEAD?
...
MORON...
YOU DON'T LIKE THAT STYLE OF LEAD?

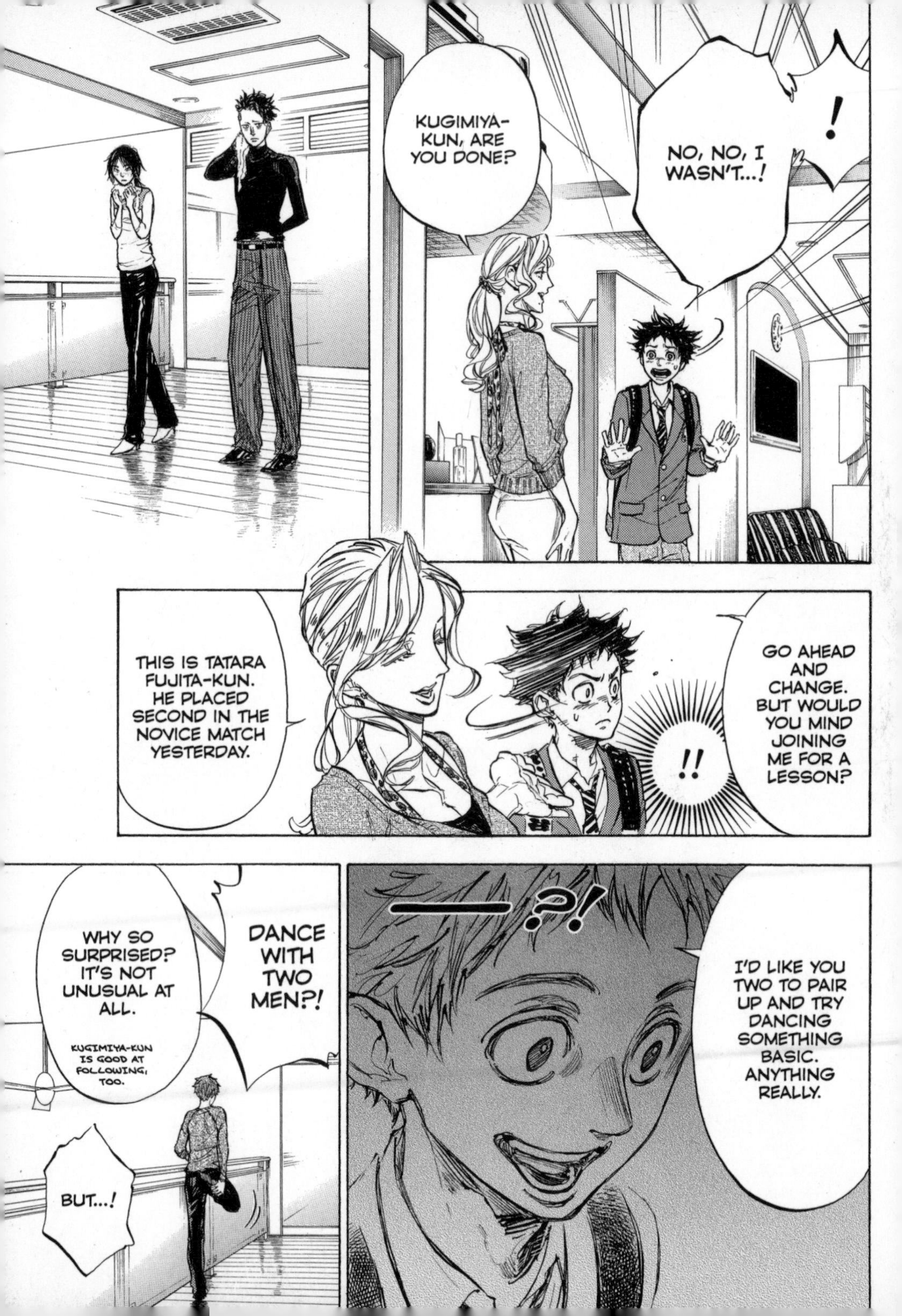
!
NO, NO, I WASN'T...!
KUGIMIYA-KUN, ARE YOU DONE?
GO AHEAD AND CHANGE. BUT WOULD YOU MIND JOINING ME FOR A LESSON?
!!
THIS IS TATARA FUJITA-KUN. HE PLACED SECOND IN THE NOVICE MATCH YESTERDAY.
——?!
I'D LIKE YOU TWO TO PAIR UP AND TRY DANCING SOMETHING BASIC. ANYTHING REALLY.
DANCE WITH TWO MEN?!
WHY SO SURPRISED? IT'S NOT UNUSUAL AT ALL.
KUGIMIYA-KUN IS GOOD AT FOLLOWING, TOO.
BUT...!

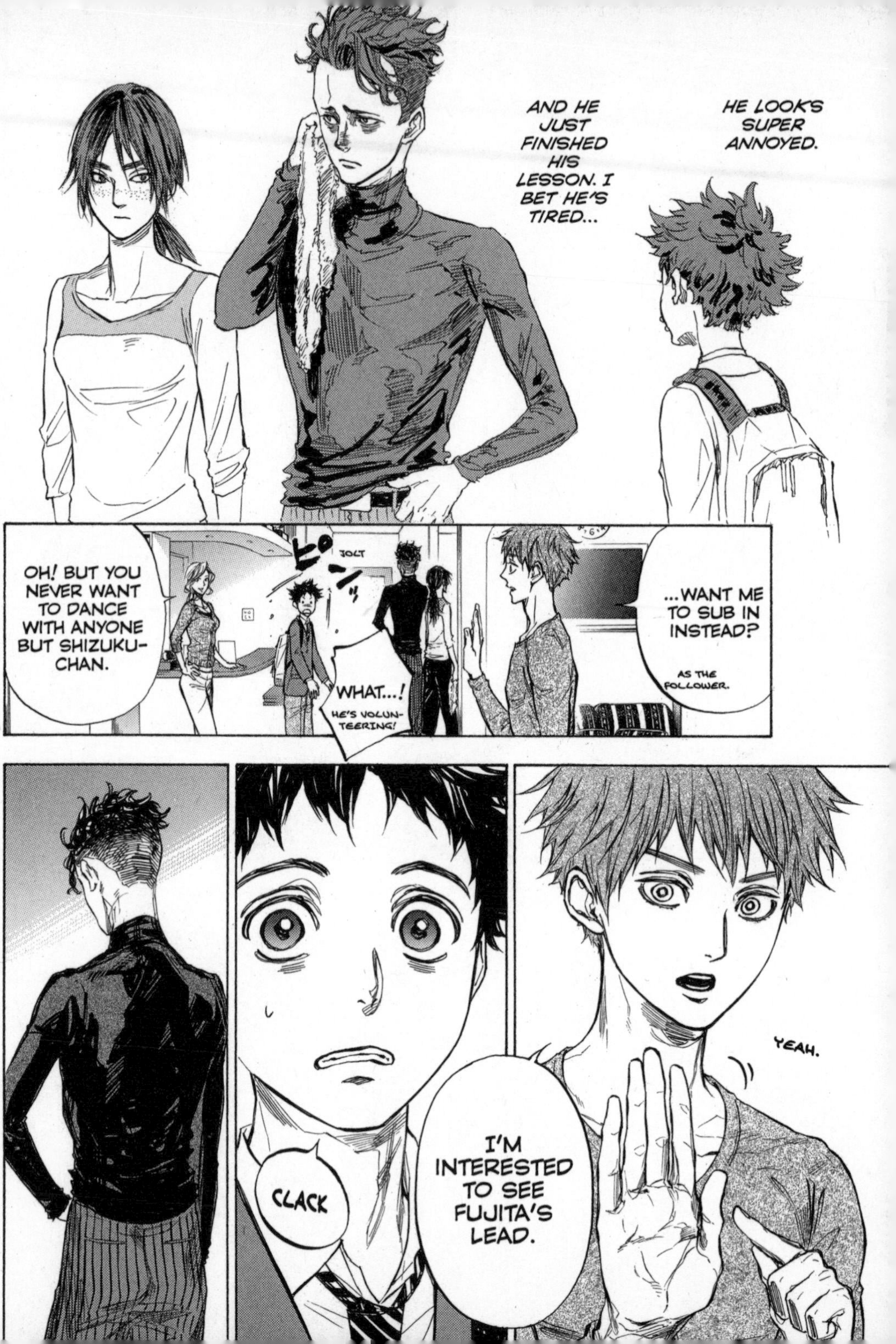
HE LOOKS SUPER ANNOYED.
AND HE JUST FINISHED HIS LESSON. I BET HE'S TIRED...
...WANT ME TO SUB IN INSTEAD?
AS THE FOLLOWER.
JOLT
WHAT...!
HE'S VOLUNTEERING!
OH! BUT YOU NEVER WANT TO DANCE WITH ANYONE BUT SHIZUKU-CHAN.
YEAH.
I'M INTERESTED TO SEE FUJITA'S LEAD.
CLACK

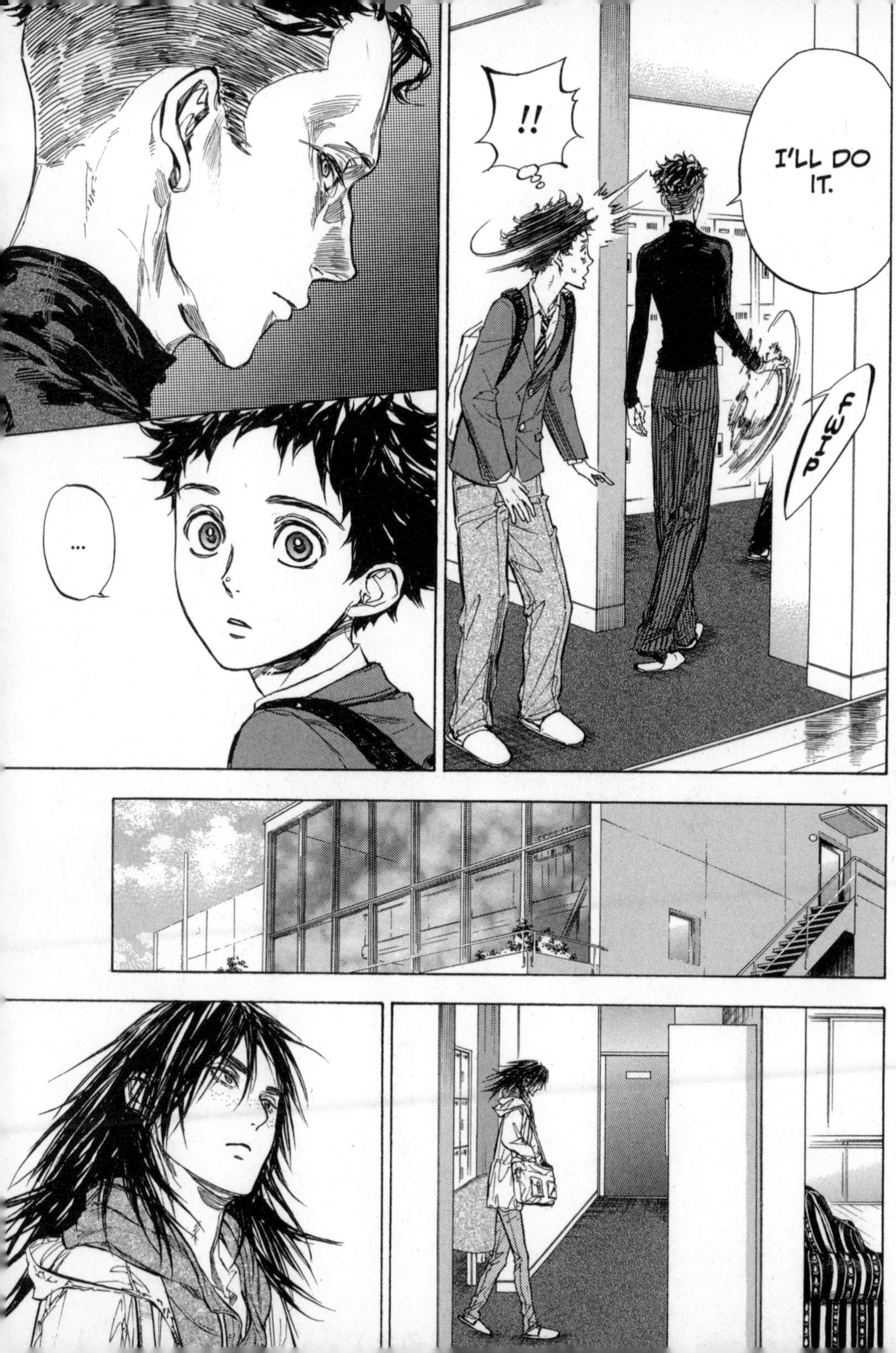
I'LL DO IT.
!!
FWIP
...

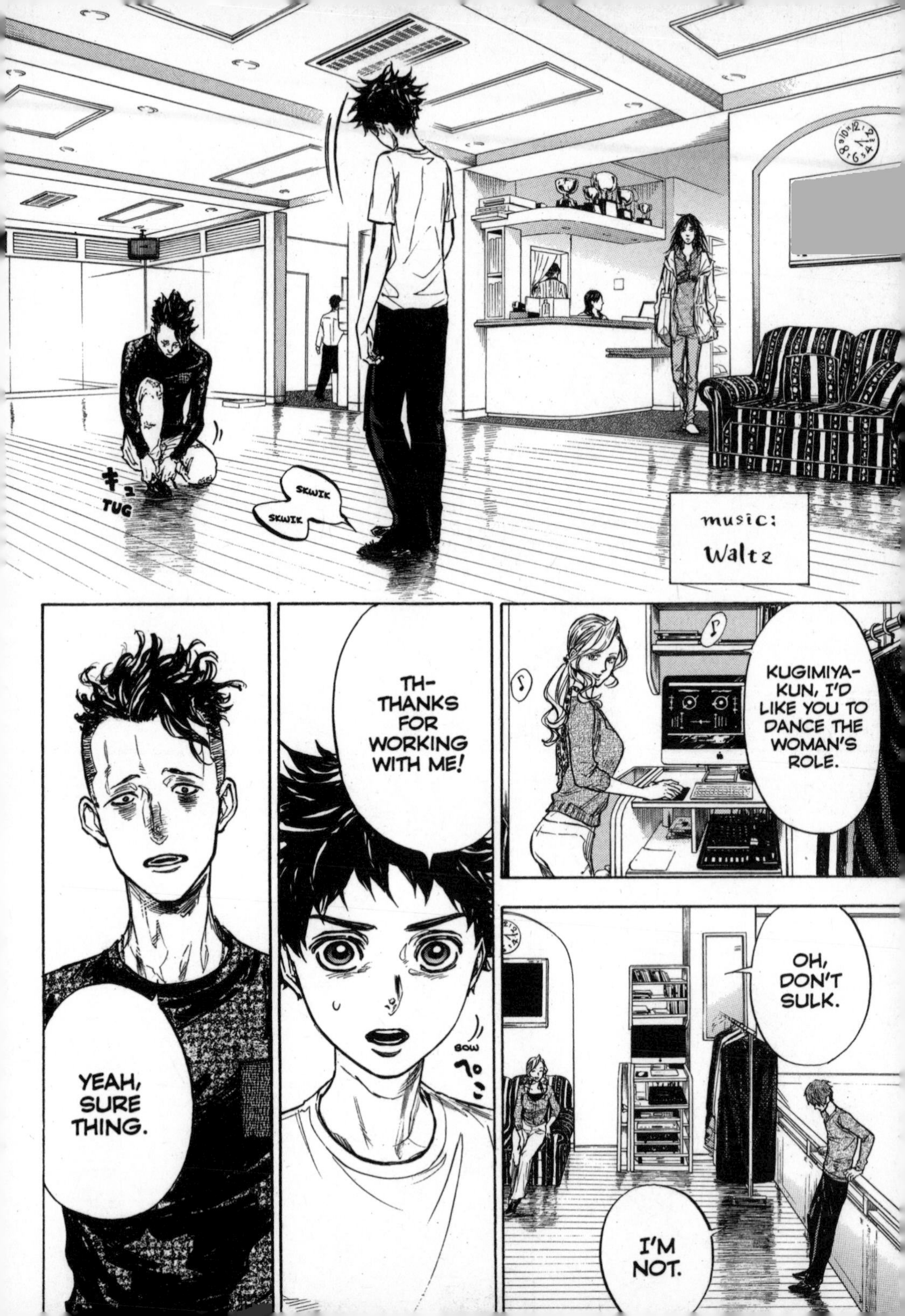
music:
Waltz
SKWIK
SKWIK
TUG
KUGIMIYA-KUN, I'D LIKE YOU TO DANCE THE WOMAN'S ROLE.
OH, DON'T SULK.
I'M NOT.
TH-THANKS FOR WORKING WITH ME!
BOW
YEAH, SURE THING.

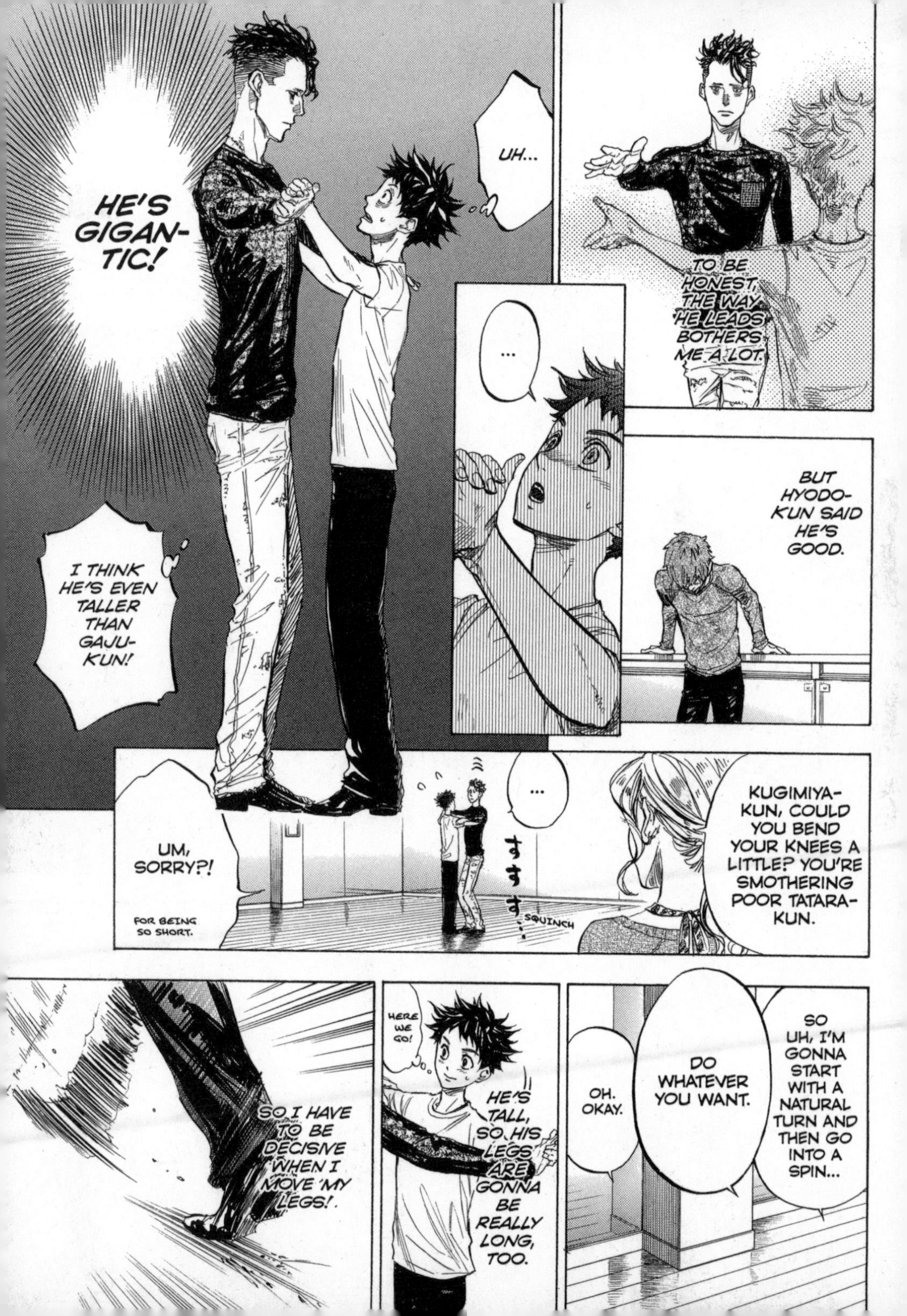
TO BE HONEST, THE WAY HE LEADS BOTHERS ME A LOT.
BUT HYODO-KUN SAID HE'S GOOD.
...
UH...
HE'S GIGANTIC!
I THINK HE'S EVEN TALLER THAN GAJU-KUN!
KUGIMIYA-KUN, COULD YOU BEND YOUR KNEES A LITTLE? YOU'RE SMOTHERING POOR TATARA-KUN.
...
すすす
SQUINCH
UM, SORRY?!
FOR BEING SO SHORT.
SO UH, I'M GONNA START WITH A NATURAL TURN AND THEN GO INTO A SPIN...
DO WHATEVER YOU WANT.
OH. OKAY.
HERE WE GO!
HE'S TALL, SO HIS LEGS ARE GONNA BE REALLY LONG, TOO.
SO I HAVE TO BE DECISIVE WHEN I MOVE MY LEGS!

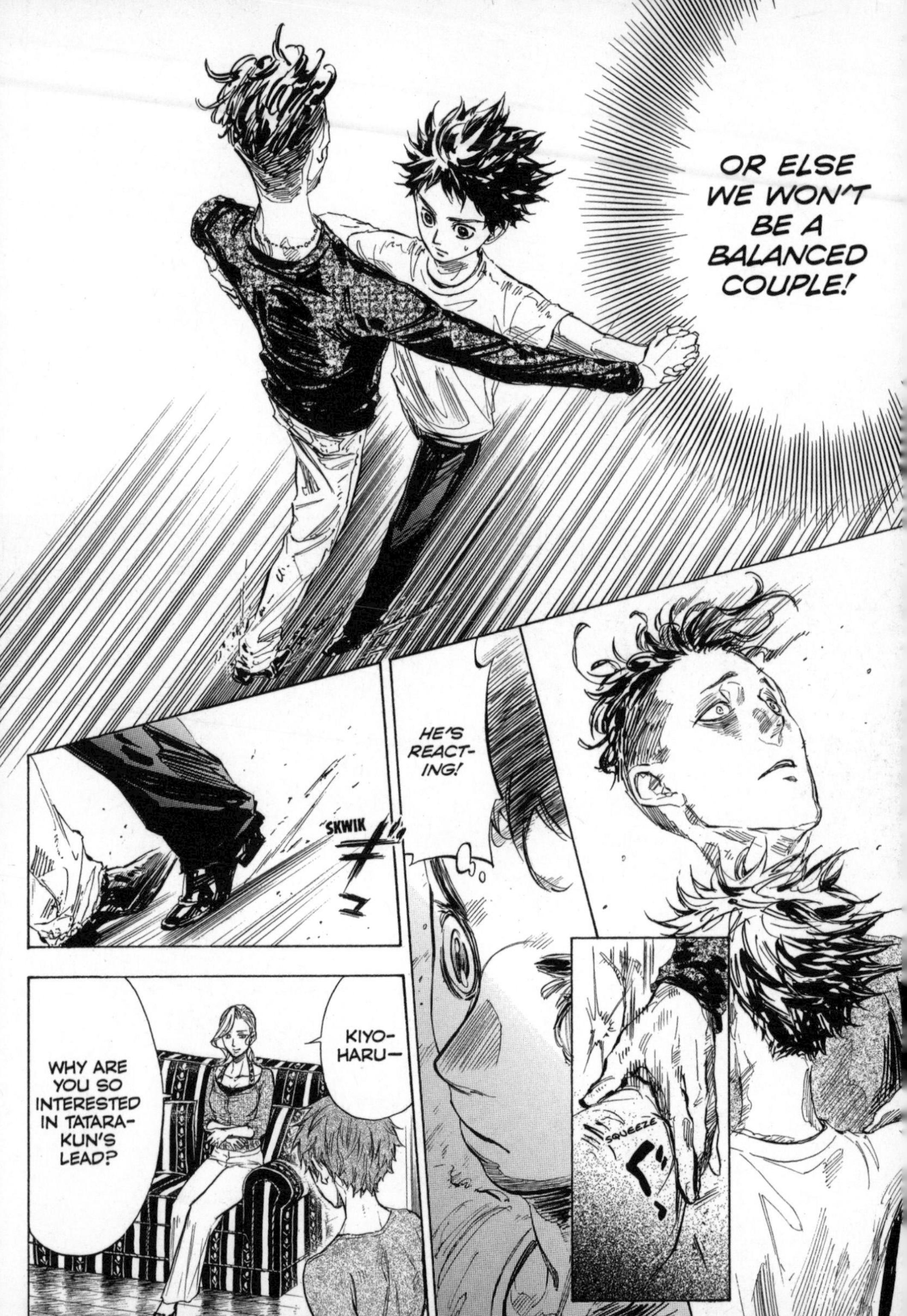
OR ELSE WE WON'T BE A BALANCED COUPLE!
HE'S REACT-ING!
SKWIK
SQUEEZE
KIYO-HARU—
WHY ARE YOU SO INTERESTED IN TATARA-KUN'S LEAD?

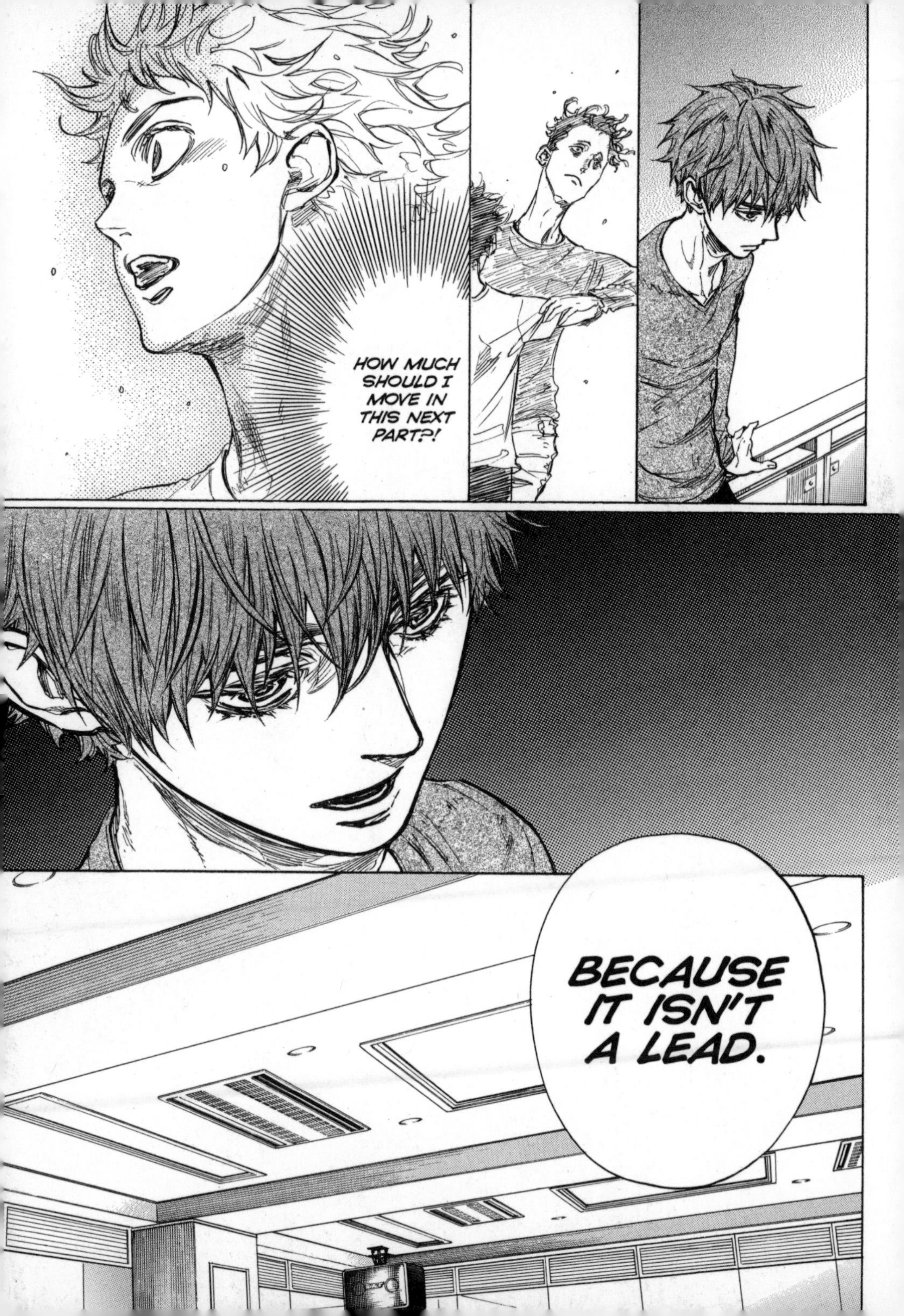
HOW MUCH SHOULD I MOVE IN THIS NEXT PART?!
BECAUSE IT ISN'T A LEAD.

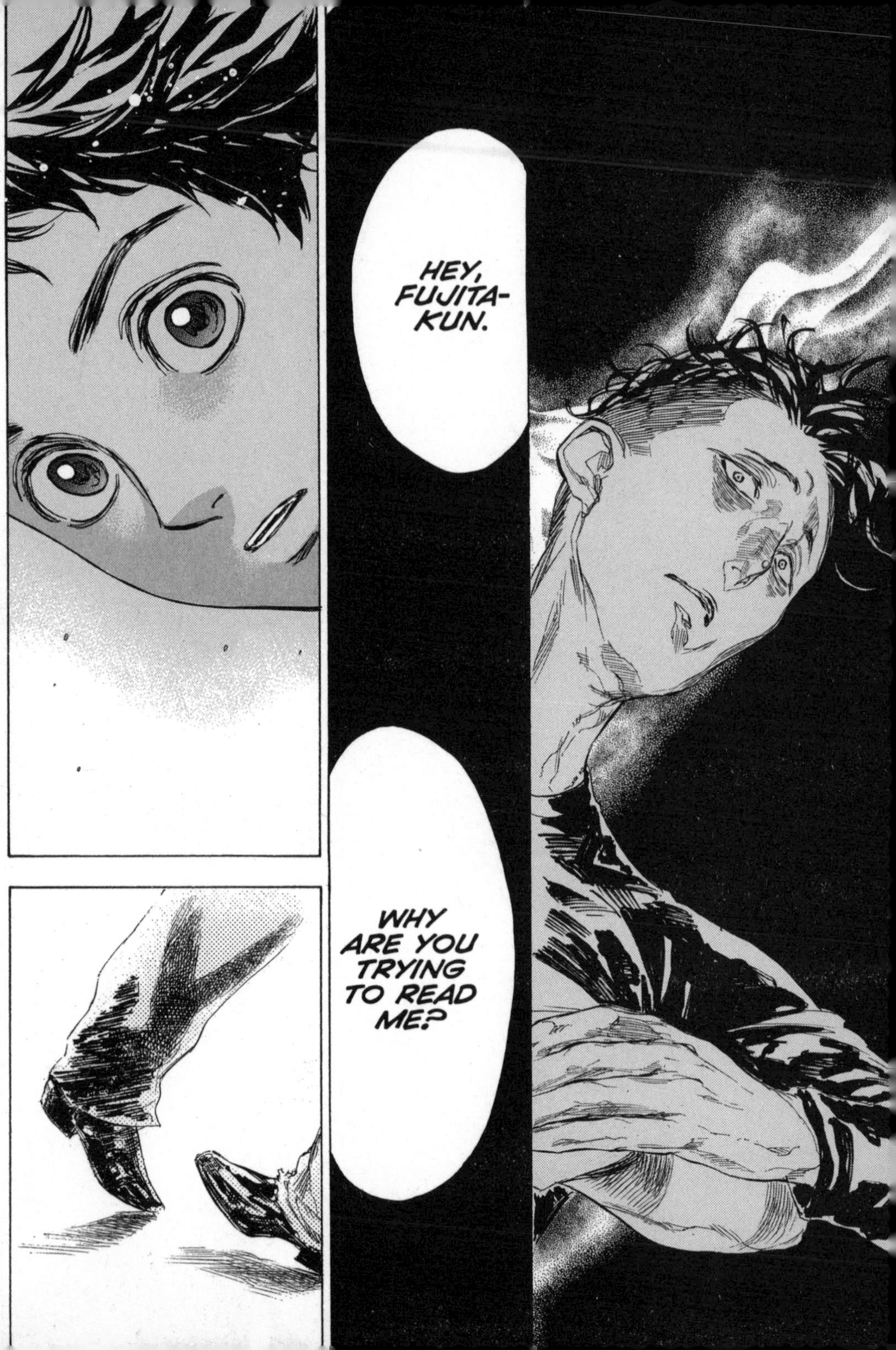
HEY, FUJITA-KUN.
WHY ARE YOU TRYING TO READ ME?

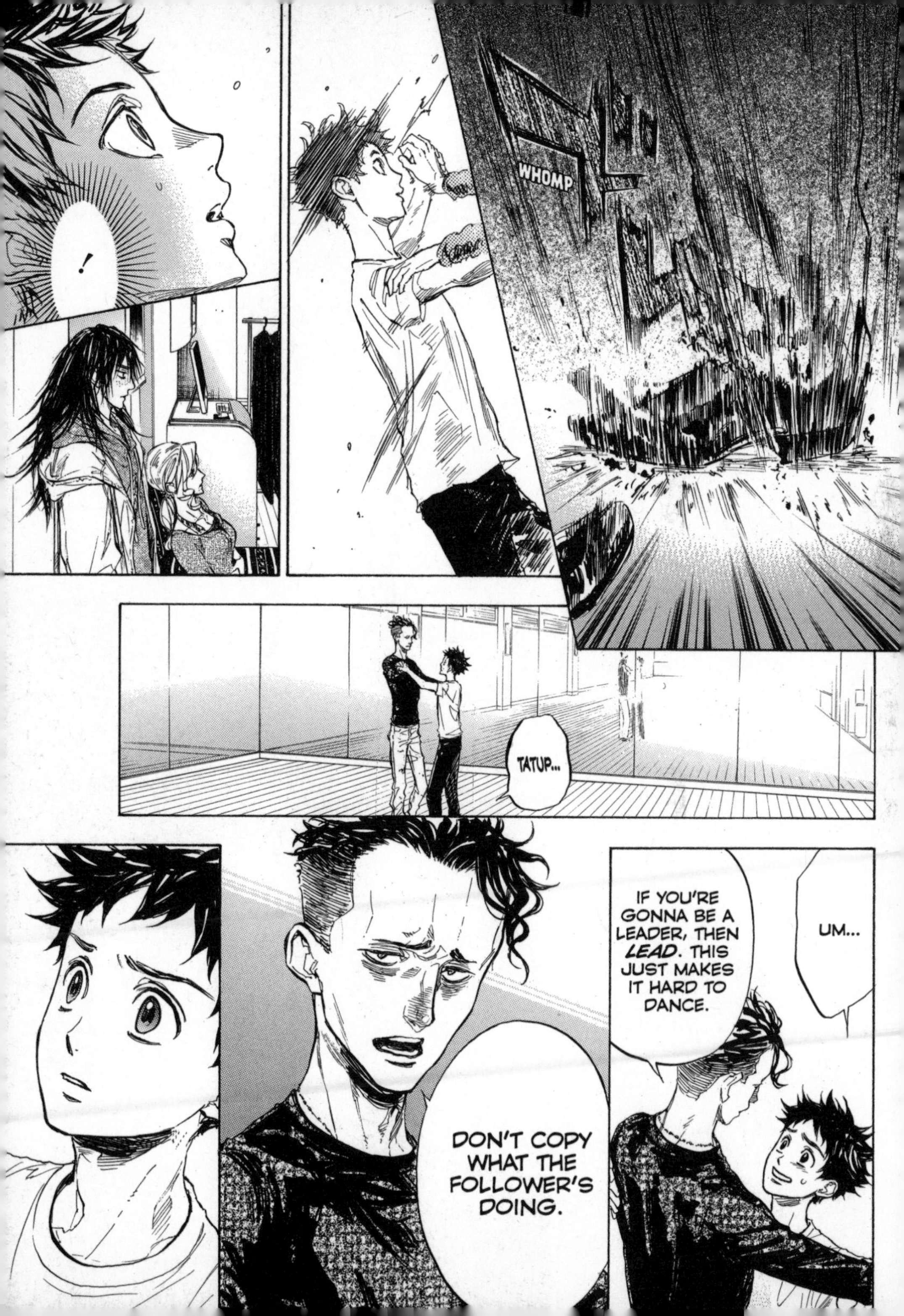
WHOMP
!
TATUP...
UM...
IF YOU'RE GONNA BE A LEADER, THEN LEAD. THIS JUST MAKES IT HARD TO DANCE.
DON'T COPY WHAT THE FOLLOWER'S DOING.

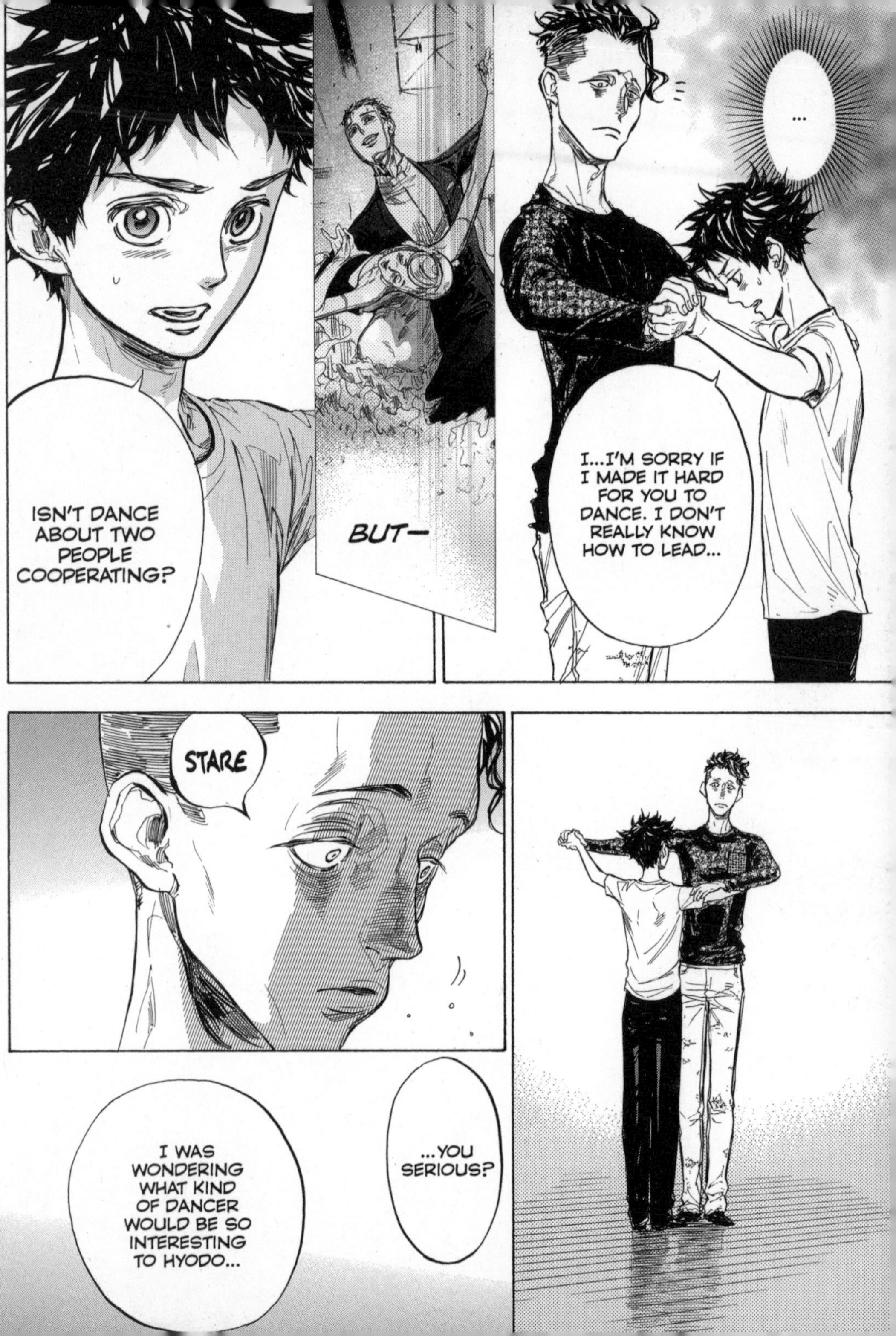
...
I...I'M SORRY IF I MADE IT HARD FOR YOU TO DANCE. I DON'T REALLY KNOW HOW TO LEAD...
BUT—
ISN'T DANCE ABOUT TWO PEOPLE COOPERATING?
STARE
...YOU SERIOUS?
I WAS WONDERING WHAT KIND OF DANCER WOULD BE SO INTERESTING TO HYODO...

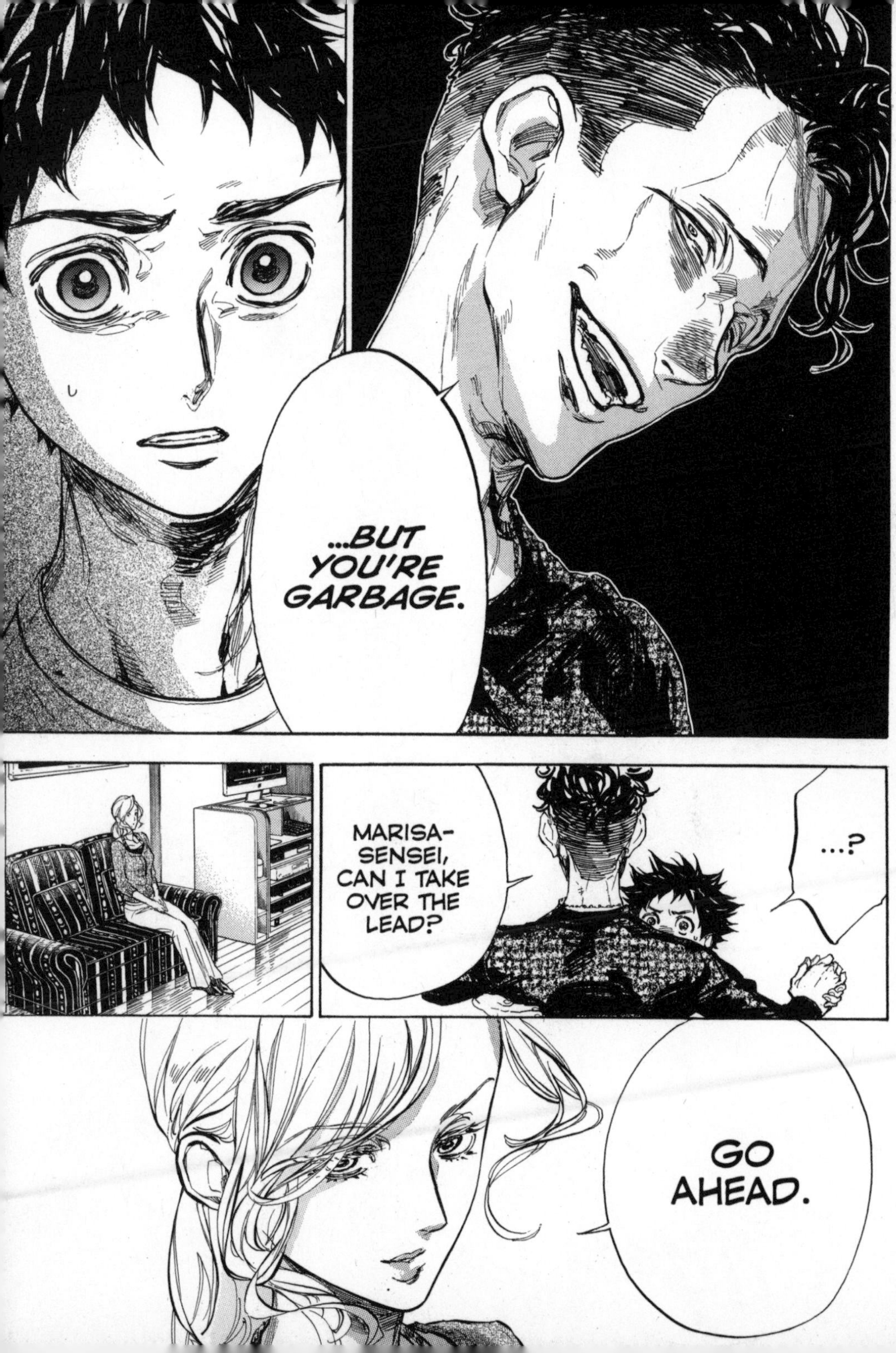
...BUT YOU'RE GARBAGE.
...?
MARISA-SENSEI, CAN I TAKE OVER THE LEAD?
GO AHEAD.

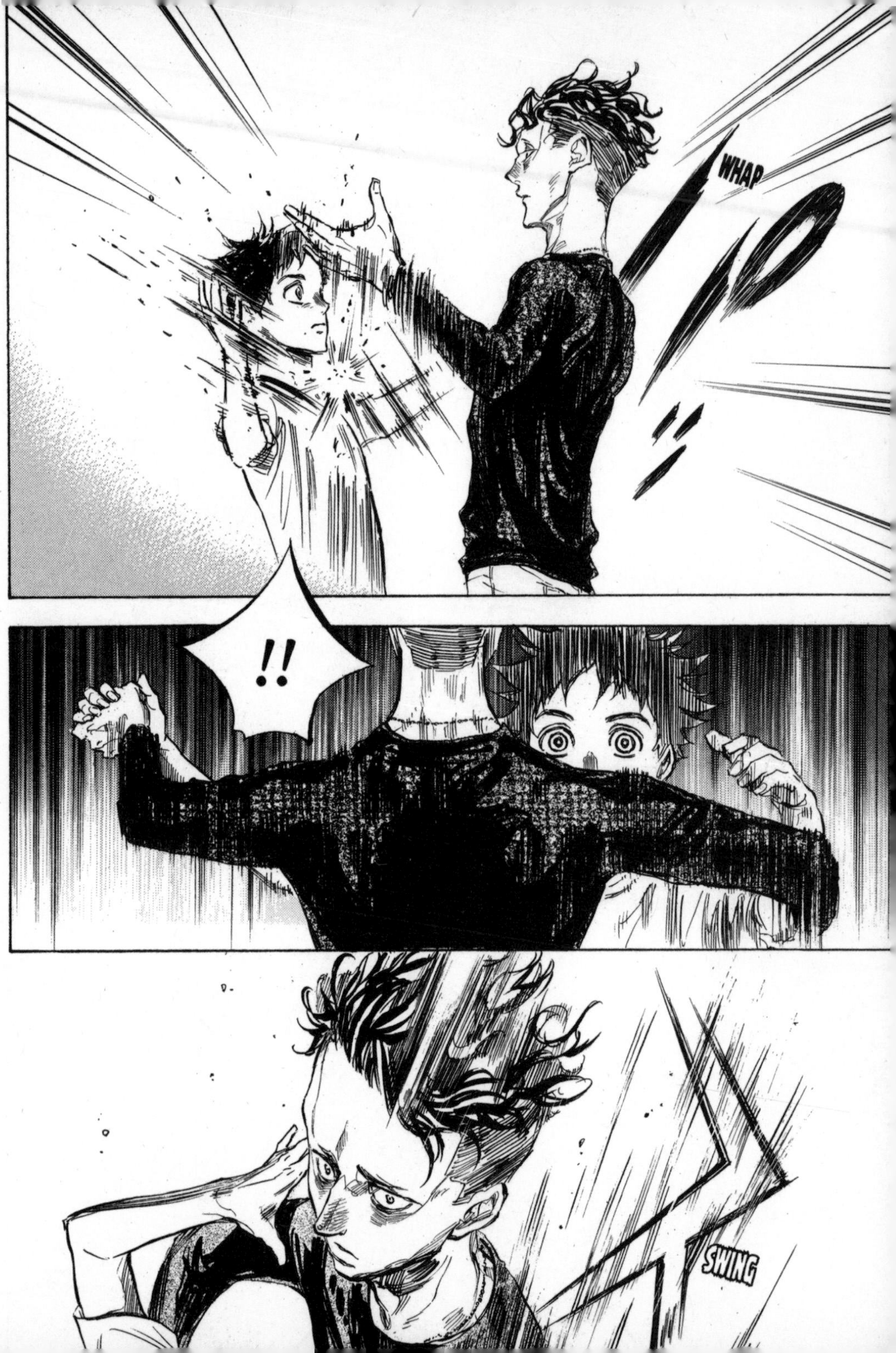
WHAP
!!
SWING

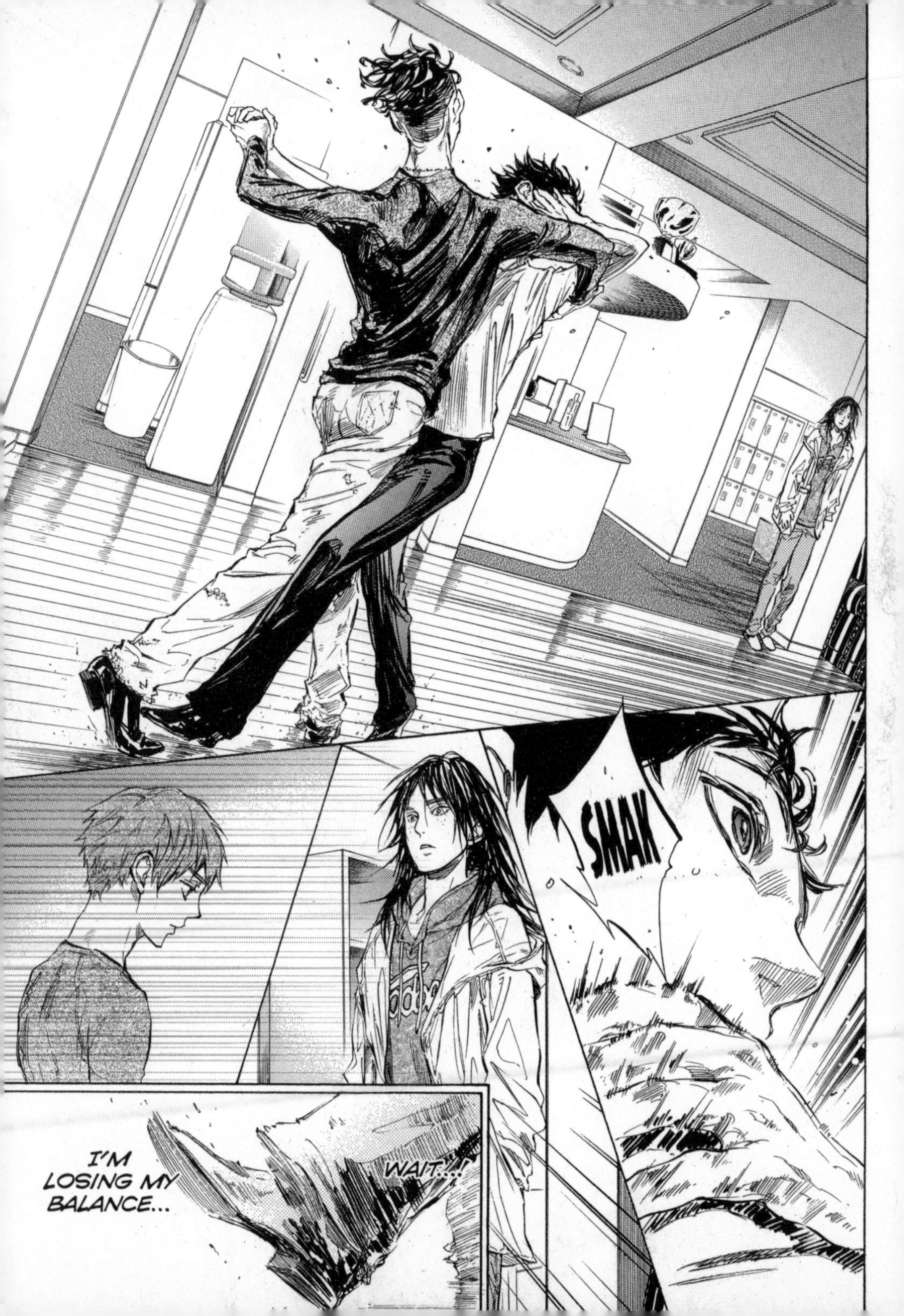
SMAK
WAIT...!
I'M LOSING MY BALANCE...

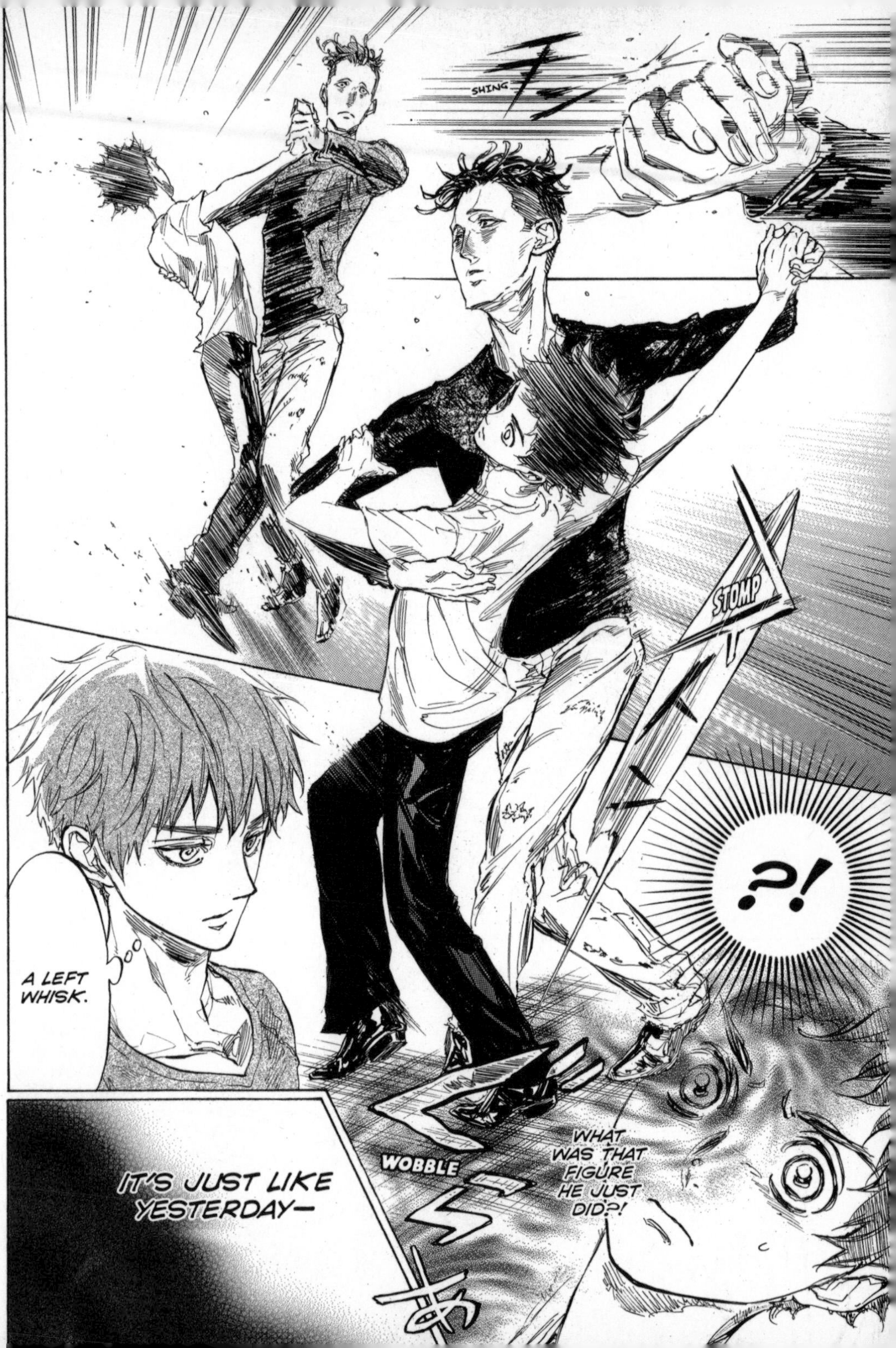
SHING
STOMP
?!
A LEFT WHISK.
WHAT WAS THAT FIGURE HE JUST DID?!
WOBBLE
IT'S JUST LIKE YESTERDAY—

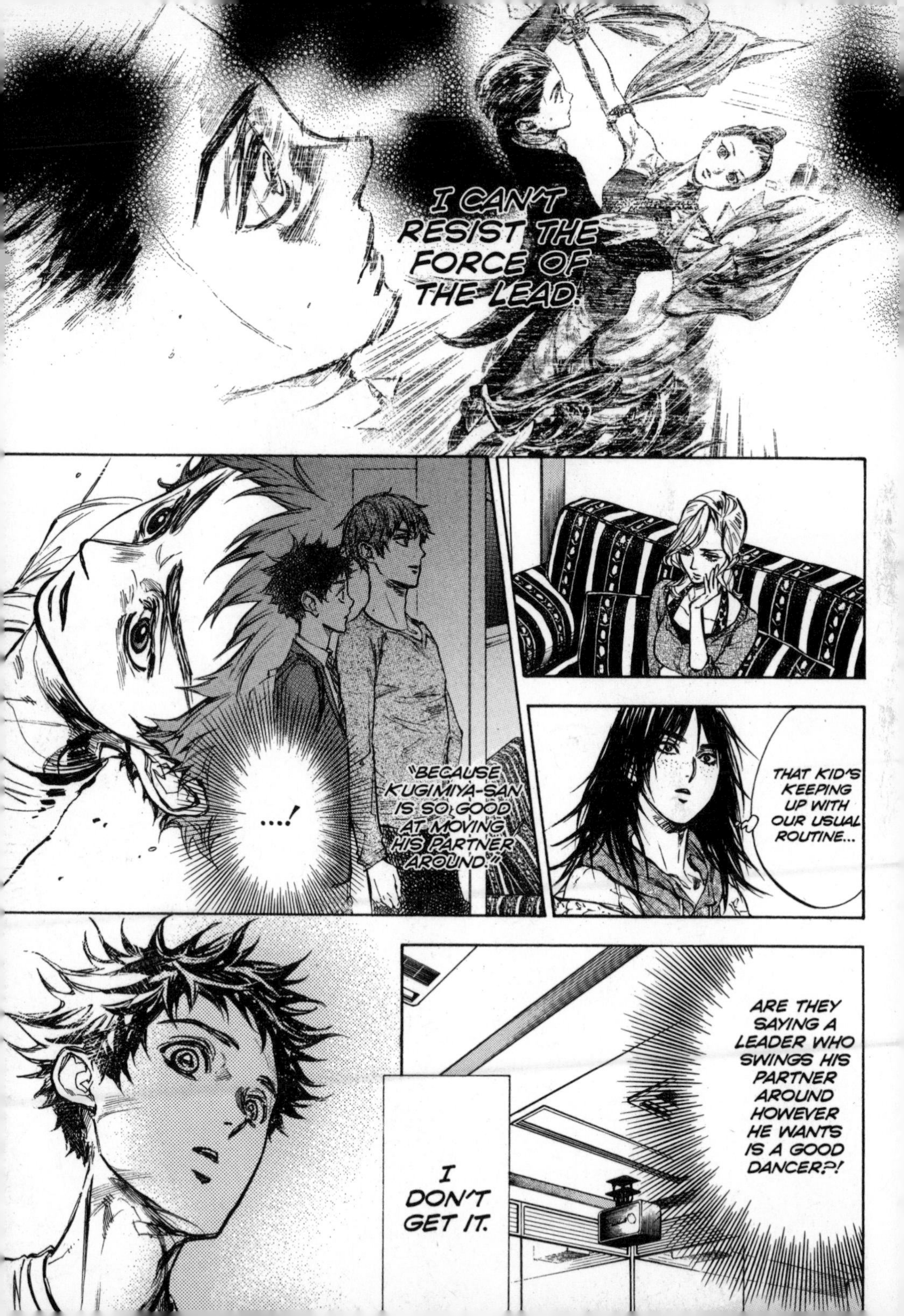
I CAN'T RESIST THE FORCE OF THE LEAD.
THAT KID'S KEEPING UP WITH OUR USUAL ROUTINE...
"BECAUSE KUGIMIYA-SAN IS SO GOOD AT MOVING HIS PARTNER AROUND."
...!
ARE THEY SAYING A LEADER WHO SWINGS HIS PARTNER AROUND HOWEVER HE WANTS IS A GOOD DANCER?!
I DON'T GET IT.

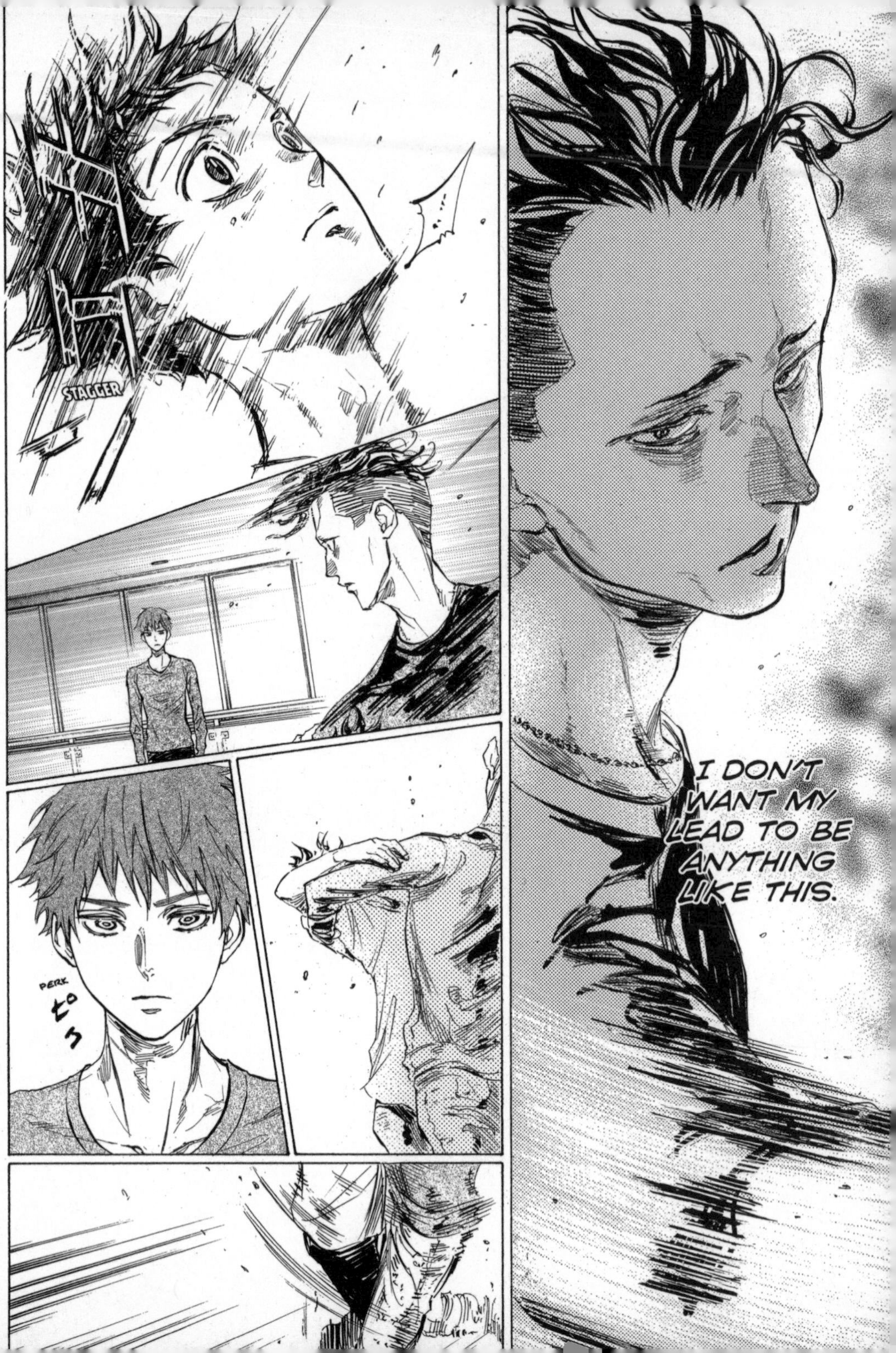
I DON'T WANT MY LEAD TO BE ANYTHING LIKE THIS.
STAGGER
PERK

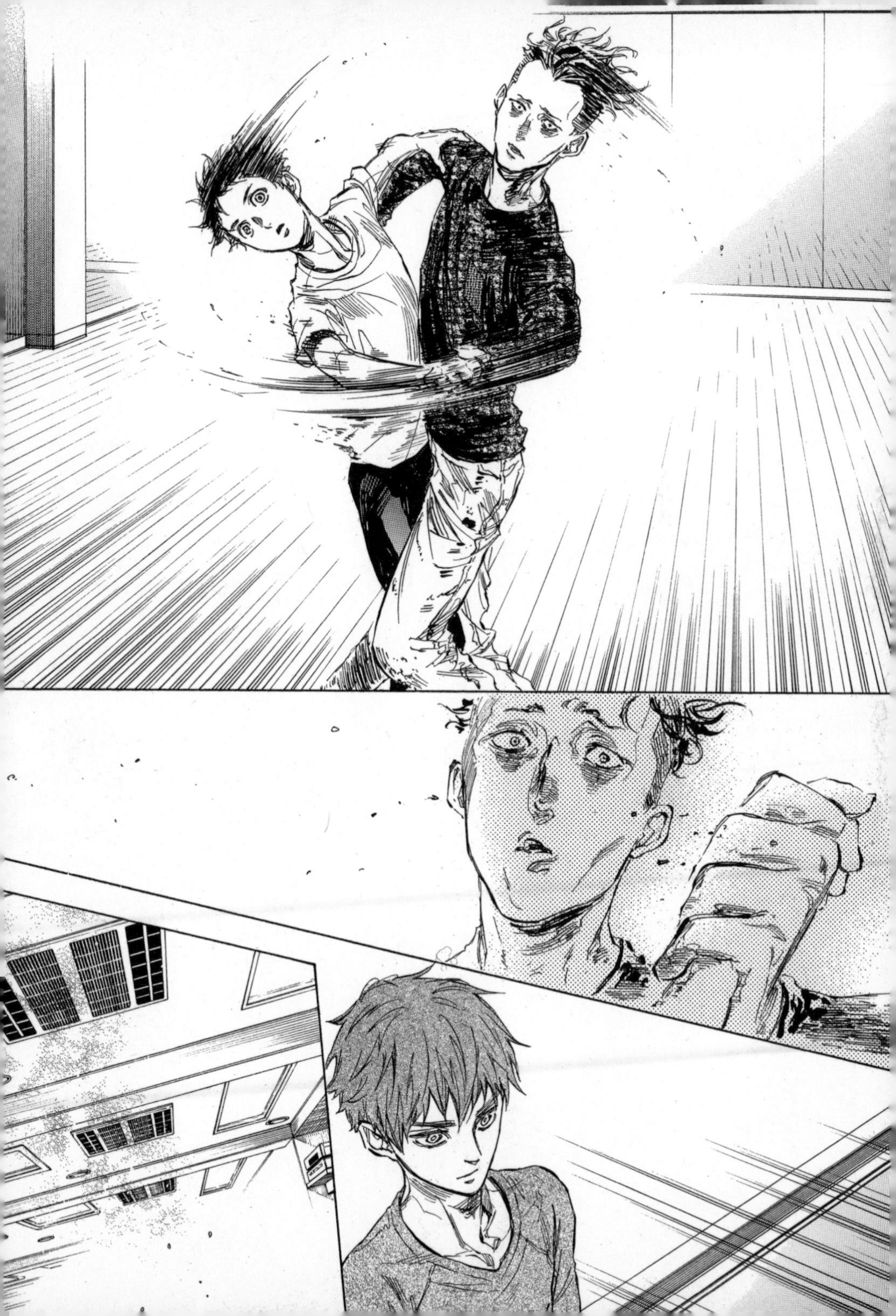

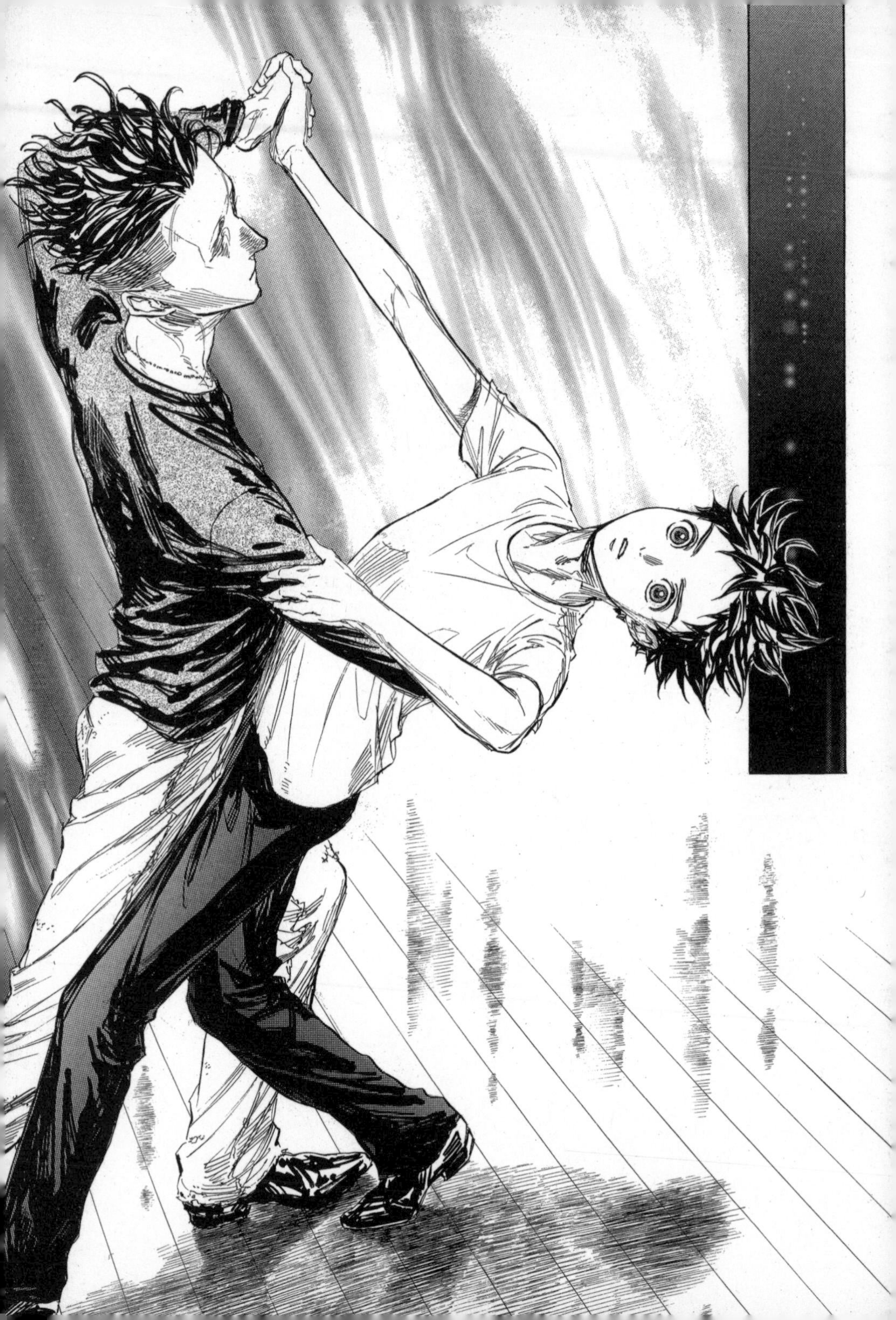

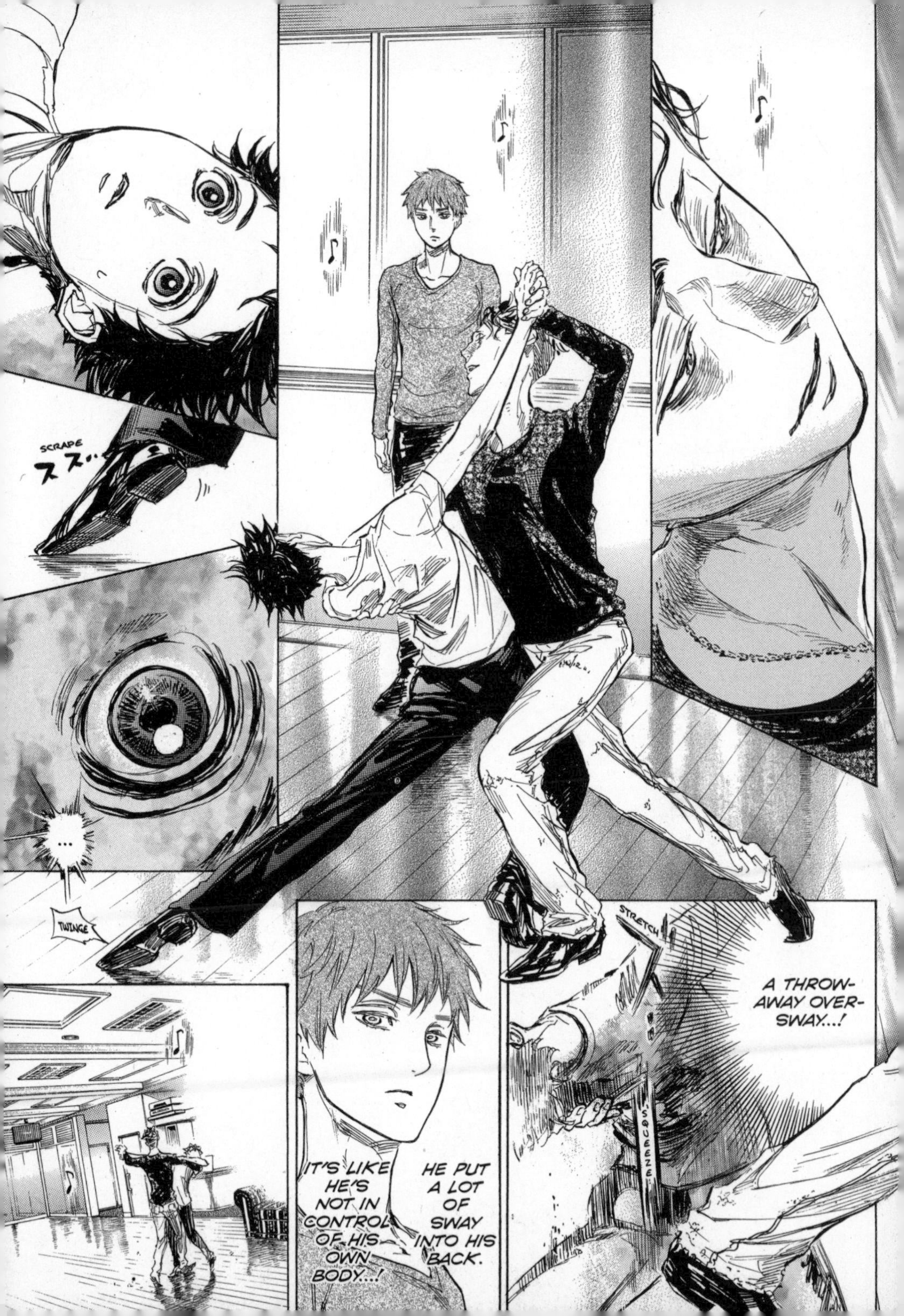
SCRAPE
スス…
...
TWINGE
STRETCH
A THROW-AWAY OVER-SWAY...!
SQUEEZE
HE PUT A LOT OF SWAY INTO HIS BACK.
IT'S LIKE HE'S NOT IN CONTROL OF HIS OWN BODY...!

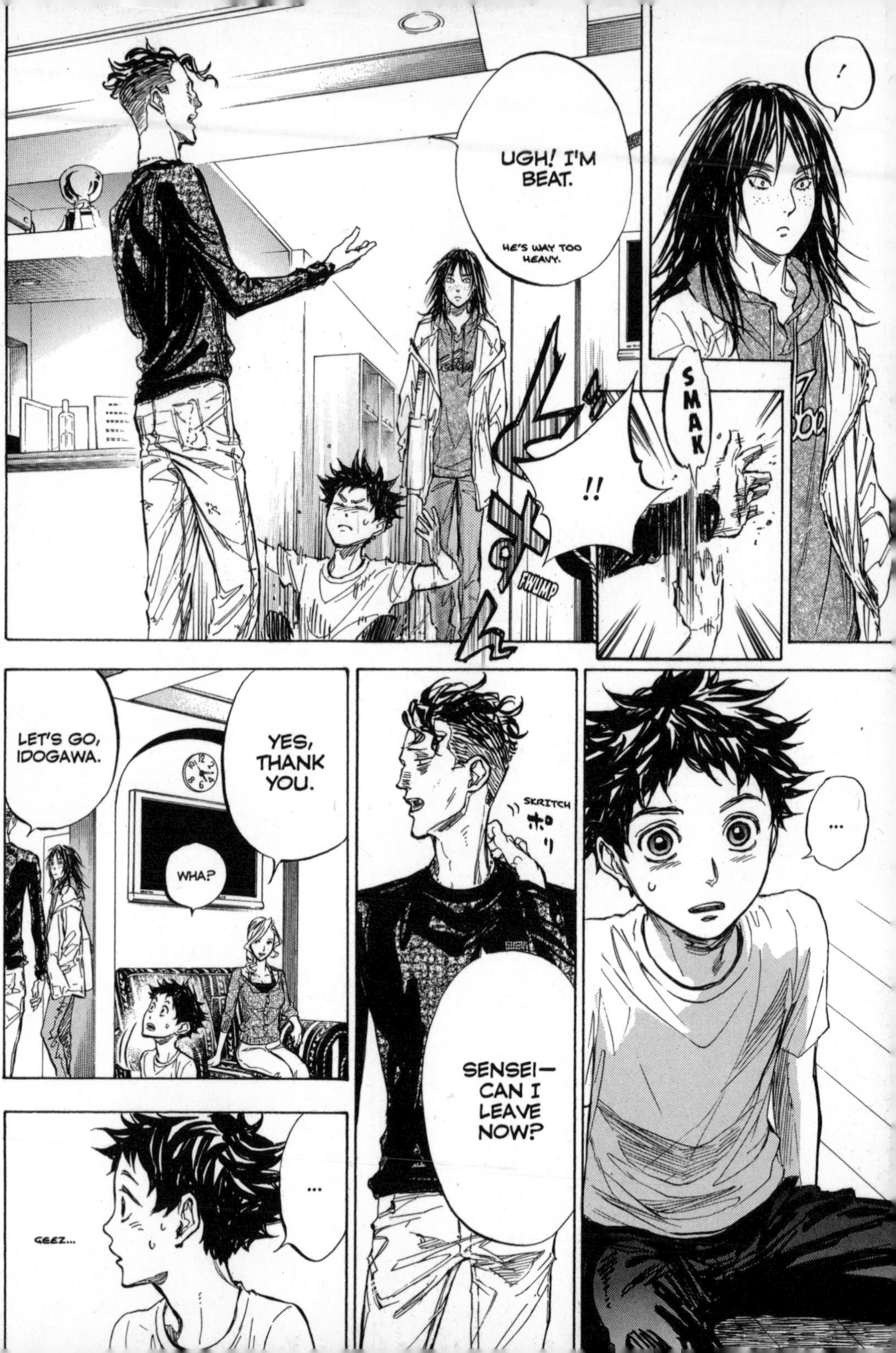
!
SMAK
!!
FWUMP
UGH! I'M BEAT.
HE'S WAY TOO HEAVY.
...
SKRITCH
SENSEI— CAN I LEAVE NOW?
YES, THANK YOU.
LET'S GO, IDOGAWA.
WHA?
...
GEEZ...

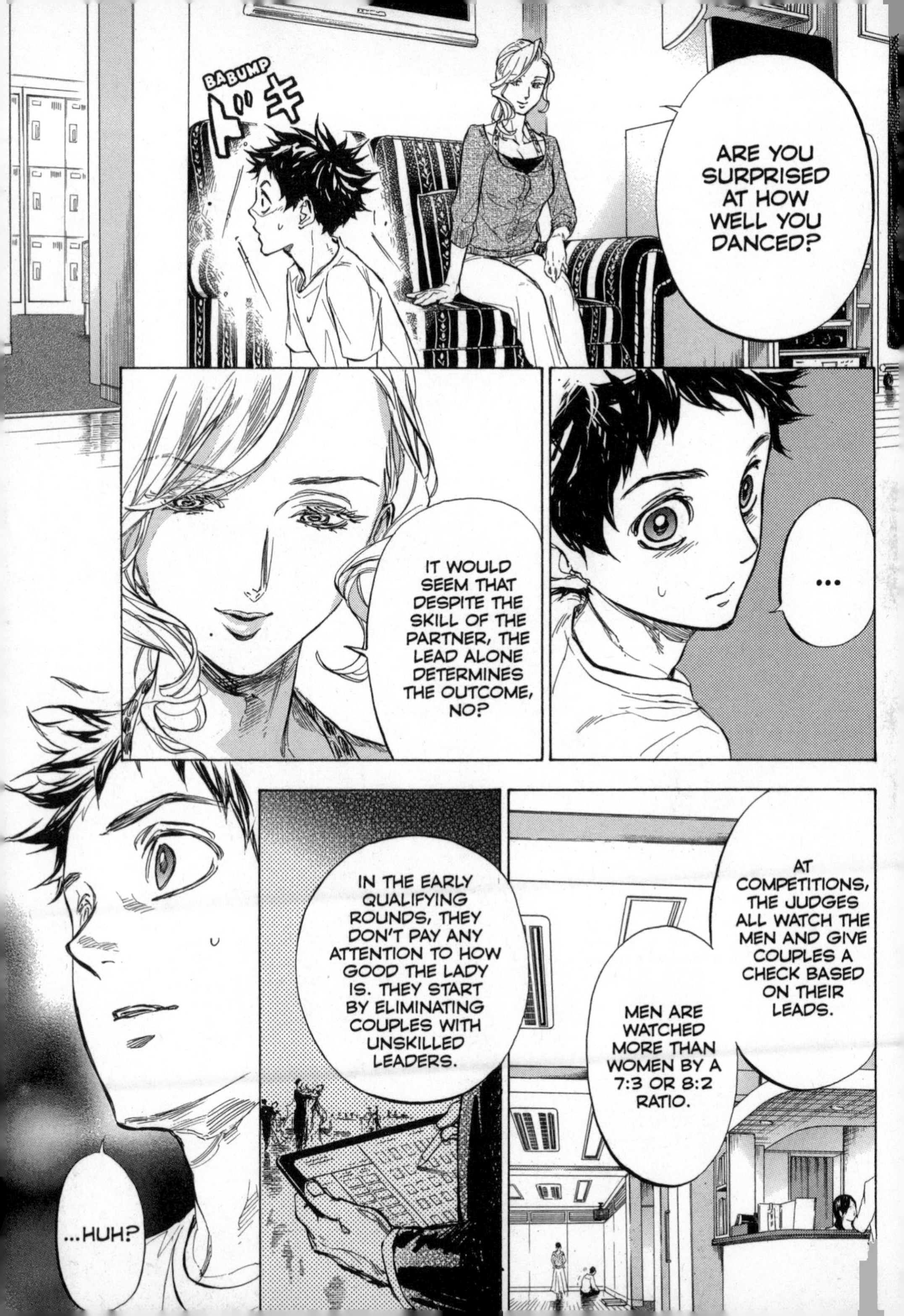
ARE YOU SURPRISED AT HOW WELL YOU DANCED?
BABUMP
ドキ
...
IT WOULD SEEM THAT DESPITE THE SKILL OF THE PARTNER, THE LEAD ALONE DETERMINES THE OUTCOME, NO?
AT COMPETITIONS, THE JUDGES ALL WATCH THE MEN AND GIVE COUPLES A CHECK BASED ON THEIR LEADS.
MEN ARE WATCHED MORE THAN WOMEN BY A 7:3 OR 8:2 RATIO.
IN THE EARLY QUALIFYING ROUNDS, THEY DON'T PAY ANY ATTENTION TO HOW GOOD THE LADY IS. THEY START BY ELIMINATING COUPLES WITH UNSKILLED LEADERS.
...HUH?

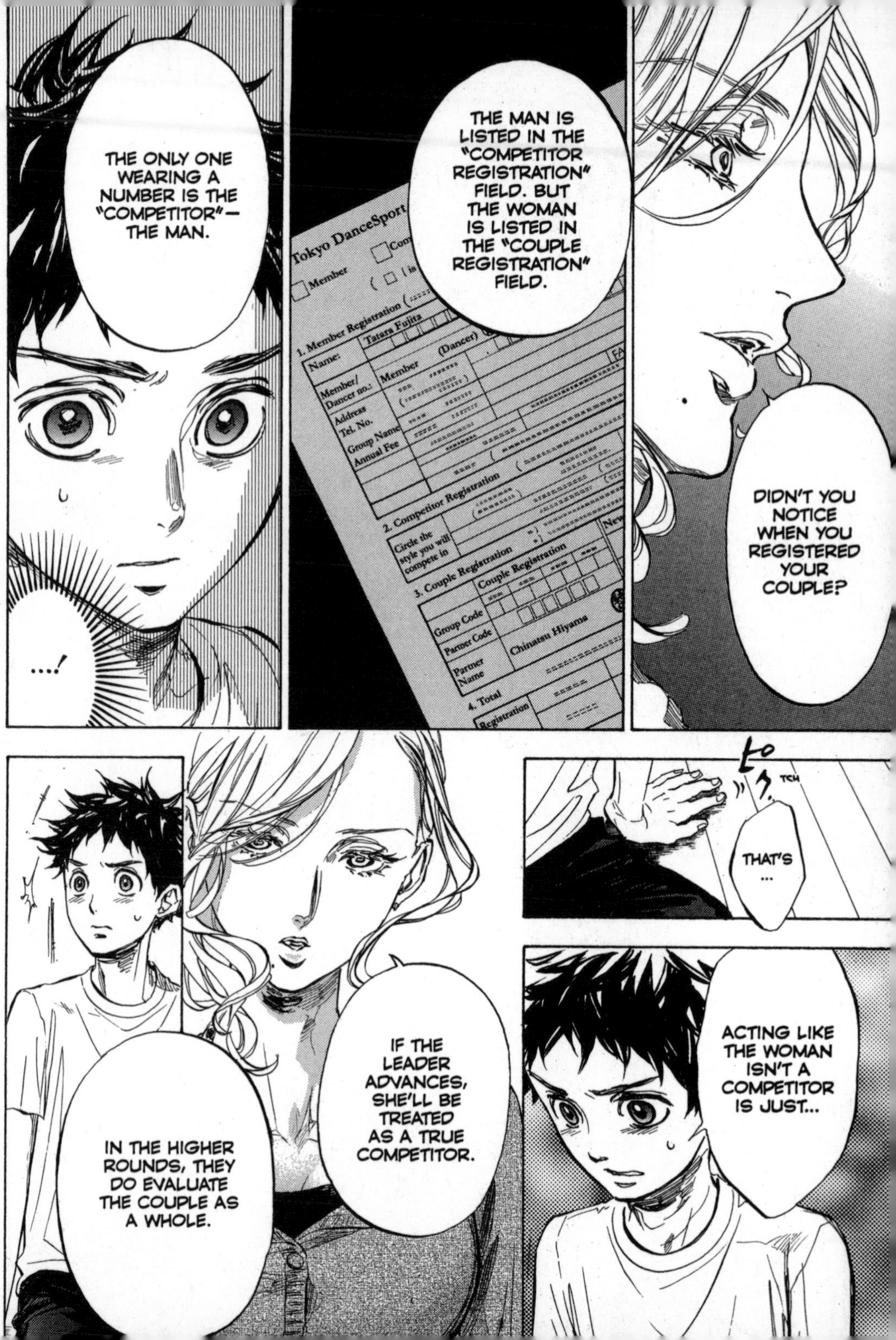
DIDN'T YOU NOTICE WHEN YOU REGISTERED YOUR COUPLE?
THE MAN IS LISTED IN THE "COMPETITOR REGISTRATION" FIELD. BUT THE WOMAN IS LISTED IN THE "COUPLE REGISTRATION" FIELD.
Tokyo DanceSport
Member
1. Member Registration
Name:
Tatara Fujita
(Dancer)
Member/ Dancer no.:
Member
Address Tel. No.
Group Name
Annual Fee
2. Competitor Registration
Circle the style you will compete in
3. Couple Registration
Couple Registration
Group Code
Partner Code
Chinatsu Hiyama
Partner Name
4. Total
Registration
THE ONLY ONE WEARING A NUMBER IS THE "COMPETITOR"— THE MAN.
...!
TCH
THAT'S ...
ACTING LIKE THE WOMAN ISN'T A COMPETITOR IS JUST...
IF THE LEADER ADVANCES, SHE'LL BE TREATED AS A TRUE COMPETITOR.
IN THE HIGHER ROUNDS, THEY DO EVALUATE THE COUPLE AS A WHOLE.

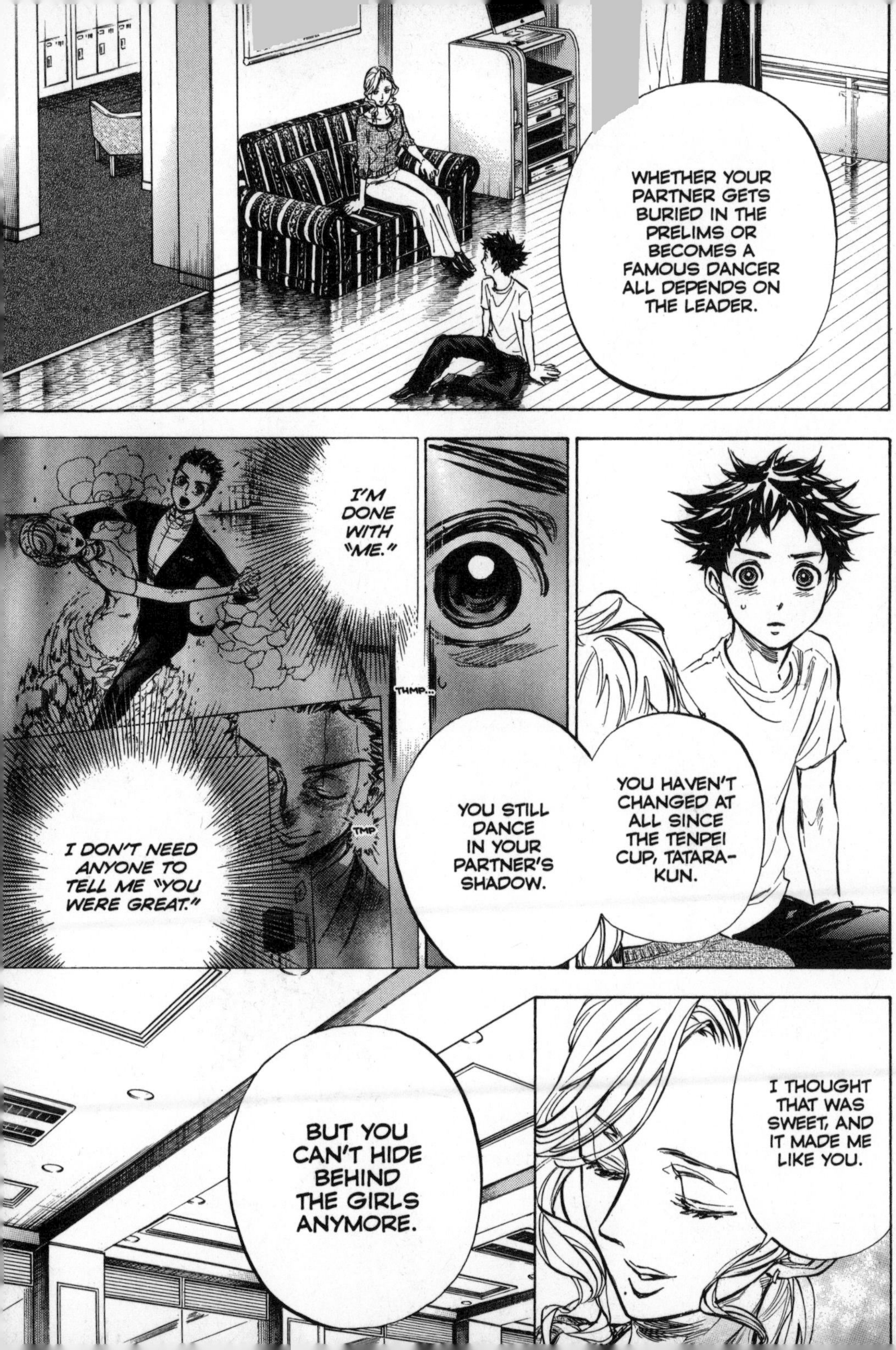
WHETHER YOUR PARTNER GETS BURIED IN THE PRELIMS OR BECOMES A FAMOUS DANCER ALL DEPENDS ON THE LEADER.
YOU HAVEN'T CHANGED AT ALL SINCE THE TENPEI CUP, TATARA-KUN.
YOU STILL DANCE IN YOUR PARTNER'S SHADOW.
I'M DONE WITH "ME."
THMP...
TMP
I DON'T NEED ANYONE TO TELL ME "YOU WERE GREAT."
I THOUGHT THAT WAS SWEET, AND IT MADE ME LIKE YOU.
BUT YOU CAN'T HIDE BEHIND THE GIRLS ANYMORE.

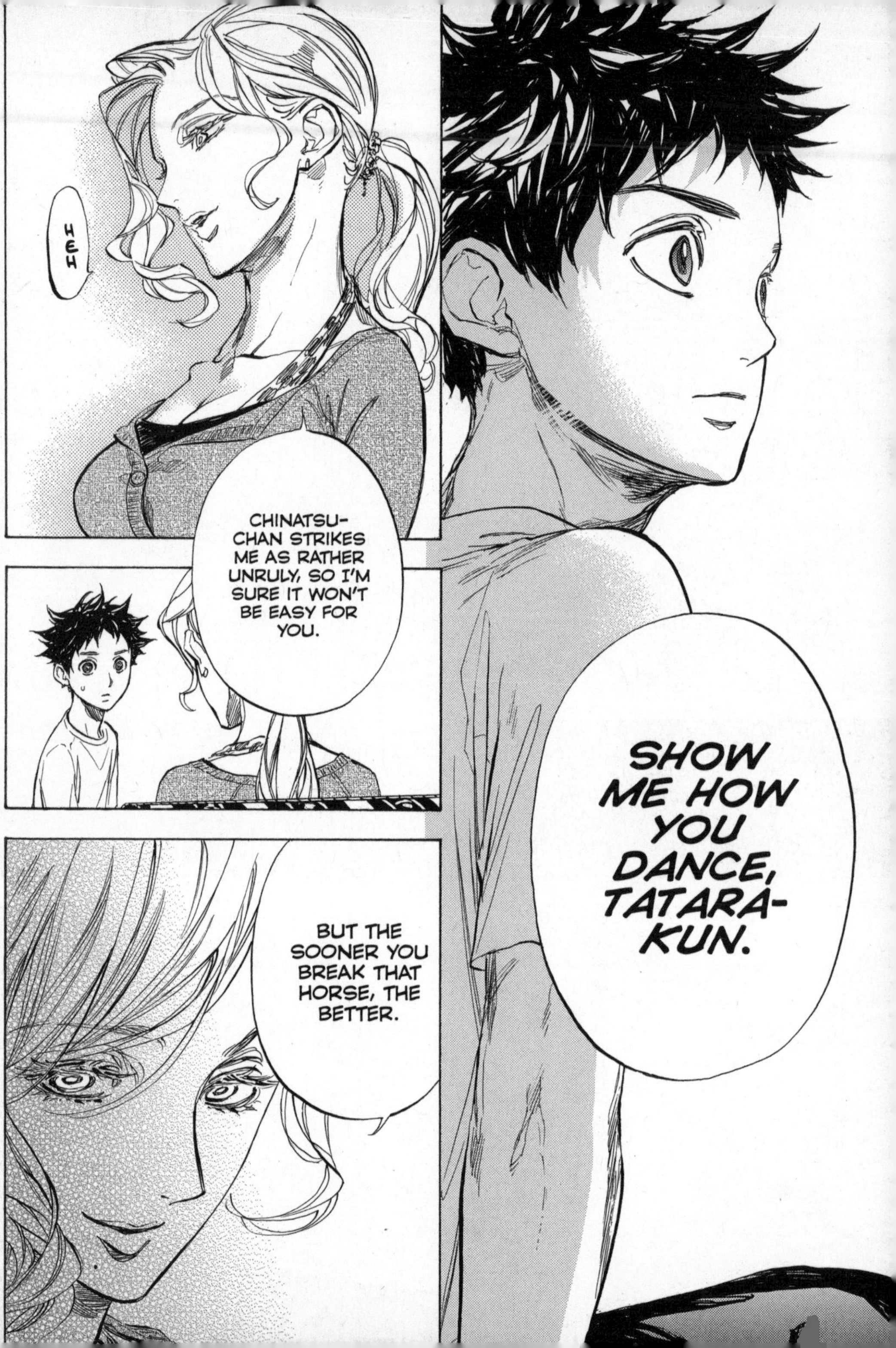
SHOW ME HOW YOU DANCE, TATARA-KUN.
HEH
CHINATSU-CHAN STRIKES ME AS RATHER UNRULY, SO I'M SURE IT WON'T BE EASY FOR YOU.
BUT THE SOONER YOU BREAK THAT HORSE, THE BETTER.

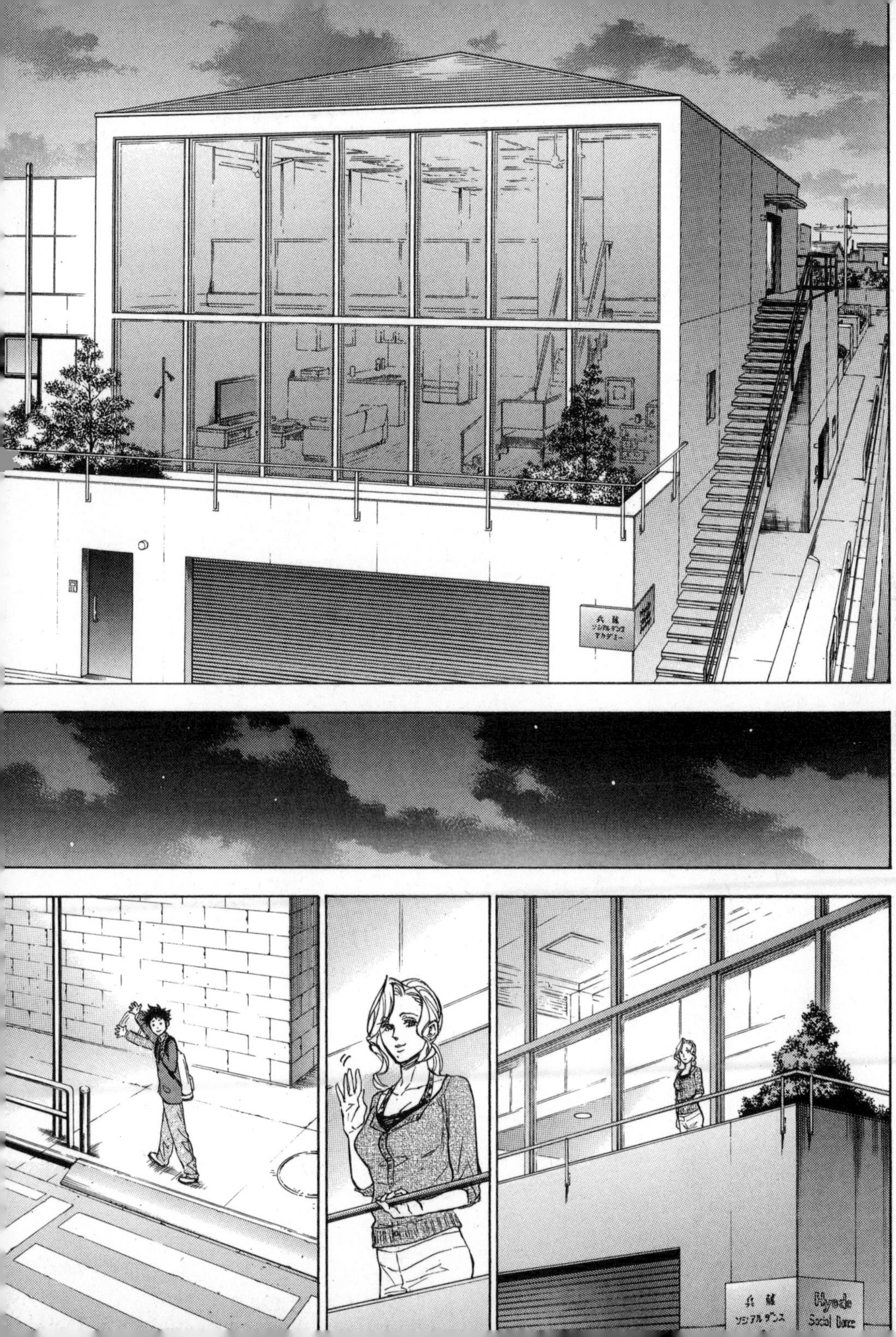
兵藤
ソシアルダンス
アカデミー
兵藤
ソシアルダンス
Hyodo
Social Dance

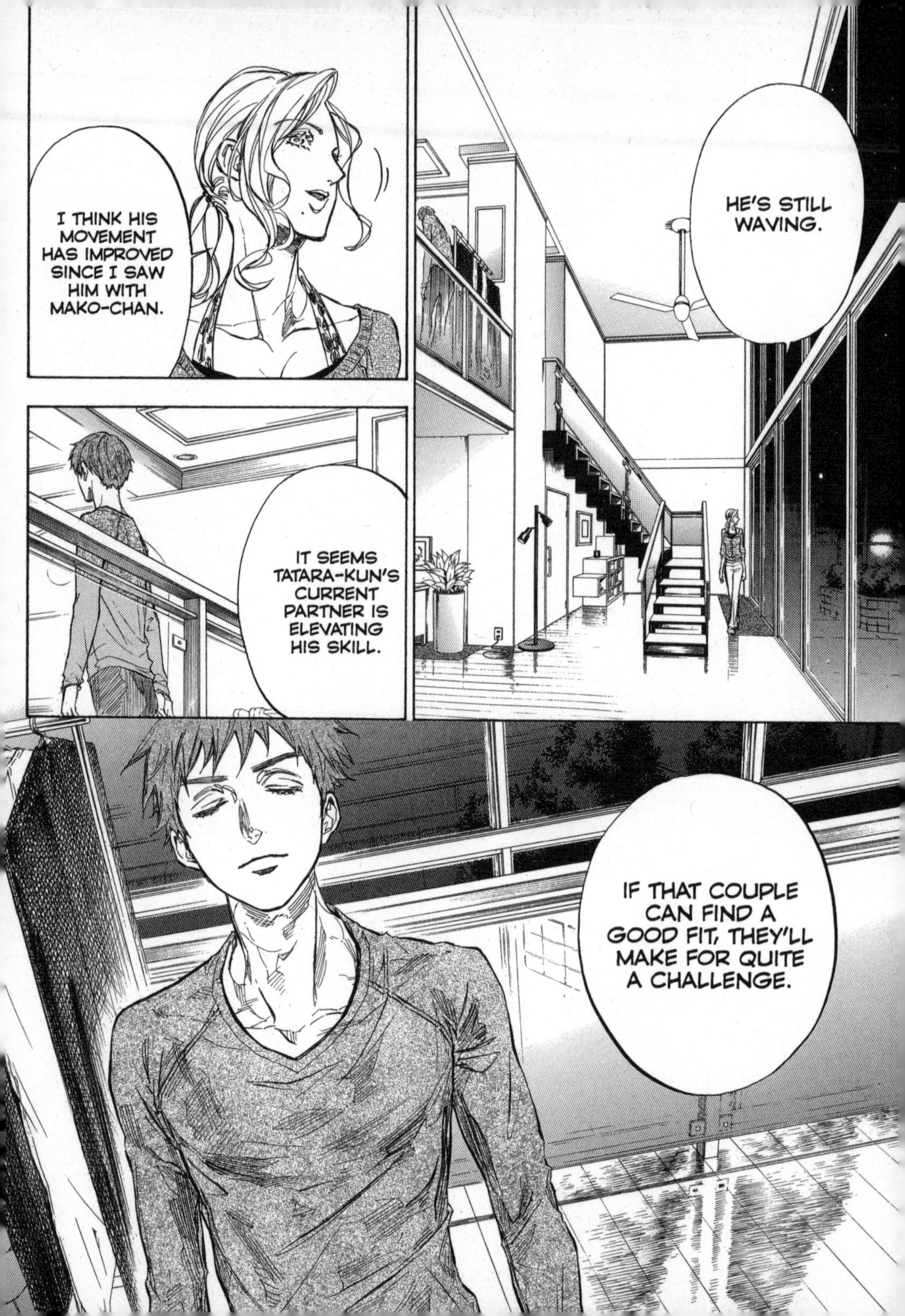
HE'S STILL WAVING.
I THINK HIS MOVEMENT HAS IMPROVED SINCE I SAW HIM WITH MAKO-CHAN.
IT SEEMS TATARA-KUN'S CURRENT PARTNER IS ELEVATING HIS SKILL.
IF THAT COUPLE CAN FIND A GOOD FIT, THEY'LL MAKE FOR QUITE A CHALLENGE.

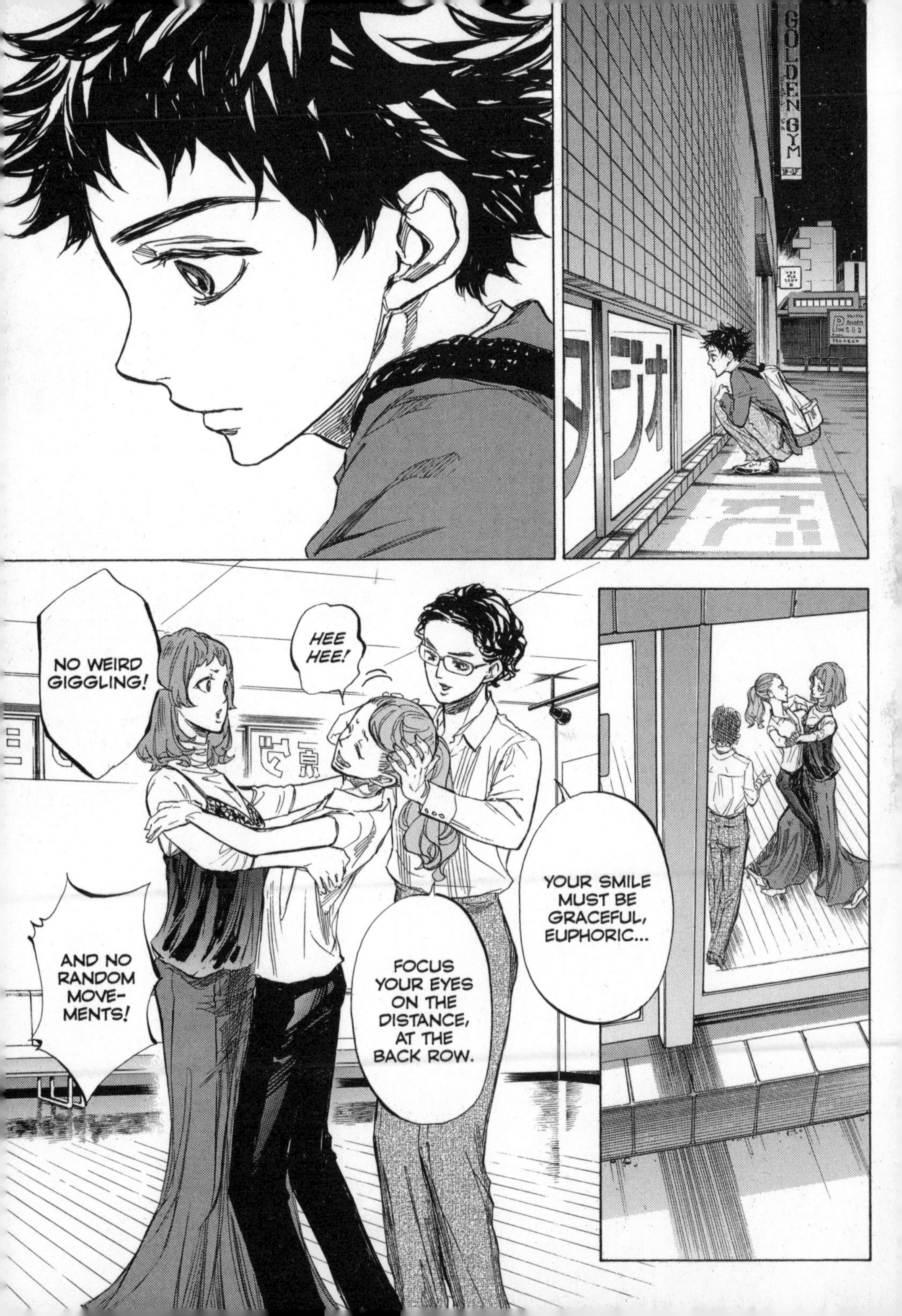
GOLDEN GYM
YOUR SMILE MUST BE GRACEFUL, EUPHORIC...
FOCUS YOUR EYES ON THE DISTANCE, AT THE BACK ROW.
HEE HEE!
NO WEIRD GIGGLING!
AND NO RANDOM MOVE- MENTS!

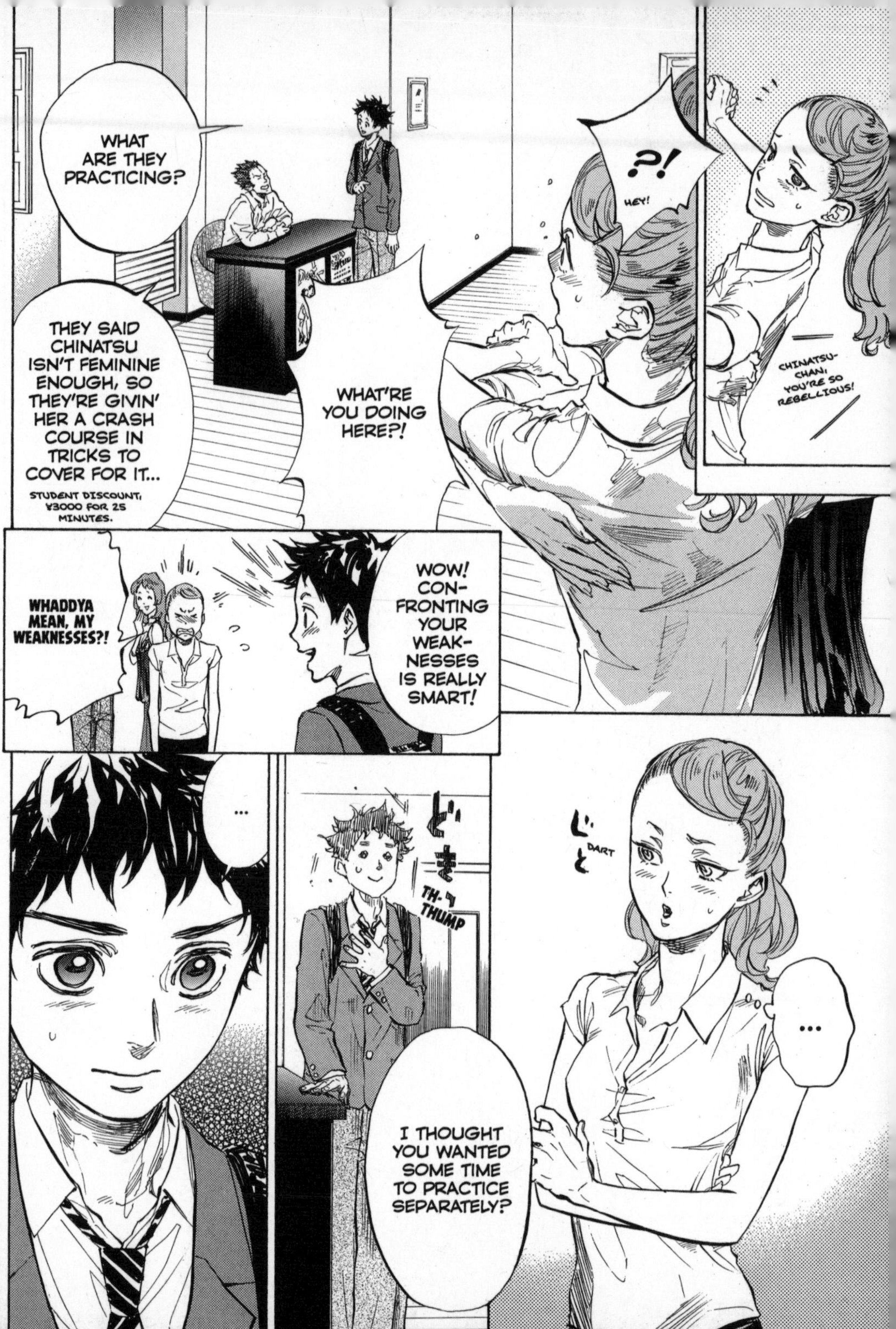
CHINATSU-CHAN, YOU'RE SO REBELLIOUS!
?!
HEY!
WHAT'RE YOU DOING HERE?!
WHAT ARE THEY PRACTICING?
THEY SAID CHINATSU ISN'T FEMININE ENOUGH, SO THEY'RE GIVIN' HER A CRASH COURSE IN TRICKS TO COVER FOR IT...
STUDENT DISCOUNT, ¥3000 FOR 25 MINUTES.
WOW! CON-FRONTING YOUR WEAK-NESSES IS REALLY SMART!
WHADDYA MEAN, MY WEAKNESSES?!
DART
...
I THOUGHT YOU WANTED SOME TIME TO PRACTICE SEPARATELY?
TH-THUMP
...

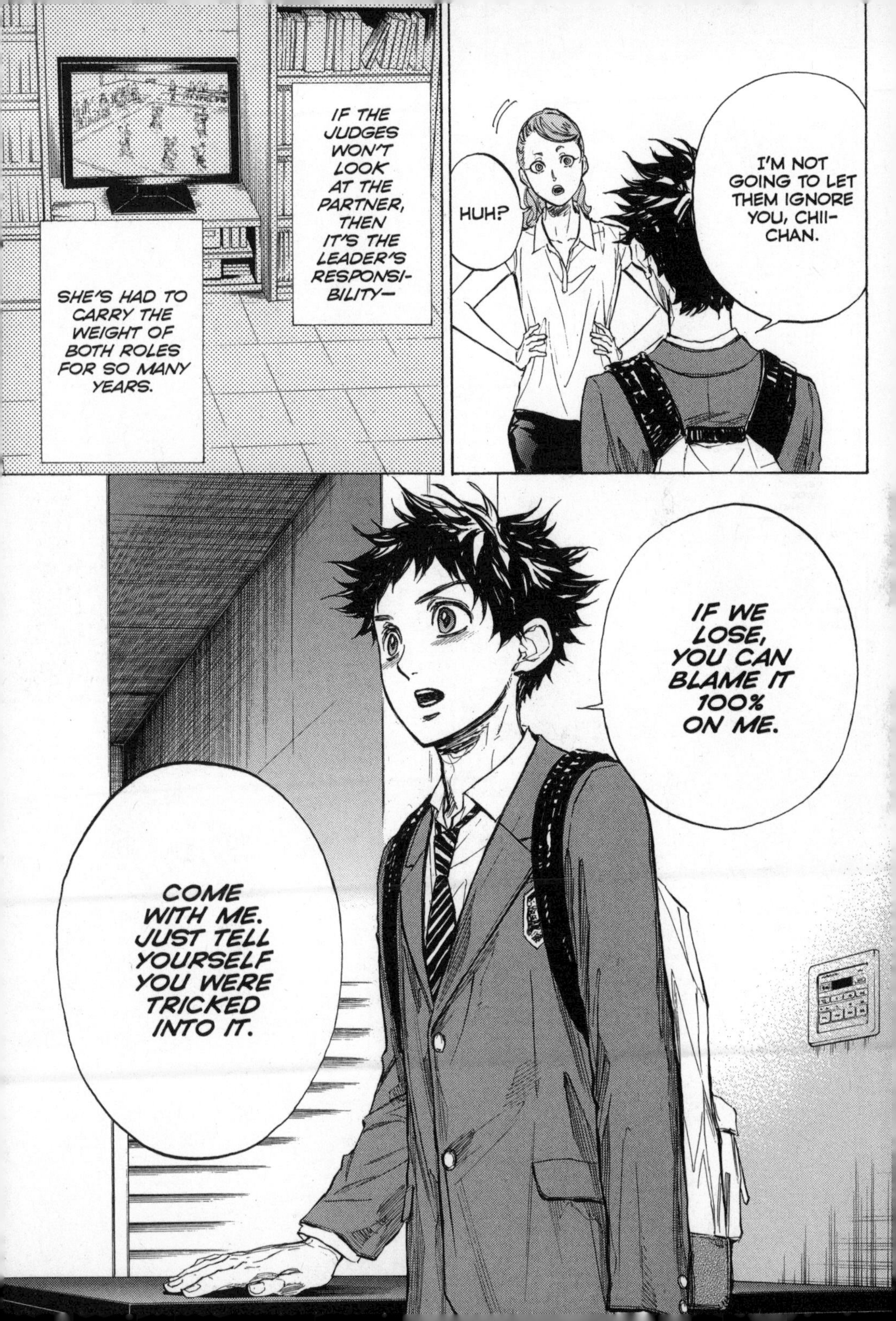
I'M NOT GOING TO LET THEM IGNORE YOU, CHII-CHAN.
HUH?
IF THE JUDGES WON'T LOOK AT THE PARTNER, THEN IT'S THE LEADER'S RESPONSI-BILITY—
SHE'S HAD TO CARRY THE WEIGHT OF BOTH ROLES FOR SO MANY YEARS.
IF WE LOSE, YOU CAN BLAME IT 100% ON ME.
COME WITH ME. JUST TELL YOURSELF YOU WERE TRICKED INTO IT.

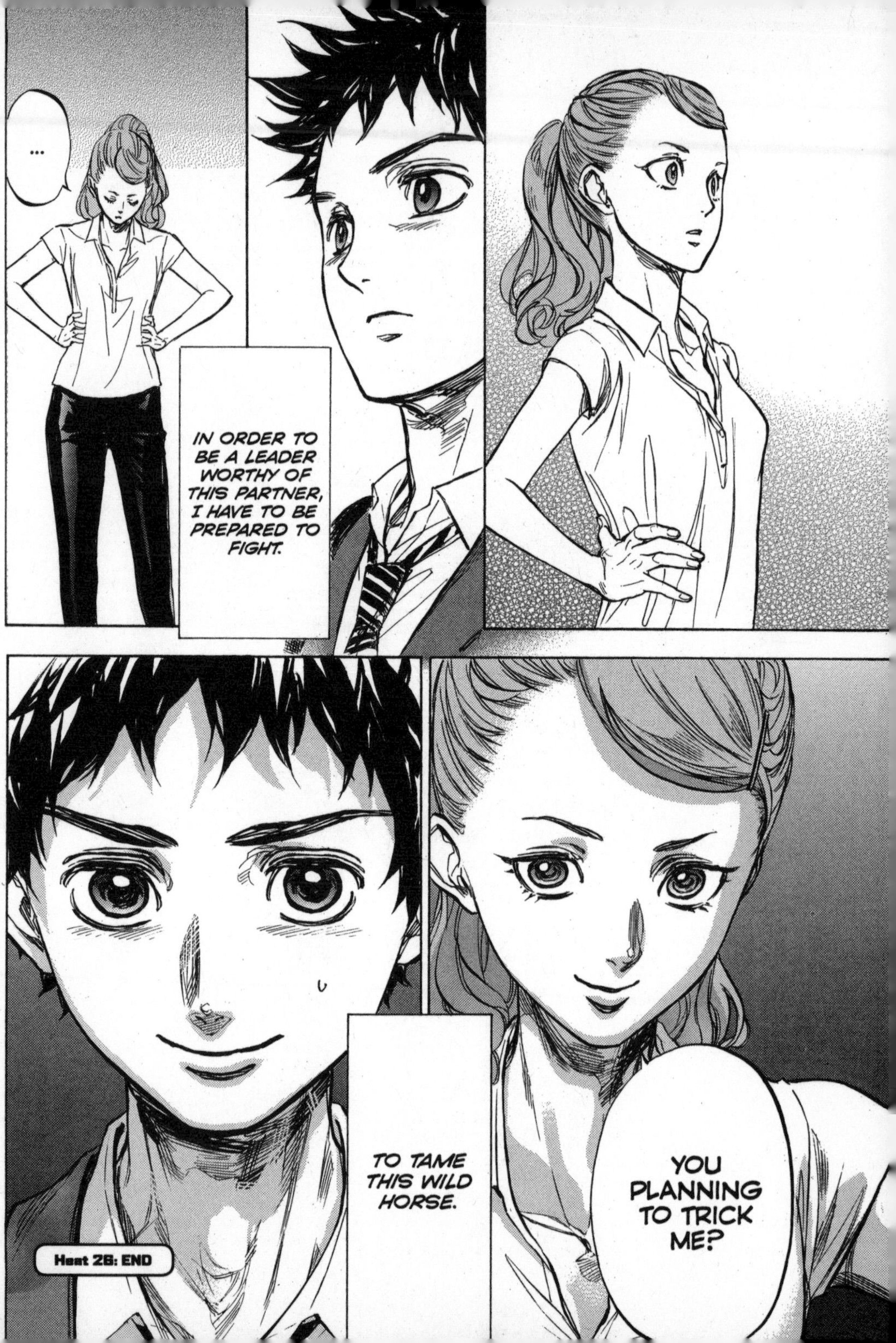
IN ORDER TO BE A LEADER WORTHY OF THIS PARTNER, I HAVE TO BE PREPARED TO FIGHT.
...
YOU PLANNING TO TRICK ME?
TO TAME THIS WILD HORSE.
Heat 26: END

*Special Thanks!*

***For help with interviews***
*Mr. Yoshihiro Miwa*
*Ms. Tomoko Miwa*

***For help with background***
*Sakane Dance School*
*Café Pousse*

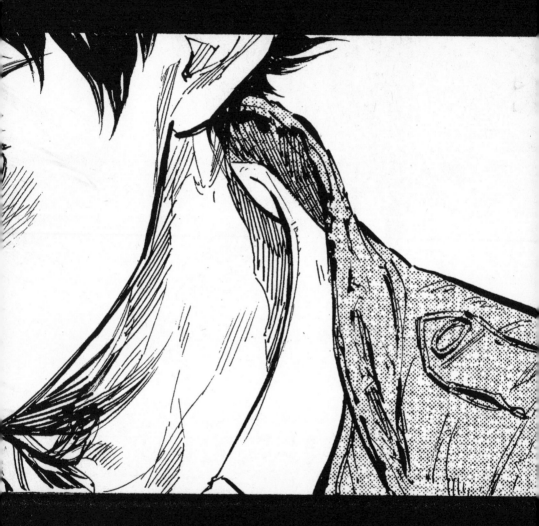

TATARA BEGINS HIS TRAINING AT THE HYODO SOCIAL DANCE ACADEMY...

...KNOWING THAT THE APPROACHING GRAND PRIX COULD DETERMINE HIS FUTURE AS A DANCER!

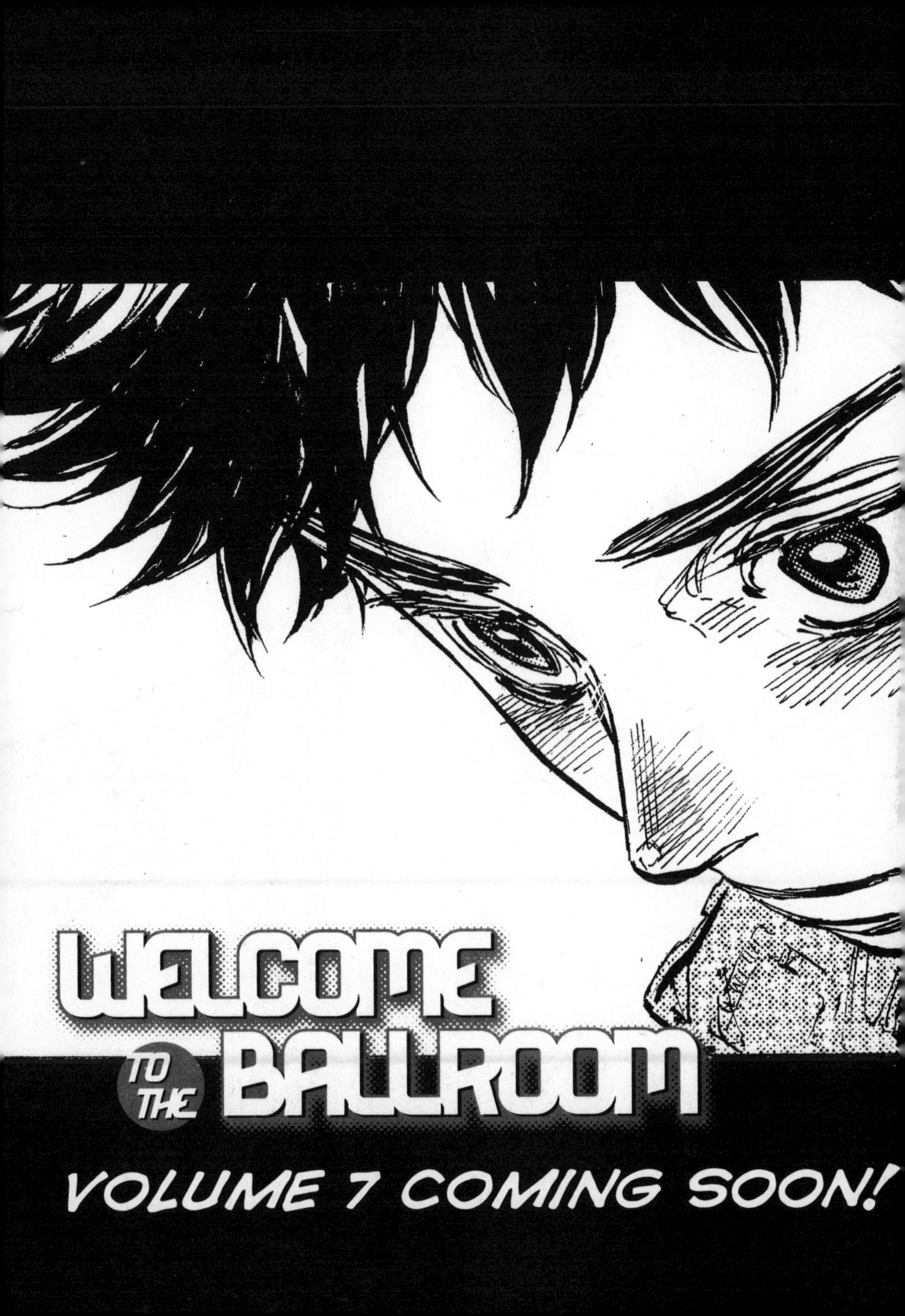
WELCOME TO THE BALLROOM
VOLUME 7 COMING SOON!

*Welcome to the Ballroom* volume 6 is a work of fiction. Names, characters, places, and incidents are the products of the author's imagination or are used fictitiously. Any resemblance to actual events, locales, or persons, living or dead, is entirely coincidental.

A Kodansha Comics Trade Paperback Original.



Published in the United States by Kodansha Comics, an imprint of Kodansha USA Publishing, LLC, New York.

Publication rights for this English edition arranged through Kodansha Ltd., Tokyo.

First published in Japan in 2014 by Kodansha Ltd., Tokyo, as *Booruruumu e Youkoso* volume 6.

ISBN 978-1-63236-446-3

Printed in the United States of America.

www.kodanshacomics.com

9 8 7 6 5 4 3 2 1

Translator: Karen McGillicuddy
Lettering: Brndn Blakeslee
Editing: Paul Starr
Kodansha Comics edition cover design by Phil Balsman